Doggett

THE MERCURY CAPSULE

The Bookshelf
for Boys and Girls

Prepared *under the Supervision of*

THE EDITORIAL BOARD
OF THE UNIVERSITY SOCIETY

VOLUME VII

Nature and Science

THE UNIVERSITY SOCIETY, INC.

Educational Publishers since 1897

NEW YORK

1963

ACKNOWLEDGEMENTS VOLUME VII

Grateful acknowledgement and thanks are extended to the following publishers and authors for permission to reprint copyrighted material:

Childrens Press—"Traveling in Space" by John Lewellen, illustrated by Winnie Fitch and Joe Phelan, from *You and Space Travel* by John Lewellen, copyright, 1951, by Childrens Press. Reprinted by permission of the publisher.

Golden Press—Frontispiece photo of Space Capsule from *The Astronauts, Pioneers in Space.* Published by The Golden Press, Inc., New York, and copyright, 1961, by Time, Inc.

McGraw-Hill Book Co., Inc.—"How the Television Picture Is Made" by Jeanne and Robert Bendick, from *Television Works Like This* by Jeanne and Robert Bendick, published by McGraw-Hill Book Co., Inc., copyright, 1949, 1954, by McGraw-Hill Book Co., Inc.

William R. Scott, Inc.—"Electricity" by Herman and Nina Schneider, illustrated by Bill Ballantine. Reprinted with permission of the publisher, William R. Scott, Inc. from the book, *More Power To You*, copyright, 1953, by the authors, Herman and Nina Schneider. "Levers, Pulleys and Wheels" by Herman and Nina Schneider, illustrated by Bill Ballantine. Reprinted from the book, *Now Try This*, by Herman and Nina Schneider, copyright, 1947, by William R. Scott, Inc.

Franklin Watts, Inc.—"Saving Our Natural Resources" by F. C. Smith, from *The First Book of Conservation* by F. C. Smith, copyright, 1954, by Franklin Watts, Inc. Reprinted by permission of the publisher.

Illustrators of this Volume

DIMITRI ALEXANDROFF, *Saving Our Natural Resources*

BILL BALLANTINE, *Electricity; Levers, Pulleys and Wheels*

JEANNE AND ROBERT BENDICK, *How the Television Picture Is Made*

R. I. BRASHER, *Birds: Animals That Fly*

WINNIE FITCH, *Traveling in Space; Man Explores Outer Space*

JOE PHELAN, *Traveling in Space; Man Explores Outer Space*

With the exception of "Trees" and "Flowers," all the other illustrations in this volume are by ROY K. WILLS.

A Word to Parents about this Volume

NATURE AND SCIENCE

THE study of nature and science takes us from the basic beginnings of the universe to the horizon of our foreseeable tomorrows — a range of billions and billions and billions of years. In this journey we consider the stars, the sun, the moon, rocks and sand, mountains and valleys, the earth, the skies, the seas, and all that in them is: plants, animals, man and all his works.

It is a subject so vast that scholars have written countless volumes on just one or another aspect of it: how old the earth is, for instance, or what the floor of the ocean is like, or how electricity works, or how fast a rocket can travel.

Here, in this one volume, a child can see the whole panorama unfolding with all the excitement of the most dramatic wonder-story. Probably never before has so much dependable information on nature and science been covered in a book for readers as young as ours — and surely it has never been made so easy for them to understand or so interesting.

To have been able to do it is the contribution of the book's chief author, KARL HESS, whose wide professional knowledge of science and nature only partially explain his success in this field. What makes his writing for children so thoroughly delightful is his sure understanding of what interests them. It is a natural gift enhanced by his experience in teaching natural history and science to children, especially to his own young son to whom he has been an inspiring father.

There *are* nature books gaudier than this one — books filled with blown-up pictures in both natural and unnatural colors, but short on information. The primary intention of this book is to *inform* the child but to do so in a way that he will thoroughly *enjoy*. The illustrations, therefore, are meant to *help* the child visualize the meaning of the text, not to divert him from it.

It is our belief that Mr. Hess's stories of nature and science provide his young readers with word-pictures vivid enough to last them through life.

For good measure, the illustrations, most of them by ROY K. WILLS, enliven the word-pictures and make them even more graphic and understandable to young readers.

Table of Contents

Life's Building-Blocks

LIVING things are the most wonderful and amazing things on earth. No metal machine made by men is as perfect as the living machinery in even the tiniest insect. No jewel can have the beauty of the colors in, say, the wings of some birds. But most important of all is the fact that no matter how much men have learned about stones and earth and stars and even atoms, things that are not alive, men have never been able to explain the real secret of living things. We do know quite a good deal about what makes up living things, but we cannot *make* life the way we can *make* machines. Life has to make itself. Flowers have to grow from the seeds of other flowers. Birds must come from the eggs of other birds. Babies must come from mothers, whether those babies are baby lions or baby boys or girls.

1

WHAT IS LIFE?

Most people in the world, including most scientists, feel that the real secret of life is a religious fact. The holy books of religious faiths all over the world tell of the creation of life by a Supreme Being.

Scientists, however, can take over from there. They can show us all the parts that must be put together to make up the miraculous thing we call life.

First of all, we know there is one substance that is present in absolutely every living thing on the earth. This substance is called *protoplasm.*

In finding out about living things, there is no more important word than protoplasm. The word itself comes from the Greek language and is made up of two words. One word is *protos* and means "first." The other word is *plasma* and means "form." So the word protoplasm means "the first form."

That's just what it is. It is the very first and most basic building-block of life. Nothing that lives can be without it. Nothing that doesn't have it can be alive.

When we talk about life's building-blocks, of course we do not mean that the things animals and flowers are made of are shaped like blocks. They aren't at all. We mean that protoplasm and the things made from it are like building-blocks in this way: When a child plays with blocks, he piles one block on top of another. Then he may put more blocks on the side and then add some more here and there. When he is finished, he may have a little house, or a fort, or something else. But he has taken the blocks and made them into something they weren't before. They used to be just a jumble of blocks and he has made them into a house.

The building-blocks of life that we talk about here are like that too. They come in every shape imaginable, but they are put

2

together to form whole new things. When protoplasm is put together it may form a flower or a man or woman or any other living thing. That is, men and women and flowers are built out of the protoplasm. That is why we say we are talking about life's building-blocks in this part of the book. We are going to tell you about how protoplasm builds all living things.

You are alive. So you must have protoplasm. Of course you can't see it. When you look in the mirror you see your face. Well, your skin has protoplasm in it. Your eyes have too. But all protoplasm in your body is turned into living building-blocks which, in turn, make up skin and bones and blood and muscles and all the rest of the living human body. Building-blocks made of protoplasm make up the bodies of the bees and the birds and the animals. Others make up the flowers and trees. And some even make up the germs that make us sick.

HOW LIVING THINGS ARE FORMED

We'll start building with protoplasm so that you can see how living things are formed.

Our protoplasm is the first building-block, as we have said. It is alive. Just to look at it, even through the most powerful microscopes in the world, it wouldn't seem like much. First of all, it is a liquid. More than half of any protoplasm you would look at under the microscope would be plain water. But in the water, not really dissolved but just suspended, or hanging, there are other things.

These other things, it seems, make the protoplasm thicker than water. Sometimes it is only as thick as olive oil. Other times it

is about as thick as cranberry sauce. Nobody is absolutely sure why it changes like that. But it does.

Protoplasm doesn't really have a color, but under the microscope it might appear to be sort of pale blue-gray. Scientists put stains and dyes on protoplasm so they can see it and study it.

The reason we say protoplasm is alive is that it can move, nourish itself, grow, and make more protoplasm.

Scientists know what protoplasm is made of. First, it contains important chemical elements like carbon, nitrogen, hydrogen, and oxygen. It also has other chemical elements in it like sodium, iron, phosphorus, sulphur, magnesium, calcium, and chlorine.

Those chemicals make up other things that are in the protoplasm. One very important part of the living protoplasm is made of carbohydrates. One of the most important things the carbohydrates do is to turn parts of food into heat energy.

In the protoplasm, also, are fatty substances which store as well as make energy.

Another thing in protoplasm that may sound familiar to you is *protein*. You can see that word on lots of foods. Milk and fish and meats and eggs are sometimes advertised as having lots of protein. This substance is very important for several reasons. It is a main source of nitrogen inside living things. Nitrogen, like oxygen, is needed by all living things. It also makes living things able to grow.

The protoplasm also contains hormones and vitamins. You have probably heard a lot about vitamins, and you may even take them to help keep you energetic and well. Inside the protoplasm, vitamins seem to be the substances that carry some of the special values of separate foods. Some vitamins help you grow. Some help keep you healthy. Scientists aren't quite sure of *why* they do it, but they know *that* they do.

The hormones in the protoplasm may not be as familiar to you, although people talk about them more these days than ever before. This substance in the protoplasm is a "messenger." In its own way it links together all the protoplasm in a living thing so that it can work as it should.

Finally, there are substances in the protoplasm called enzymes. The enzymes dissolve food particles so that they can be used for building energy in living things.

Now we have our first building-block. It is the liquid called protoplasm with all the things it contains. It is alive. And it is the basis of all life.

WHAT PROTOPLASM DOES

Before we see how larger things are built with protoplasm, and finally *everything* from flowers to boys and girls, let's pretend to watch some of the protoplasm through our powerful microscope in the laboratory and see what it *does*. For, like all living things, it *does* something.

That, in a way, tells us what life is: Living things can *do* something. Rocks can't. They just lie there, until moved. Living things can *do* something on their own. Trees grow and their leaves stretch out to reach the sunlight. So do the petals of flowers. People and animals, of course, *do* even more things.

Now, what does the protoplasm do? The protoplasm takes part in the digestion of food. Digestion is the way that food inside the body is prepared to build new parts of the body, make it grow, or provide it with the energy it needs to move about. Then comes what a doctor or a scientist would call respiration. You might call it just plain breathing. It means getting oxygen into living things. The oxygen has to be there to release energy from foods. Protoplasm takes oxygen and combines it with parts of food to produce energy.

The other thing that protoplasm can do that things that aren't alive *can't* do, is to

*Protoplasm and how it grows
and replaces itself*

4

make more of itself. Protoplasm adds material to itself, grows and then separates into two pieces where there used to be only one piece. In this way the living material in living things keeps growing and replacing itself.

WHAT HAPPENS WHEN PROTOPLASM SHAPES UP AS A "CELL"

Now we can see the next building-block. It comes from protoplasm, of course. When a certain amount of protoplasm comes together, it forms something called a "cell." Protoplasm just in its original form, as a shapeless liquid or jelly, couldn't be used to actually build a body or a plant. It has to form into a more solid shape, a shape that can be used to build with. The shape it forms is called a cell.

The first man to use the word cell in talking about the way living things are built, was Robert Hooke, 'way back in 1665. He used it in describing the way cork, which comes from a tree (the cork oak), is built. Corks, as you may have guessed, if you have ever broken one taking it out of a bottle, are very light because they have a lot of very tiny air spaces inside them. You can't really see those spaces with just your eyes, but when you break a cork you can tell because of the crumbly way it comes apart.

When Robert Hooke studied his piece of cork, he decided to call the tiny air spaces cells. Later the word came to mean portions of protoplasm.

The portion of protoplasm that makes up a cell can be of many different sizes. The smallest is so tiny that it would take a half million of them to fill a teaspoon. The largest cells are the yolks of bird's eggs.

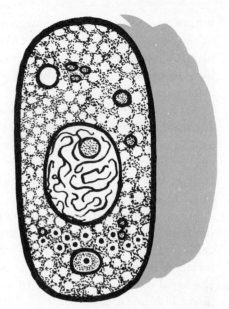

A cell

The thing that is the same in both the tiny portion of protoplasm that forms the smallest cell and the larger portion that forms a cell in the egg is that the protoplasm inside the cell is all one portion *with a wall of thicker protoplasm substance holding it together.* That thicker wall around the protoplasm is what makes it possible to build with cells.

The way these cells build up bodies and plants is to line up together to form different and stronger substances, like the skin, or muscle, or bones.

Scientists, by the way, call this tough outer part of the cell a *membrane* if it is a cell from an animal, and if it is a cell from a plant they call it a *cell wall.* Besides making it possible to build with the protoplasm, this tough outer coating of protoplasm makes it possible for the cells to enclose different things within the wall or membrane so that the cells can do different jobs and build different substances. That is how some cells can build our red blood while

5

others can build white bones, and still others can build green leaves. We'll see about those differences and also see just how these cells do the different jobs in a later part of this book.

When these cells join to form another substance, the cells are pressed together and may have many different shapes. An egg yolk cell can change shape too, of course, as when an egg flattens out as you put it in a pan to fry it.

What we have now is this: protoplasm is the basic material of life. Protoplasm forms cells. The cells make up all the other materials of living things, the stems of plants, the wool on lambs, the sap in trees, the blood in human beings.

Scientists call the cells "organisms" because, after all, a cell is really just "organized" protoplasm. That means it is a unit of protoplasm which is able to feed itself, and grow, and even make more cells. It is "organized" to do things inside its protective wall. But these organisms behave differently from that point on. Some always get along alone. Others flock together to form new substances.

The number of cells used to build living things can be anywhere from one to billions.

Living things that have only one cell as their entire body are called *protozoa*. Most of them are very tiny—so tiny that it would take 100,000 of them to fill a teaspooon. You may remember, though, that we mentioned some cells that are five times tinier—it would take a half million (500,000, or five times 100,000) to fill a teaspoon.

The difference is that those smaller cells always are part of substances formed by putting a lot of cells together—like bones or skin or blood. When we find something that is alive and moves all by itself but *still* is only made up of one cell, it's always a little larger. And that is just the case with *protozoa*. Some of these one-cell *protozoa* even grow as large as a quarter-inch in length and look like tiny jellyfish.

One form of protozoa is called an *amoeba*. Perhaps you have heard that word because many people think the amoeba is the only living thing that is made up of only one cell. Actually it is just one of many kinds of protozoa. The different kinds of protozoa are named according to their shapes, where

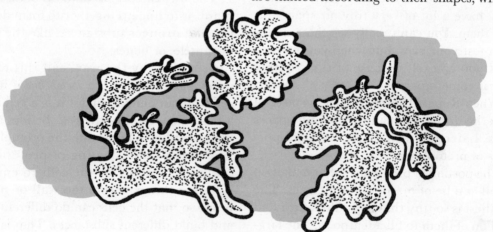

How the amoeba changes its shape

6

caused by the race between them to see which side can grow faster and produce more new cells to carry on the fight.

These one-cell living creatures, like the protoplasm from which they are formed, can reproduce or duplicate themselves. They do this by simply splitting. After they have split, there are two cells instead of one. Each of these two cells then grows and when each of them reaches a certain size, *they* each split and the two cells become four cells. The same process takes place among the cells that grow together to form other substances, like hair or wood. They too split as they grow, to form new cells.

Living things grow as the cells that form the substances of the body or plant divide and make new cells.

But the one big difference between animals and plants is that plants can make their own protoplasm which, in turn, makes cells. Animals can't do that. They have to eat plants, or other animals that have fed on plants, in order to get the material for making protoplasm. (The way green plants go about making their own protoplasm, from the air and from the things they take from the ground, will be part of the story about plants that you can read later on in this book.)

BILLIONS AND BILLIONS OF CELLS

But you probably still want to know how many cells it takes to make up the living things you are more familiar with.

A good example is your own brain—the wonderful brain that lets you understand about cells and be curious about them. How many cells are there in your brain? Scientists figure that there are about nine billion cells in just one human brain. Of course,

they live, or what they eat. The amoeba, for instance, is one that keeps *changing* its shape.

It is among these one-cell organisms also that we can find many of the things that cause sickness. Fevers, like malaria — the fever that so many soldiers got when they fought in jungles—are caused by protozoa that attack healthy cells in the blood. That stomach-ache people sometimes get when they eat "something bad" can be caused by certain one-cell organisms in the "bad" food. When these particular cells go down into our stomachs they start fighting the healthy cells there and we get a stomach-ache! A lot of the trouble we have when harmful cells and healthy cells meet is when you remember that some of those tiny one-cell creatures are so small that a hundred thousand would fit in a teaspoooon, nine billion cells doesn't seem too many to make up a brain. But just so you'll know how big a number nine billion really is, look at your two hands. There are ten fingers. Now, ten times that would be one hundred. Ten times *that* would be a thousand. And if you took one thousand of those "thousands" and multiplied by still *another* thousand you would have one billion. And the human brain has *nine* billion cells of protoplasm in it!

Of course, protoplasm and the cells it forms haven't always been around in such complicated forms as human beings with their nine-billion-cell brains. Some scientists believe that there was a time on earth when the only living matter was protoplasm in single cells. The only living things on earth then were protozoa, one-celled creatures. They could move. They could eat and grow and make new protozoa. Sooner or later these single-celled units of protoplasm got together and formed new things with, say, two cells apiece. From then on, over

Rock with fossil remains

millions of years, the groups of cells got more complicated and larger until, finally, they began to form tiny creatures and plants. Some of the first were like jellyfish and worms, and the plants were like seaweed.

Just how long ago the very first living protoplasm appeared on earth is not known. But we have a good idea of when the protoplasm formed itself into groups of cells to make living creatures.

The way we can figure this is by thinking about the kind of substances that were formed from earth and mud and, over millions of years, hardened into rock. When the earth or mud held living creatures or plants the remains of those creatures or plants sometimes stayed in the mud and then in the rock as it hardened. These traces of ancient plants and creatures are called *fossils.*

Scientists have also figured that certain types of rocks belong to certain periods of time, for in each of these periods, different types of fossils are found.

WHAT FOSSILS TELL US ABOUT THE AGE OF THE EARLIEST FORMS OF LIFE

The oldest period in which rocks containing fossils are found is called the *Proterozoic Era.* This period of the earth took place about one billion years ago. Remember how many a billion is? In rocks from a period called the *Archeozoic Era,* which was perhaps a half-billion years earlier, there are no fossils. Of course, if only one-cell creatures lived in that time, they may not have even made marks on the mud that we could find as fossils today. They would have been too tiny and jelly-like to leave marks.

Cave man

The oldest fossils, from that time one billion years ago, are sorts of worms and tiny plants like those that today form a green scum on some ponds and lakes.

From fossils, therefore, we can figure that some form of life has been on earth for at least a billion years.

HOW OLD IS MAN?

What about man, though? How long have there been men, even the earliest cave men, on earth? From the skeletons and other remains of ancient men that have been found, and from the sort of rocks under which they are buried, scientists have figured that the most ancient man lived about a million years ago.

Compared to the time in which other forms of life have been on the earth, that isn't very much time at all. One million is just one one-thousandth of a billion! And, as you may read in another part of this book, the earth itself, with or without living things on it, has been in existence at least *three billion* years.

So, as you can see, men are really just newcomers on the earth. Hundreds of millions of years before men there were the tiny worms and plants, and single cells.

One of the first animals to leave the water

WHY THE FIRST LIVING THINGS LEFT THE OCEAN FOR THE LAND

At first, as far as we can tell, the earliest creatures lived in the oceans.

It took millions of years for living things to leave the oceans and go to live on dry land. We can only guess why the creatures and plants went on to the land. We can only guess why some forms of life chose to stay in the oceans. Perhaps some of the tiny worm-like animals of a billion years ago found they could no longer easily feed themselves in the ocean. Some may have eaten all of the plant life in their neighborhood in the ocean. Without that plant life, then, they would have had no way of rebuilding their own protoplasm. So, perhaps some struggled away from their old areas and some just sort of stumbled up onto the land. Even earlier, perhaps, some of the plant life in the oceans had grown closer and closer to the shore until, one day when a very low tide may have left them high and dry, they just rooted in the land and stayed there. It would have been those plants that the tiny animal creatures would have found to nourish themselves with as they moved out onto the land.

Now those things are all *perhaps*. What we know for *sure* is that life left the oceans and *did* move onto the land. And when it did, the simple globs of protoplasm and cells that started it all began to develop more and more into the sort of animals and plants we know of today. We'll learn about them next.

Ancient Animals

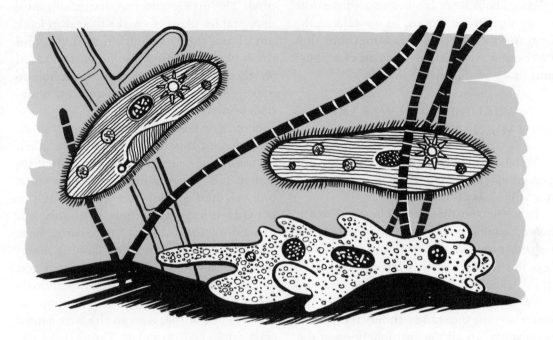

Earliest known animal

SOMEWHERE around a billion years ago life began to develop on the earth. But scientists to this day can't be sure of exactly when the first life was created on earth. There simply aren't any traces of what scientists believe were the very first living things. They were tiny one-celled organisms something like the ones we can see today in a drop of water if we look through a microscope.

After many centuries, when living things developed into creatures with hard shells or bones, they left traces. The marks of these ancient creatures, some of them still very tiny, were left in mud. Then, over millions of years, the mud turned to stone.

If the mark hadn't been disturbed, as it might not be in a deserted swamp for instance, then the mark of the ancient creature remained in the stone. We call those marks *fossils*. A bit of the creature itself remaining in the rock is called a fossil too.

Now, the very oldest remains of any fossils that scientists have found seem to be about a half-billion years old. But many scientists think that even before there were these creatures that could leave marks, there must have been others—like the one-celled bits of protoplasm. (You can read about them in the chapter of this book called *Life's Building-Blocks.*)

So, we can figure that somewhere between

a half-billion and a billion years ago, life began on earth. Don't forget that we are talking about *when* life began and not *how* it began. How it began, as we said at the beginning of the book, is something that has been accounted for in terms of religion and never explained by science.

WHAT THE EARTH WAS LIKE WHEN LIFE FIRST APPEARED

What was it like when the first life appeared on earth? We can only guess, but it might have been like this:

It is believed that great clouds of steam floated around the earth as it formed. These turned into rain and began to fill the valleys of the earth with what later became great lakes and oceans.

We are quite sure that life began in the water or in the mud under the water. Somewhere, in all the vast loneliness of the world, a creature came to life. It was probably a single tiny cell of living matter or protoplasm. And it was probably a *plant* cell—that is, a cell provided with chlorophyll, the green coloring matter of plants that enables plants to make their own food, out of air, the energy from sunlight, and water. With nothing else on earth to feed on, those first cells must have been able to make their own food out of the raw materials present in the world.

Sooner or later many of these cells probably drifted together. It may have taken thousands of years. When they drifted together and began living together, or when one cell had grown and split enough to provide many cells, there probably appeared on the waters of the world, here and there, patches of green floating material, like the algae or the green scum you see on ponds today. The algae then floating on the water could provide food for other types of life, and so the first *animal* cells appeared on earth. From these developed all the animal life. From the algae came all the plants.

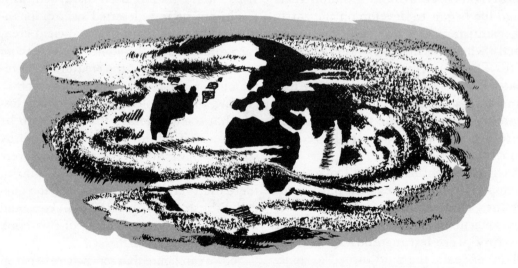

Great clouds of steam floating around earth

WEEDS, WORMS, AND INSECTS

Some of the green floating algae developed into seaweed-like plants that waved along the bottom of the water. The animal cells, meantime, developed and changed into worm-like creatures.

For more thousands of years both the plants and the animal life changed and changed. Some of the plant life near the shores probably began to grow up onto dry land, and before long fern-like plants began to appear in clumps here and there. The tiny, worm-like creatures in the water developed into starfish and jellyfish and finally into hard-shelled creatures that looked rather like centipedes. Sooner or later even some of these creatures began to follow the plants out onto dry land.

It was more than three hundred million years ago that the first creatures began to leave the water to live on land. Scientists can tell this by the fossils of these creatures. If the fossil is found in rocks that must have been out of the water millions of years ago, then the scientists can figure that they have a dry-land fossil. Then, by comparing that rock with rocks whose age has been carefully tested and is known, they can tell when the fossil's mark was made.

By about fifty million years after the first creatures went onto the land, some more familiar forms of life had begun to develop. Insects, many of which have hardly changed over hundreds of millions of years, began to appear.

The process by which all this came about is called evolution, and although it may appear very strange, it really isn't. It is easy to see, for instance, how a worm-like creature in the ocean might flop out onto land and begin living there. Perhaps it

Early forms of starfish, jellyfish and centipede-like creatures

could find more food there. Perhaps it wanted to escape other creatures that were hunting *it* to eat.

Once out on land and able to live there, the worm-like creatures would start raising new families and each one would be better

Glacier period

used to living on land than the one before. One family might even produce some children with legs—tiny ones, of course—to make it easier to get around. Those first ones would be sort of accidents of birth. But the nature of living things is such that if an accident like that turns out to be very helpful, it may become a regular part of the next generation. So, from wormlike creatures in the sea we might get lizard-like animals on the land.

Besides the appearance of insects, and frog-like and lizard-like animals, some of the animals that stayed in the water developed into fairly familiar forms. The shark, for instance, is a sort of fish that developed back in this period hundreds of millions of years ago and has hardly changed at all since its first appearance some two hundred and fifty million years ago.

At about that time, also, the living things on the earth began to have great troubles. The earth, which had once been steaming hot, began to have long periods of thousands of years in which great thick sheets of ice, or glaciers, covered most of the world. When the glaciers came, very few animals could live in the icy climate. Many kinds of animals died out and became extinct during the periods of the glaciers and there were no more like them. But many other kinds kept on living and developing.

THE TIME OF THE DINOSAURS

Then, about one hundred and fifty-eight million years ago, in a time called the Triassic Period, some of the animals had grown and changed into the strange and frightening creatures we lump together as *dinosaurs*. The word dinosaur actually means "terri-

14

ble lizard." It describes most of the dinosaurs very well, for, in the first place, they belonged to the reptile family as lizards do. And they were terrible because they were so large, some of them being more than 60 feet long. When we think of reptiles today, we think mainly of snakes. But actually the animal family of reptiles includes many different animals, like lizards and turtles and crocodiles and alligators. It is easier to think of the dinosaurs as reptiles when we think of alligators as reptiles. Many of the ancient dinosaurs, in fact, looked a bit like today's alligators, except that they were larger. They had hard armored scales on their body, they could swim in water or walk on land with their short legs, and they laid eggs instead of having live babies.

Some of the creatures of the dinosaur age that we sometimes see pictures of to-day are the *stegosaurus, brontosaurus, ptero-dactyl, triceratops,* and *tyrannosaurus.*

The *stegosaurus* had a body rather like a rhinoceros, heavily armored. But its head was more like an alligator's head. It had a long powerful tail like an alligator's too, but its legs were longer and it could move on land better. The thing that makes this creature easy to remember is that all along its back in a double row were big flaps of armored skin. Along the tail these flaps changed into long spikes.

The *brontosaurus* was one of the largest of the lot, much larger than today's elephants. Some remains of these creatures show that the brontosaurus could grow to 60 and 70 feet long and be twelve feet high or twice as high as a tall man. Besides its size, the brontosaurus was quite noticeable for having a neck that was almost as long as

Brontosaurus

its body. The brontosaurus looked a bit like a fairy-tale dragon, except that it had a smooth dark skin, didn't snort and puff smoke (no *real* animal ever did), and lived on plant life alone, never eating any other animals.

The *pterodactyl* was much smaller, five or six feet from head to tail, but for a reptile it was perhaps the strangest of all. It could fly. Instead of this kind of reptile developing legs for walking or flippers for swimming, it had developed a wide thin area of skin that it could use for wings. But if it could fly, why not call it a bird? The reason is that all birds have feathers. The pterodactyl didn't. It was just like any other reptile, except that it could fly.

Triceratops was one of the fiercest of the great terrible lizards. It was built very much like a modern rhinoceros except that it was more heavily armored and from its head came two great horns jutting out almost straight like swords.

The very fiercest of all the animals in this age of reptiles, however, was *tyrannosaurus*. His name means the tyrant. And he *was* a tyrant, ruling over the other animals, eating any he wanted. There was no enemy powerful enough to stop him.

Tyrannosaurus stood upright on great scaly legs. He had a long powerful round tail and a fierce large-mouthed head. From tip of tail to top of head the tyrannosaurus measured about fifty feet.

AFTER THE DINOSAURS CAME THE MAMMALS

After ruling the earth for perhaps as long as one hundred million years, the great reptiles, the dinosaurs, began to disappear.

Tyrannosaurus

The giant brontosaurus turned out to be just too big. He had trouble finding food, he had trouble running away from smaller but fiercer meat-eating dinosaurs.

Tyrannosaurus, gobbling up everything in sight, may have eaten himself right out of existence.

At any rate, there came a time fifty or sixty million years ago when there were no more dinosaurs left. Instead, a new animal that had been developing while the dinosaurs had been ruling the earth, began to grow stronger and more plentiful. This new sort of animal was the mammal—warm-blooded, with hair, and having live babies instead of laying eggs. While they grew more plentiful, so did the few reptiles that survived from the age of the dinosaurs, but these were all smaller than the giants. They were the reptiles like the ones we have today: snakes, turtles, alligators, and so forth.

Mastodon

MAMMALS WITH A MODERN LOOK

The mammals that were taking over the earth looked much more like animals we have today than like dinosaurs. There was the *arsinotherium* for instance. He looked a lot like a rhinoceros. But, you may remember, so did some of the great reptiles, like the triceratops. But the arsinotherium had thinner skin, though still plenty thick compared to most animals, and on this skin in some places were patches of hair. Too, he was born and bred on land and wasn't like the great reptiles who were just a few reptile eras removed from having lived in the water. This meant that he could live on the land much better. All in all, he looked and acted much more like a modern animal than the dinosaurs.

Then there were small horse-like animals, like the *orohippus* and *mesohippus*. There were great wolf-like animals like the *hyaenodon,* and tiger-like cats such as the *dinictis*.

By the time thirty-three million years ago had rolled around, the world was in what some scientists call the Golden Age of Mammals. By this time there were great elephant-like creatures such as the *trilophodon* and later the *mastodon* with its tusks curving and twisting far longer than any elephant's. But there also were smaller animals, like rabbits and cats and even monkeys. For every animal we know of today there was some sort of fairly similar animal during this Golden Age of the Mammals.

17

But then all the animals had another time of terrible trouble as ice formed again and began to move in great sheets across the earth as it had done many millions of years before. Half the world, at least, was completely frozen. Many of the animals died. Only the toughest and the best equipped lived. Some developed fur that enabled them to live in cold climates—the bear for instance. Some lucky ones escaped to parts of the world that didn't freeze. Many of the animals in Africa today are thought to be Ice Age survivors who escaped from colder parts of the world where they once lived.

Finally the ice melted and the world settled down to what the scientists call modern times. These "modern" times started almost two million years ago. By then just about all the animals we know today had developed about as far as they could, and instead of changing some more, they settled down and stayed just about the same.

Color shows area of the earth covered by glaciers during the Ice Age.

MAN

The final part of this story of the development of life on the earth started only one million years ago. In the long march of evolution that is a very short time indeed.

New kinds of mammals began to be seen here and there on the earth. Some of the other animals may have thought they were just another kind of big ape or monkey. They were quite hairy and walked on two legs. But these new mammals started doing things that no other living creature had ever done. They began making things, like spears to help them hunt, and sharp pieces of stone to help them cut.

Over many thousands of years, as these strange new mammals walked straighter and began to cover their smooth skins with hides skinned from animals, they made other useful things — nets to catch fish, needles out of bones, threads out of pieces of animal muscle.

Some of them lived in caves but some built huts of wood and leaves.

They told stories to one another. They were human beings.

Man's age on earth had begun. And it is still here.

Early man making first tools

19

How Animals Grow

WE HAVE seen how living things can change. Now we will see how they grow.

The growing things that you probably wonder about the most are animals—and people. When we talk about people we know what we mean. But when we talk about animals, we might get mixed up.

If a scientist said "animal" he might mean something entirely different from what you or I would mean. The scientist might mean anything alive that wasn't vegetable. (By "vegetable" he would mean plants and trees and flowers and such things as cotton and, of course, the foods we call vegetables anyway.) To scientists the world breaks down into three great parts: animal, vegetable, and mineral. The mineral part means all the rocks and stones and dust and dirt and air and everything *not* alive.

Now, when you think of "animals" as a scientist does, "animal" would include all the insects and even germs. Usually we don't think of those as animals. When we say "animal" we usually mean something like a cat or a dog or an elephant.

For most of us, the word "animal" means a very particular kind of animal. It means that part of the animal kingdom called mammals. Let's see what mammals are.

Animal   *Vegetable*   *Mineral*

HOW DO MAMMALS
DIFFER FROM OTHER ANIMALS?

In the first place, all mammals have some sort of hair or fur. Just as all birds have feathers, mammals have hair or fur. Of course, there may be some time during the mammal's life that you can't see the hair or fur—but some time during its life it *will* be there. (Men and women are mammals, as well as most animals that we think of as animals.)

What else about mammals? Well, another thing is that practically every mammal has a special way of giving food to its babies. The mother, in practically every family of mammals, can make milk in her body to feed to her baby. Cows are the mammals best known for this because they have enough milk left over to feed young human beings and grown-ups as well.

Another thing about mammals is that most of them have live babies rather than eggs from which the babies hatch. In Australia, Tasmania, and New Guinea, however, there are three sort of mammals that *do* lay eggs. One is the Duck-Billed platypus. You may have heard about platypuses because they are so odd. Besides being mammals that lay eggs, they have webbed feet, a bill like that of a duck, and fur like a beaver. The other mammals that lay eggs are two types of spiny ant-eaters that live in the same lands.

But before you decide that it is easy to recognize a mammal, you had better know about some of the largest and strangest animals of all—the whales, sea-cows, and dolphins. They don't live on the land like other mammals. They live in the oceans, and you might think they were fish. But they aren't. Unlike real fish, these swimming mammals do not lay eggs. Their babies are born alive, just the way a calf is born to a cow or a child to a human mother. They can give milk. There are some spots on their bodies where they have hair, and their temperature is higher than that of real fish. Mammals, in general, have some warmth to their bodies. Living things that aren't mammals, like fish and snakes, don't have nearly as much if any.

The whale is the most amazing mammal in one way. It is the largest living creature on earth. Not all whales, of course, are such gigantic creatures. In fact some types of whale are not any larger than some of the large fish, like sharks. The type of whale that is the real giant is called a Sulphur-Bottom or Blue whale. It is not only the largest animal now alive on the earth, but it is even larger than the great dinosaurs that lived millions of years ago.

This kind of whale grows to be as much as 100 feet long. This makes it as long as about six automobiles parked bumper to bumper. And this great whale weighs as much as 300,000 pounds, about the weight of about nine *big* automobiles!

On the other hand there are such mammals as the tiny shrews, mouselike animals that don't weigh as much as a toy soldier, and are only about as large. As we said, it is these animals, these mammals, that you probably wonder about most because, after all, *you* are included in all this. You are, so far as the scientists are concerned, a mammal.

So, when we answer the question in this part of the book, about how animals grow, we really are going to answer the question of how *you* grow.

To begin the answer you should remem-ber the first of this book about the cells that are the building-blocks of all living things. There you read about living things made of only one cell. They are called *pro-tozoa*. All other living things made up of more than one cell are called *metazoa*. Mammals, of course, are made up of billions of cells. You may remember that we said that a man's brain alone has more than nine billion cells in it.

The story of how you or any other mammal grows is the story of how all cells grow because cells are what form muscles and skin and bones and blood.

22

HOW MAMMALS ARE BORN

Let's start at the very beginning. All mammals start with a particular kind of cell that the scientists call a *germ cell*. They don't mean the kind of germ that gives you a sickness. They mean what the Romans meant when they first used the word "germen" which means to sprout.

That's just what these germ cells do, too. They sprout. We'll learn about the ones that sprout plants later. Now we are interested in the ones that sprout animals!

The germ cell starts to grow in a special place inside the mother—whether it is a mother lion or a mother cat or a mother who will have a little boy or girl. The cells begin to grow and to split to make other cells. Soon all of the cells have formed a small pouch. Into this is taken nourishment from the mother's blood stream. In it, also, new types of cells begin to collect and start growing.

These cells are the ones used to build bodies. Scientists call them *somatic cells* to separate them from the *germ cells* that start the process of growth.

Working on the pattern set by the germ cells, these new cells begin to form themselves into the shape of a baby—baby cat, baby lion, or any sort of baby. Depending on the pattern set by the germ cells, they will form a baby boy or a baby girl.

When the shape is formed enough, the baby is born. It is brought out to live.

HOW MAMMALS GROW

Now, with the baby born and growing by itself, we can learn more about how it grows. We can see how all the billions of cells get together and do their jobs. They do it by forming *tissues*.

You may think of the paper tissues you use when you have a runny nose. The tissues formed by cells are quite different. A tissue of that sort means simply a grouping together of cells to form different special substances that do different special jobs. Their pattern is set by the germ cells too, as the baby first takes form. That is why

some babies grow to be tall men or women and some short, and why some have red hair and some black and some blond.

OUR TISSUES

One kind of tissue is the kind that forms skin. Another kind forms bones. Another forms muscles. Another forms the nerves that connect all the other tissues and, in a way, tell them what to do. For instance, the nerves running through your skin are what make your finger hurt when you touch something very hot. They send the pain message to your brain which acts like a switchboard for the nerves. The brain sends a message back along other nerves to your muscles, and the muscles jerk your hand away so it won't get badly burned. All this happens more quickly than the time it takes to blink your eyes.

How message travels to brain when finger touches a flame

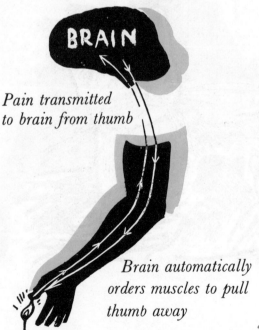

BRAIN

Pain transmitted to brain from thumb

Brain automatically orders muscles to pull thumb away

Knowing about those four basic forms of tissues we can now go on to the things we call *organs*. Then we will be very much closer to the answer of how we grow.

OUR ORGANS

The organs are simply groups of tissues that act together to do a special job. The tissues, you remember, are just cells that act together to do a special job.

Your legs are an *organ* of movement. They let you move. They are called an organ because they have skin tissue covering them, bone tissue making them straight and strong, muscle tissue making them able to move fast and powerfully, and nerve tissues carrying messages to them.

For growing, however, there are even more important organs. These organs are inside of the body. They are the organs that take food and turn it into energy to keep you alive, and also into new tissues to make you grow!

THE DIGESTIVE ORGANS

First there are the digestive organs, which center around the stomach. The job the digestive organs do is to change food into liquids and absorb those liquids into the blood. From there another group of organs, called organs of circulation, take the good part of the food throughout the body. We'll get to that next. But now, let's follow the *digestive system*.

First, the food comes in through the mouth. If the food is a liquid, like milk, it goes down easily. If the food is solid, like meat or candy or vegetables, the teeth break it up so it can be swallowed. While the chewing is going on, the food is mixed

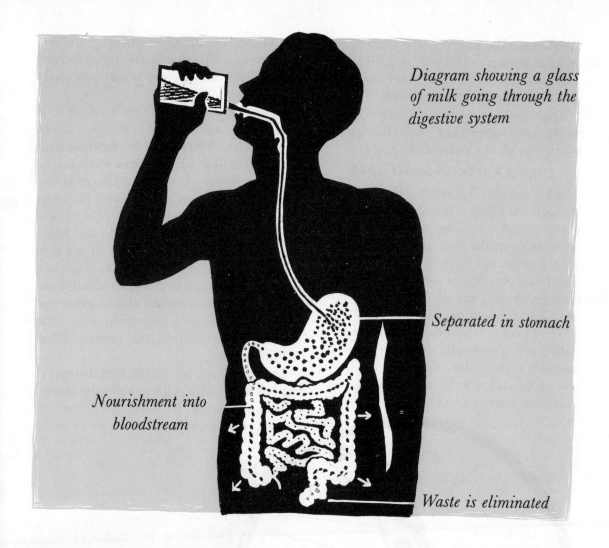

Diagram showing a glass of milk going through the digestive system

Separated in stomach

Nourishment into bloodstream

Waste is eliminated

with and softened by the saliva in the mouth. This helps start the digestion that is the job of the digestive system.

Next, the food goes into the stomach where it is mixed with liquids that always are being formed by the cell tissues there— liquids made up of special cells. Their job is to mix with the food and dissolve most of it. When it is dissolved it goes into the intestine. From there it seeps right through the walls of the intestine and is taken into

the blood to be carried throughout the body. The part of the food that the body can't use, both liquid and solid, is passed out of the body.

THE ORGANS OF CIRCULATION

Now we come to the circulatory system, the organs of circulation that carry nourishment throughout the body. From this nourishment, the cells in the tissues of bone grow and make us taller. The cells in our muscles use the nourishment to grow and make us stronger. The cells that make hair grow also use the nourishment and make us need hair cuts or hair ribbons.

The *circulatory system* also carries oxygen, which our lungs take from the air we breathe to all the parts of the body.

THE BLOOD DOES MANY JOBS

The circulatory system does all this through the blood. The blood goes through every part of the body, carrying the nourishment from the food and the oxygen to all the cells that form the various tissues. The blood also carries away waste products cast out by the cells after they have fed on the food and used the oxygen.

The blood cells that carry the oxygen are called red blood cells. Actually they are sort of a bluish color when they are inside the veins and arteries of the body. The veins and arteries and blood vessels are the tubes carrying blood. When exposed to air, as when you cut your finger, the cells turn red and that is why the blood you see is always that color.

In the blood also are other kinds of cells called white cells. These cells take care of your health. They do it by fighting and actually eating up bacteria that might otherwise make you very sick. Bacteria is a word that scientists use to name the one-cell organisms that cause many of our worst sicknesses. Bacteria also include some helpful one-cell organisms, however. It is a certain kind of bacteria, for instance, that brings nourishment to plants. Without those bacteria we would not be able to grow our food. Other bacteria make milk sour. Still others can turn certain fruit juices or alcohol into vinegar.

In doing their job in the blood stream, the red and white cells actually use themselves up very fast. Red cells are formed in the marrow of the bones at a rate of more

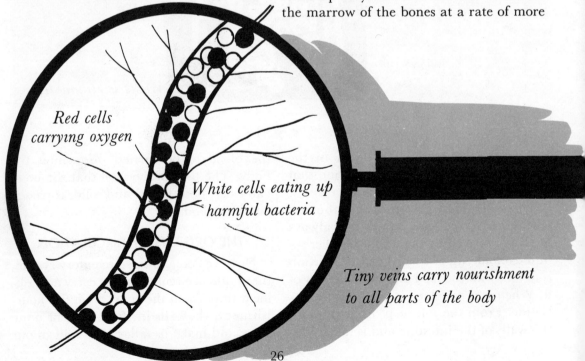

Red cells carrying oxygen

White cells eating up harmful bacteria

Tiny veins carry nourishment to all parts of the body

than one million every second! The white cells are produced by special glands. A gland is just an organ whose job is to make special cells.

Sickness is usually a race between the white cells and the bacteria to see which can produce the most cells. If the white cells win, they gobble up the bacteria and you get well. If they don't then the bacteria can spread and you get sicker.

THE ORGANS OF BREATHING

Next we come to the *respiratory system* which just means the organs of breathing. The main part in mammals, of course, are the lungs. In fish the gills do that job, and insects have tiny holes along their body that take care of breathing for them. Earthworms breathe right through their skin.

As we have seen, from the circulatory system, the big job for the lungs is to take the good oxygen out of the air and into the body. But the lungs also have to get rid of

Good part of air taken into bloodstream

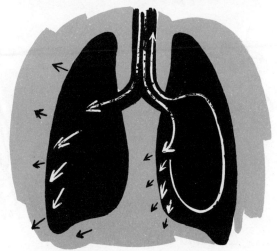

*Remaining carbondioxide
is breathed out*

the bad part of the air that is left over—the part called carbon dioxide. The lungs do that every time you breathe out. You breathe *in* to bring air with oxygen into the lungs. You breathe *out* to get rid of the carbon dioxide that is left.

Because of this, if you were in a room that was closed up absolutely tight, you could breathe only as long as there was some unused air in the room. After a while your lungs would have removed all the oxygen from the air and the room would be full of carbon dioxide. That is a very good reason for making sure that there always is some way for new air to get into wherever you are. Don't worry too much about it, though, because just opening the door of your house a few times a day is enough, and in most houses enough air leaks in around the windows and under the doors. Where people get into trouble is when they get locked into tightly closed places like old ice-boxes.

THE OTHER ORGANS
THAT KEEP US ALIVE

The other systems that make up the organs that keep us alive are: the *muscular system,* which gives us the strength to move around, jump, run, and walk; the *skeleton system,* which includes the bones to which the muscles are attached and which keep our bodies straight; the *excretory system,* which takes away the wastes we can't use from the food we eat and the liquids we drink; the *nervous system* that carries all the messages that make our muscles move and all the organs work properly; and the *reproductive system* that takes care of the germ cells with which the miracle of birth and growth begins here on earth.

27

Animals
around the World

WE HAVE learned a good deal about how animals grow. Now it is time to start taking a close look at these animals, one by one. We'll begin with the mammals, whose growth we talked about. Then we'll meet some other families of animals.

First let's think about the animals we call *domesticated,* because they live with human beings and help them. Domesticated animals are not wild animals. We'll meet the wild animals later.

We can start right around home and around our own town and then work our way out into the fields and finally across the oceans into the jungles and mountains of foreign lands.

When you think of animals that live close to man and help him most, you probably think first of the dog or cat. We call the dog man's best friend. Dogs certainly are friendly. Some cats are too.

A CHILD'S MOST IMPORTANT ANIMAL FRIEND—THE COW

But, if you stop to think for a moment, there is one other animal that really is closer to your life than any other. It is an animal that helps keep you strong and healthy every day of your life. It is the first animal, in fact, that plays an important part in the life of most boys and girls. This amazing animal is the plain, ordinary cow. It gives us milk. Some scientists say that milk is the perfect food. They mean that it

has everything in it that a person needs to grow and stay healthy.

If we live in a city, the cows probably do not live very close to us. They live on farms. But every day the milk that the cows make comes to homes in the city.

The way a cow makes that milk is a wonderful story in itself.

As we learned earlier, all mammals, the mothers that is, can make milk to feed their children. The cow makes *its* milk to feed its calf. But some sorts of cows have a lot of milk left over after they have fed their own calf and even after the calf doesn't need any of the milk at all. These are called milk cows or dairy cows. A dairy farm is a farm where cows are raised for milk.

The making of the milk starts when the cow eats. The cow's stomach is able to separate the proper things from the food the cow eats and to make milk from them. Per-

Cow and Calf

haps you have seen cows eating or grazing on grass. If you have seen them in a barn, they have been eating the dried grasses and plants that we call hay.

A cow gets minerals, like calcium and iron, vitamins, proteins, and all the other things needed to make milk, from the food she eats. That is why dairy farmers are very careful to have their cows eat the right things, the best grass, and the best hay. If the cows didn't eat right, then the milk wouldn't be made right.

When the cow first chews her food she doesn't do a very good job. She just grinds it a couple of times between her teeth and then swallows it. It goes into the first part of her stomach. It comes back into her mouth in the shape of balls of food. Now she lies down or just stands somewhere where she won't be bothered, and chews the food all over again. This time she does a good job, chewing and chomping the balls of food very thoroughly.

This ball of food that gets the second chewing is called a "cud." When you see a cow standing, chewing, as though she had a mouthful of chewing gum, she is just chewing her cud.

Scientists think the reason certain animals, like cows, eat like this is that it was once a safety factor. Thousands of years ago, when all animals lived in the wilds, it might not have been safe for them to spend much time eating out in the open fields, for other wild animals might have crept up behind them and pounced on them. So the cow gobbled down her food very fast and then went off to a safe hiding-place to chew it thoroughly.

Animals that eat like that are called *ruminants,* and chewing the cud is called

Ruminants

29

ruminating. Ox, sheep, deer, goats, and even antelopes, camels, and giraffes are cud-chewing animals like the cow.

After the cow has chewed her cud, she swallows the food for the second time. Now the food is very well chewed up. It goes to another part of the stomach. In this part of the cow's stomach, the food is tumbled around and ground so that the different things in the food begin to separate. The minerals and the vitamins and other important elements are taken out and prepared for being put together to make milk.

Finally the food moves into the last part of the stomach where the different parts are finally separated all the way. Because the separate parts are mostly white, the milk they make will be white too.

The food particles needed to make the milk are now in liquid form. The liquid moves from the stomach into the cow's intestines, which are like long coiled tubes leading from the stomach. Those parts of the food that the cow needs for herself are taken into the bloodstream and carried to the places in the body that need nourishment.

The parts that are left for making milk are carried directly to the cow's udder, the milk-bag underneath the cow. The calf can get the milk from the udder by sucking at one of the four finger-like teats that come from the udder. The farmer gets the milk by squeezing them.

The main types or breeds of dairy cows are: The *Ayrshire,* the *Brown Swiss,* the *Guernsey,* the *Holstein,* and the *Jersey.*

In the northeastern states you will see a lot of dairy cows called *Ayrshires.* The best of these are reddish with big splotches of white on them. Some are mostly white with the darker colors up toward their shoulders and head. Others are brownish with white. The cow weighs 1,200 pounds in good condition, and the bulls, the males, weigh about 1,800 pounds. The horns are medium size. Ayrshire milk contains on the average about four per cent butterfat. This is just about the average for all the milk we get in America. An Ayrshire cow, on the average, will give about 4,500 quarts of milk during one year, though some have given more than twice that much.

The *Brown Swiss* is a sort of cow that was brought to this country from Switzerland just after the Civil War. Just as its name says, this is a brown cow. It has a black nose and the tips of its medium-size horns are tipped with black. These cows give just a bit more milk, on the average, than the Ayrshires, but the butterfat content is about the same.

One of the richest sorts of milk comes from the *Guernsey* cow. This type of cow was brought to America from Guernsey, one of the Channel Islands off the coast of England. Another breed, the *Jersey,* came from another Channel Island, Jersey.

The Guernsey's milk averages almost five per cent butterfat and is known for its rich golden color. The cow itself is about the color of a young deer, a very light yellowish brown. It has white markings. These cows are about the same size as the others we have talked about so far and give about the same amount of milk on the average.

The largest of the dairy cow breeds in size are the black and white *Holsteins.* Their milk isn't as rich in butterfat as the others we have talked about, but each cow gives, on the average, abut 7,000 quarts of milk each year. The cows weigh about 1,500

Hereford

Longhorn

Holstein

Brahman

pounds and the bulls 2,000 pounds, which is a ton. The calves, when they are born, weigh from 70 to 100 pounds.

The Jersey cow is the smallest of the breeds. Like the Guernsey, its main color is a light brown or fawn, sometimes with white markings. The Jersey's milk is rich, just as is the Guernsey's, but a Jersey does not give quite as much on the average. The cows weigh only about 1,000 pounds and the calves may weigh as little as 40 pounds when they are born.

The kinds of cows we have been talking about are raised mainly for their milk. But some cows—the kind the cowboys herd in the West—are raised mainly because of their meat. They are called beef cows because we get beefsteak, roast beef, and other forms of beef from them.

Although beef cows and dairy cows and bulls may be about the same size, the beef cattle have to be a lot stronger because they usually live on the open range, finding their own food, until it is time for them to be fattened up for market.

The cows that the old-time cowboys used to drive in great herds across the western plains were a tough, very powerful breed known as *Longhorns*. And their horns really *were* long. Many were six and seven feet long, from the tip of one to the tip of the other. Today's beef cattle aren't quite as fierce looking as that. In fact, they are fairly tame, not very different from the milk cows.

Some of the beef cattle that you may see are the all-black *Black Angus*, the reddish *Hereford* with its white face, and the light colored *Brahman* with a great big hump on its shoulders.

Even though the cow may be the most important animal for you, the one you probably like the best is either a cat or a dog. We'll talk about dogs first.

Dogs, or at least animals resembling dogs, appeared on earth many millions of years before anything that looked like a man. The first man-like creatures came no more than a million years ago. The first animals that scientists say were like dogs appeared between forty and sixty million years ago.

The first dog-like creatures probably looked more like bears than the dogs we are used to seeing now. Gradually, though, as all the animals in the world went through the changes we learned about earlier, dogs began to look like, well, like dogs. By the time man himself had got around to making tools and weapons out of stone, in what is called the Stone Age, about 50,000 years ago, the dog had already become a good friend of man. At least so it would seem, for when the bones and stone axes of the ancient Stone Age men have been found, the bones of dogs have often been found nearby. This means that men and dogs lived close together even then.

Unfortunately, men didn't begin to write down what happened to them until about 6,000 years ago. By then, dogs were just as important to men as they are today. In some ways they were even more important. For, then as now, they helped men hunt. But back then, hunting was the most important means of getting meat for the table.

Helping men to hunt came naturally to dogs, for in order to live dogs themselves had to be hunters even before there were any men on the earth. When the dog teamed up with man to hunt, the two of them together became the best hunting combination the world ever has known. No wild animals anywhere are as deadly hunters as are a man and a dog. The man has the best brain. The dog has his wonderful sense of smell and hearing and sight. Together they can outsmart any other animals and, unless they are careless, no other animals can outsmart them.

It wasn't too long, apparently, after man and dog teamed up to hunt that women and children discovered something else about dogs. They found dogs were very friendly and that it was good to have them even when there wasn't hunting to do. Children found them to be wonderful playmates.

Today, in countries like America, where hunting is a sport and not the only way of getting meat to eat, most dogs are pets even when they are also used for hunting.

The kind of dog that is probably loved as a pet by more people than any other is no particular type at all, really. It is just dog, a mixture of many breeds. Some are little white and black ones with a shrill bark. Others are big floppy ones with shaggy coats. In between there are many other different kinds.

Many dogs, of course, are of one certain breed, or type, and have been raised to do a special job. Some of the very smartest dogs are the ones used to help herd animals. Many dogs have been trained to keep sheep and cattle, and even chickens, from straying. But several kinds of dogs have made a specialty out of it. The ones you probably know best are the *Collie* and the

32

German Shepherd or *German Police dog*.

The German Shepherd has also been trained to help the police and to guard buildings and, very wonderfully, to guide blind persons.

When it comes to hunting dogs, the kind we usually think of is the hound. There are many different kinds of hound, but one thing they have in common is that they locate game animals by scent, by smelling them, and then follow or "hound" them,

German Shepherd

Collie

until the hunter can come. The most popular of the hounds today is the little *Beagle,* with his long ears and short sturdy legs. The Beagle's specialty is hunting rabbits.

One of the largest of the hounds is the *Bloodhound*. He has a great wrinkled face that looks very sad. His ears droop. In many parts of the world, including the United States, the Bloodhound is used by policemen to help find people who have either got lost or who are running away after doing something bad. The Bloodhound helps find them by sniffing after their scent.

Other hounds specialize in hunting certain things. There are many hounds, for instance, called *Coonhounds* because they like best of all to hunt raccoons.

Then there is the funniest of all the hounds, the friendly little *Dachshund,* or badger hound. People always make jokes about the Dachshund because he looks so very much like a hot dog on legs. But there is nothing funny about the way this wonderful little dog can hunt. He specializes in hunting for badgers. The badger is a very strong and tough animal that is almost as large as the Dachshund himself. The Dachshund's short legs make him especially good at hunting Badgers. They let him wriggle down into the holes where Badgers hide.

Another very important type of hunting dog is the *Retriever*. The special job that the many kinds of Retriever do is to fetch back game that has been shot. When a duck hunter shoots a duck over the water, he might never get the duck if it weren't for the Retriever that jumps into the water and swims out to bring back the duck. Other Retrievers bring back birds that have been shot and fallen into thickets and woods where a man might not be able to find them.

Pointers and *Setters* also are special dogs used for special hunting jobs. Both of these types of dog are used in hunting birds in the field. When the dog spots a bird, like a quail or a pheasant, he stops so still that he looks like a statue. Not a muscle moves. The dog actually points at the bird with his head. Then the hunter can come along, ready to shoot when the bird flashes up, flying away.

Another important type of hunting dog is the *Spaniel*. These are generally smallish dogs with nice long coats. They are very good for finding rabbits as well as for finding birds and making them fly up into the air where the hunter may have a shot at them. The *Cocker Spaniel* is one of this type although now he is almost always kept as a pet rather than a hunting dog.

There is another kind of hunting dog, like the *Greyhound* and the *Whippet,* that has been used to chase game rather than just to find it. Hundreds of years ago, one of the sports that many Kings liked best of all was to watch dogs like this race after deer or other game. Many just liked the race itself, for the dogs very often were trained to come back as soon as they had caught up with the game and not to hurt it at all.

Of course there are a lot of dogs that really aren't specialists at anything at all except looking pretty or cute or doing tricks to make people happy. The tiny *Chihuahua,* which is small enough to fit in a lady's

Chihuahua

pocketbook, is one dog like that. The *Poodle* with its funny haircut is another.

Some dogs that are usually pets now, once had very special jobs in certain parts of the world. The big, sad looking *St. Bernard* won its fame in the Great St. Bernard Pass through the mountains between Switzerland and Italy. When travelers became lost in the pass, St. Bernards were used to find them. Around their necks, sometimes, were tied little bundles of food or casks of brandy for the stranded travelers.

Terriers are another group of dogs that used to be used for hunting but now are kept most often just as pets and to enter in dog shows. Terriers are usually small dogs. They used to help hunt rabbits and foxes. Perhaps because they remember their old hunting days, many terriers today still act as though they were always on the alert to go dashing off on a chase. The little Scottie, or *Scotch terrier,* is a good example of this as he trots along on little short legs with his shaggy black coat almost touching the ground but with his head held high and a little cockily.

Sometimes you may see a larger dog that looks a good deal like the Scottie, particularly in the squarish cut of his muzzle and the whiskers around it. But this dog, larger, with longer legs and a sort of black-blue fur, is called a *Kerry Blue terrier*.

Airedale is another familiar dog name and it too identifies a terrier. The name comes from the river Aire in England where the first ones were raised. It has a tough rough fur that is black across the back and tan everywhere else.

Some of the terriers are called wire-haired because their hair is short and very tightly curled all over them. One of these is the

Kerry Blue

Fox terrier, a black and white terrier that is larger than a Scottie but also has the Scottie's square muzzle, or nose and mouth, and whiskers. The *Boston terrier,* one of the terriers that was raised in this country, has a fairly smooth coat of hair and is brindled. Brindled means that it has dark splotches or streaks of fur against a lighter (grayish or brownish) coat.

The *Great Dane,* which is the largest dog we see nowadays, once was a mighty hunter of the most fierce animals, even bears. Later Great Danes were used to trot along beside the carriages of noblemen. Now they are kept as pets and to be seen in dog shows.

The fierce-looking but really gentle *Bulldog* once was used in a cruel sport known as bull-baiting. The dogs would be put in an arena to fight bulls. Their flat faces meant that they could get a better tighter grip when they bit the bull. This sport has been stopped now, and the Bulldog is a wonderful pet.

There are some dogs, like the *Boxer,* that have gone through a lot of changes and served a lot of purposes before ending up as the big frisky flat-faced pets that they are today. The dogs that came first, in the

Boxer line, were two types of hunting dogs. One type was the sort that chases game. The other was a type that finds the game for the hunter. Later, the dogs that resulted from breeding those two types were used to fight bulls, the way the Bulldogs were. But these particular ones were smaller and lived in Germany rather than in England like the regular Bulldog. Today, the Boxer has come a long way from a fighting dog to a home dog. One good reason for calling them Boxers, by the way, is that they pounce on things with their front feet, hitting them the way a boxer might. Sometimes the Boxers kill mice and snakes just by pouncing on them with their front feet. Most of the time, though, they pounce on stones to knock them around as though they were playing a game.

One of the strangest jobs a dog has these days is the job that has been given to the *Dalmatian.* This is a white dog with lots of

Dalmatian

big black blots on it. These dogs once were very popular as coach dogs. Noblemen liked to have these clean-looking black-and-white dogs trot alongside their coaches when they went traveling. The Great Dane, remember, also was popular for this. The dogs were just one way of proving that the nobleman was very wealthy. After all, not many people could afford to have a coach and feed the coach horses, much less have a bunch of dogs trotting alongside just for decoration!

But today the Dalmatian has turned out to be the dog that, more than any other, you see around the firehouses where the hook and ladder and the fire-engines are kept. Firemen seem to like these dogs more than any others. And on many a fire-engine racing to a fire you can see a Dalmatian sitting right up with the driver or snuggled up on the floor of the fire-engine. Perhaps the fire-house near your own home has a Dalmatian that the firemen would show you.

THE CAT WALKS ALONE

Cats are loved by people just as dogs are. But there are so many differences between cats and dogs that, as you would expect, they are loved in a different way too.

Cats don't frolic in the fields or help people hunt and cats don't go out and bring in the sheep or cattle. But, as pets most people love them for just about the same reasons they love dogs. They keep people company. Their fur is warm and soft to pet. They are pretty to look at.

But also there are many cats that do useful jobs. In fact there are probably more useful cats than there are just pet cats. The important job that cats do is to catch mice and rats.

If it were not for cats in large cities, some scientists claim, the rats and mice would run around so free and increase so much in numbers that they would overrun the city.

The United States Government keeps cats in Post Offices to catch the mice that might gnaw mail sacks. Other public buildings too have cats to guard against rats and mice.

Because of this valuable service they can perform, whole new families of cats have been bred. For instance, cats that can stand very cold temperatures have been bred to act as guards in cold storage plants. When we say an animal is "bred" to do something this is what we mean: If you want to have cats "bred" to stand the cold, you have to find mother and father cats that don't seem to mind the cold as much as other cats. When these cats have children, you pick out the children that also seem to be especially at home in the cold. When these children grow up, other cats that can stand the cold are mated with them. This keeps on through one family after another until, finally, all the kittens that are born, each time, are more at home in the cold than anywhere else. We then say it is a new "breed" of cat. It has been especially "bred" to stand the cold.

The most familiar cat, for most of us, doesn't have *any* name more special than just "cat." Usually this is the common straight-haired cat. It comes in just about every color and combination of colors that you can imagine. Some are striped, some are gray, some are black, some are yellowish, some are mixed.

When you look at any of these ordinary cats, you might not think they were related to the great ferocious-looking lions and tigers. But if you watch any cat in your neighborhood as it goes hunting, you certainly would be reminded of a lion and a tiger. For just like the lions and tigers, which are the biggest of the cats, the little cats that live in your neighborhood are wonderful hunters. Unlike the dog, they do all their hunting for themselves. Only certain large cats, in the jungle, ever have been trained to help men hunt. Cats are known as creatures who walk alone. They hunt alone too.

Today, the main families of cats kept as pets in this country are the *Persian* or *Angora*, the *Siamese*, the *Abyssinian*, the *Short-Haired*, the *Manx*, and the *Maltese*. Here is what they are like:

The Persian cat has very long fine hair.

people called them Angora cats after the town of Angora in Turkey. We now call this town Ankara and we call the cats Persian to distinguish them from another sort of cat with not quite so long hair that we call the Turkish cat. Also, we know now that all of these cats could not have come from the single town of Angora.

The Siamese cat has short hair with a very beautiful color. Its body is a very light fawn, which is a light creamy brown. The face, legs, and tail, however, are a rich chocolate color. People who have a lot to do with big exhibitions where cats are shown and win prizes because of their beauty and intelligence, often say that the

Persian Cat

Siamese Cat

Its color ranges from white to blue and to black. Many people have got into the habit of calling almost any long-haired cat a Persian. These beautiful cats came originally not only from Persia but from India and China as well. Native traders passed some of the cats on to the men of the great American sailing ships that went all over the world in the 1800's. At first, when these cats were brought back to America, most

Siamese is the smartest of all household cats.

The Manx cat is one of the easiest to tell from all other cats—and not because of its color either. The color, as a matter of fact, can be just about anything. But the Manx cat doesn't have a tail. Scientists think that the Manx cat came to be a cat without a tail in this way: First of all there were (and still are) a lot of types of cat in the Far

East, in China and Japan and Malaya, that have pretty short tails. It is thought that some of these cats were put on board the great Spanish fleet of warships called the Spanish Armada which sailed against England just a hundred years after Columbus got to the New World.

Some of the ships of this great fleet were wrecked on the Isle of Man off the coast of England. The cats got loose on the island and made their home there. As the cats raised new families, the tails of each new generation of Manx (or Isle of Man) cats got shorter and shorter. It was a sort of breeding process, like breeding the cats that can stand the cold. Cats with short tails had kittens with short tails. These kittens grew up and had families of their own, and because both the mother and father had short tails and there were no mother and father cats in the family with long tails, the tails of each generation of kittens kept getting shorter. Finally these Manx cats, from the Isle of Man, just didn't have any tails at all.

The Abyssinian cat is another short-haired cat. It is a dark brown cat specked with black. Down its back there is a black stripe.

The Maltese cat is blue or slate-colored. Its name would make you think it comes from the Island of Malta, but it doesn't. People just have called bluish cats Maltese cats although nobody knows why and the name has stuck. Many bluish cats that have been called Maltese have come from as far away as Iceland.

Perhaps you have noticed that one sort of cat has not been mentioned. That is the "tabby" cat. Many people think that the tabby cat is a special sort of cat. Actually,

the word tabby means a special sort of color and not a particular kind of cat. Tabby means a cat with light-colored fur that has darker stripes or bars or spots. Some tabby

Maltese Cat

cats are yellowish with orange stripes or bars or spots. Some are gray with almost black stripes. Some are silver with bluish bars. All cats like that are tabby cats, and all of the cats that come in different colors can also come "tabby" colored. Some people call certain African wildcats tabby cats, but mainly it just means the color of a cat.

ANIMAL FAMILIES

So that we may get an idea of the way that animals are grouped together in families, we'll meet the most important members of the "cat family" right now.

The broadest word used to cover animals like cats is "carnivore." This means all animals that eat meat. Not only cats but also dogs and bears and wolves and every other animal that eats meat. So we have to narrow that word down a bit if we want to talk about only the "cat family." We do that by saying that all cat-like animals be-

38

long to a family called *Felines.* In the Feline family are all of the cat-like animals. The "cat family" is the Feline family of animals, and it includes about 50 species or separate sorts of animal.

The several kinds of house cat that we have been talking about are not the only animals in the feline family.

IS THE LION REALLY THE KING OF BEASTS?

Next to the household cat, the cat-like animal we probably think of or hear about most is the lion. Almost all the lions we know of today—except the ones in zoos— live on the great plains of Africa. A few others are known to live in a forest called Gir in the western part of India.

The lion is a proud looking animal. The male lions have great ruffs of tawny hair framing their faces. Because of the way he looks, the lion is called the King of the Beasts. Actually, the lion may not deserve that title. It is true that no other animals in the jungle go out of their way to get into trouble with lions. But there *are* animals that lions do not scare.

The *elephant,* the largest land animal in the world, has little to fear from a lion. The tough *rhinoceros* with its armored skin and sharp horn does not seem afraid of the lion either. The *Water buffalo,* with its curving sharp horns, also can hold its own with a lion. Even the friendly *giraffe* can send a lion running away by kicking at it with its sharp hooves.

There is a small animal in the jungle too that can send a lion running away whenever it appears. This animal is called a *Zorille.* But it is just an African version of a

plain old *skunk.* Not even lions want to be around when a skunk-like animal decides to squirt some of the terrible-smelling fluid that it uses to protect itself.

Lion

All of this does not mean that the lion is not a strong and powerful animal. He is. But it might not be really fair to call him the King of Beasts. People who live in Africa, for instance, say that the elephant comes closer to deserving that name.

Lions are great hunters, as are almost all members of the cat family. The lion does

not hunt for sport. He hunts for food. He eats that food until it is all gone before he kills another animal. Each lion in Africa kills about one animal each month for food. When the lion is not hungry and hunting he is quite friendly to other animals and may often be seen drinking at the same water hole with different kinds of antelopes, though when a lion is hungry, an antelope would make one of his favorite meals.

The member of the family that does most of the hunting is the mother lion. The handsome big father lion, the one with the great ruff of fur, either lies lazily in the sun while the mother lion hunts or he stalks through the tall grass scaring animals and making them run away. He tries to make them run toward the waiting mother lion who does the actual killing.

Usually, lions do not bother men at all, unless the men bother them. Sometimes, though, an old or wounded lion may be unable to hunt the animals out on the great plains. If a man happened to pass close to one of these lions, the disabled lion might attack in order to get a meal. But only rarely do lions attack people as readily as they do animals.

THE BIGGEST OF THE CATS ARE THE TIGERS

Although we often think of lions as the largest of the cat family, they are not. The largest of the cat family is a *tiger*.

The largest lions are about ten feet long from the tip of the tail to the tip of the nose. A lion that big has a body between six and seven feet long.

The largest tigers are about eleven feet long. Their bodies alone can be as much as eight feet long. They can weigh as much as 500 pounds, or a quarter of a ton.

These very large tigers are found in the

40

icy northernmost parts of Russia, in the frozen wastelands and mountains near the Arctic Circle. They have black stripes on orange-reddish fur, like most other tigers. But they also have very long-haired fur to keep them warm in the frozen snowy lands where they live.

Most pictures we see of tigers show them in hot jungles in Africa, or the lands in and around China and India. Actually, even the tigers who live there are bothered by the heat and spend much of their time in the water to keep cool.

The first tigers—great beasts with big jutting teeth called Saber-Tooth tigers—lived millions of years ago in the cold lands where the largest tigers are found today. The tigers that live in the warmer jungles came there much later.

Although most tigers are the orange-and-black combination we mentioned above, quite a few have been found with very light fur and some are white with black stripes.

Like lions, most tigers prefer to stay as far away from men as possible. But, also like lions, when tigers are wounded or old and mean, they may try to attack men.

One thing about tigers that is different from most other animals who get their food by hunting, is that the tiger has a very poor sense of smell. He hunts by ear—that is, by following the sounds made by whatever animal he is after. Men have found that if they stand very still, not making a sound, tigers will pass right by them in the tall grass and not even know they are there.

Even though the tiger is the largest of cats, he still isn't a King of Beasts. Packs of wild dogs kill many tigers. And elephants, who live in India as well as Africa, have little trouble in destroying a tiger who may

dare to challenge them.

LEOPARDS—BLACK, WHITE AND SPOTTED

Next to lion and tiger, the name we know best among the big cats is *leopard*. Leopard, familiar as the name may be, is a very confusing name. People are always getting it mixed up with the word *panther*. Black leopards are called Black panthers.

Just what is a panther and what is a leopard?

Here is the way men who study animals have worked out the differences between the two names. They do not use the name panther for any particular animal. Rather, they use the name panther for a group-name for all the big cats that can roar. So, when you say "panther" you could mean a lion or a tiger as well as the sort of big cat called a leopard.

Now, what about the leopard? The most common leopard is the spotted cat, about the size of a large dog, that lives all over Africa and in Asia too.

Very often when a litter of these leopards are born, one of the little leopards will be pure black. These black leopards are the ones that most people call Black panthers. But there is no such thing as a special animal called a Black panther. There are only the Black leopards.

Many hunters in Africa say that the leopard is the most dangerous of the cats, more dangerous than the lion. One reason is that the leopard doesn't seem to be particularly afraid of men. Leopards like to eat baboons but if a man comes by when the leopard is hungry, the leopard will just as likely attack the man as he would a monkey.

41

When the leopard is fighting, too, he is considered the fastest of all large animals.

Besides the black leopards, the color of

Leopards

branches of trees. The brownish dried-grass color of the lion is about the same with all lions because most lions live in the great grassy plains where that color is the most common of all.

Some of the most remarkable examples of protective coloration are found among the insects. These tiny creatures sometimes have more than protective colors that make them seem actual parts of bushes and trees. They often grow in shapes that also make them seem a perfect part of the background wherever they live. They are described in the part of this book dealing with insects.

Birds, too, have tricks of protective coloration. Even some fish are shaped and colored so that they blend perfectly into the places

Zebra

leopards may change according to where they live.

In grassy open areas, they often are light-colored to blend in with the surroundings and their spots may not be so noticeable. In the great forests, however, they often are dark with a lot of big black spots, like the mottled shadows the sun casts through the jungle trees.

Animals whose color help them to hide in the places where they live, are said to have a "protective coloration." This means they have a color to protect them.

The leopards are examples of animals that are found with different colors depending on where they live. Other animals, like zebras, for instance, are all colored alike. The zebra's protective coloration, dark and light stripes, help it to stand unnoticed anywhere where there are stripes of shadow cast by the sun coming through the

Walking Stick

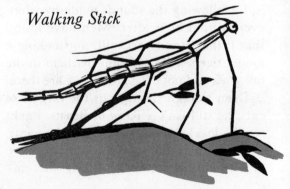

where they live. The birds and fishes are also described in another part of this book.

In the cold northern parts of China and India the ordinary leopard is not found. But there is another member of the leopard family that does thrive there in the snow. It is called, because of that, the *Snow leopard*.

The fur of the Snow leopard is more woolly than that of the others, and it is pure white on the underparts and sort of yellowish gray along the back and sides. The spots are not so clear as those of the other leopards. These leopards have bodies about five feet long and tails about three feet long. Leopards that live on grassy plains are sometimes about that size too. But the leopards that live in the jungles are usually smaller.

The third member of the leopard family lives much closer to us than the others. This is the leopard known as the *jaguar*. It is the largest of the leopards. Some weigh almost as much as a tiger, about 500 pounds. But their bodies do not quite reach the eight-foot length of the biggest tigers.

Not many years ago there were many jaguars in our southwestern United States, in California, Arizona, and New Mexico.

Jaguar

Today most of them have moved so that Mexico is as far north as we ever find any great numbers of them. From there on south through Latin America, there are jaguars.

Besides the fact that it often grows larger than any of the other leopards, there is a difference in the spots of the jaguar too. The jaguar's black spots are arranged in a series of rings like (O's made of dots) rather than just scattered over the fur. Another thing about the jaguar is that of all the big cats, he is the best climber of trees. All of them can climb trees, although the lion and tiger are rather clumsy about it. But the jaguar can race up a tree just about as easily as a house cat.

Almost as though to make sure that everybody will get mixed up about leopards, the people of Latin America usually call the jaguar, which is a leopard, a "tiger." The name for the jaguar in those countries is "El Tigre."

THE MIDDLE-SIZED CATS DON'T ROAR

Next to the big cats we have just talked about come a group of middle-sized cats. The scientific name that covers these cats is *profelis*. The lions, tigers, and leopards are grouped as *panther* because they can roar. The *profelis* can't roar very much, if at all.

The common house cat as well as all other small cats are grouped under the name *felis* and, as we mentioned, all cats are in the *Feline* family.

Among the medium-sized cats, the *profelis*, there is one that still lives in considerable numbers in this country. This one is the *Mountain lion*. A more correct name for the Mountain lion is *puma*. Other names the Mountain lion sometimes goes by are *cougar* and *catamount*.

Instead of roaring, the puma has a high-pitched cry that sounds like a woman crying out. Pumas live in Latin America as well as North America. In the United States, pumas once lived everywhere but now are mostly found west of the Rocky Mountains. Some have been seen in Florida.

For some strange reason, pumas seem to like to follow men in the woods and mountains but they rarely, if ever, attack men. In fact there have been so few times when pumas have attacked men that for all practical purposes this largest of North American cats might be called the most harmless. There are smaller cats, sometimes called wildcats, that are far more dangerous. We'll learn about them later.

Another member of the middle-size cat family is the *Clouded leopard*. It lives in Asia. It grows a little larger than the puma, sometimes being about as large as a regular leopard. Its color is gray tinged with yellow and its black spots are more squared than the round blotches of most leopards. These leopards like to sleep in trees and their main food is small birds.

The other two members of the middle-size cat family are very much alike except for where they live. They are both called *Golden cats*. One lives in Tibet and Burma and the other lives in Africa. They have reddish-brown fur. The one that lives in Asia has sort of gray spots while the one that lives in Africa has black spots. The largest of these Golden cats is not as large as just a fair-sized leopard.

THE SMALL CATS—TAME AND WILD

Now we come to the smaller cats. These include the household cats with which we are familiar. There are more cats in this group than in any of the others.

Some of the smaller cats are spotted so that they look rather like little leopards. The *ocelot* is one of these. It lives in Latin America and grows to be about the size of the largest house cats.

In practically every warm country in the world there is some form of cat with leopard-like markings. Often they are simply called *Leopard cats*. There are some other small cat-like animals that are spotted like leopards but that are in a class all by themselves. One of these classes is the *Serval*. This is a long-legged leopard-spotted cat that lives in the hottest parts of Africa. Because of their long legs they look more like dogs with cat's fur and a cat's head than any of the ordinary spotted cats.

Another spotted African cat in a class by itself is the *cheetah*. They look almost exactly like small leopards. But they have at least one thing about them that isn't cat-like at all. Their claws are like those of a dog and cannot be pulled out of sight into the paws like the claws of a cat.

Cheetah

A cat's claws are called "retractile" because they can be "retracted" like the landing gear of an airplane.

The cheetah often is used to help men hunt and can be tamed fairly well—as can most cats. The cheetah can help in hunting because he is very possibly the fastest four-footed animal on earth. Men in cars have driven beside cheetahs at speeds of 60 miles per hour. In this country, cheetahs brought from Africa, have been used to help run down coyotes in the West. The cheetahs have been found to be the only animals that can catch the wolf-like coyotes.

There are some other spotted cat-like animals but they belong to a family that is not really the cat family at all. We'll meet them later. They are called *Viverrines*. We'll get to them after we round out our look at the cat family. We have only two more groups to look at first. One is the *jaguarondi* and the other is the *lynx*.

The jaguarondis live in Latin America. They look a bit like small pumas except that not all of them are the sandy light-brown color of the puma. Some jaguarondis are grayish. All of them, however, have a black line that goes from the corner of the eye down to the mouth.

The lynxes will be much more familiar to you because among the lynxes are the small tough cats we call wildcats. Many people use the name wildcat to describe any small cat that is a mean or vicious fighter. But the lynx deserves the name most of all.

In this country there are two kinds of lynx. One is called a lynx, the *Northern lynx*. These grow to be a bit larger than the largest house cat. They are light-colored and

they all have tufts of fur growing from the ends of their ears. That is how you can tell

Bobcat

them. Other lynxes live in many other parts of the world. Canada is the home of most of them on this continent. Some live in Europe. And in the frozen wastes of Russian Siberia where the largest tigers are found, there are some lynxes that are more than three feet long.

The lynx found most often in the United States is called a *Bobcat*. He differs from the Northern lynx by being smaller and by not having such noticeable tufts of fur on his ears. The name Bobcat refers to the short tail that many types of lynx have. The tail looks as though it had been "bobbed," or cut off short.

Other lynxes, usually called *Jungle cats*, live in most of the jungles of the world. They have tufts of fur on their ears too. In the jungles, many of the lynxes have families in which one of the parents is a regular house cat that has gone out into the jungle.

45

Other Jungle cats, without the tufts of fur on their ears, are called Tabby cats in parts of Africa. (Remember, though, that when we are talking about house cats—as we learned earlier—tabby just means the color and not the sort of cat.)

Another member of the lynx family that lives in Africa is the *caracal*. It has long ears, with very long tufts of fur, and a coat of short reddish-brown fur. At one time, caracals were trained to hunt, but the even faster cheetah has taken over in that field now. The caracal, though, is so fast that it often gets its food by leaping up and swatting down birds that are flying past.

CAT-LIKE ANIMALS THAT AREN'T REALLY CATS

We mentioned just a while back that there are some cat-like animals that aren't cats at all. They are members of one of the most mixed up of all animal families, the group called Viverrines. Sometimes these animals are called half-cats. But that is only half right, for many of them do not even resemble cats. To give you an idea of how mixed up and different the members of this family are, one, the genet, lives in Africa and looks just like a tiny dark leopard-spotted cat. But another member of the family is the weasel-like, fearless *mongoose* that is so famous for being able to kill the *cobra,* one of the deadliest of all snakes.

The most famous mongoose is the storybook mongoose named Rikki-tikki-tavi who was the hero of one of Rudyard Kipling's great stories about India. Actually there are several sorts of mongoose. The mongoose that is so quick and smart that it can beat the cobra is called the *True mongoose.*

He is between a foot and a foot-and-half long and has tough shaggy fur. Some are brown, some are gray, and a few have white speckles on them.

The way these little animals kill deadly snakes has nothing to do with their being able to stand the bites of those snakes, the way some people think. If the snake ever bit the mongoose, the poison would be as deadly as it would be to any other animal. The secret of the mongoose's fighting is its speed and its strange knowledge of how snakes act and fight. No one knows why the mongoose likes to fight snakes, but that is the fact. There are mongooses like this in both India and Africa.

Other kinds of mongoose include the *Banded mongoose* of Africa. It has stripes across its body. There also is a very small or *Dwarf mongoose* in Africa. All in all there are eleven different kinds of mongoose.

All of them are rather small and have rather pointed heads with little ears. Their tails are fairly furry and start out thick tapering down toward a thinner end.

One very famous expert on animals, Ivan Sanderson, says that a mongoose really looks just like what a child would draw if he just wanted to show "an animal." Maybe the next time you draw a small animal with four legs, a rather pointed head, and a long tail, you can call it a mongoose and let it go at that.

Another member of the strangely mixed Viverrine family is the cat-like *civet*. Although they have bodies rather like cats, civets have faces more like foxes. There are different kinds of civets in different parts of the world. One sort, that lives in both Asia and Africa, is called the *True civet.* These little animals produce a butter-like material from a gland in the back of their body. This is called civet just the same as the animal. The odor of the butter-like civet material is very strong but very pleasant. Natives in many places where the civet is found take this material from the little animals—almost like milking them—and pack it up to be shipped all over the world where people use it as the base for many wonderful perfumes.

HYENAS

Closely related to the *Viverrine* family are the *hyenas*. One of the hyenas, called an *aardwolf*, lives in Africa and is the animal that links the mongoose-genet-and-civet group of animals with the hyenas. But we really mean the *Spotted hyena* of Africa. Like all hyenas, this one would just as soon find a dead animal to eat as have to kill one. The hyenas are rather cowardly. The spotted ones, however, travel in large packs and will attack other animals if they can sneak up on them. Usually they can be scared away by anything that acts as though it might put up a good fight. Hyenas are among the few sorts af animals anywhere in the world that actually let themselves get dirty.

There is another hyena, the *Striped hyena*, that lives in part of Africa and also in India. These hyenas travel alone but are as cowardly as the spotted ones, preferring to eat dead animals rather than have to fight and kill them.

DOG-LIKE ANIMALS (CANINES)

Just as there are many cat-like animals there are many dog-like animals beyond those familiar ones we know as "man's best friends."

Because dog-like animals are known to have lived as far back as sixty million years ago, such animals are actually among the oldest forms of mammals on earth.

Dog-like animals are members of the *Canine* family of animals. Remember that the cats were members of the *Feline* family?

The Canine family is split into two main groups. One is called the true canine group. It includes the kinds of dogs we keep as pets and use for hunting. It also includes *foxes, wolves,* and *jackals.*

WOLVES

Many scientists feel that the dogs we now keep as pets are merely types of wolves that have changed according to the sort of climate in which they live and the sort of jobs men have kept them to perform.

When it comes to the animals we now call wolves, the ones that live in the wilds and hunt sometimes alone and sometimes in packs, there are really only two kinds. One we call just *wolf.* They are like large dogs, with faces rather like the German Shepherd dog. Their fur can be of many colors. There are white, black, gray, red, brown, and yellow wolves. Wolves live in just about every part of the world and in every sort of country from the mountains to the deserts.

The second kind of wolf is called a *coyote.* This is a sort of wolf that is very plentiful in the western part of our country. The coyote is particularly different from the wolf in that the coyote always prefers to live on the open prairies.

There is one very special member of the

Coyote

Canine family that fits in between the animals we call dogs and the wolves. This is the *dingo* of Australia. Dingoes are short-haired, yellowish dog-like animals. There is no particularly good reason for not calling them dogs except that they are found only in Australia and are believed to be a very ancient breed of animal.

FOXES

Another dog-like animal that you may recognize right away from the many stories that have been written about them is the *fox*. Although foxes are found in nearly every kind of country, even in frozen Iceland, their favorite home is in bushy areas where there are plenty of small animals for them to feed on. There are many foxes, especially *Red foxes,* all over the United States.

In stories, foxes are usually shown to be so smart that they can trick most other animals. We even use the word *foxy* to describe a person who is very sly or crafty. Actually, the fox isn't any smarter than any other animal. The dogs kept as pets usually seem much smarter.

The fox is what is called a burrowing animal, it digs or burrows into the ground to make a home. Of course, if a fox can find a little cave between rocks or under an old tree, he may use that for a home instead. He's smart enough not to dig his house if there is any easier way of getting one just as good.

Although foxes do a lot of damage around farms by stealing chickens, they also do a lot of good out in the bushes where they live. They eat many of the mice and rats that otherwise would eat the grain and other things around the farm. All in all, the fox probably eats more animals that do damage than animals that do good.

Besides the Red fox of America, there are at least a dozen other kinds around the world. There are, in fact, three other kinds in the Western Hemisphere alone. In the northern plains there is a small fox, about a foot-and-a-half long, that is light yellowish in color. It is called a *Kit fox.* Even farther north there is the *Arctic fox,* which is a dull brown in color in the summer but changes to either a white or a very dark blue in the winter. These two winter colors are called color "phases." The Black panther, which is really a black leopard, is just a color "phase" of the leopard—remember? The Red fox that we talked about first also has a color phase. Some of these foxes are black. The other fox in this country is the *Gray fox.*

FENNECS, JACKALS, DHOLES, AND OTHER ODD MEMBERS OF THE DOG FAMILY

One of the dog family that seems closely related to the foxes is called the *fennec.* This little animal lives in Africa. It looks like a toy version of a fox with fluffy, light-colored fur and big eyes.

The member of the dog family that is perhaps the least likable of all is the *jackal.* These dog-like creatures are smaller than wolves and live in the hot, tropical parts of Asia and Africa.

The thing that jackals do that makes people dislike them is the way they follow after the great cats, the lions, leopards, and tigers. When the great cat has killed an animal and eaten all he can for the moment, the jackals will sneak in and steal some of the food. Because of this, people say that anyone who sneaks in to benefit from another person's efforts is a "jackal." Also, jackals, when very hungry, will sometimes band together and hunt down larger animals, killing the other animal simply by overwhelming it with weight of numbers.

There are some jackals, or at least jackal-like animals, that live in Latin America, but scientists are still arguing about just how to classify them. They can't make up their minds exactly what names they should be given or with which group of the dog family they should be included. So don't be surprised if you can't figure out what family some animal in the zoo belongs to.

The remaining portion of the dog family is really a bunch of left-overs. They don't fit into any other family but the dog family, and yet they certainly aren't dogs.

One, the *dhole,* which lives in Asia, looks very much like a dog but with a fox-like face. But these animals have two less teeth than the 42 that almost all other members of the dog family have. Also, the dholes have long fur between the pads of their paws, and the mothers have twelve or fourteen places on their bodies for the young ones to get milk rather than the ten that other members of the dog family have. Another thing about this strange member of the dog family is that, so far as anyone knows, a dhole can't be tamed. Even wolves and foxes, if caught early enough, can be tamed somewhat, but not a dhole. They are very fierce hunters and can bring down animals many times their size.

Another of the odd members of the dog family is called simply the *Hunting dog.* This dog-like animal lives in Africa. His scientific name is *Lycaon.* He hardly needs a scientific name, though, to keep from getting mixed up with any other hunting dog.

One of the first things you would notice about this "dog" is that its ears are like no dog ears you have ever seen. They are very large, but not at all floppy. They are oval and stand up straight, and each one looks just about as large as the dog's head. The fur of the Hunting dog also is very strange for a dog. It is black, white, and orange. One of the reasons it doesn't fit with most of the dog family is that it has only four toes on each of its four feet. Other members of the dog family have five toes on the front feet and four on the hind or back feet. When you see a dog's track, however, you will see that the prints left by the front feet look as though they had only four toes. This is because the fifth toe is so high that it doesn't leave a mark.

The Hunting dog got its name for the very good reason that it is one of the most fierce hunters in Africa. These dogs run in large packs. They will even chase lions, although usually they pick old lions.

A pack of Hunting dogs will chase an animal until the prey gets tired and drops exhausted and unable to defend itself. Then, Hunting dogs that are not tired come up to make the kill. The pack always runs so that some of its members will be ready and fresh at the end of the chase.

The two other odd members of the dog family are the *Bush dog* of Latin America and the *Bat-eared fox* of Africa.

The Bush dog certainly looks odd. It has the shape of a *dachshund*. Remember the dachshund? It looks rather like a sausage with legs. The Bush dog looks like that too. But it has a very bushy tail!

The Bat-eared fox looks like a small fox with silvery gray fur. Its teeth make it different from the other dog-like animals. It has more teeth than any other member of the dog family. While most members of the dog family have 42 teeth, with the dhole having only 40, the Bat-eared fox has 46 or 48.

BEARS

The animals that are closest to the dog family but with a family of their own are the *bears*. Their family is called the *Ursine* family.

One of the members of the bear family, the *Alaskan Brown bear,* is the largest meat-eating animal that lives on land today. The elephant, the largest of all land animals, eats leaves and vegetables, not meat. Certain kinds of sharks and whales that may be 50 feet long and weigh several tons are the largest meat-eating animals anywhere. But, of course, they don't count as land animals. So the Alaskan Brown bear is left as the largest meat-eater on land.

Alaskan Brown Bear

This big bear grows to be about eight feet tall and weighs around 1500 pounds. That's three-quarters of a ton. The easiest way to tell this huge bear from any other is by its size. Color alone isn't a very good way to tell bears apart. The Alaskan Brown bear, for instance, can have fur of just about any color from a yellowish brown to a very dark brown. Some of these bears have grizzly fur—that is, fur tipped with silver. Because of that, some people call them *Grizzly bears* and, so far as the color goes, they are right. But, as we said, color isn't the big clue to a bear's identity, or a bear's name either.

There *is* a kind of bear that *should* be called the Grizzly bear. Many people, in fact, think the Grizzly bear is the biggest of bears. But it isn't. The Alaskan Brown bear is.

The Grizzly bear is a sort of brown bear

that often, but not always, has a coat of grizzled fur. Some of these bears live in Alaska, but some live all the way down the Pacific Coast of Canada and in the northern part of America in such states as Montana and Wyoming. Like the Alaska Brown bear which isn't alway brown, the Grizzly isn't always grizzled. Some are a yellowish brown, others are dark brown, and a few are almost all black. They do have one mark that helps make them look different from other bears. They have a hump of muscle above the shoulders.

Some grizzlies grow as large as seven feet tall, but they weigh only about 800 or 900 pounds at the most. That means they are about half a bear lighter than the giant bears of Alaska.

Although there are many terrible stories told about ferocious bears, they usually try to avoid men if they can. But they do fight fiercely if cornered. Some people say that bears don't like the taste of people and that they will take only one bite out of a person. But other people, who make more sense, point out that one bite would be too much for *them* whether the bear liked it or not!

Another bear that lives in America is the *Black bear*. This bear is the real proof that naming bears after colors is pretty hopeless. The Black bear, which lives everywhere in America except in the very middle states, is best recognized as merely the smallest bear of our country. The largest Black bears are about five feet long. Most of them aren't much taller than a twelve-year-old boy and weigh only about 200 pounds. The color of Black bears is really something. In the East, where this bear usually lives in forests and swamps, it generally *is* black. In the West, where it usually lives in the mountains, it is generally

Polar Bear

a cinnamon color and people often call it the *Cinnamon bear*. Farther up the West Coast, in Canada, many of the Black bears are almost all white. In certain parts of Alaska there are Black bears that are a light blue. People call them *Glacier bears*.

The last kind of bear that may be found in our part of the world, although you would have to go where the Eskimos live to find it, is the *Polar bear*. Here, at last, is a bear where color really counts. This one is white. And white is just the color it should be, too. For the Polar bear lives in the white world of the frozen north, the snow kingdom of the "pole" or top of the world.

The Polar bear is about the size of the Grizzly bear but, probably to guard it against the very cold weather where it lives, is better padded with fat and weighs more than the Grizzly.

The favorite home of the Polar bear is very strange. Rather than living right on the land, like other bears, it prefers to live on the big pieces of ice that float in the waters of the far north. These are called ice floes. They are really floating islands of ice. From them the Polar bear dives for the fish that make up most of its meals.

Bears don't live only in America and Canada of course. Kinds of Brown bear, for instance, are found in many of the mountains of Europe and in Russia and China. Strangely, though, no one has actually found any bears in Africa, the greatest animal land of all. People have heard stories of bears living in mountains in the northern part of Africa but no one has been able to prove the stories.

Although bears may seem to be sort of clumsy as they walk along with a sort of

shuffle, they actually are very fast and powerful animals. All of them can climb trees and even swim very fast. In the places where bears live there usually isn't any animal that bothers them at all and, except for men, they have no real enemies in the animal world.

Black Bear and Honey Bees

One weakness that most of them have, however, is a sweet-tooth. They love sweet things to eat. Honey is one of their favorite foods, and many bears decide to live in a certain place just because it has a good tree-full of honeybees nearby. Perhaps because they are so used to hunting honey, bears can go right into a swarm of bees and act as though they are not being bothered a bit. In fact, they hardly ever get stung by bees.

Just before cold weather sets in, bears eat more than usual, storing up extra fat on their bodies. When it gets very cold, the bears find a cave, or scoop one out under the snow, and settle down for a nap that lasts until the snow begins to melt.

When the bear takes this nap in a snow cave, the moisture of his breath freezes all around the inside of the snow cave and seals the bear in. Most baby bears are born during the nap-time and, if the mother is very fast asleep, her babies may be born without her even waking up. Baby bears, by the way, are very small considering the size of the parents. Even the babies of the giant Alaska Brown bear are only about the size of a kitten.

Where there isn't snow and the winters aren't so bad, the bears may nap for only a few days at a time or just lie around lazily. When they do sleep for a long time, however, this long nap is called "hibernation," which means sleeping during the cold winter months. Some of the other animals we will talk about also hibernate.

Besides the Brown bears that are found so many places in the world, there are other kinds of bears that live in other lands.

In the Andes Mountains of Latin America there is a small, black bear with light colored rings around its eyes. These rings look like glasses and, because of that, this bear is called the *Spectacled bear*.

In Asia there also is a small black bear with a light-colored face that is called the *Sun bear*. Perhaps because this bear has a very kind-looking face, it often is kept as a pet and, like many bears, may be trained to do tricks. Most bears are able to do one thing that looks like a trick and do it without any training at all. They can stand on their hind legs. Sometimes they do this when they are about to attack some other animal or when they are taking a good look around the countryside. Because of this, bears may be taught to walk so that they look like men in great big fur coats.

Just north of where the Sun bears live in Asia there is a bear called the *Moon bear*. This one is a larger bear but also is black with white marks around its face and chest. These bears eat less meat than most bears and seem to have a taste for fruits and vegetables as well as for that bear favorite, honey.

In India there is another black bear with a different sort of appetite. This bear is called a *Sloth bear*. It has a very long nose which it uses for rooting down into ant and termite houses in the ground. It loves to eat these insects.

ELEPHANTS

Since we have been talking about large animals that live on the land we might as well get right to the largest of all—the *elephant*.

The elephant has an animal family all its own. This family is called *Proboscidea*. Sometimes an elephant is called a *pachyderm*, a word meaning "thick skin." Any animal with thick skin, like a rhinoceros, for instance, can be called a pachyderm.

The real name for the elephant family, *Proboscidea*, is much better. The word is a combination of two Greek words which mean "for feeding." But the word proboscis, which comes from those words, has come to mean snout or nose and, of course, the elephant's long snout or trunk is not only what he uses to eat with, but it is also one of the things about elephants that is the most unusual.

The elephant's trunk is his nose. There are other animals, like ant-eaters, that have long noses which they use for eating, but there is nothing like the elephant's nose anywhere on anything. The main use of the elephant's trunk is to rip off the tree leaves that are the chief part of his meals. The elephant also uses the trunk to squirt water when he bathes and to squirt dust on himself as a way of clearing off insects.

The end of the elephant's trunk is so movable that it can pinch together like fingers and grab a tiny pebble—or a peanut in your hand at the zoo. The elephant's trunk is so strong that it can curl around a log weighing hundreds of pounds and lift it up.

Elephant
Squirting Water

In India and Burma particularly, elephants are trained to carry logs for men. Besides lifting things, elephants can push tremendously heavy wagons and move great stones from places where men want to plant farm crops.

Circus elephants often are trained to help the circus by pushing heavy wagons into place and by lifting the poles needed to put up tents.

There are two kinds of elephants. The largest is the elephant that lives in Africa. The other kind of elephant is the Indian elephant. In India, by the way, the elephant also is used as a means of transportation. It carries people, particularly for hunting. Instead of riding on the back of the elephant, the way a cowboy rides on the back of a horse, the people who ride Indian elephants sit or stand in large boxes, called howdahs, that are strapped to the elephant's back. The elephant kneels down so that people can climb into the howdah. A man sitting on the elephant's head guides the elephant by tapping it on the side toward which he wants the elephant to turn.

The huge elephants that live in Africa have been found as large as twelve-and-a-half feet tall—or twice as tall as a very tall man.

It would seem that the Indian elephant, even though it is smaller than the African elephant, would certainly also be the largest sort of land animal. Actually, the Indian elephant rates as third among land animals. The largest Indian elephant known was about ten-and-a-half feet tall. But the *White rhinoceros* of Africa, although it doesn't grow that high, actually weighs more than the Indian elephant, generally, and is counted as the second largest land animal.

Just as the elephant's nose is developed into a trunk, two of the elephant's teeth have developed into something quite different from most teeth. These are the two tusks

African Elephant *Indian Elephant*

of the elephant which stick out beyond its mouth on either side of the trunk. The tusks are made of ivory, a shiny, bone-like substance that is very valuable and is used to make beautiful pieces of jewelry or wonderful carvings. Because of the valuable ivory tusks, elephants have been widely hunted. Now there are very strict laws to prevent people from hunting elephants just to get their tusks.

The tusks of African elephants grow as long as 11 feet and can weigh almost 300 pounds apiece. Indian elephants have smaller tusks. Indian elephants also have smaller ears, which is a good way of telling the two kinds of elephant apart.

There are some things about elephants that many people believe, or at least talk about, that are not true at all. People say that elephants have the best memories in

the world, and that "an elephant never forgets." That isn't true. Elephants have about the same sort of memory that boys and girls have. Some pretty good, some pretty bad.

People also say that there is a mysterious place in Africa that is a special graveyard for elephants. This place is supposed to be hidden so well that men cannot find it. If they did find it, the story goes, they would find so much ivory that they would be very rich. That story isn't true either. Many elephants, when they get old and sick, do go far off by themselves. Others, apparently trying to keep cool when they are sick and feverish, go into swamps where, if they die, they sink from sight. But many elephants have been found dead in many parts of Africa and there is nothing at all that in any way indicates a special place where they go to die.

There is one true thing about elephants, though, that is even stranger than those two things that aren't true. This is the way that elephants seem to understand human talk better than any other animal.

Generally speaking, the elephant is very smart and has a large brain. But there are other smart animals that don't seem to have anywhere near the ability to understand people that elephants do. Even dogs, who obey commands, are thought to be obeying certain sounds rather than understanding the actual words. Elephants, on the other hand, may be talked into doing things by people using different words than those used most of the time by the elephant's trainer. The elephant seems to understand the conversation in general rather than certain words in particular.

Strangely enough, even though elephants do work so closely with men, they have never become really domesticated like dogs or horses. Most elephants that are kept in a zoo or held captive some place to do work do not have families.

WHALES

When we started talking about elephants, we said that the elephant is the largest mammal that lives on the land. Do you remember about another mammal that doesn't live on land? It's the largest animal that ever lived, larger even than the dinosaurs of ancient times. It is the *whale*.

It is hard, at first, to think of whales as mammals or as animals like dogs and cats and elephants. The whale lives all its life in the water. We think of it as the biggest of all the fish. But it isn't a fish at all. It is like a fish only because it lives in the water.

Fish lay eggs. The whale has its babies alive, just as a cat has kittens or a dog has puppies or a mother has a baby. The whale has a tough smooth skin but many also have some hair or hairy bristles at various places

The Whale

on their bodies, rather than scales like a fish. The whale's blood is warm while the fish's blood is cold. And the whale has to come up now and then to take air from the surface of the water while the fish can take the oxygen it needs right out of the water.

Perhaps strangest of all is the fact that the whale mother, just like any other mammal mother, is able to feed her young with milk from her own body. It is hard to imagine a whale feeding her young the way a mother dog feeds hers—with all the little puppies lined up, eagerly taking their milk. But it happens. When the whale is ready to feed her young, she turns over on her back in the water, with her stomach above the surface. The babies poke their heads up out of the water and are able to reach the places where they can get their milk. And the milk they get is very much like rich cow's milk.

There are several things most people think of first when they think of whales— and probably the last thing most people would think of would be a baby whale nuzzling up to its mother for lunch.

56

The first thing a person might think of is the great size of the whale. And that would be quite right, for among the whales, as we have said, are the largest animals that ever have lived on earth. That largest of whales and animals is a special whale, however. It is the *Blue whale*.

The largest Blue whale that has been measured was 113 feet long and weighed more than 170 tons. Think of that, 170 tons! That weight is the same as two-and-a-half dozen full grown elephants, or nearly 100 automobiles.

Not all whales, of course, are as large as the Blue whale. There are about 300 different kinds of whales in the oceans of the world. The smallest ones are only about five feet long.

Just as there are big differences in the sizes of the whales there is quite a lot of difference in what they eat. Fortunately, perhaps, the very largest ones eat very small things. The largest whales thrive on little shrimp-like sea creatures that are only about an inch long. Of course they scoop them up by the hundreds of thousands, but, anyway, it is rather comforting to think that the largest animal that ever lived doesn't have an appetite for anything larger—say for something about the size of a dog or a cat.

Other whales feed on even tinier creatures in the sea, also scooping them in in vast numbers and straining them through special fringes in their mouths which we will describe a little later.

Other whales, however, go in for really substantial food like octopuses and squids and even other whales. The Sperm whale, which even if not the largest, is still quite a large whale, has developed a particular taste for such tid-bits as ten-ton giant squids. Perhaps the appetite of this whale more than makes up for the dainty taste of the most gigantic ones.

One thing that all these whales have in common is the position of their tail flippers. On fish, as you can see whenever you go past the fish counter at the store, the tail fin is straight up and down. On whales the tail fin is crossways.

Even when we can't *see* a whale, we sometimes can see another trademark of this amazing sea-going mammal. That trademark, of course, is the great spout of water that seems to be coming from the top of the whale's head in most pictures of whales.

Actually that isn't a spout of water at all. This is what happens to make that spout: Because the whale is a mammal and has to breathe air just as we all have to, it must come to the surface of the water every now and then and clear its lungs to take in fresh air.

Because some whales can hold enough air in their lungs to stay under water for as much as an hour and dive beneath the waves as deep as a mile, it is easy to imagine how they feel when they come to the surface. Their lungs are full of air from which all the health-giving oxygen has been removed. The air, in fact, is almost all carbon dioxide, and living things cannot stand to be full of that for long. Also, the whale's lungs have put a lot of moisture into the air and the warmth of the whale's insides have heated the air.

So, when the whale comes to the surface, eager to get a good breath of fresh air, it just blasts the old air out as fast as possible through its nostrils which are high on its head. Then out comes the old air, hot and wet, a great spout of mist shooting up out of the water.

All of the 300 different kinds of whales are divided first of all into two main families. These are the family of *Baleen whales* and the family of *Toothed whales.*

The Baleen whales are the ones with the strainers in their mouths to catch the thousands of tiny sea creatures as the whale swims along with its mouth open like a giant scoop. These strainers are formed of a substance that is about the same as the material from which our fingernails are made. The substance, in whales, is called *baleen* and hangs in rows from the roof of the whale's mouth. Along the bottom of the baleen there is a fringe of the substance that serves as a strainer for the whale's food.

When a lot of tiny morsels have been collected on the baleen fringes, the whale simply closes its mouth, squeezes the water out between its lips, and then swallows its meal.

The giant Blue whale is one of the Baleen whales, and it and its cousins of the Baleen family are the most important ones so far as the whaling industry goes. The hunting of whales, by the way, is still a regular business today just as it was when the old sailing vessels and their harpooners sailed the seas in our grandfathers' and great-grandfathers' times.

Whales are particularly valuable because of the valuable oils that are taken from the great layers of fat or blubber beneath their skins.

In the days of old whaling ships, the sailors had a simple way of describing whales. They were called *Wrong whales* or

Right whales. The Right whales were the ones that stayed afloat after being har-

Right Whale

pooned and could be brought to the ship easily because of that. The Wrong whales were the ones that sank from sight when killed. The Blue whale by those standards, is a Wrong whale. If the harpoon can't hold it, it is lost.

The other major family of whales is the family of *Toothed whales.* The thing that sets this group apart isn't really that its members have teeth—because some of the Toothed whales have just bony jaws and not teeth. But these whales *don't* have baleen. That is why they are all in a family together so far as the scientists are concerned.

The most famous member of this family is the *Sperm whale.* If you know Herman Melville's story of Moby Dick, the greatest even if not the most accurate story ever written about whales, you may know that Moby Dick was a Sperm whale.

The largest of these whales seen today are only about 60 feet long, or about half the length of a Blue whale.

During the days of the sailing ships, the

Sperm Whale

hunting of Sperm whales was one of the most important ventures in America. Oil from these whales, called sperm oil, was as important for lighting lamps in those days as gasoline for running cars today.

Perhaps because the Sperm whale has such a terrific appetite for large sea creatures, like giant squids, its digestion is very poor. In fact, Sperm whales all seem to have very bad stomach trouble that causes them to throw up a most amazing material called ambergris. Grayish and hard, the ambergris comes up in large wads. It is amazing because it has a most wonderfully pleasant scent and is a substance more highly prized than any other for making perfumes.

One of the Toothed whales is "toothed" in a very unusual way. This is the *Narwhal*.

Narwhal

When this whale is young it has a few teeth that just seem to be put here and there helter-skelter in its gums. As the whales grow, all but one or at most two of these teeth drop out. And then a most amazing thing happens. The tooth that is left begins to grow. It grows straight out and as it grows it begins to look like a long spike that has been twisted to make it look grooved like a screw. Some of these teeth or tusks grow as long as ten feet and make the Narwhal look ever so much like a sea-going version of the fairy-tale unicorn.

Down the list of Toothed whales we come to a group that most people don't think of

as whales at all but rather regard as a separate sort of "fish" altogether. These are the *dolphins*.

DOLPHINS AND PORPOISES

Among the dolphin part of the whale family we can find the most amazing extremes in behavior of any animals in the world. One of the dolphins is one of the most fierce animals on earth—to judge by the savage way it kills its food and the amount of killing it does. Yet, another one of the dolphins is a frisky friendly animal that people have trained to leap out of the water and do tricks. There have been many films made of these playful dolphins. Perhaps you will recall one you may have seen.

The terrible monster of the dolphin group of whales is called the *Killer whale*. It isn't anywhere near as large as the truly great whales. Killer whales only grow to be about thirty feet long—of course *that's* about as long as two automobiles. But they are the fastest of all the whales.

Killer Whale

Killer whales have huge mouths that open straight across. This huge mouth looks like a terrible trap when it is open, for there are sharp curved teeth all around the inside. These particular members of the dolphin branch of the whale family live in both the Pacific and Atlantic oceans and are so fierce that they even attack the giant whales that are three or four times as large.

When they attack one of the large whales, they sometimes just swim like a torpedo at the big whale, bite out a great piece, and swim away.

Like some fierce meat-eating animals that live on land, the Killer whales hunt in packs, slashing through schools of fish and swallowing them whole as they go. Fish as big as men can be swallowed whole by these Killer whales. Seals, lying on top of ice floes have been eaten by these terrible ocean killers. The Killer whales just smash through the ice and grab the seals!

The nice member of the dolphins makes up for the bad reputation given by the Killer whale. This friendly dolphin is the *Beaked* or *Common dolphin.*

These dolphins are the "fish" that people often see traveling ahead of ocean liners, jumping high in the air as they swim and frolic to the amusement of the watching passengers. Actually, of course, they aren't fish at all. They are mammals. They must breathe air. Sometimes, when one of these dolphins has been hurt, other dolphins have been seen shoving and pushing the wounded one up to the surface where it can get life-giving air.

Another thing that is nice about these dolphins is that they seem to love their children just as much as human mothers and fathers love their own babies. Underwater microphones have recorded the sounds of a dolphin family and when you listen to these records you hear the parents making the same sort of loving sounds to their little dolphins as human parents make to their babies.

In several places in Florida where very large and deep pools have been built especially to hold ocean creatures—sort of like deepwater zoos—the dolphins usually steal the show every day.

Some are trained so that when a bell is rung at the edge of the pool, the dolphins come streaking up from the bottom of the pool and leap high out into the air. When a keeper holds fish out to them, they leap right up and take them from his hand—without so much as a nip of the fingers.

Others have been trained to leap out of the water and go right through a hoop held out for them.

The only time you might hear complaints about these playful dolphins, which are about the size of a smallish man, is from swimmers with whom the dolphins have tried to play. Sometimes when a dolphin decides to play around a swimmer, jumping and splashing out of the water around him, the swimmer may wish that the dolphin would go a bit farther away from his fun. But, all in all, these dolphins are about the nicest animals that live in the sea.

One of the things that separates the dolphins into a special place in the whale family is that they tend to have longer heads than the blunt, sometimes flat front that we usually think of when we think of whales. Although many whales don't have perfectly flat fronts like that, the dolphins, in general, do have a more streamlined look with their head sloping forward and sometimes ending in a sort of snout-like slant.

Oddly enough, though, one of the other small whales that does have a generally blunt head is often confused with the dolphin. At least people keep getting the names all mixed up. This other small mem-

60

ber of the whale family is the *porpoise*. Perhaps you have heard people talking about porpoises leaping in front of ships and doing tricks. They really were talking about dolphins.

Harbor Porpoise

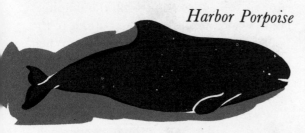

Perhaps because porpoises live close to shore their name has become familiar to a lot of people and they just use that name for any small member of the whale family.

The porpoise, however, does have one very interesting trait all its own. Do you remember about the stomach of a cow, and the way it is divided into separate compartments so that food may be swallowed and then digested later on? Well, the porpoise has a stomach rather similar to the cow's, with a special compartment in it in which food eaten earlier is put to be digested.

So far we have talked about some of the most useful and familiar mammals as well as the largest and strangest. There are, of course, many more that we should meet. Perhaps you would like to make a list of all the animals that you can think of that should go in this section about mammals.

61

Birds: Animals that Fly

FROM day to day, as we go to school, run errands, or just play outdoors, we probably see more birds than other kind of animal. Even in large cities, birds such as the little gray and brown sparrows and the big slate-colored pigeons are seen every day, everywhere. Around homes where there are trees, gardens, and shrubs, birds are heard singing all summer long, and even in the coldest winter a few hardy birds may be seen scratching for food such as seeds that may have fallen to the ground during the summer.

Look about you some summer day. No matter where you are, there is a good chance that you will see or hear a bird.

One reason why birds are seen everywhere is that the world in which they live, the air, is not claimed by other animals. Perched high in trees, nesting on limbs far above the ground, and flying through the air, birds usually have things pretty much to themselves.

Even birds that nest on the ground, like pheasants and bob-whites, or ducks that live on lakes and along shores, have a special advantage over other animals. When danger threatens, they can take to the safety of the air. This shows why birds live almost everywhere in the world. Many, called migratory birds because they migrate—that is, move from place to place—travel thousands of miles each year in order to find the safest and best homes for themselves. These birds often spend their summers far north, some going as far as the lands of the Eskimos. In summer, even in the far north, the weather is mild enough for birds to find food and raise their young. Then, as the cold weather comes, they take to the air in

vast swarms and travel south, stopping along the way wherever the food and climate suit them best. Such birds as these go so far as to cross the oceans in their yearly travels from one home to another.

HOW DO THEY FLY?

BEFORE we do anything else, let's answer the question most often asked about birds: How do they fly?

The key to the answer is in the two things birds have that other animals do not have: feathers and wings. Birds have feathers and wings just as all mammals have hair.

Everyone who has seen a bird flying realizes that birds fly with their wings. But most people imagine it is the *beating* of the wings, up and down, that pushes the bird up into the air and keeps him there. Actually, until

not too long ago, many scientists thought that too. But when cameras were made that could actually take pictures of a bird's wings in flight, we got the real story of how the wings and feathers work.

First, let's see how the wings really move.

The wings of a bird are in many ways like the wings of an airplane. They keep the bird in the air the way an airplane's wings keep it in the air. They do not simply flap up and down.

The shape of an airplane's wings (as is described in detail in the part of this book about airplanes) is more curved on the top than on the bottom. When air passes over the wing, it goes faster over the curved top part than over the bottom. When air moves like that there is less pressure on the top of the wing than on the bottom. The

63

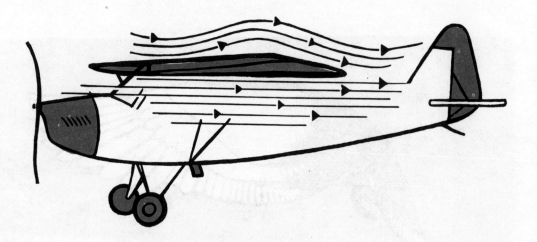

greater pressure on the bottom keeps the wing in the air, holding the airplane up.

Now, an airplane with its spinning propeller goes roaring off down the airport runway until the air is rushing over the wing fast enough to make the airplane rise into the air.

But a bird's wing has to work differently. A bird has no propeller to take him rushing along the ground until the air is moving over his wing. So the bird has to move his wing through the air.

Do you see the difference? The airplane moves, wings and all, until the air is rushing over the wing. The bird just moves its wings. It can do this while standing still and then soar off into the air. Once the bird is in the air, he can hold his wings still and just glide or move them and fly.

But the bird does not just flap his wing in moving through air. If we looked at a pigeon flying in slow motion, for instance, here is what we would see his wing doing: First the pigeon raises its wings straight up over his back. Then it starts moving its wings down.

Because of the feathers that make up his wing, the pigeon can change the shape of his wing very easily. As the wing starts its downward motion, the pigeon keeps all the feathers close together and curved on top. His wing then is shaped very much like an airplane wing. As the wing goes down in the first part of the flying motion, the pigeon tilts it a bit so that instead of flapping down flat, it knifes down at an angle making the air rush over it the way air rushes over an airplane wing.

As the pigeon's wing goes down farther, it is moved straight ahead a bit to make the air rush over it even more. At the end of the downward part of the flapping motion, the wings are thrust all the way forward and are actually out in front of the pigeon's head. As the pigeon brings its wings back to start another flapping motion, it makes its feathers open up so that the wing can move through the air very fast to get ready for another downward swoop.

TRY IT YOURSELF

When people try to imitate the way a bird's wings flap, they usually just flap their arms up and down. But from what we have learned, you can imitate it much better and more accurately than that. Instead of just flapping up and down, your arms should be held right up over your head and then swooped down and *forward* until your hands clap together way out in front of your chest.

Some birds are so heavy that even though their wings move like that, they have to take a running start along with the flapping before they can get into the air. When ducks take off from water where they have been floating, they have to paddle along in the water a little way before they can get into the air. They do this to overcome the drag of the water. When they do, it looks almost as if they are running on the water before they flap up into the air.

As we have said, all birds have wings and feathers, but some birds cannot use them to fly. The *ostrich,* the largest of birds, weighing as much as 300 pounds, has wings that just aren't big enough to get him off the ground. To make up for it, the ostrich has long powerful legs that let him run so fast it almost looks like flying. There are other birds too, like the *rhea,* which are just too big to fly. The *penguin,* because it lives in the cold part of the world at the South Pole, has stopped using its wings for flying and instead has learned to dive under the water for fish which is the only food to be had in that icy part of the world.

Now, here are some of the most interesting members of this family of animals with feathers and wings.

WATER BIRDS

PELICAN

If you don't know what a *pelican* looks like—just look at the picture! Have you ever in your life seen such a bill on a bird? Seems as if it would give him a headache just to carry it around. But the pelican doesn't mind, as he finds it very convenient indeed for holding fish. He can stow a good-sized fish away there, and eat it at his leisure.

Pelicans are big birds—four or five feet long—and look very awkward indeed as they sit on the shore or waddle along. But once in the water, with that cavernous beak opened wide—the fish had better look out!

CORMORANT

When a *cormorant* gets after a fish, it doesn't have much chance—that is, the fish doesn't. Look at the picture and you can see why. With its strong webbed feet and blunt wings a cormorant can swim rapidly, even when under water, and its beak is shaped almost like a fish-hook. So, what chance has the fish?

Cormorants are wonderful divers as well as swimmers, but are not much on flying, so they frequently build their nests on the ground. You can see them on the rocks out in the Pacific, near San Francisco, or off the coast of Maine; and in winter they go as far south as the Gulf of Mexico. They are about three feet long, and are a greenish-black, with coppery wings.

PETREL

TERN

The *petrel* is another bird familiar to everyone who crosses the ocean, for it is found far out of sight of land. It is not a big bird, like the gull or the tern, but a tiny little fellow no larger than a swallow. How brave they must be to venture so far out!

Instead of tucking their feet in their feathers when they are flying low over the water, they let them hang down, so that they seem actually to walk on the surface of the water. That is why they are called "petrels," which means "little Peters." You remember how the Apostle Peter walked on the Sea of Galilee.

Petrels are a sooty shade of brown, and the one shown in this picture has a white streak on its tail pinions.

There are over fifty species of *terns,* so you see it is a rather large family. They are also kin to the gulls, and others of the long-legged swimmers. They are sometimes called "sea swallows," as with their slender bodies and long powerful wings they can dart through the air as swiftly as swallows.

And what wonderful endurance they have! Terns have been known to fly from the Arctic Circle clear down to the Antarctic—and back again. That's from one end of the world to the other—thousands upon thousands of miles!

Terns are of many colors. This one in the picture is as white as snow, except for its black cap. They are about the size of the gulls, but longer and more slender.

67

RAZOR-BILLED AUK

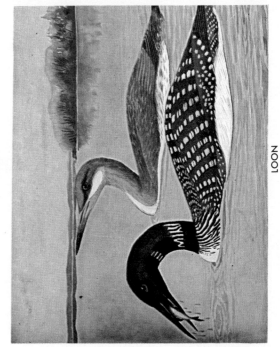

HERRING GULL

PIED-BILLED GREBE

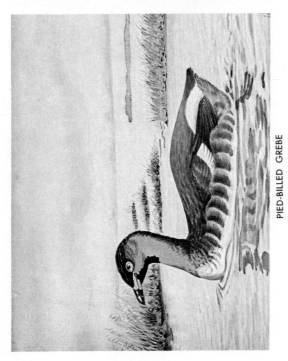

LOON

68

GREBE

People often say, "He swims like a duck." But here is a bird that swims better than a duck. The *grebe* is just about the best swimmer ever.

This picture shows a common variety called the *pied-billed grebe,* because of the peculiar markings on its bill. It lives so much in the water that it has been nicknamed the "water-witch." It has other names in different parts of the country, for it roams over a good deal of ground — or rather, water. Some folks call it the dabchick, and others the dipper.

If it wants to hide, the grebe can sink down under the water until only its eyes and the point of its bill stick out. Then nobody can find it, even the sharp-eyed hawk is baffled. This grebe is about a foot long, and of a dark brown color.

LOON

You may have heard someone called "as crazy as a loon"—although I hope not. But as for the *loon* itself, it is a smart bird. Maybe people call it crazy because it has a funny kind of long-drawn-out cry which can be heard a long way off. It may make you shiver, the first time you hear it.

Loons are found in the upper part of the United States and Canada, especially where there is plenty of water. They even build their nests right at the edge of a lake or stream, and the chicks learn to swim before they know how to walk. The loon's chief food is fish, so of course it can swim and dive well. But it is not so good in flight, and still worse when it tries to run on dry land. Maybe that's when it's crazy. Some loons are quite large, from two to three feet long, and they are variously marked.

AUK

This bird with its curious-shaped beak is a member of the numerous *auk* family. It is called the *razor-billed auk* because it bites so sharply. Auks live up north, from southern Greenland down as far as the coast of Maine or farther. They are very active and like to fish. They rest on the water as light as a cork, and if they see a fat fish down under the water, quick as a flash they go after it, so neatly as to leave scarcely a ripple. And they can fly as well as swim.

Flocks of auks are seen far out to sea. If you ever should see one, you could easily tell it by its bill and its black back and white shirt. It is about a foot and a half long.

GULL

If you have ever been to the seashore, you have doubtless seen the *gulls.* They are everywhere, swooping around in graceful circles, or resting easily on the water. They can even sleep there in calm weather, and gulls will stay out at sea for days at a time, coming in only when there is danger of a storm.

The *herring gull* shown in our picture is the most common species, and it varies in color from pure white to a grayish blue. Some of them are nearly two feet long, but as they wheel past, they look much smaller. They are fond of fish, oysters, clams, and in fact almost anything in the shape of food. They will follow a ship for days, to catch anything the cook throws overboard.

CANADA GOOSE

EIDER DUCK

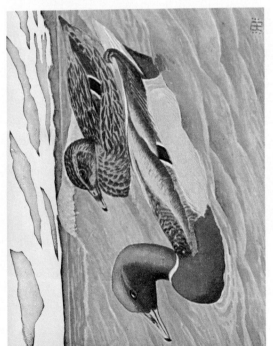

MALLARD DUCK

WHITE IBIS

70

MALLARD DUCK

Of course you know what a duck looks like—so whenever you hear of a *mallard duck,* just remember that it is a wild cousin of the barnyard fowl. But it is far stronger, handsomer, and more resourceful than the tame one. It can fly for long distances, going from north to south with the approach of winter, and returning north the next spring. But it is a hardy bird, and if it can find a sheltered cove where the water does not freeze over, it may remain north all winter.

This duck is about two feet long, and is beautifully marked with green head, grayish-brown back, chestnut breast and red feet.

CANADA GOOSE

Have you ever seen a flock of wild geese in flight? It is a wonderful sight. They pass by a mile above us, flying at faster than express-train speed and in a wedge-shaped mass. An old gander leads them, making the point of the "V," and the others spread out behind him. And how they do fly! In a night they can go from Maine to Florida.

The most common variety is the *Canada goose,* shown in the picture, a big bird, three or three and a half feet long, that you would never think could fly so fast and so far. As these geese fly they cry "Honk, honk!" And when the farmers up north hear them in the fall, they say: "Well, winter's coming."

WADING BIRDS

EIDER DUCK

The *eider duck* is about the same size as the mallard, but very different in looks. Its neck and back are white; its tail and lower body brown or black. It often has a dark cap over its eyes.

The eider duck has a curious habit. The mother bird will tear the downy feathers from her own breast in order to make a soft lining for her nest. These feathers are so fine that they are highly prized by people for filling pillows and comforters; so the birds are tamed and kept for this purpose. Eider ducks are found in both America and Europe, but in larger numbers abroad, as there they are protected and tamed instead of hunted.

WHITE IBIS

Now we are going to tell you about some of the wading birds, and the first one here in our pictures is the *ibis.* Of course, being a wader, the ibis has long legs and large feet —the feet serving to brace its rather ungainly body and also to keep it from sinking deeply into ooze or mud. It has a long bill, which is likewise of great use in searching about in shallow water for food.

This species is a beautiful white, with black-tipped wings, and it is a pretty sight to see a long file of them flying together. They like to live in the south. They are about two feet long and quite as tall.

| CRANE | EGRET |

The *crane* is built for deeper water than some of the other waders. It has long legs, is four feet in length, and has a wing-spread of over six feet. The one shown in the picture is called a sandhill crane because of the sandy plateaus where it is often found.

When it flies, the crane seems all legs, wings and neck. It likes to live in Florida and Louisiana, and despite its long legs which seem just made for wading, it really likes to hunt for its food on dry land. But here its legs still stand it in good stead, as it can see the approach of an enemy a long way off. When cornered, it fights fiercely, as many a hunting dog has learned to its sorrow, for the crane's beak is sharp as a dagger.

The *egret* has had a sad story. Its beautiful plumage has been its undoing. You will see in the picture the long white plume-like feathers which adorn its back. Well, people have wanted these feathers to put on women's hats,—"aigrettes," they are called — and so the poor birds have been slaughtered by the thousands.

The egret is a tall graceful bird of the heron tribe, and stands over three feet high. It has a long bill of dark color. The legs are also dark. The National Association of Audubon Societies has done a noble work in keeping egrets from being killed.

GREEN HERON

NIGHT HERON

The *green heron* is comparatively small, only about a foot-and-a-half long. At its name implies, it is a rich green in color on its back, with a neck of chestnut hue.

It is not a sociable bird, and does not live with other members of its family in flocks as some birds do. Instead, it builds its nest off by itself—a mass of sticks in some lonely bush or low tree.

The green heron is fond of small fish and finds its long, swordlike bill of great use in spearing them. Fingers may have been made before forks, with persons, but the heron carries his fork along with him.

The *night heron* doesn't stay up all night, as you might think from its name, for it likes the daytime too. But along about twilight, it wakes up to the fact that it is rather hungry and a nice mess of fish would taste good. So with a loud and hoarse "Quawk!" it proceeds down to the nearest pond, swamp, or river.

The night heron has been nicknamed the *quawk,* or *qua-bird* from its cry. This heron is finely marked, with a black crown and back and white underparts. Its wings and tail are gray, and it is about two feet long.

SANDPIPER

WOODCOCK

The *sandpipers* are like the *snipes* and are also members of the wading family. They can go around in the mud and water all day long without having their mothers say, "Don't stay in there too long, I'm afraid you will catch cold." The sandpiper boys and girls do have some advantages.

There are ever so many different kinds of sandpipers, such as the *red-backed,* the *purple,* the *stilt,* and others so called from their plumage or form. The one shown in this picture is a *spotted sandpiper*—you can see why. It looks as if someone had tattooed its shirt all over. These birds are about nine inches long.

The *woodcock* belongs to the family of *shore birds or waders.* It doesn't mind getting its feet wet on occasion, but if food is plentiful on dry land, so much the better. A nice dish of angleworms or grasshoppers suits it to a T. It has lots of nicknames—*big eyes* (because its eyes do seem a size large for it), *pewee, mud snipe, bog bird,* and several others.

The woodcock is found in many parts of the country, from Nova Scotia to Florida. It is not quite a foot long, with brown and orange chest. Two or three broad stripes on its head and a long, business-like bill, with its big bright eyes, make it easily remembered.

BIRDS OF LAND AND FOREST

WILD TURKEY

MOURNING DOVE

When the first settlers came to this country and it was a wilderness, there were thousands of *wild turkeys*. The Indians used to hunt them, and at the first Thanksgiving dinner the Pilgrim Fathers had wild turkey to eat. So persistently have these birds been hunted ever since, that they have almost disappeared from our fields and woods.

A full-grown wild turkey is quite large, measuring nearly four feet to the end of its fan-shaped tail. It looks and acts very much like the tame ones you see in the farmyards but is far more active. Flocks of them by the hundreds used to fly for long distances seeking new feeding grounds, but almost no one ever sees one in America any more.

If you should be walking through the woods and hear a heartbroken sort of moan coming from a tree a little way ahead—a sound as if there were no more joy in life at all and one might as well die and be done with it—the suffering bird would be the *mourning dove*. "Ooo!" it wails; "Ooo-oo, ooo-ooo! That last grasshopper was tough!"

But the bird is not really as sad as it sounds. It is blue-gray in color. It has a long neck and an extra long tail. It measures a foot from tip of beak to tip of tail, though you wouldn't think it. Farmers like this dove, as it eats many insects and bugs that would otherwise destroy the crops. It is especially fond of weed seeds.

TURKEY VULTURE

BLACK VULTURE

The *turkey vulture* is one of the ugliest of birds, and you wouldn't want one for a pet. Vultures' habits are, to say the least, not refined. They feed on the dead bodies of other birds and mammals; but they are very useful for this very reason, as they keep the countryside clean and free from offensive odors.

While ungainly and awkward on the ground, they are graceful in flight. Their powerful wings have a spread of six feet, and they can hover in the air for hours at a time. They are extremely keen of sight, and can locate a dead rabbit from more than a mile away.

Some people call this vulture a *carrion crow*. It is smaller than the turkey vulture and in some ways resembles a crow. It is of blackish color, with a naked head and neck and white feet.

These vultures are quite tame as nobody ever molests them. In some southern cities they can be seen calmly walking up and down the streets looking for stray bits of food. So efficient are they as street cleaners, that people down there throw out garbage, instead of putting it in a can, knowing that within a few minutes the carrion crow will find it and clean up every speck.

BALD EAGLE   HAWK

Every good American, little or big, knows what a *bald eagle* looks like as it is our national bird. What an air of majesty and power it has! Its eye is so sharp that we call all such "eagle eyes." Its wings are so broad and powerful that it can fly farther and higher than other birds and carry an animal as large as a lamb away with it. Its wing-spread sometimes exceeds seven feet.

High up on the side of a cliff an eagle may build its nest—a rough affair of sticks —and the father bird will fly, perhaps for miles, bringing their supper—which may be a rabbit or choice fish—to the mother and the young ones.

"As sudden as a hawk," the saying goes, and it is an apt one, for the *hawk* is nothing if not sudden. Picture a peaceful farmyard on some sunny afternoon. The chickens are scattered about feeding or sunning themselves. Suddenly a dark shadow is seen on the ground, coming with express-train speed. Their dreaded enemy, the hawk, drops like an arrow, seizes a half-grown chicken, and is gone—all within five seconds!

Hawks have powerful wings, spreading out three feet. They can carry off rabbits too, and their sudden attacks make them the most dreaded of the birds of prey.

SPARROW HAWK

OSPREY

There are a good many hawks, big and little, but the *sparrow hawk* is the smallest and most peaceful. In fact, it is inclined to be friendly with man. It will build its nest in the hollow of some old tree near the farmhouse, and it keeps the premises pretty clear of mice, grasshoppers, caterpillars, beetles, and other "small fry." So, when the farmer hears its cry of "Killy-killy-killy!" he doesn't get his gun, as he does when the big chicken hawk comes around.

In other words, the sparrow hawk pays for his board and keep. He is less than a foot long and has a chestnut-colored back.

The *osprey* is often called the *fish hawk*. If you ever see one, you will know why. It is the most patient fisher of all the birds—and successful too.

The osprey will fly high in the air over the water, and so keen is its sight that it can see a long way down under the waves. When it has located the particular fish it fancies, down it will dart—often many feet below the surface—fasten its long talons into the fish's back, drag it up, and fly away with it. So you see, it is a strong as well as an agile bird.

It is dark brown above and white below, and is about two feet long, but has a wingspread of five feet.

SCREECH OWL   GREAT-HORNED OWL

Suppose you were going through a wood some dark night, when all of a sudden, right above your head, somebody said: "Whoo? whoo, whoo-oo?" Wouldn't you jump and shiver! Some people call this little owl, which gives such a mournful note, the *shivering owl,* and probably that's a better name than *screech owl.* Its call is soft and wailing, and it hasn't much of a screech.

There are lots of owls, and this is one of the commonest. It has round, staring eyes —as all owls have—which see better in the night than in the day. So the owl usually sleeps in the daytime, and goes hunting at night—for mice and such tidbits.

The *great-horned owl* is a larger bird than the screech owl, and is also called the big hoot owl. It has a couple of tufts, like horns, on its head—hence its name.

This owl is nearly as destructive as the hawk, for it is likewise a hunter, and as it does its hunting after dark, it is doubly dangerous. It will carry off chickens, ducks, and even small turkeys. Rabbits and partridges also fear it, for its lightning-like swoop, with clutching talons and cruel beak, offers little chance of escape.

It has a mottled plumage of dusky brown color and stands two feet high.

BELTED KINGFISHER

CUCKOO

We don't see a *cuckoo* as often as we see some other birds, for it has a shy and retiring disposition. But often out in the country you can hear one—a long, throaty wail. "That's a rain crow," says the weather-wise farmer. "We'll have rain tomorrow sure."

Why the cuckoo knows anything about the weather or why they call him a crow, nobody knows. He certainly doesn't look anything like a crow. He isn't black but brown and white—a slender little bird about a foot long, and half of that length is tail.

The cuckoo eats stacks and stacks of caterpillars, and so saves much fruit and grain for the farmer.

Isn't this *belted kingfisher* a cocky-looking little bird? It looks and acts, in fact, as if it were "cock of the walk." Note that perky little crest on the head, the smart white collar around the neck, and the sharp-tailed evening coat! And the belted kingfisher is as smart as it looks.

As fishermen these birds are about the best ever. They will sit out on the limb of a tree, fifty feet above the water and see, down in it, a minnow the size of your finger. Down they will drop like plummets, hitting the water hard. But with a sudden dive, up they come and that minnow comes right along.

Belted kingfishers can be easily recognized. They are about a foot long from the tip of the short tail to the end of the long beak.

DOWNY WOODPECKER

RED-HEADED WOODPECKER

A little black and white bird, with a sharp bill but friendly ways, is the *downy woodpecker,* which is found in many places east of the Mississippi River. It isn't much more than six inches long, but those six inches mean business! Watch one pecking away industriously into the side of a tree. It has found a decayed spot, and its keen scent tells it that under that wood is a borer that has no business in that tree.

Tap, tap, tap! Come out, you borer! And he usually comes out, to be snapped up by the sharp little tongue inside the sharp little beak of the woodpecker.

If you can't see the downy woodpecker easily, you certainly can't miss its red-headed cousin. In his uniform of red, white and black he could be found even if he didn't do that noisy tapping on the side of a tree.

But the *red-headed woodpecker* is not at all bashful. He's handsome and he knows it. In addition to his pounding on a tree, as all his tribe do, he's noisy in his talk — a terrible gossip, who likes to talk things over with his neighbors and doesn't care who overhears him.

He is a little larger than the downy woodpecker and sometimes varies his diet of bugs and grubs by trying the farmer's fruit.

FLICKER

WHIPPOORWILL

The *flicker* is another member of the wood-pecker family, and is larger than the red-head. He has been called the *golden-winged woodpecker* (which will give you an idea of his coloring), also the *yellow-shafted wood-pecker* and a lot of other names.

He makes friends readily with other birds, such as robins and bluebirds, and if you provide him with comfortable living quarters, he may live right in your yard. You can always tell a flicker by the crescent on his breast and the gay crest of red feathers on his head.

You'll remember this bird's *name,* at any rate; and if you ever hear its strange cry, around about twilight, you won't mistake it. "Whip-poor-Will!" it implores you in three long whistled notes that will be re-peated time after time with a stop to take breath. Once I counted seventy-seven times, and after a pause of about half a minute the bird was off again. But no matter how long you may hear the cry, you will rarely see the speaker himself.

The whippoorwill is a very shy bird that only becomes bold enough to approach a house when it gets dark.

BLUEJAY

CROW

Here is a bird that you would never accuse of being modest or retiring. The *blue jay* struts around in his "baseball suit" as if he owned everything in sight. And to hear him arguing with the other birds, you would be sure he does think so.

He has an ugly, hoarse call of "Jay! Jay! Jay!" But with all his faults he is a handsome bird, and he stays around up north all winter when most of the other birds are gone. The flash of his smart blue coat is a welcome sight. But he has a bad reputation with other birds. They call him a thief, and say he robs their nests.

Speaking of thieves, this is one of the worst ever. The *crow* is the pest of the farmer. It delights to tear up the young corn, and when the farmer rigs up a scarecrow, the bird often laughs at it.

The crow is black—of course, you know that—and is saucy, bold, active, and full of tricks. It knows right away if the farmer is carrying a gun, and will then give him a wide berth.

Another familiar feature about the crow is its call—a long, searching "Caw! Caw!" which you can hear for a mile or more. Crows like to flock together. Sometimes you will see a field fairly black with them.

| BOBOLINK | MEADOWLARK |

If you should chance to see a little bird about seven inches long, with a black and white coat and a bluish black shirt, and this bird sang as if it were trying to split its head open, that would be the *bobolink*. It actually seems to go crazy singing.

The bobolink is a great traveler and goes under various names. In the south it is called the *rice bird* and the *reed bird*. It eats rice so greedily that it becomes quite fat, and so pays the penalty of its gluttony by being shot.

The *meadowlark* is about the size of the bobolink, and, like that bird, is a great singer — but doesn't take singing quite so seriously. Out in the open fields you may see the meadowlark, whose fine yellow breast is set off with a crescent of glossy black. As it rises into the air its melody rises with it —a particularly charming song.

Sometimes it will stay north all winter, cheerfully enduring the snow and cold, and making its meals off dried weed seeds. When it wants to vary its diet it hunts up a cater-pillar.

ENGLISH SPARROW

CHIPPING SPARROW

What a perky little bird this one is! It doesn't hesitate to attack feathered neighbors twice its size, and it usually wins.

The *English sparrow* came to our shores as a visitor and since then its family has grown so large that it can be found almost everywhere. Nobody likes it very much, it is so saucy and impudent, but little it cares what anybody else thinks. It is so sturdy that it stays north right through the winter, and you will often see it hopping about over the snow looking for seeds or crumbs.

The *chipping sparrow* is far more popular than its English visitor. For one thing, it is tame and of a gentle disposition. For another, its song, while brief, is sweet. It likes to build close to the house, and has been called the "hair bird" from its fondness for using horse-hair in its nest.

It is about the size of the English sparrow, but is not quite so bright in color. Its coat is a rusty color, and its breast a dull gray.

GOLDFINCH

JUNCO

Still another small bird, about the size of the sparrow, is the *goldfinch*. He is a beauty, and I fancy he knows it, but it doesn't hurt his disposition. If you should see a flash of yellow dart through the air and come to rest on a tree or fence, and he should show black wings and tail, you would be safe in calling him a goldfinch. Some people call him the *wild canary*, for he looks a good deal like the caged variety and his song is quite as sweet. Sometimes he says, "Tic-o-ree! ric-o-ree!" and sometimes "Per-chic-o-ree!"

That's a funny name for a bird now isn't it?—*junco!* But you will like *snowbird*, which is his ordinary everyday name. This sociable little bird, which is about the size of the sparrow, is one of the hardiest. It is found clear up in Alaska, and doesn't seem to mind a bit how cold it gets.

Members of his family are of several colors. One is called the slate-colored junco—you can see why from the picture. But there are black and blue and white snowbirds—all a jolly lot as they jump about and chatter. Put out some crumbs for him, won't you, when winter comes?

SONG SPARROW

CARDINAL

The *song sparrow* is not quite so friendly as the chipping sparrow. It prefers the quiet of some thicket or a fence corner to the porch or barn which the chipping sparrow may seek.

But in its quiet retreat it composes a whole lot of music—and such music! Opening its little throat it fairly pours itself forth in song. And passersby stop and listen with delight.

The song sparrow is found in many parts of this country, in Canada, and even in far-away Alaska. It is a little over six inches long, and is brown, black, and white. But its song is pure gold.

You know there is a shade of red called "cardinal," because the high Church officials wear robes of this color. Well, here is a high priest of song who flaunts his coat of red with the best of them.

You can tell a *cardinal* as far as you can see one—and somehow, just the sight of one makes the day seem brighter. There is no more strikingly handsome bird in all the woodland. And he is just as cheery as his coat. He calls out, "Cheer, cheer, cheer!" Or maybe it is a "Hip, hip"—just as if he wanted you to add the "Hurrah!"

He is over eight inches long, and is found generally in the eastern part of the United States.

SCARLET TANAGER

GROSBEAK

Do you want to know how to tell a *scarlet tanager* from a cardinal? Well, the tanager has black wings and tail. If the flash of red which darts across the road has these, you can safely call it a tanager. And it is quite as beautiful and arresting as the cardinal. Some people call it the *black-winged redbird*.

When the farmer does his plowing in the early spring, this bird gets busy too, and follows along in the fresh furrows, picking up the grubs and worms that have been dug up. Later on in the summer it is lazier, but does not disdain a nice mess of caterpillars.

There are several kinds of grosbeaks, but the handsomest of the lot is the *rose-breasted grosbeak*. It is about the size of the cardinal, and is strikingly marked with red, black, and white. The red or rose color is in a little patch on its breast, like a badge.

The grosbeaks are not frequently seen, however, as they like the thickets. But their song is well worth hearing, it is so rich and mellow.

The bird has a terrible nickname—the "potato-bug bird," because he is particularly fond of these pests of the potato vine. So all the farmers welcome him.

PURPLE MARTIN

CLIFF SWALLOW

The *martins* belong to the *swallow* family. They can be told by their forked tails. This one is also called the *house martin,* as it likes to live in houses built for it by its human friends.

Down south, in front of small cabins, you will often see empty gourds hung up on poles or in trees, and in there the martins go housekeeping quite happily. They are sociable with each other. They like to live in colonies, and some martin houses have five or six stories. Don't you want to build a home for a family of them before next spring?

This *swallow,* unlike its cousin the martin, doesn't wait for somebody else to build a home for it. It prefers to plan and build its own—and it makes a good job of it too. It gets a quantity of mud together and molds a bottle-shaped house, with a round hole for a front door, and the whole thing is fastened under the eaves of the barn, or in some crack of a cliff.

This bird, also called the *eave swallow,* is only six inches long, and brightly marked in contrasting blue, white, and reddish tints.

BARN SWALLOW

CEDAR WAXWING

A friendly and familiar figure around farms and gardens is the *barn swallow*—so called because it likes to build its nest on the projecting beams of the barn. The nest is a queer mixture of mud, straw, grass and twigs, and is lined with feathers.

The swallow flies in a peculiar darting manner, and this and its forked tail easily identify it. It has a steel blue coat and is about seven inches long. Now that the old barns are disappearing in favor of new garages, the barn swallows are hard put to it to find a convenient home.

This is an aristocrat among small birds. If you should see one, you would catch your breath and exclaim, "My, what a beauty!"

Indeed it is beautiful. First of all, there is a charming crest, then a blending of soft colors—drabs, browns, slates, pale blues, with a fringe of gold, and a touch of red— all united, with its graceful form and air of distinction, to make it one of the loveliest of birds. It is said that the *cedar waxwing* is so polite that if ten of them are sitting on a limb and one finds a cherry, it will pass it on to the next, and so on down the line to the end.

BOB-WHITE

RUFFED GROUSE

Some time when you are out in the country you are likely to hear a cheery whistle. It sounds like, "Bob White! Wheat's Ripe!" So persistently does the call come, that the bird has long since been called the *bob-white*.

In the north some folks call it a *quail*, and in the south others say, "There's a *partridge* calling." But the bird disputes them both, insisting, "My name's Bob White!"

The bob-white's dusky white and chestnut coat blends perfectly with the grass and leaves. But hunters with dogs come looking for bob-whites in the fall, as they are very good to eat. When the hunters come too close, away they go like a shot.

Bob-whites are about ten inches long and quite plump.

The ruffed grouse is another beautiful game bird, so wild that only the keenest eye can see it in the woods where it hides. But sometimes the farmer boys hear a distant beating like the sound of a muffled drum, and eagerly they will creep up to get a sight of the drummer. If they are *very* lucky they may see the grouse, but more often the bird sees them first. Then with a thunderous roar of wings the grouse is gone. He is as large as a medium-sized turkey, and is sometimes called a *pheasant*. His reddish-brown plumage makes him very hard to see—but that suits him first rate. He is "not at home" to just anybody.

91

MOCKING-BIRD

THRASHER

When we think of singers, here is one that beats them all, for the *mocking-bird* has a long list of songs that it will cheerfully sing for you, and when it runs short of them, it will begin to imitate some other bird. In fact, you can listen to the mocking-bird— as it is called, from this curious habit of mocking others—by the hour. There have been songs written about this bird, and it is one of the most familiar and best loved of all.

The mocking-bird is good-sized—about ten inches long and has a brownish-gray coat and white and gray vest; just a quiet bird to look at, but my, how it can sing!

This bird is often called the *brown thrasher* and the picture tells you why. It has a long tail, which brings its full length to eleven inches. It jerks its tail up and down in a quick, nervous way, which reminds one of the way farmers used to thresh out grain with flails; and that is probably how it got its name.

The brown thrasher is quite a songster, and has a trick of repeating the same refrain over and over again, as if trying to memorize it. Some people call it the *brown mocking-bird,* and others the *brown thrush;* others still, the *song thrush.* But under any name it just keeps singing along.

92

WREN

MARSH WREN

The *wrens* are among the smallest and most fidgety of birds. They are never still a minute when away from home. They seem always to be going on an errand and being twenty minutes late.

The *winter wren,* shown in the picture, is only about four inches long, but that's the busiest four inches you ever saw. It is reddish brown in color and looks like "Jenny wren," as the house wren is called, but is even smaller than the fussy Jenny. It has a sweet, high song; but if anything bothers it, that song will change to an angry chatter.

There are two varieties of the *wrens* that live in bogs and marshes—the *short-billed* and the *long-billed.* The last-named like to live among the cat-tails along the shores of some sluggish river or bay, and they build remarkable houses which look something like coconuts, fashioned of interwoven rushes. These houses are so well built that they are almost waterproof.

Inside is a downy little room, where the mother wren sits patiently upon the tiny speckled eggs until they are hatched. These wrens are only five inches long, and have perky tails.

NUT-HATCH

TITMOUSE

The *nut-hatch* family, of which there are several members, have a curious habit. They like to walk upside down. If you should happen to see one, like the white-breasted nut-hatch shown in the picture, as likely as not it would be marching head-first *down* a tree instead of walking *up*. It must think this is a topsy-turvy world!

The nut-hatches are small birds, no bigger than the wrens. They have sharp bills for searching in the cracks of trees for grubs, and a very inquisitive eye. They are friendly and tame if you do not disturb them, but they are *very* busy.

Still another tiny bird is the *titmouse*. The tufted fellow shown in the picture is a cousin of the *chickadee,* and is smart and brimful of curiosity. He is dressed in soft gray, with a fine, showy, pointed crest. He probably thinks he is a drum major.

The titmouse is easily tamed, and has even been known to fly right into a house, through an open window, in search of a good place to build a nest. It has a loud and clear note, and doesn't stay still for a single minute. For such a small bird, the titmouse is wonderfully self-important.

CHICKADEE

KINGLET

The *chickadee* got its name from its cheery chirp—"Chickadee-dee!" It is a little bit bigger than the wren, though not much, and has the same quick, inquisitive, important ways that all these little feathered friends seem to have. It is a hardy bird, seeming to prefer the snowy wastes of Canada and New England to the warmer states.

The chickadee is especially fond of red cedar berries, and makes itself at home in the dense evergreen forests. Here, if you could peep in, you would see whole flocks of them darting about for all the world as if they were having a game of tag.

You would have to be personally introduced to the little *kinglet* in order to know it. For one thing, it is quite small—a hop-o-my-thumb of a bird (about four inches long)—and for another thing, it lives a good part of the time away up in Canada.

The *golden-crowned kinglet* comes south in the wintertime. The *ruby-crowned,* which has a dash of red on its head, seems to enjoy the bitterest and stormiest of weather. For such a tiny creature, with only a coat of feathers, this seems astonishing. But the kinglet shows us that we can get used to anything.

ROBIN

BLUEBIRD

Of course you know the *robin*, that commonest and best liked of all our song birds. How we love to watch the friendly robin hopping about over the lawn, flaunting that bright red breast or searching out some likely spot for a nest! And how cheery is the robin's song!

The robin is easily the best known of all the birds, and endless stories and songs have been made in its honor. The male robin's clothes are brighter than the female's—just as if he wore new garments and made her wear the old faded ones. A robin is about ten inches from tip to tip—and one of our most welcome signs that spring is here.

Next to the robin, we know and love the *bluebird*. We now have a saying that the bluebird stands for happiness. Bluebirds are also messengers of spring and when we see their fine blue coats and note their gentle manners, we greet them as old friends.

Like the robin, the bluebird is found nearly all over the United States. It is not quite so large as the robin (about seven inches). If you have an orchard near your house, look there for bluebirds, as they like to build nests in gnarled apple-tree trunks. Yes, bluebirds are happy birds, and it makes us happy just to look at them.

Reptile Families

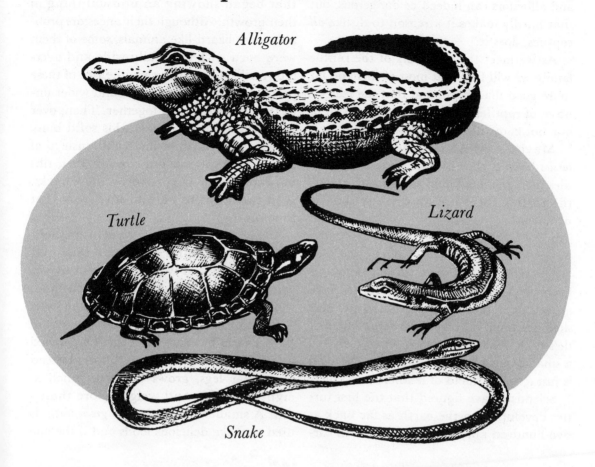

Alligator

Turtle

Lizard

Snake

IF YOU were asking questions about animals, you would probably discover that one particular kind is quite hard to find out about—the kind in the family called *Reptiles*.

People who know a lot about lions and tigers and dogs and cats, and even camels and whales, often don't know very much about reptiles. Perhaps when we say which animals belong to this family, you will understand why.

There are four kinds of animals in the reptile family. There are the turtles. There are the lizards. There are the snakes. And there are the crocodiles and alligators. They are not the sort of animals we see around every day—no matter where we live. Most of them live very hidden lives.

Just as it is with many other things that are not familiar to us, some people are scared of reptiles. That is a shame. For if something is strange-looking or unfamiliar, that is certainly no reason to be afraid of it. In fact, of all the hundreds of different kinds of turtles, lizards, and snakes, there are very few that really do people harm. Crocodiles and alligators can indeed be dangerous, but that hardly makes it a reason to dislike *all* reptiles, does it?

As we meet the members of the reptile family we will find that most of them do far more good than harm and that the fear we have of reptiles is really just the result of our not knowing enough about them.

Maybe it would be good to start with *turtles* because they include some of the reptiles that are often found as pets and, among the turtles, there are hardly any that do us harm.

TURTLE TANKS

The moment you see a turtle, you notice his most distinctive feature. All turtles have a shell over their backs. Sometimes this shell is a bone-hard roof all across the turtle's back, making him look very much like a small armored tank. Sometimes the shell is just a tough shield of leathery substance.

Scientists have figured that the first turtles developed on the earth as far back as two hundred million years ago, much ear-

lier than even the dinosaurs. These ancient turtles were members of the reptile family that began showing an unusual thing in their growth. Although their ancestors probably were lizard-like animals, some of them were born with especially wide and overgrown ribs. Over the years, the ribs of these particular animals got wider and wider until they actually grew together. Then, over more thousands of years, this solid bony growth marked all of them and, instead of being inside them as our ribs are, their ribs became a shell that covered their backs. And turtles were here to stay from that time on.

Today one of the best ways of distinguishing turtles is to find out where they live. Some live only in water, some can live in water but also spend some time on land, while a few live on land almost all the time.

Some of the turtles that live in water, in the ocean to be exact, are huge. One, called a *leatherback turtle,* has great flippers instead of regular legs, grows to be as much as eight feet long, and weighs more than a ton! A smaller sea turtle, the *green turtle,* is used to make delicious foods and is the one

Leatherback Turtle

Box Turtle

people use for that delicacy, turtle soup. That turtle, too, has flippers rather than legs.

Another turtle that people often know because of its use as a food, is called the *diamondback terrapin*. The *diamond* part of the name comes from the diamond-shaped furrows on the turtle's shell. *Terrapin* is the name of a whole group of turtles that live in the fresh waters of North America. Even though they do live in the water, however, they do not have flippers. They have legs but with webbed feet like a duck's.

TORTOISE IN A BOX

If the children of America, which is a country that has as many turtles as any other place in the world, were to vote for their favorite kind of turtle, they would probably choose a certain tortoise. That word, *tortoise*, is familiar to everyone who has read the wonderful story about the slow steady tortoise beating the harum-scarum rabbit in a race. Scientists use the word tortoise to refer generally to turtles that spend a lot or most of their time on land.

The tortoise that so many children like is the *box-turtle*.

It is called a *box-turtle* because it can duck all the way inside of its shell as if it were getting into a box and snapping the lid.

Besides the hard shell on their backs, turtles have a hard flat plate underneath them too. But most turtles do not have their top and bottom shields so arranged that they can close them together like a box. Usually, some part of the turtle sticks out here or there, and with many turtles the top and bottom shields are very small compared to their whole bodies. It is as though you had little saucers on either side of your hands with all the fingers sticking out.

With the box-turtle, however, the top and bottom plates come together in a perfect fit. When the turtle pulls in its head under the top shell, a hinged part of the bottom shell snaps up to close the box tight.

Scientists call the top shell of a turtle the *carapace*. The bottom plate is called the *plastron*.

99

Box-turtles have pretty yellow lines all over their shells, and they are very good natured. Kept as pets for any length of time these turtles get so that they don't even bother to hide in their shells when people come around. They just stick out their heads and stare, seeming as curious about the people as the people are about them. Like so many land turtles, this boxed one can live quite nicely on vegetables and fruit although grasshoppers and other insects are also welcome in the diet. It is by eating insects that turtles and many other reptiles help keep the balance of nature—making sure that the insects don't increase to an alarming degree.

Unfortunately, in spite of all the interesting and harmless turtles of the lakes, rivers, and fields, there are also dangerous turtles, and it is because of their very bad reputation that some people fear all *turtles*.

SNAPPERS

The dangerous turtle is the *snapping turtle*. There are two kinds of snapping turtles in North America. Both live in the water. Both have shells that aren't nearly large enough to cover them, particularly underneath where they have only a small rounded cross-shaped section of shell, covering only about half their undersides.

Although you wouldn't guess it from some of the terrible stories that are told about these turtles, they have no teeth. Turtles just don't have teeth. They have bony ridges instead of lips with which they chew their food. The snapping turtles, however, have such powerful jaws that the bony ridges of their mouths can rip and tear a fish or, to show you what they could do to an arm or a finger or a foot, they can snap a broomstick right in two.

The most widespread of the two kinds of American snapping turtles is called the common snapping turtle and grows to about a foot-and-a-half in length and weighs about 30 pounds.

The other snapper is even larger. It is called an *alligator snapper* because it is so fierce in appearance. Like the common

Snapping Turtle

Alligator Snapper

snapper its shell is marked by pyramid-shaped bumps. It is the largest of all the turtles that live in water. Full-grown alligator snappers weigh as much as 150 pounds, which is probably more than your mother weighs.

Either of these two turtles, lying in wait just below the surface of some muddy stretch of water where they can't be seen, can haul down a large wild duck and make a feast of it. The largest could be dangerous to a swimming human, but, like most animals, they will usually shy away from humans. Like other animals, also, they are most dangerous to humans when annoyed or when they might feel that they were being attacked.

One of the most common mistakes made about turtles is to call all of them snapping turtles when there are only so few that really are. People often imagine that any turtle is a "snapper" because when picked up, it will open its mouth and snap or even hiss. Actually, unless the turtle is one of the water-living snappers we have described, it is just trying to defend itself. Like any other living thing with a mouth, all turtles can clamp onto a finger when trying to protect themselves. But they certainly don't "snap." In fact, a pussy-cat can bite many times harder than most turtles.

STORM SNAP

There is another mistake about turtles that you may hear. That is that if they do "snap" they won't let go until it thunders. First of all, of course, even if a turtle did "snap" you, unless it were one of the big real snappers you could just pull your finger away. And if you think about it for a minute you will realize that there is no possible connection between thunder and a turtle's frame of mind. Of course that notion doesn't make sense.

101

FAMILY RESEMBLANCE

You may wonder what it is that puts turtles into the Reptile family. Well, first of all, they have backbones (and that separates them from such animals as crabs and lobsters and the insects). Their blood is not warm (and that separates them from mammals in general). When we say their blood isn't warm, we mean that the blood in their bodies is about the same temperature as the outside air or water in which they live. *Our* blood, because of the way we turn our food into energy, is warmer than the air around us.

Because of their particular make-up, reptiles are very sensitive to heat and cold. When temperatures go to extremes, the reptiles do too. Reptiles that live in very hot places, like deserts, stay out of the sun when it is at its hottest and many of them just sleep right through the very hottest parts of the year while reptiles that live in

Turtle asleep in cold climate

colder climates, do the opposite and sleep through the coldest parts of winter.

Another interesting thing about reptiles is that their young develop from eggs. Most of them, like turtles, actually lay these eggs and the young hatch from them just as chickens hatch from the eggs of a hen. Some turtles, however, keep their eggs inside their bodies until they hatch and then it almost always seems as if the mother reptile were giving birth to her young in the same way that mammals do.

Scientists sometimes say that reptiles are very closely related to fish and that, except for the fact that fish have fins, it might be very hard to say where one family ends and the other begins.

LOOKING BACK AT THE LIZARDS

An easy way to imagine what the world must have been like many millions of years ago is to look at a *lizard*. Today, of course, most lizards are quite small. But in the age

Lizard asleep in desert climate

of the dinosaurs many of them were huge. (The word *dinosaur* itself means "terrible lizard.") Imagine, then, a world in which there were giant lizards roaming everywhere, each of them three or four times the size of a man.

Even when people don't imagine things like that they imagine some other fantastic things about lizards—even the little ones of today. For lizards, which are members of the reptile family are especially strange-looking animals. And some people are afraid of anything that looks strange to them.

FEAR AND FACTS

Let's look at the lizards closely, as we did at the turtles, and see just what there is to be afraid of. It certainly isn't size. The largest lizards alive in the world today some-

*Common
lizard of today*

times grow to be ten feet long. There are many, many animals that are larger. There are even some dogs that weigh as much as the largest lizards. For another thing, those largest of lizards live only on a couple of islands in the Pacific—and they aren't even harmful there! What's more, when put in cages in a zoo they soon become quite tame.

Well, then, is it that *some* lizards, large or not, are terribly fierce and dangerous?

Of all the 2,500 different kinds of lizards known all over the world, only two—remember that, only two—are known to be poisonous and therefore dangerous to man.

BRIGHT MONSTER

One of those poisonous lizards is a three-foot brightly colored fellow frighteningly called a *Gila Monster* that lives in the dry western part of the United States. The other is a similar lizard that lives in Mexico. Both are covered with shiny smooth bright red and black bumps as though to warn people to stay away—but, amazingly enough, both of them calm down when put in cages and, like the giant lizards, can become quite tame. They use their poison just to defend themselves from things that try to hurt them.

All of this does *not* mean that you should go out and make friends with any old lizard. But it does mean that when someone says

*Giant lizard of
prehistoric times*

Gila Monster

in a frightened voice that you must beware of all lizards because they are so poisonous, you will be able to tell them that they are talking about just two members of a family of 2,500—and that those two members are so brightly colored that no one would be likely to pick them up by accident.

Actually there may be some hope for lizards and people getting along a little better these days. In the United States for instance, a prickly looking little lizard called a *horned toad* (a flattish animal with jagged ridges all over him and with a spiny fringe around his sides) is being kept as a pet by more and more people who have learned to ignore the fact that he is so fierce looking and are just amused by his funny way of scurrying around and his very tame attitude toward people. Come to think of it, you might try to imagine some time how people, towering way up in the air, must look to a tiny lizard. Perhaps it takes some effort on *their* part to get over being scared of us!

CHANGEABLE CHAMELEON

There is one form of lizard that has been kept as pet for more years than the horned toad. That lizard is the *chameleon*. Many children who have been to a circus, particularly in the United States, have become familiar with the American chameleon because this tiny, soft, quickly moving type of lizard is often sold as a pet there.

But children everywhere have probably heard about this amazing animal. The reason is that the chameleon has a special trick: His color changes to blend in with his background, thus helping him to escape the notice of animals that might want to harm him.

This changing of color is usually automatic. The color changes slowly as the animal moves from a brown leaf onto green grass. But the changes can be caused by other things too. Temperature can affect the chameleon's color and so can excitement. When the chameleon is excited it may change to a color altogether different from the one of its background.

CHEMICAL SKIN

The color of a chameleon changes because of its unusual skin. In a chameleon's skin are thousands of tiny splotches of oil of a special sort. Light reflected from the surrounding ground or leaves affects these, causing the chemicals in the splotches to shift and change. When that happens, the color of the chameleon's skin changes too—just the way you can change the color of a glass of grape juice by adding a lot of water

American chameleon

—to make it pale—and then adding more grape juice to make it dark again.

Actually, the smooth little pet sold in circuses is called an *American chameleon* and is far different from the true chameleons of Europe and Asia. They are usually much larger and with more heavily beaded skins. Too, they have eyes set in remarkable cone-shaped bumps that can move in separate directions. One eye can look straight ahead while the other looks backward. These true chameleons also have amazing tongues, long slender whiplike things that they can lash out quicker than the eye can follow in order to snare a passing insect.

THE LIZARD LOOK

In trying to figure out just what makes a lizard a lizard and not a snake for instance, scientists sometimes have a little trouble. Here are some of the things they run up against. Most lizards, to be sure, have something that snakes don't. The lizards usually have four short legs on their sometimes very snake-like bodies. But some lizards *don't* have any legs at all. A quick look and you would say they were snakes.

Most lizards have eyelids that move, sort of like yours. Snakes never have them. But then *some* lizards don't either.

Most lizards have at least a trace of an ear showing outside their head. Snakes don't. But then, again, *some* lizards don't either.

Then how do the scientists tell them apart? One way is by the kind of "skin" that covers them. Both snakes and lizards are covered with scales, as they are on their undersides. The under part of a snake is covered by long narrow scales laid one after the other in a single row. The underneath part of a lizard is covered by at least several rows of scales or of a bumpy covering.

CROCODILES AND ALLIGATORS

Perhaps, as the lizards have been described, you have thought of other members of the reptile family that certainly also look like lizards and like giant lizards at that. Those would be the *crocodiles* and *alligators*.

Actually they are not lizards. They form a part of the reptile family all by themselves. In many ways they form the very

Eyelids

Ear openings

Head of lizard emphasizing basic characteristics

worst part of that family. For, although the hides of these animals are very useful to people in making belts, luggage, shoes, and many other things, there is nothing else about them that appeals to us generally. Fortunately, they are the very smallest part of the reptile family.

VILLAINS?

In stories about Africa, the crocodile is often shown as a terrible villain, making some people imagine that these big lizard-shaped, armor-skinned reptiles did nothing else all day but slide into the water to attack unfortunate humans. In fact, however, they are quite lazy and, like most animals, would not go out of their way to attack anything as large as a human if there were any smaller food to be had at all. In Africa, for instance, far more people are killed and injured each year by the roly-poly hippopotamus than by the terrible-looking crocodile.

When you hear these stories about Africa,

you might listen carefully to see if the creatures that slither into the water are called alligators. If they are, then something is wrong, for alligators are found in only two places on earth—in the Americas and in China. They have broad snouts. The crocodiles, which *are* found in Africa, have narrow snouts.

So far then, the score for the lizards, and even for alligators and crocodiles, isn't too bad; is it? Two kinds of lizards are poisonous—but not numerous. The alligators and crocodiles—which are rather easy to avoid —can be quite dangerous, but they are not a major threat even to the people who live near them.

SNAKE FRIGHT

Now, finally, we come to the part of the reptile family that causes the most trouble when it comes to people having the wrong ideas about them. These are, of course, the snakes or serpents.

Just a mention of the name *snake* is

106

Alligator at edge of river

enough to make some people want to leave the room and not listen any more. Some people can't even stand to see a picture of a snake. Many think they would faint if they saw a live snake, and some actually would. Many would either run or try to kill the snake.

Of all the animals on the face of the earth no other is as generally feared as is the snake. Yet, just as there are many different kinds of people, some of whom you like and some of whom you don't, there are many kinds of snakes.

Some of them you wouldn't and *shouldn't* like because they are poisonous. Their poison makes them far more dangerous than even the most ferocious lion or tiger. But the majority of snakes are *not* poisonous. They do *not* harm humans. Instead, they help us.

As with all the other members of the rep-

tile family, the first wise thing to do is to understand the snakes and not be afraid unless there is real cause.

Now, let us meet the snakes—not as frightful creatures, but just as animals, some bad, most good, all deserving of our attention.

SNAKES

Some people don't like snakes simply because of the way they move. Snakes slither. That is, they wriggle along the ground in a curvy sliding sort of way. But snakes don't do that for any scary reason. The snakes slither for the simple reason that they have no legs, no arms, no limbs at all which would let them move in any other way. People walk because they have legs. Snakes slide because they haven't. There is nothing stranger about the snake's way of moving than there is about ours.

WHAT PEOPLE HAVE AGAINST SNAKES

Some people say they don't like snakes because they are slimy. People who say that have probably never held a snake. Most snakes aren't slimy at all, unless they have just come out of the water. Snakes have a slick clean skin formed of scales that usually lie flat and smooth. Fishes, on the other hand, do have a slimy feeling when they are taken from the water. But few people seem to mind that.

Other people don't like snakes because they are so cold. They *are* cold in a way, but only sometimes. They are among the animals whose blood temperature stays about the same as the outside air. So, when it's cold or cool outside, the snake is cold or cool. But when the weather is warm, the snake is warm too. Not much to be afraid of on that score either.

Then there are people who feel that the snake is a very bad animal because it stares in what they think is an evil manner. Well, the snake doesn't stare to frighten you. The snake stares the way it does because it doesn't have any eyelids to blink or to close the way some other animals do. Instead of an eyelid, the snake has a transparent cover, almost like a plastic lens, over each eye. It sleeps with its eyes just as wide open as when it is moving about.

Just to give you some more ideas of how many strange things people have come to believe of snakes, here are some not-at-all-true stories that millions of people are ready to tell as absolutely true.

THE UNREAL WHEEL

There is supposed to be a snake, called a *hoop snake,* that bites its tail, forms a wheel, and rolls away whenever there is danger. The snake also is supposed to have a sting at the end of its tail. Well, the truth is that no snake can roll like a hoop; no snake has a "sting" at the end of its tail; in fact, no snake has a "sting" anywhere. Snakes have teeth.

Talking about the wrong idea that snakes have "stings" brings up the equally foolish idea that snakes can "bite" with their tongues. Because snakes have long thin whip-like tongues that they keep flicking out—to catch insects and to "feel" things in front of them—some people think those tongues must carry poison.

Snakes have teeth with which they can bite—like most animals. *Some* snakes are poisonous. When those snakes bite, they use their poison in either of two ways. Some expel the poison from tiny holes inside their mouths and let it splash into the wound they have made with their teeth. Other snakes have two hollow teeth through

Snake "slithering"

*This is something snakes
never really do*

which the poison is squirted when the snake bites. But they have *no* "stingers" and no poison tongues!

There is supposed to be a snake that is just like glass. It is supposed to break into a lot of pieces when hit with a stick. There is no such snake. There are lizards, however, whose long tails can be snapped off very easily.

FRIENDS, NOT MILKERS

There is supposed to be a snake that can milk cows. There isn't. With teeth as sharp as most snakes have, a cow would not be likely to stand around and let the snake take its milk. The snakes that are called *milk-snakes* are often found around farms.

They don't live on milk at all. They feed on rats and mice and are among the farmer's best friends because of that.

Some snakes are supposed to swallow their young in order to protect them. Some *do* eat their young—but not to protect them. On the contrary, they eat them just as they would any other food.

Now, finally, we have to talk about the one thing that is bad about some snakes—the poison. First of all, remember that most of the 2,500 different kinds of snakes in the world are not poisonous at all. And the poison of those that are isn't bad enough to do more than make a person sick. In the United States, for instance, there are many

109

different kinds of snakes, and only four kinds have any poison at all.

THE FEARFUL FOUR

Those four are the *rattlesnake,* the *coral snake,* the *copperhead,* and the *cotton-mouth moccasin.* The *rattlesnake* is one of the most easily recognized snakes in the world. Every kind of "rattler" has a shell-like tip at the end of its tail. When this tip is shaken by the snake, its parts rub together and make a dry buzzing sound, like a child's rattle being clicked very fast.

The *coral snake,* although it is the most deadly of all the poisonous snakes in America does the least damage because it doesn't like people and avoids them whenever possible. If you tried to find one, you would have a hard time, and even coming across one by accident is rather rare. Even so, the coral snake gives plenty of warning because of its bright colors. It is a thin small snake but it has bright bands of red, yellow, and black all around its body. There is a perfectly harmless kind of snake with bands of those colors too. In the poisonous one, however, the bands of red touch the

bands of yellow. In the harmless one the red bands touch the black bands. There is a rhyme to remember this:

Red touch black, good for Jack.
Red touch yellow, kill a fellow.

The *copperhead,* with a coppery skin and sort of hour-glass shaped splotches of darker color along its back, lives in many parts of the country, but even when one bites a person it usually just makes the victim sick for a few days.

The *cotton-mouth* lives in the water, in the South—the part of the country where the coral lives also. The cotton-mouth's name is a good one. The inside of its mouth is very white, and it looks even whiter because the outside of this snake is very dark.

KRAITS AND MAMBAS

The most poisonous snakes in the whole world are ones that most people hear little about. India, for instance, has a small snake called the *krait* whose poison can kill in just a matter of seconds. Africa has a big snake called the *black mamba* that is one of the few snakes that will stand its ground and fight against practically any animal rather than

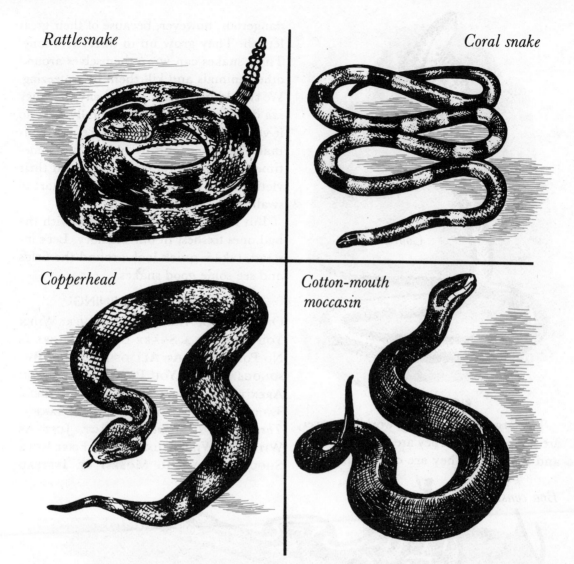

Rattlesnake

Coral snake

Copperhead

Cotton-mouth
moccasin

try to escape. And its poison is very deadly.

HOODED SPITTER

Perhaps the most famous of the poisonous snakes is one found in many hot countries of the world—the *cobra*. There are many stories told about these snakes. The most famous of the cobras, probably, are the big, light-colored members of this fam-

ily that are able to flatten the skin behind their heads into wide, oval-shaped hoods that give them a very fierce and deadly appearance as they hold their heads up, weaving and waiting to strike. Three kinds of cobra don't even have to strike to be dangerous; they can actually spit their poison through the air for a distance of several feet. If it hits the eyes of another animal it will sting and blind.

Cobra

dangerous, however, because of their great length. They grow up to thirty feet long. These snakes can wrap themselves around other animals and kill them by squeezing. We should be careful only to say that they *can* do this, because they actually *don't* do it very often. These snakes, like most animals, kill their food by biting. But sometimes they wrap themselves around their victim while they *do* bite and then start to swallow it.

But let's not leave the snakes with the bad ones freshest in our memory. Let's instead, take a quick look around the fields and see some good snakes.

BIG BOAS

The largest snakes in the world, however, are not poisonous. They are the *pythons: boas* and *anacondas*. They are often considered

A WORD OF WARNING

One Word of Warning, However: When You Do Find a Snake Be *Sure* There Is No Possibility At All of Its Being Poisonous Before You Pick It Up. If You Aren't *Sure*—Because You Haven't Been Taught About *That Particular* Snake— *Then Leave It Alone.* In Fact, Just As With All Wild Things, Your First Rule Should Be *Not* To Molest It. Instead

Boa constrictor

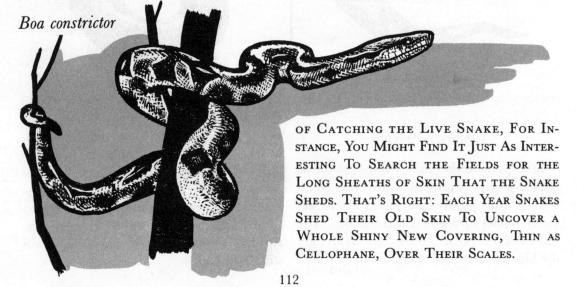

of Catching the Live Snake, For Instance, You Might Find It Just As Interesting To Search the Fields for the Long Sheaths of Skin That the Snake Sheds. That's Right: Each Year Snakes Shed Their Old Skin To Uncover a Whole Shiny New Covering, Thin as Cellophane, Over Their Scales.

112

In many Southern rivers of the United States there is a black snake with reddish blotches along its underside. Some people think it is the hoop snake we described as a myth on a previous page. Actually this is the *mud snake* and it does a lot of good by feeding on eels that might be harmful to the fish in the water.

This harmless useful snake also has a hard pointed tip on its tail. As you can imagine, people who don't really know about snakes will say that this is a "stinger". We've described how wrong that is.

FAVORITE SNAKE FRIEND

One of the favorite snakes of boys and girls is the shiny bright little *green snake* that grows to be about a foot-and-a-half long and eats pesky insects. The *garter snake* about which you may hear, is about the same size but has dark stripes running the length of its body.

Unfortunately, however, those snakes are like most other snakes and just don't get along very well at all in captivity. When you catch one, therefore, be sure to let it go after a while unless you have all the things you need to feed and keep it. In the United States, there is no fear about poison from such snakes. There simply are no poisonous snakes living wild in the United States that are all shiny green or have stripes up and down their bodies.

There is a ferocious-looking snake sometimes called the *puff adder* that scares some people into thinking it is poisonous by its loud fierce hissing. But then, if the person doesn't run away, the snake just rolls over and plays dead. Actually they are about the most gentle of all snakes.

Corn snakes, which look a little like copperheads, are found around many farms and do a good job in hunting down rats and mice. Some *blacksnakes* are good at that also —although it is true that an occasional baby chick also finds its way into their diet.

Most farmers figure that every single non-poisonous snake like that is worth actual dollars in work done toward killing pests on the farm. Many farmers have learned the all-important lesson about snakes: the more you know about them, the less you fear them and the more you can see how helpful they can be.

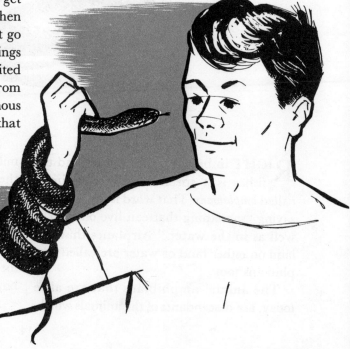

Pet snake

Amphibians:
The In-Betweens

Frog

RIGHT in between the reptiles and the fishes is a special family of animals called *amphibians*. That word is just a way of saying "something that can live on land as well as in the water." Airplanes that can land on either land or water are called amphibians too.

The animal amphibians that are alive today, are descendants of the animals which, millions and millions of years ago, first left the water to try and live on land. Today, most amphibians are still a bit better off or more at home in the water than on land.

Perhaps when you meet the most familiar of the amphibians you will be surprised, for he is a very familiar animal to most boys and girls. He is the *frog*.

Like all amphibians (and there is only

114

one other common kind, which we will meet later) frogs lay eggs that look like little dots covered in clear jelly. When these jelly eggs hatch, they produce small fishlike creatures called *tadpoles*. (Scientists call them *larvae*, the same name used to indicate the young stage of insects too).

These tadpoles, which may be seen swimming in summer brooks and lakes, quickly grow into frogs.

BOOM AND PEEP

Full grown frogs come in many sizes and colors. The largest in North America is the big, green *bullfrog* whose deep-voiced croaking is a familiar sound all summer long. Bullfrogs are sometimes as much as six inches long. The tiny spring *peeper,* whose high piping sounds almost like a bird-call in the summer night, is hardly ever more than an inch long and, instead of being green, is brown with a blackish cross on its back.

Perhaps you have heard a sort of clicking sound in the woods near a stream at night, like pieces of metal being clicked together. Those are *cricket frogs,* little brown and green fellows whose name is given to the toys that make a clicking noise when you press them.

Frogs feed mainly on insects which they trap by darting their tongues and flicking the insects right off a twig or even right out of the air.

The croaking or piping of the frogs is made by blowing up a flexible sort of pouch they have at their chin. The pouch acts almost like a loudspeaker for their noises.

TREES AND TUNNELS

When it comes to places to live, however, frogs have many different ideas as to which place is best. Some burrow backwards into the ground and just sit there at the end of their tunnel until they come out to feed—usually at night. Others dig down into the mud beside streams or lakes. Some hide under rocks, others live in the grass. And, most surprising of all, some live in trees.

Tadpole

Toad

TOADS

Usually, the ones that live most of the time on the land, and even climb trees to make their homes, are called *toads*. Perhaps the very mention of toad reminds you of something not nice. People used to say that you would get warts if you touched a toad. One reason for that, perhaps, is that toads have very bumpy or wart-like skins themselves. Another reason may be that during certain times of the year, when the toads are starting to produce eggs, a whitish liquid oozes through their skin. If this gets in the eyes or mouth of another animals or a person, it can be quite poisonous. Otherwise, however, toads are among the most easily tamed of all the frogs and often are kept as pets. No matter what, they will *not* give you warts!

SALAMANDERS

The other common group of amphibians look more like lizards than like frogs. They are the *salamanders*.

One of the first differences between salamanders and lizards is that lizards have scaly skins and salamanders have smooth slick skins. Also, salamanders are usually little tiny creatures that live in damp places under rocks and logs near water.

Children all over the world have found these little creatures scurrying into hiding in the woods. Because they do look so much like little lizards, or even like tiny inch-long dragons, many fairy tales have been made up about salamanders. (Even though most are tiny, a few kinds of salamanders, like

116

Salamander

the ugly wrinkled *hellbenders* that you can see in tanks in the zoo grow to be almost two feet long).

FIRE FABLE

One of the strangest stories told about salamanders used to be told in the days before people had taken the time to find out about the lives of animals, and especially the tiny ones. The story involved fire. It was thought that some salamanders actually lived in fireplaces, playing in the fire and never getting burned. The truth probably was that the little creatures were some-times seen scurrying away from fireplaces in the days when houses had dirt floors. From that, people might have made up stories and finally believed them.

If they had only known then what we know about salamanders today, they wouldn't have had to make up stories. For these creatures are remarkable enough without having any fairy tales made up about them at all. Just think—like the frogs, the little hurrying salamanders that you may find under a rock are echoes of that very long ago day when certain animals, adventuring out of the water, became the first moving things to set foot on dry land!

Other Underwater Creatures

Octopus

THERE are many other forms of life, beside fishes, under the surface of the waters of the world—so many that scientists are not yet sure they have discovered all of them. But we can meet a few of the outstanding ones here.

Stories about one of the strange undersea creatures are usually scary—and for a good reason. What other kind of story *could* be told about a creature with eight long rub-

bery legs lined with openings that are used as suction cups to grasp the things it eats? And that's not all. This creature has a stomach on top of its head! It has a parrot-like beak that can rip and tear! It can squirt out an inky liquid that blackens the sea around it so that its enemies cannot see. That creature, of course, is the *octopus*.

Fortunately, most of them are fairly small —so small that a swimmer could grab one with a single hand and bring it safely to the surface. But sometimes, in the ocean, there are huge ones, and those are just as frightening as the stories say they are.

TWENTY THOUSAND LEAGUES

People who have read Jules Verne's amazing story of the submarine *Nautilus* and its trip, "Twenty Thousand Leagues Under the Sea," will remember another relative of the octopus, the *squid*. Although Jules Verne's story was mostly make-believe, the part about the giant squid was partly true. There are no giant squid, so far as we know, large enough to destroy a large submarine, but there *are* some about the size of rowboats.

The squid has ten legs, two more than the octopus. It also has a differently shaped body. While the octopus has its legs emerging from a plate-like body underneath its bag-like stomach, the squid's legs emerge from a bullet-shaped body. But in both animals the stomach is above the head.

Both the octopus and the squid, by the way, are highly prized by many people, in almost all countries, as having delicious meat for eating.

STRANGE STONES

One of the strangest "animals" in the entire undersea world is one that many people never really realize *is* an animal. They think of it as some sort of stone. This strange animal is a tiny one with a tube-like body and little waving arms or tentacles that are used for fanning the water to obtain the even tinier bits of sea life that it eats. These tiny creatures stay in the same place their entire lives building the limestone compartments in which they live. Most of these creatures build their little compartments side by side, millions upon millions of them together. Sometimes these structures form great reefs or underwater ridges or even islands in the ocean. Sometimes they form branching tree-like struc-

Branched coral   *Brain coral*

Starfish

tures. All these things are called *coral*. You've heard of coral reefs? Well, coral reefs are these millions upon millions of tiny compartments built by the little coral animals. Even when the little creatures die, the hard stony compartments remain and it is because of them that many people come to think of coral only as stone-like structures beneath the water or as jewelry.

DEEP STARS

Also familiar to practically everyone who goes to a seashore are the strange hard-skinned creatures called *starfish*. Some of them are shaped like a five-pointed star and others more like a sunburst. These animals, although harmless to most creatures, are fond of feeding on clams and oysters around which they wrap and cling. Because

many sea-creatures—and humans too—consider oysters and clams so good to eat, starfish are generally considered an underwater pest no matter how fascinating it may be to find one of their hardened, dried, star-like bodies on the beach.

SPIDER KIN

Crabs and *lobsters,* cousins of the spider family, are also nippily familiar along sea shores. A freshwater lobster—much smaller than the ocean kind—is found in many streams and is called a *crayfish.* (Some people call them crawdads, or crawfishes too).

Of all the sea creatures, perhaps the ones best loved by people at a seashore, are the ones that live in lovely shells.

120

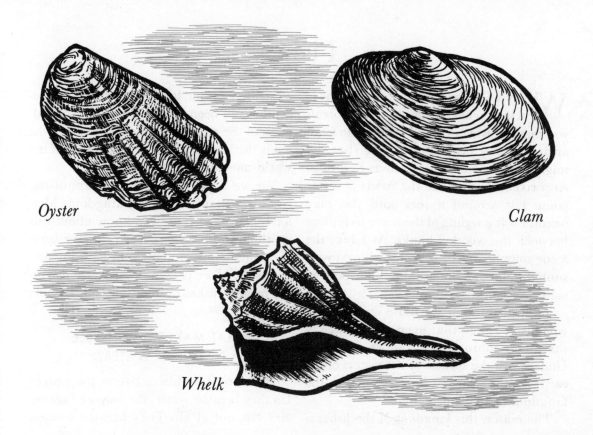

Oyster

Clam

Whelk

SEA TREASURE

Shells, washed on to the beach, are like jewels just waiting to be found. And each time the tide washes anew on the beach, new jewels are thrown there to be found, carried away, and treasured.

Some of the shells are from underwater *snails* and are like big, white versions of the familiar snail shells of the garden. There are the big, trumpet-like shells of the *whelk* and *conch* which, when held to the ear, make you think you are hearing the rushing of the ocean. Actually, you can hear the same thing by cupping your hand or a glass to your ear—but just as some words sound better when they are rhymed in a poem, so does the sound seem much more exciting when produced by a shell. Then there are the small many-colored shells that are like plates for some fairy dinner. There are long twisted hornshells and dark narrow mussel shells and, of course, the grey shells of oysters which, no matter how dull on the outside, always shine with the mysterious possibility that the oyster may have made a gleaming pearl inside.

The whole ocean, really, is like that. Except for the white frosting of its waves and the deep moving valleys of its thousands of miles of water, the top of the ocean is like a lid under which, if we just could peak, we should see all kinds of gleaming strange treasures and marvelous sights unlike those anywhere else in the world.

Fishes

WHEN YOU look at the ocean or a river or a lake, what do you see? At the ocean you may see waves capped with white foam and you may hear the roaring that the mighty ocean makes as it moves and rolls. At a river you may see the swirls of water going fast around a rock and you may hear the soft gurgling of the water as it slides between the wooded banks. At a lake the scene may be one of peaceful stillness with sunlight shining on a calm blue pool of water.

Yet, just underneath those waters lies a world so strange that even the surface of the moon could hold no more surprises. Underneath the surface of the waters of the earth lies the strangest kingdom of all—the kingdom of the fishes.

The reason this kingdom of the fishes is so strange is that men have only very recently even been able to look into it. Of all parts of the earth, the kingdom beneath the sea is the least explored. It is the part of the world most mysterious to men.

Yet we do know quite a bit about the creatures that live in that kingdom. Men have had good reason to know about fish for thousands of years. For fish have been and remain one of mankind's most important foods. More people in the world live on the meat of fishes than on any other single thing.

WHAT MAKES A FISH ABLE TO LIVE IN WATER?

How are fish able to live in the water? Do they breathe water, the way we breathe air? No, not at all. They breathe oxygen

Underwater view of ocean with fish and plant life

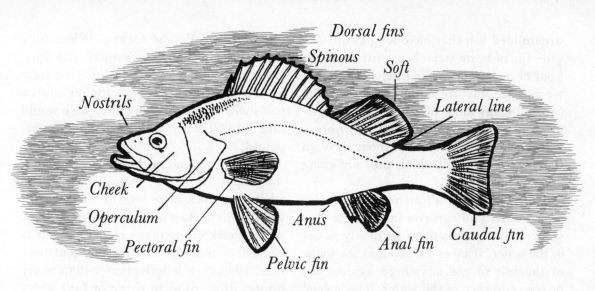

Dorsal fins
Spinous
Soft
Lateral line
Nostrils
Cheek
Operculum
Pectoral fin
Pelvic fin
Anus
Anal fin
Caudal fin

Features of fish enabling it to live in water

just as we do. But the fishes are able to take this life-giving substance out of the water. Other animals cannot.

The part of the fish that takes the oxygen from the water is called its gills. Usually you can tell where these gills are by the two flaps or slits that are easily seen back of the eyes of the fish. Under those flaps or slits are delicate layers of tissues that literally strain oxygen from water. If you have ever seen a fish just taken from the water, you may have noticed how it seems to open and close its gill covers, like the breathing of a person out of breath. The fish is no longer taking oxygen from the water as it should do. Suddenly it is in a world full of oxygen and all the other gases that make up the air we breathe. A fish cannot manage to control the "ocean" of oxygen in which it finds itself. It "drowns" in the air.

To live in their watery world, fishes have other special features besides gills—features that enable them to move easily in the wa-

ter. If you have ever tried dragging your hand quickly through the water, you will know what a problem that makes for a fish. Because water is so much heavier than air, it resists movement much more. A fish, therefore, has to be the most streamlined of animals in order to move swiftly through the water.

Also, instead of legs or wings fishes need special "limbs" to move with. The "limbs" with which fishes move are called fins. These are the thin vane-like projections on the top, bottom and sides of a fish and at its tail end. With a sort of wriggling motion that causes its entire body to swish back and forth and its tail fin to sweep rapidly like an oar, a fish can zoom through the water at speeds of up to 70 miles per hour— far faster than any but the very fastest racing boats can go.

HOW FAST CAN A FISH SWIM?

The very fastest of the fishes are the *swordfishes* and *broadbills,* two large very streamlined fish that have long sword-like growths of bone stretching out from the front of their heads. The little *minnows* that we can see darting about in any stream (we call many kinds of very small fish minnows) only go about nine miles an hour. But when you watch them shoot through the water you would think they are going about a hundred.

Goldfish travel about seven miles an hour. Why, you can run faster than that yourself! But you couldn't go nearly as fast in the water. It takes the fins and the shape of the fish to get anywhere against the heavy resistance of the water. The special bodies of the fish also resist the great pressures deep in the ocean where the pressures are so great that even a submarine would be crushed by them.

HOW DO FISH RANGE IN SIZE?

Just as there is a great difference in the speeds of different fishes, there is a vast difference in their sizes. The smallest fish in the world is a tiny one called the *goby* that lives in the lakes of the Philippine Islands, far off in the Pacific Ocean. When fully grown, a goby is not quite a half-inch long. Look at a ruler and then imagine fully grown fish that never get longer than a half-inch. When it comes to weight, it would take 15,000 goby fish to make just one pound!

At the other end of the size scale there is the largest fish of all—the *whale shark*. The whale shark is a huge brownish fellow with yellowish checks and spots on his hide. A whale shark sometimes weighs as much as 150,000 pounds and reaches lengths of more than 50 feet—a length greater than many houses and equal to three or four automobiles in a row.

In spite of the huge size and the frightening name of the whale shark, it is as harmless as any fish in the ocean. Its entire food supply comes from tiny sea creatures that float and swim near the surface of the ocean —most of them so small you'd hardly see them without a magnifying glass. The whale shark couldn't even swallow a good-sized fish (the size of the kind you might have for dinner) if it wanted to. Its food comes to it through large strainers of bone in its mouth. Those strainers let only the tiniest things pass through.

Whale shark

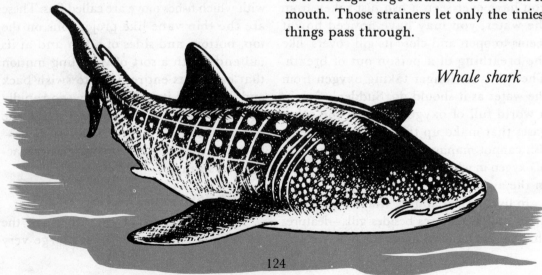

124

When we mention the whale shark as the largest of all fishes, you must not get mixed up by wondering if there aren't whales larger than that. Of course there are whales much larger than the whale shark. But ordinary whales are not fish. Whales are mammals. Whales have live young babies, just the way cats, dogs, and people do. Most fish lay eggs although some hatch those eggs inside themselves and produce live young fish that way. Whale mothers have milk for their young, just the way other mammal mothers do. Whales have little tufts of hair. All mammals have hair. No fish do. Fish blood is cold—always just the temperature of the water in which the fish is swimming.

The other part of the whale shark's name —shark—brings up another matter. The shark is a fish, and, of all the fish in the world, perhaps the one that is talked about most. For the shark is one of the deadliest creatures in the world, and in every country frightening tales are told about it.

FISH THAT PEOPLE TELL "FISH STORIES" ABOUT

Actually, of all the many kinds of shark, only a few are what are known as "man eaters," dangerous enough to harm a man in the water. Of these man-eaters, the 30-foot-long great white shark of the warm Pacific is perhaps the most often spoken of as "THE man-eating shark."

Sharks are among the oldest living things. Scientists who have studied them carefully say there has been little change in them over the last hundred million years! Perhaps there has been little need for change, for it seems the shark is perfectly fitted to his underwater world.

First of all, sharks are about as streamlined as anything could be, from their pointed snouts back along their sleek hard-hided bodies to their powerful tails that can shoot them through the water at up to 35 miles an hour. And, although that is not as fast as some fish can swim, it is plenty fast enough to allow sharks to grab all the food they need. Even the smaller sharks—those that could do no harm to man—are so well adapted to their life, and so tough, that they have few enemies to fear except other and larger sharks.

There is another fish that is talked about almost as much as the shark—but for a much more pleasant reason. That is the *flying fish*. Travellers on both the Atlantic and the Pacific who have seen these amazing fish never forget them and often delight in telling their stay-at-home friends all about them. The friends may find some of the stories hard to believe.

The truth about these fish is that they do *not* fly. The only animals that actually fly are birds. Other animals that are *said* to fly actually glide. The flying fish is like that. It glides. Instead of regular fins like other fish, the flying fish has wide long wing-like fins on the side of its body, near its head. It plunges through the water very close to the surface. Suddenly it will break through the surface and start swimming right on top. Like almost all fish it can stand being out of the water for a few minutes.

When a flying fish swims on the surface of the water, it stretches out its wide wing-like fins. Suddenly, as the fish goes faster and faster, the wings will send it hurtling up off the water and into the air where it glides forward for as much as several hun-

"Flying fish"

dred feet. It is no wonder that travellers who see these foot-long fish up in the air like that believe they are flying.

FISH WE ENJOY CATCHING

Away from the oceans and in the streams and lakes of the forests live some of the fish most interesting to men who get so much quiet pleasure in catching them. (Catching the giant fish of the ocean is fun too, but it is usually very hard work and often quite dangerous.)

Children in many parts of the world delight in catching small fish such as the American *bluegill*. Grown-ups go after such fish as the wondrous *trout* that leaps and flashes when it is caught and lives in wonderful streams where the water rushes free and clear and fast. One reason, perhaps, that so many people love to fish is that they know they are not inflicting pain on the fish they catch. Scientists have figured that fish are built so that they do not actually experience pain the way other animals

American bluegill

might. When a fish is caught with a hook in its mouth, for instance, it has been found that the fish really feels only a sort of pressure—about what you feel when you press a finger not too hard against your cheek.

The fish that is caught the most—usually in huge nets dragged between two or more large ships—is the herring, a name applied to a whole family of fishes. The *shad* is one member of the herring family that is caught by the millions for food. It is a two-foot-long, shiny-scaled fish that usually is netted as it leaves the ocean to go into quiet fresh-water streams to lay eggs.

The *sardine* is another member of the herring family that is familiar to us as food. Actually, the fish you usually find inside a can of "sardines," is the *pilchard herring*. Although there are several other kinds of small herrings that are sardines too, it is the pilchard that usually ends up in the can.

The member of the herring family that is just called *herring* grows to be about ten inches long. They are most easily netted as

they leave the deep parts of the oceans to find places for their eggs along the coastlines.

ODD FISH

Before leaving the world of fishes there is one more member of the underwater community that should be introduced. It is the oddest fish of all. It is so odd, in fact, that most people wouldn't even recognize it as a fish. It is the *seahorse*.

The seahorse can be anywhere from two to eight inches long, or, rather, we should say *high* because the seahorse doesn't go about head-first, stomach-down like other fish. It moves upright on its tail—head up, tail down.

First, imagine what it looks like—in case you haven't seen its picture before. It has a bony head shaped like a horse's head. Then it has a heavily ridged bony body with a puffed-out chest and a long bony tail that curves forward so that the tip of it can point right up to its chin.

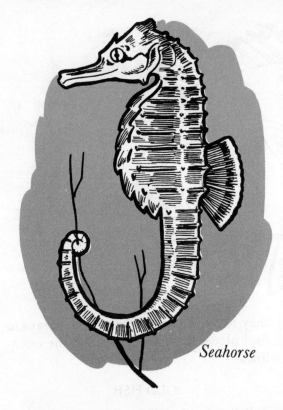

Seahorse

Although the seahorse may be the strangest looking fish—because it doesn't even look like a fish—there are plenty of other odd members of the community that lies below the surface of the seas.

In the very deepest parts of the ocean—parts, as we have said, so deep that the water there would crush a submarine—there is a fish with a lantern. That's right: a lantern. This fish has a long flexible rod-like growth coming from its head. On the end of this rod, dangling almost like a piece of bait on a fishing line, is a blob of material that glows in the pitch blackness of the deep world. When other fish swim toward this strange glowing thing in the darkness the *lantern fish* gulps them down.

Other fishes have other strange ways of getting their meals. Some lie quietly near the surface of the water waiting for insects to fly by. When they do, these fish squirt a little stream of water up into the air and knock the insect down. There are other fish that just lie in rocky places with their mouths wide open waiting for smaller fish to swim in. And then there are fish like the flat *flounders* that lie still on the ocean floor seeming to be just part of the sand or mud, unnoticed by their enemies as well as by the sea-creatures they then find easy to snap up for their meals.

Then there are some fishes that are just plain odd even though their shape is like that of a fish in general and not altogether different like the seahorse. There is the *pipefish* that is about as thin and round as a pencil. There is the *sea robin* that walks along the bottom of the ocean using its two side fins like legs. There is the *sturgeon* with great bony knobs on its tough sides. (The

When the seahorse moves, a tiny fin on its back helps it. It swims head-up so that it looks like a tiny horse dashing through the water. When the seahorse wants to remain still, it just curls its tail around a blade of underwater grass or some other growth and hangs on.

When the female seahorse is ready to lay eggs, she doesn't just let them go into the water or attach them to underwater plants or scoop out a nest in the sand for them the way most fish do. No indeed. The mother seahorse deposits all the eggs in a little compartment built right into the father seahorse, just below his chest. There the eggs hatch. When they do, the father seahorse opens his pouch and puffs the tiny babies out into the water where they can take care of themselves.

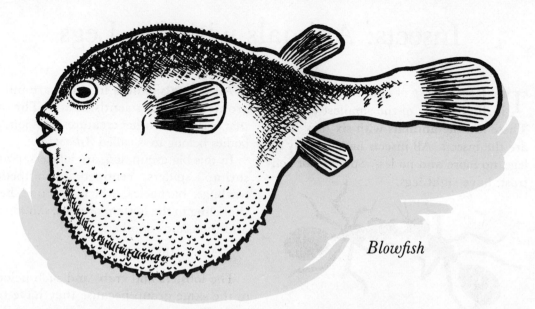

Blowfish

eggs of that fish, the sturgeon, are the delicious food we call *caviar*). There is the ocean *sunfish,* shaped like a slightly oval pie and with only top and bottom fins—no tail and no side fins! And this odd plate-like fish weighs as much as 1,000 pounds when fully grown!

Then there are the *blowfishes,* covered with spiny needles that are sometimes poisonous. They can puff themselves up into balls with their needles bristling every which way as protection.

When you think of the familiar animals of the dry land and then think of the strange animals of the water world, you will probably agree that just beneath the surface of ocean, stream, river, or lake there stretches a frontier as wild and wonderful as any we know.

Insects: Animals with Six Legs

THE largest *group* of animals in the world includes some of the smallest animals. These are the animals with six legs. They are the insects. All insects have exactly six legs, no more and no less. Spiders, for contrast, have eight legs.

Ants Feeding

More than a half-million different kinds of insects have been found and named by scientists so far, and many scientists think *ten times* that many will be discovered.

There are more of these tiny creatures on earth than any other form of animal life that we can see without the help of a microscope.

WHAT AN INSECT IS— AND WHAT IT ISN'T

First of all we have to learn just what an insect is and what it isn't. When scientists start out separating animals into different groups, they start with the most noticeable thing that sets certain animals apart from others.

In the case of insects and animals like insects, the first thing that sets them apart is that their bodies are jointed together as separate parts instead of being in one piece inside of a skin like ours or like a puppy dog's. That is, the various parts of an insect's body are hinged together. The legs of these creatures also are jointed.

All animals jointed like that are put in groups called by scientists *Phyla*. The one that insects and other creatures with jointed bodies belong to is called *Arthropoda*.

In this big group, too, are lobsters, crabs, shrimp, spiders, centipedes, millipedes, sowbugs, barnacles, which are the shells that cling to the bottom of ships, sand fleas, and thousands of others.

TEN-LEGGERS

The lobsters and crabs and such belong to the same group because they have ten legs. They are part of a group called *Crustacea.*

Lobster

The spiders, with their eight legs, all belong together in a group called *Arachnida*. The group that insects belong to is the six-legged group and it has the easier name of *Insecta,* just insect with "ah" on the end.

Once we have found a creature with six legs—an insect—we still have quite a way to go before we know what kind of insect it is. The big groupings we have just mentioned are called *Classes* by scientists.

After the *Classes* come groupings called *Orders*. This is where we first start separating the insects, or anything else, on the basis of resemblances that we can see. All butterflies, for instance, belong to one Order. All beetles belong to another Order. Beetles may come in many sizes and shapes, but they all have some things very much in common. That is, they have more in common than just the fact that they have six legs like all other insects.

After the Orders come even finer separations called *Family* and *Genus*. We won't worry much about those fine divisions. First we want to learn about separating the various kinds of insects into the different Orders —that is, to classify them. That will be fun.

There are insects everywhere in the world, even in the middle of the city or out on the farthest farm. Everybody has a chance to study them. That is why you may find insects the most interesting of all nature studies.

To classify insects the way scientists do— and don't forget that anyone, including you, who studies things on a systematic basis is a scientist of sorts—we have to learn about the different parts of insects.

WHAT THE JOINTS JOIN

We know that insects have six legs. They also have three parts to their bodies. These parts are joined by joints but *not* connected inside of a skin the way our bodies are.

The first part of the insect body is the head. It has a mouth that can do special jobs. Some insect mouths are made to chew. Others are made with needle-like straws to suck juices from plants or blood from animals. Others are made just to lick.

The kind of mouth an insect has helps to tell us what kind of insect it is.

The head also has eyes. With insects there are two different kinds of eyes in the head. First there are the simple eyes, which are something like human eyes. Then there are the compound eyes, made up of many different lenses all put together. They are built so that instead of letting light through a single opening, as ours and all simple eyes do, the compound eyes let light through hundreds and even thousands of separate tiny openings. The simple eyes of an insect are usually at the top of the head while the compound eyes are usually at the side of the head, but looking forward.

Also on the insect's head is a single pair of feelers or *antennae*.

The next part of the insect after the head is the chest or thorax, which is itself made up of three parts. Often the parts of the chest, however, are so smoothly fitted to-

Grasshopper

gether that you don't notice the different parts or you may think only that the chest has some lines on it separating it into sections.

The legs of the insect come from the chest section. There is one pair of legs to each of the three chest sections, thus always giving an insect six legs.

When the insect has wings, the wings also are attached to the chest part. So we can say that this part of the insect is the part that makes him go. It is where all of his organs of motion, the wings and legs, are attached.

Finally there is the stomach or *abdomen* part of the insect.

The way we classify the insects is on the basis of their wings, their mouths, and the way they grow. Let's start.

HARD-WINGED INSECTS

The largest group, or Order, of all is the group called *Beetles*. The scientists call them *Coleoptera* which, like most scientific names, is easier to say than to spell.

All beetles have wings that have hardened into thick covers over their backs. There is another set of wings underneath but they are thin and folded up. The mouths of beetles are made for chewing. All beetles grow up in four stages. Because many other insects also grow in these four stages, we will stop now and describe them.

The four stages are these: First there is an egg. The egg hatches a worm-like creature called a *larva*. Some of these larvae (adding an "e" makes it mean more than one larva) are known to us as caterpillars. When you see a caterpillar, remember that it is simply one stage in some insect's growing up.

After the larva comes a stage called the

pupa. The pupa is a stage where the insect just sleeps and grows. Sometimes in this stage it wraps itself up in threads, like spider webs, and we call it a *cocoon*. After this stage the insect is fully grown.

Beetle

Insects either grow up that way, in four stages, or they grow up like any other animal that comes from an egg. That is, they hatch out as tiny insects and grow up to be larger insects of whatever kind they are.

Now, what are beetles? We'll go back a bit. They are insects with one set of wings that have turned into thick covers over their backs. Their mouths are built for chewing. They grow up in four stages. Scientists throw in a few more fancy differences like the number of joints in the antennae (10 or 11) and the joints in the bottom part of the leg (5). Imagine counting the joints in an insect's foot and ankle!

THE STINGERS

One of the Orders that most of us are very familiar with is the Order that includes all the bees, wasps, and ants. Scientists call this group *Hymenoptera*. If you glance back, you may notice that both the big name for beetles, *Coleoptera*, and the big name for ants, bees and wasps, *Hymenoptera*, end with the same group of letters—*ptera*. That word-ending is from a Greek word meaning wings. Coleoptera really means "sheath wing." That is, the beetle has hard wings that form a sheath on its back. A sheath is something that protects, like the sheath of a knife or the sheath of hard wings on the back of the beetle.

The ants, bees, and wasps all have two pairs of very thin filmy wings. And the name *Hymenoptera* is made up of two Greek words that mean just that, thin wings.

Wasp

Perhaps you don't think of ants having wings, and most of the time they don't. But ants do have wings during a certain time each year. It is when they are looking around for mates to form new families with. After they settle down together and start making eggs, they drop their wings.

The mouth parts of the ants, bees, and wasps are made for chewing or for sucking. All of these insects develop in four stages, eggs, larva, pupa, and adult.

Some of them have one thing that no other insect has. They have stingers. Anyone who has been stung by a bee or a wasp knows about these stingers. An easier way to learn about stingers is to read about them and we'll do that later.

WOOD-EATERS

An insect that looks just like the ants but is not a member of their group at all, is the *termite,* the little insect that actually eats wood. Termites have an Order all their own and it is called *Isoptera*. Sometimes they are known as white ants, even though they aren't ants at all. Unlike the ants, for instance, the termites just grow from their eggs, from little termites to grown-up termites. Ants, as we now know, grow in the four stages of egg, larva, pupa, and adult.

CHIRPERS AND JUMPERS

Grasshoppers are another familiar sort of insect. The Order that includes jumping grasshoppers also includes chirping crickets, katydids, and locusts. Sometimes even cockroaches and the long wingless insect called the walking stick are lumped together with the grasshopper group, though in very exact classifications they are put in an Order of their own.

The thing that sets the grasshoppers and others in the group apart from other insects is this: they have leather-like front wings and back wings (four altogether) that fold up in pleats, like a lady's fan.

TWO WINGS AND TROUBLE

One of the most annoying and dangerous groups of the insects, so far as man is concerned, is the group called *Diptera*. It includes the flies, gnats, and mosquitoes. All members of this group have just two wings (two is what the *Di* part of their scientific name means). They develop in four stages. When people speak of *maggots,* for instance, they are really talking about the larvae of flies.

The most dangerous thing about flies and

mosquitoes isn't just that they often make people itch where bitten. When we say one of these insects bites we really mean that it pierces the skin with a needle-like part of its mouth. It does that in order to suck up some blood. That is its food. The real danger is that when they bite people, they often leave germs behind that cause the people to get sick. Flies sometimes carry germs on their feet and just leave the germs wherever they happen to walk. If they touch your food, they may leave germs there. That is why people are so eager to keep flies out of the house.

BEAUTIFUL BUTTERFLIES

Some of the insects make up for the trouble some others cause us. The butterfly, of the Order called *Lepidoptera,* is like that.

Describing butterflies is like trying to tell someone what a sunset looks like. You might try that some time. You will find that ordinary words are never as pretty as the real thing. Only poetry can make words paint such beautiful pictures.

Butterfly

Butterflies come in the most beautiful colors. In the sunlight, their large wings, covered with what looks like velvet, flash with many colors. Different types of butter-

flies have different combinations of colors. Some have glittering red dots on shimmering cream-like wings; others have bright yellow streaks against a velvet-black background. Even a less popular group of the butterfly family, the moths, sometimes have wonderful colors in their wings. We'll meet them later.

Now that we have seen how some of the main Orders of insects are classified, we can start traveling around in this strange and wonderful world of the six-legged creatures. First we'll see how the young insects grow.

EGGS FIRST

The eggs of insects, just like the eggs of other animals, are produced inside the females. When the female insect is ready to get rid of the eggs she sends them out of her body through a part called the *ovipositor.* Sometimes this is nothing more than an opening in the body. Other times, though, it is a little tube, and the eggs can roll down through it to wherever the mother wants to put them.

One sort of female fly has a tube like that three inches long. Why does a small fly have to have a tube as long as that? Well, it's a special sort of fly that has to put its eggs deep down inside old logs. The reason for this is that when the eggs hatch they have to eat the young of *another* kind of insect that lives inside the logs. The mother fly can't tunnel into the log herself so she just drills down into the wood with her long egg-laying tube and lets the eggs drop down through it.

TWO-WAY TUBE

The bees and wasps have an egg-laying apparatus that can also be used for stinging. When these insects use this tube to sting with, they sometimes drop down a liquid that hurts your skin. That is why such a sting can be so painful.

The honey-bee has an egg-laying stinger that gives everybody trouble, including the honey-bee. When the honey-bee uses the tube just to lay eggs, everything is all right. But when the tube is stuck as a stinger into the skin of some larger animal or a person, the honey-bee simply can't pull it out because of little notches along its end. In order to get away, the honey-bee actually has to pull loose from the stinger and, most times, this kills the honey-bee. Other insects in this group, however, can use their stinger over and over again, dropping down the painful liquid when they sting and just as easily dropping down eggs when they want to do that.

Some of the insects, particularly some of the flies, hatch their eggs right inside of their own bodies so that when they let the young insects out of their body, they seem to be giving birth to little worm-like larvae rather than laying eggs. One of the wasps has a terrible problem along those lines. If the mother wasp can't find a place to leave the larvae after the eggs have hatched in her body, the larvae will simply eat her up!

Ichneumon Fly

Usually, to get the eggs started growing inside the body of the female insects, some cells from a male insect have to be put inside the female. But there are some flies and wasps and a few other insects that don't have to do this at all. The females of insects like that can just make eggs all by themselves.

WALKING-STICK "WOMEN"

The walking-sticks, those long, green stick-like insects we sometimes see, are practically all females in the United States where they are able to make eggs without any males around at all. Farther south, in Latin America, the same sort of insect does have to have males to help make its eggs.

Bees and wasps show us another sort of egg-making. When a bee or wasp lays eggs that have not started with cells from a male, the eggs will hatch all right — but all the baby bees and wasps produced from those eggs will be males. If that kept up all the time, then the wasps and bees would disappear from the earth because there would be no more females left to lay eggs of *any* sort.

Bees and ants have still another thing when it comes to producing eggs. Some of the bees and ants are called workers. These are older females who have not laid any eggs. If they finally do lay some, all of those eggs produce female insects.

If the young insects from the mothers' eggs, the larvae, are fed enough, they can develop into females who can lay many thousands of all sorts of eggs. The females of ants, wasps, and bees that specialize in laying eggs, and can lay both female and male eggs, are called queens. We hear most often about queen bees.

Usually, a whole part of the insect community, an insect town, is built around a queen, and the main job of everybody else is to feed her, fertilize her eggs, and then feed the young so that the community can keep on with new members being born and raised all the time.

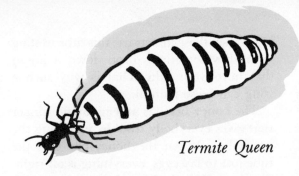

Termite Queen

EGGS BY THE MILLION

The number of eggs an insect can produce changes greatly from one kind of insect to another.

Some female beetles can produce only three or four dozen eggs during an entire lifetime. A female Japanese beetle, like the ones that eat so many things in a garden, lays only about fifty eggs during its entire lifetime. Those eggs, by the way, are put under the ground through the beetle's egg-laying tube.

Insects that live together in hives or colonies, like ants and bees, can produce thousands of eggs, from a single female, in a single day.

The champion of all, however, is the termite. Queen termites, in warm climates where they live most comfortably, have been known to lay more than 5,000 eggs in a single day, and a single queen in her lifetime may lay as many as three million eggs.

When the eggs are from insects that do not grow in four stages, the creatures that hatch from such eggs are just like tiny versions of the adult insect.

The little insect is called a *nymph*. Sometimes, when you think you see a very small grasshopper, you may actually be seeing a nymph or baby grasshopper.

The nymphs have a special problem in growing. All insects have fairly tough skins —tough compared to the rest of their bodies at any rate. In order to grow they have to shed this skin every now and then. It can't grow along with them the way our skin can. All insects have to shed their skins, but the insects that grow from nymph to adult have to do it most often because it is the nymph's *only* way of growing. Other insects have the larva and pupa stages to help them grow.

HOW AN INSECT CHANGES ITS SKIN AND ITS SHAPE

When the nymph is ready to shed its skin and grow a new and larger one, the old skin splits in half and the insect simply walks right out of it. While its new skin is hardening, the insect tries to drink a lot so as to be as large as possible when the skin hardens. When an insect hasn't any other way to make itself bigger at this time, it may simply draw in a lot of extra air and puff up as big as it can so as to fill up the new skin. It takes just a few minutes for the new skin to harden so that the insect doesn't have to stay puffed up like that for very long.

With the new skin on and all hardened, the insect is ready to eat and eat until the skin begins to pinch it and it is ready to go through the shedding process all over again.

Sometimes you may find a shell-like skin clinging to a tree or rock. You will know, next time you see one, that the skin is an old one left by an insect that was growing larger.

The most complicated way that insects grow up is the four stage way. Scientists sometimes call this "complex development" and complex means complicated.

After the egg has been dropped by the mother, the larva is hatched. This is the time when the young insect does much of its feeding and growing. Some just take it easy during this time and never move at all. The larvae of bees are like that. They just rest in a part of the wax honeycomb where the eggs are laid. Grown bees bring them all the food they need. That kind of larva doesn't have legs because it doesn't have to do anything.

The larvae of flies, as we said, are called maggots and are tiny, white, wormlike creatures.

Mosquito larvae are called wrigglers and live in clusters hanging in the water of still ponds and other water.

Beetle larvae are usually called grubs but one, the larva of the click beetle, is called a wire worm.

Larva of the White-lined Sphina

CATERPILLAR APPETITES

The larvae most people know about are the larvae of moths and butterflies. These are the caterpillars. Some are quite large and some quite small. It is the small larvae of some moths that make holes in woolen clothes. Many people put the blame for these holes on fully grown moths—the kind we sometimes see flying around on summer nights. Actually it is the caterpillar or larva of the moth that eats the clothes.

Because caterpillars have to get out and look for their own food, they have stubby little legs on their wormlike bodies. Because most caterpillars eat the leaves of growing plants, they are often harmful to gardens and farms. That is why many gardeners and farmers don't care at all that the caterpillar may grow up to be a beautiful butterfly. They don't want the caterpillar to eat up their crops in the meantime, and you can hardly blame them.

But, when the caterpillar finally does develop into a butterfly or moth, the result can be really wonderful.

The differences between the caterpillars and the butterflies are so amazing that we might stop here to describe some of them.

FROM CATERPILLARS TO BUTTERFLIES

One of the most beautiful of butterflies is the giant *swallowtail*. It's a large insect, with a body about an inch long and wings that open up to about four inches across. The wings are a very deep leathery dark brown, but down the wings on the outer side and across them on the front part are rows of golden splotches that look as though someone had spilled sunlight along the

137

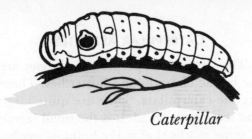

Caterpillar

edges. But the caterpillar of this butterfly is another matter. It has a thick brown body with a back of mottled yellow and brown. Up near its head the back swells into a hump. On top of its head are two red horns.

The *monarch* is a familiar and beautiful butterfly. It has wings that are mostly orange. But the edges are very dark and dotted with light colored spots. The caterpillar of this one is colored and striped just about the same as a tiger.

The *buckeye* butterfly has dark brown wings shading to orange at the edges but with purplish spots that look like three eyes on each wing. The caterpillar is yellowish with a thick dark brown stripe down the side.

One of the most common families of butterflies has the funny name of *fritillaries*. They are the medium-sized butterflies with orange or red colors on top of their wings and with lighter spots on the bottom of the wings. The caterpillars of this group come in many different colors, from brown to purple, but all of them have rows of little spikes all along their backs.

One of the funniest caterpillars is that of the *spicebush swallowtail*, a dark butterfly with a delicate green shade across the back of its wings, as though someone had blown the dust of emeralds there. The caterpillar of this butterfly is a thick green fellow with a light underpart. The thing that makes him sort of funny to see is that he has a pair of great big false eyes on the top of his body up by his head. The eyes, purplish

and yellow, are used to scare birds and other creatures that might eat caterpillars. But they also give this little creature the most amazing expression, as though it had eyes just about as big as its head.

When it comes to moths, we are used to little dusty gray creatures. But there are some that are larger and quite beautiful. *Sphinx* moths in many parts of the world have red, black and white bands on their wings or yellow spots along their bodies.

THE SILK-MAKERS

Some of the silk moths have delicate pink wings.

It is the caterpillars of these moths, by the way, that spin cocoons made of silk when they are ready to turn into butterflies. We get silk for clothes by unraveling those cocoons.

Now that we have mentioned cocoons again, it is time to watch the next stage of the four stages that butterflies and similar insects go through as they grow. The next stage is the third stage, in which the larva turns into a pupa to get ready to become a full-grown adult.

Among many insects, this pupa stage involves spinning a cocoon of delicate threads. Among others it means making a hard shell-like covering around the larva.

The larvae of moths, the caterpillars of moths, spin real silken cocoons—some of them, as we said, spin the sort of silk we use in clothing. Butterfly caterpillars, however, just cover themselves with a tough film.

Ant larvae spin paper-like cocoons. Often, when people show you ant eggs, they are really showing you the tiny cocoons of ant larvae. The ant eggs themselves are just like little white pinheads. But the cocoons of ant larvae *do* look like tiny eggs.

The larvae of flies, like those that buzz around your house in summer, make a hard woody shell to protect them during the pupa stage.

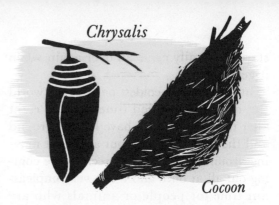

Chrysalis

Cocoon

WONDERFUL GROWING

It is in this stage that the miraculous change from wormlike larva to adult insect takes place. Inside the cocoon or other covering, the pupa rests and changes until it is ready to come out. The cocoon or other covering is cracked. Insects that spin cocoons have help in this because they can produce a special liquid that eats away the cocoon. Once the covering of the pupa is thrown off, the insect is free, grown, and ready to start its own life and family.

To watch a caterpillar spin a cocoon or shell around itself and then, after just a few days or weeks, come out as a beautiful butterfly or moth, is one of the most wonderful things in nature. If you find a cocoon or other pupa and keep going back each day to see it, you may be lucky enough, sometime, to see the miracle happen right before your eyes. If you are careful, you may even be able to remove the branch that a pupa is attached to and put it in a small cage where you can watch it in your own room until the adult insect is ready to come out. It is much harder to find the pupa of ants and other insects who spend that part of their lives inside logs or under the ground.

SHORT LIVES AND LONG ONES

How long the adult insect lives, after it has grown up from either a nymph or a larva and pupa, is also very different among different insects. May flies, for instance, emerge from the pupa stage without any mouth at all. They don't need one to eat with because they live only a few hours, or a couple of days at the most. Yet, in that brief time, they are able to make and leave eggs that keep their family going.

At the other end of the insect life scale there is an insect called the *seventeen-year cicada*. This insect develops from a nymph rather than through the larva and pupa stages. The nymph, however, lives for 17 years! And it spends all that time burrowed under the ground. After 17 years it comes up and lives only a few weeks more as a full grown adult, looking rather like a fat, big fly.

Some members of the bee-wasp-and-ant group of insects live anywhere from one year to two or three.

SLEEPERS

You may wonder what happens to all the insects when the weather gets cold. Many of them just sleep through the winter, hidden in the ground or in trees or inside of houses. Insects that can't stand the cold usually lay their eggs so that the eggs or larvae can live through the winter and start the family cycle all over again when it gets warm.

In many of the coldest parts of the world the most insect-filled time of all is right after the snow and ice have left the ground and the insects can get out and start moving around. They usually seem to be coming out all at once and it is a very unpleasant time for people or animals who are bothered by insects.

TINY MUSIC

When there are a lot of insects in one place, we usually don't have to see them to know that they are there. The noise they make tells us. For insects make very special sounds indeed.

The most common sound they make is a buzzing of one sort or another. The buzzing comes from flying insects and is caused by their wings as they beat back and forth in the air. To get an idea of how fast insect wings can move in the air just wiggle a finger as fast as you can. About the very fastest that anybody can move any muscle is about a dozen times a second. That is the very fastest you could wiggle your finger.

The wings of some insects—mosquitoes —can move as much as *300 times a second*. And because of the speed of its wings, the mosquito makes the highest pitched sound. If you want to know how that sounds on the musical scale, you can find out on a piano. The note that matches the mosquito's buzz is D above middle C.

BUZZING AND DRONING

The bumblebee, on the other hand, moves its wings only about half as fast as a mosquito—130 times a second according to scientists who have studied it.

Down the line even further is the droning of the horsefly with wings that move only 97 times a second. To see what this sounds like compared to the mosquito, you would have to hit G in the second octave below middle C on the piano. If you aren't studying how to play the piano, perhaps someone who knows how will sound those notes for you.

The butterflies are among the slowest insect movers when it comes to how fast their wings move. Some move their wings, when they are flying, only about a dozen times a second. Fast as that is for someone to wiggle a finger, it is very slow indeed for an insect's wings to move. It makes a sound that is so low and soft that humans can't hear it at all.

SUMMER SOUNDS

Another sound made by insects that is familiar to most people is the tiny sawing noise of crickets and grasshoppers that we hear on summer nights in the country.

This sort of sound is made by the insect rubbing parts of its body together. The

Cricket rubbing wings together

parts are rough and when rubbed together they make a noise, just as you can make a noise by rubbing two rough sticks together, or by rattling a stick along a fence.

Katydids and crickets make their sounds by rubbing their wings together. The rough edges of the wings make the chirping of the crickets or the call of the katydid that sounds like someone squeaking or whistling the name "katydid."

INSECT THERMOMETERS

Because the crickets and katydids both make these noises faster or slower depending on the temperature, it is possible to use them as thermometers when you are in the woods. The cricket's chirping is the easiest to figure. First you count the number of chirps in a quarter of a minute—15 seconds. If you add 40 to that number you will have just about what the temperature is at that time. If the cricket chirps 45 times and you add 40, that would mean that the temperature would be about 85 degrees— a warm summer night.

DRUMMERS

If there are prizes for loudness among insects, then the first prize probably would have to go to the cicadas. They make the steady, high-pitched humming that is the background for all the other insect noises. People often will say that locusts are making the noise. Particularly in the United States people have come to call cicadas locusts. But that is a mistake. The cicadas look more like big fat flies than like locusts. Locusts, in fact, look just like ordinary grass-

hoppers—the insects to which they are most closely related.

The cicadas that make the noise are male

Cicada

cicadas. They don't make their noise by rubbing legs or wings together as other insects do. They have an entirely different sort of "musical instrument." The cicada's noise comes from a thin tissue in his body. This tissue is stretched like a drum inside the insect's abdomen or lower section. Muscles attached to the tissue pull it and release it so that it hums and thrums and the hollow part of the body where it is located makes the sound seem louder.

GHOSTLY TAPPERS

Certain beetles that live in the wooden parts of houses and barns sometimes make a clicking noise, like a tiny tap, when they hit their heads against the sides of the tunnels they make in the wood. Late at night when everything is quiet you can sometimes hear these tiny taps, and some people try to make us believe they are ghost noises. The tiny little beetle that causes the sound, by bumping its head, would probably think that was very funny—if beetles could understand such things, as of course they can't.

141

BILL OF FARE

When it comes to food, insects, just like other animals, have two choices. They can dine chiefly on plants or on other animals. Humans, by the way, are among the few living things that eat both plants and animals with no special preference for either one.

Among the insects that eat animal rather than plant matter, some of the most interesting and useful are the burying beetles and the carrion beetles. You may notice sometimes in the woods that you rarely see any small animals that have died. What happened to them? Well, a lot of them probably have died in places where you wouldn't see them. But a lot of them have actually been eaten or buried by beetles.

The carrion beetles are the ones that eat them. In the United States these are flat bluish beetles not quite an inch long. Some sort of beetle like this is found just about everywhere in the world. They feed on dead animals. That makes it sound as though the carrion beetles were very dirty or bad. Actually they are very helpful, for they keep the forests clean and far healthier than if there were no carrion beetles.

WHAT THE GRAVE-DIGGERS ARE UP TO

There are many kinds of burying beetles throughout the world. Most of them are fairly large, more than an inch long, and they are very well shaped, with long smooth backs, rounded chest sections, and squarish heads. Theirs is the sort of shape you think of usually when you think of beetles. Some of them have bright colors dotted along the hard wing covers on their backs.

These burying beetles also clear the woods of small dead animals. The way they do it is quite amazing. Why they do it is also surprising.

Suppose we are watching a burying beetle that has found a dead mouse in the woods. The mouse is five or six times as large as the beetle, almost as large to him as an elephant would be to a man.

Now, watch what the beetle does. He shoves and scratches at one edge of the dead mouse until he gets part of his body and his legs underneath. Then he starts digging. After a while he shifts a bit and keeps on digging. After a couple of hours he may have dug down enough to have all of one side of the mouse in a little trench.

Carrion Beetles

Then he scurries off to the other side and starts more digging.

Sometimes he may stop and turn upside down underneath the mouse and shove with all of his legs to push the mouse over or into the deeper part of the trench that he dug before. This gives you an idea of how strong insects are. It is as though a puppy dog were strong enough to push a full grown man up on his (the puppy's) paws.

By the time a half a day has gone by, a most amazing thing has happened. The burying beetle has dug away a hole under the entire mouse. Next morning, if you go back, you won't see the mouse at all because the little burying beetle has dug him down even deeper and then covered him over with dirt and leaves and twigs so that it would look as though the woods had never been disturbed in that particular spot.

Now why does the burying beetle go to all that trouble? The reason is that the eggs of the female beetle will be placed under the ground with the body of the little animal that the beetle buries. When the eggs hatch, the larvae of the beetle, little whitish wormlike creatures, will be able to use the body for a food supply until they are ready to change into pupae and then into adult beetles.

Don't forget, though, if that sounds strange or not nice, that in the scheme of nature the work of the burying beetle is very normal and very helpful in keeping the world clean and free from diseases.

Another insect that stores up animal food for its young is the wasp. Certain types of wasps specialize in hunting spiders. When they find a spider they sting it. The sting doesn't kill the spider, but it paralyzes it so that it can't move. The wasp then takes the spider to the wasp nest. The paralyzed spiders are placed in the nest so that when the wasp's eggs hatch, the larvae will also have something to eat.

That sounds cruel too, but it is just the way things are in nature. Humans, it seems, are the only living beings that get upset about these things. The wasps and even the spiders that get eaten go about their lives without worrying, doing what they have always done and will continue to do in the scheme of nature's way.

HUNGRY PRAYER

One of the biggest eaters in the insect world is the strange-looking insect called the *praying mantis*. Most children who have lived near woods have seen at least one of these remarkable animals. They are found in the woods of many parts of the world.

They are quite large, some being nearly four inches long. They are long and slim rather like the walking-stick insects except that the mantis has big slender wings folded

Praying Mantis

143

over its back. It has a very thin body part stretching from above the wings. And it has something that no other insect has: a neck that lets it move its head so that, as one famous insect scientist has said, it is the only insect that can look over its own shoulder. Its head is shaped rather like a slice of pie, and it has two very large and reddish eyes at the two top corners.

Another unusual thing about the praying mantis is the way it holds its powerful front legs. It holds them just the way you hold your arms when you kneel and clasp your hands to say a prayer. That is why some of the mantises are called praying mantises. (Their proper scientific name, by the way, is *mantid,* but mantis is used very often, particularly for the praying variety.)

The front legs of the mantis, or mantid, are equipped with rows of sharp little stickers. When another insect comes close to them, they lash out with those powerful legs that they hold up in the air. With them they can catch and hold almost any insect that goes by. Some insects prefer a particular type of other insect for their dinner, but the mantis will tackle anything and seem to enjoy it.

OTHER STRANGE INSECT APPETITES

One of the strangest appetites of all is the appetite that termites have for wood. They actually eat the wood, dissolve it in their stomachs and take nourishment from it. But they have a very strange secret as to how they can live off a food that to any other animal would seem completely indigestible.

The termite's secret is that over the ages, and through nature's strange way in these

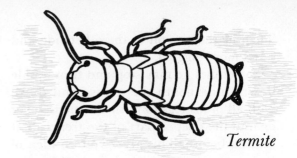

Termite

things, it has worked out a sort of "agreement" with a certain type of one-celled creature that you can see only under a microscope. These tiniest of living things live inside the parts of the termite where food is digested—where the nourishment is taken from it and sent to other parts of the body.

These one-celled creatures get *their* food from things made inside the body of the termites. In return they make a special fluid that they put into the part of the termite where food is digested. This special fluid is what dissolves the wood that the termite chews and swallows. Without the fluid the termite could not use the wood for food. And, scientists have found, the tiny one-celled creatures cannot live any place else in the world except inside of termites.

FAVORS FOR FOOD

When it comes to the insects that live on plants, there is another amazing sort of arrangement in which the insect eats the plant and at the same time makes it possible for the plant to bud and have flowers and produce seeds for new plants. This is mentioned in the section of this book dealing with plants, but here is how it works in some particular cases:

Altogether there are some 10,000 kinds of plants around the world that couldn't grow if it weren't for the insects that feed on them. The way it works is that the insects, while they are feeding on the plant, pick up some of the plant's pollen, the material with which plants grow seeds. Pollen must be carried from one plant to another plant before that plant can produce fruits and seeds. Many plants can grow seeds from pollen carried around from plant to plant by the wind—but not the 10,000 kinds that need insects.

Bees and wasps are among the greatest of the pollen-carriers in the insect world. But one of the strangest pollen-carrying arrangements is that of a certain moth and a plant called the yucca that grows in the desert. The moth is called the yucca moth. No other insect seems attracted to the yucca, and so the plant has to depend on this single kind of moth to carry its pollen from one yucca plant to another. The yucca moth has a very large mouth in which it stores the yucca's pollen. It gets a mouthful and then flies to another plant. There it puts the pollen on the part of the plant where it will cause seeds to form. At the same time the female moth places her own eggs in the flower part of the yucca plant.

Perhaps you have already noticed that this is different from the way bees and wasps go about the pollen-carrying job. They do it while they are getting food. The yucca moth doesn't eat the pollen. Then why does it carry the pollen about? The reason is strange, like so much of nature's story. The reason is that the eggs of the yucca moth can live only in a yucca plant that is producing seeds. The larvae that hatch from those eggs can feed only on the seeds of the yucca. If the moth didn't carry the pollen there wouldn't be any seeds, and if there weren't any seeds there would be no food for the young.

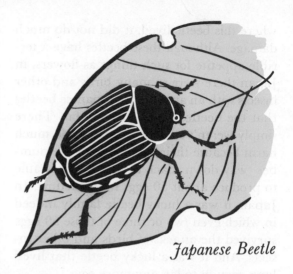

Japanese Beetle

THE PESTS

While many of the insects do helpful things like carrying pollen, many others do such destructive things that people sometimes think of all insects as bad. Where there are bad insects we call them *pests*.

Strangely enough, many of these insect pests have become pests because of mistakes made by people. There are very few insects anywhere in the world that are pests *without* those mistakes having been made. In most cases where insects do damage, there are many other insects or other creatures to fight them. These enemies of bad insects keep their numbers low enough so that they aren't a great problem. But when humans arrange it so that bad insects can get free from their natural enemies, then the bad insects can become serious pests indeed.

One of the best examples of this took place in the United States some years ago in the case of the Japanese beetle, a small beetle with a bright green head that looks almost like shiny metal.

In Japan, which used to be the only place

145

where this beetle lived, it did not do much damage. Although these beetles have a terrible appetite for such things as flowers, in Japan there were so many birds and other insects with an appetite for Japanese beetles that the beetles never got very far. There simply weren't enough of them to do much harm because their enemies kept the number way down. Each female beetle is able to produce about 50 eggs in its lifetime. In Japan, it was a lucky beetle family indeed in which even two or three of those 50 eggs survived the attacks of birds and other insects. And it was a lucky beetle that lived long enough to lay any more eggs.

Then, as ships began to go back and forth between Japan and the United States many years ago, someone made a mistake. No one thought of it as a mistake then. But someone let some Japanese beetles be carried (probably in some fruit or flowers) from Japan to the United States.

In America, there didn't seem to be a single insect or bird around that had developed a taste for Japanese beetles. As far as things in America were concerned, the Japanese beetle could go about its business without fear. It did too.

Out of every 50 eggs laid by every female beetle, all 50 eggs hatched, and all the beetles that grew up lived. Then each of the new female beetles made 50 new eggs. Those eggs produced more females and more eggs and so on and so on.

Scientists have figured out that by the time this sort of egg-hatching business had gone on ten times there would be almost two million billion (2,000,000,000,000,000) new Japanese beetles to go about eating up flowers and other plants! So the Japanese beetle is Public Enemy Number One among the pest insects in America today.

PESTS FOR PESTS

People have tried to fight insects that become pests in that way by bringing some of the insect's natural enemies into the country to control them. Sometimes this works. But every time the scientists try it they must be very careful not to bring in an insect or a bird which in turn would become a pest itself!

The English sparrow, for instance, was brought to the United States in order to

Sparrow eating caterpillar

fight a type of caterpillar that these birds feed on. But now the English sparrows have grown to such a tremendous family in most of the large cities of America that they have become pests themselves, often not leaving roosting room for the songbirds that used to live in and around the cities.

BETTER DINNERS

Sometimes an insect is just a harmless creature until man comes along and plants something to which the insect suddenly takes a fancy. There is a beetle called a potato beetle that is an example of that. It used to live on weeds in the mountains of the far western United States. Then farmers began planting potatoes where the weeds used to grow. The beetles sampled the potatoes and found that they were every bit as good as the weeds. After awhile they forgot all about weeds and just went looking for potatoes. So they became known as pests. But it wasn't really their fault at all. Men just gave them a better food.

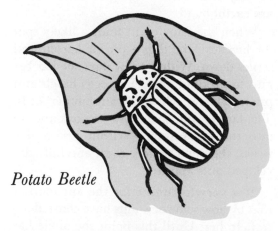

Potato Beetle

Of all the things that insects do, harmful and helpful, the way they live together has probably fascinated people more than anything else. Some of the insects, called social insects, live together in ways that few living things, except humans, do. That is, they form "societies" or groups of their own kind in which members work, play, have responsibilities, know one another, and stay together.

HOW INSECT CITIES DIFFER FROM HUMAN CITIES

Some of these insect societies, at first glance, look like a well-run human city in operation. But, actually, there is very little similarity between a group of insects and a group of humans.

In the insect city there are no private homes. Everything is operated as though everything, even the young, belonged to everyone. Humans have tried that sort of living but haven't been able to make it work. Humans like to get off by themselves from time to time and have things that are theirs alone—like babies and books and homes.

In the insect city, most things happen automatically, as though all the insects were cogs in some sort of machine. In a human city, every person is different, working differently (or not working at all) and the city operates because thousands of people are doing thousands of jobs for thousands of reasons and not just to survive—the one reason that keeps an insect city going.

But perhaps the most important difference between the insect cities and human cities is even deeper. There are no churches in insect cities, no art galleries, no schools. Beauty and faith and the way of thinking that humans have is not a part of insect life.

So, when people say that we can learn many things from watching insect cities they are right. But what we can learn is not about human cities, it is just about insect cities.

Remembering that, let's look at some insect cities, for they *are* fascinating.

An ant colony is a good place to start. Ants live almost everywhere on the earth, and their colonies or cities are pretty easy to find and watch. But, because most ant cities are under the ground, it takes special effort to see everything that goes on.

The time to start looking for what hap-

147

pens in an ant colony is during the summer when the ants are ready to start having new families. This is the time of year when the ants have wings.

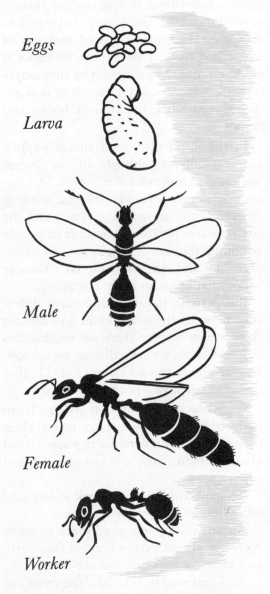

Eggs

Larva

Male

Female

Worker

On a certain day (which changes all the time) all the ants in a particular area of many square miles leave their old homes and swarms of them start to fly about in the air. These are the male and female ants, and while they are flying they separate into pairs to mate and make eggs. The ant couple will come together in the air and some of the cells from the male will be taken into the body of the female. After the male has landed back on the ground he usually dies. The female, however, starts looking for a place to set up a nest of her own. While she does this she loses her wings. If they don't drop off, she chews them off. From the day of the swarming in the air, the ants are earthbound.

When the female ant finds a likely spot for her nest, she digs a pit for herself and settles down. Within a few days she has begun to produce eggs. The eggs hatch and produce larvae which the ant mother feeds. The larvae spin their tiny cocoons and go into the pupa stage. Within just a few weeks, the pupa stage is over, and fully developed ants appear.

It is very fortunate for the ant mother that by now some new ants have come along to help her. Until this point she alone has had the entire job of caring for the eggs and feeding the larvae. But the new workers, her own children, immediately begin to help. They do the job of getting food into the nest and they even start building a better nest which, depending upon the particular kind of ant involved, may take the form of a series of passages under the ground, or tunnels in a log, or perches on leaves. From this time on, the female that started the nest has no other job but to produce eggs.

Gathering or producing the food for the ant city is one of the most amazing things done by any insects. There are ants that simply go out and gather seeds to eat, but

Ant Farm

there are others that actually have tiny
farms, others that raise insects the way humans raise cows, and others that go hunting.

HARVESTER ANTS

You might never guess that some ants
grow tiny farms and grow them just as carefully and with as much skill as human
farmers.

It took many years of careful watching
before scientists discovered this. Before that,
when a few people said that some ants
farmed crops, everybody laughed. Impossible, they said. And yet it is true, and
here is how and where it happens.

The farmer ants belong to a great section of the ant world that is given the name
Attii. Just think of your necktie and you can
remember the name. It sounds just as if you
were saying "a tie."

The farmer ants live far, far to the south
of the United States. They live in the tropical climate of South America. If you were
there to watch these amazing ants, you
could hardly miss them. When they go about
their business, they go about it by the
millions.

Out they come from their nest. They
march in a broad column and use the same
path over and over. If it is through thick
grass, the grass is actually trampled down

149

by the marching of the millions of ants, despite the fact that each ant is only about as long as your little fingernail. This well-trampled path goes straight to the trees from which the ants are taking leaves. Up the trees they go. They work like a well-trained army, each ant heading straight for a leaf with no nonsense and no hesitation.

LEAF UMBRELLAS

Once on its leaf, each ant begins to saw at the leaf with the sharp prongs of his jaws. Sawing away like that, each ant soon has cut out a tiny circle of leaf. As the ant gets to the last cut of this circle, he yanks on the part he is cutting away and holds it firmly in his jaws. After a yank or two it comes free and the ant begins to march back down the tree, with the piece of leaf waving from his jaws. Each piece of leaf is about the size of a dime. Sometimes, when there is a breeze blowing, these pieces of leaf being carried by the ants look like little umbrellas over the heads of the ants as the breeze makes them puff up. Because of this some people call them Umbrellas, or Parasol Ants.

Why do the ants want these bits of leaf? They don't eat them. In fact they are very careful not to even give them an extra munch of their jaws after they have taken them from the trees. They are determined to get the pieces of leaf back to the nest.

When they do get them back to the nest they do two sorts of things with them. One use for the pieces of leaf is to line the rooms that they dig to live in underground. For a long time people thought that was the *only* thing they used the leaf bits for.

But, deeper down in the tunnels and rooms that the ants dig in the ground, they use the leaves for something much more amazing. There, deep in the earth where the temperature stays just about the same all year round no matter how cold or hot it is on the ground above, the ants tend their farms.

Umbrella Ant

150

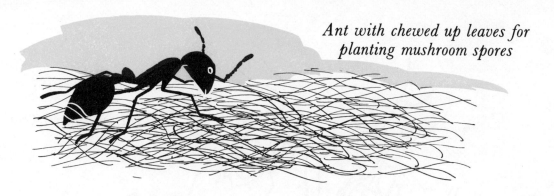

Ant with chewed up leaves for planting mushroom spores

THE PLANTING BEGINS

Down there, hundreds and thousands of ants collect the pieces chewed from the leaves and very carefully begin to mash them up with their jaws. Still, they don't eat them. As each ant finishes chewing and chewing on his particular piece of leaf, he carefully puts it onto a layer of chewed leaf on the ground. Soon, this layer of chewed leaves is like a flat, well kept farmland before the seeds have been put in. And that is just what happens next. Somehow, and we don't know how even now, these ants get the seeds or spores of mushrooms and plant them in the chewed-up leaves. Then the careful farming begins.

Some of the ants dig shafts from the farming chambers all the way to the surface of the earth. Most of the time these shafts are blocked off with bits of dirt. But, when the slowly-growing mushrooms down below need just a little bit more air, some of the dirt is taken away and a little air seeps down.

During the slow growth of the mushrooms other ants keep roaming back and forth across the fields of chewed leaves making sure that no other seeds that might have been mixed in with the mushrooms get a chance to grow.

Soon they have their mushrooms all ready to eat. They are not mushrooms just like the mushrooms we know in the fields. Rather, they are slender rootlike growths called *mycellium*. These root-like growths are the main part of all mushrooms even though we prefer the big button-like growths that pop up above the ground. The ants just like the roots and never let them grow up far enough to produce the part of the mushroom that people eat.

Once the farming ants have their food farms growing they can go on just about forever. All they have to do is keep bringing in fresh pieces of leaves every now and then to fertilize the crops. And from that time on, for all the ants, all the millions of ants, in each of the nests of this amazing family, there is plenty to eat.

Now, does this mean that the ants you see right in your own backyard just aren't smart enough to grow farms the way these ants do? It doesn't mean that at all. It just means that the ants in your backyard like another kind of food and have another kind of way of getting it. If we watch very closely, and if we could get right down in the ground with those backyard ants, we would find that what they do is every bit as interesting as the things that the farmer ants do.

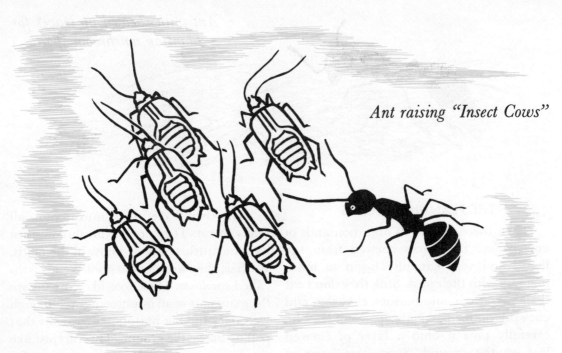

Ant raising "Insect Cows"

PIN-SIZE "COWS"

There are some ants that go in for another form of farming. You might call it dairy farming, for, to all intents and purposes, these ants seem to be raising insect-cows. But instead of getting milk from them, they get a sweet sugary syrup that is their favorite food.

There are several kinds of ants that go in for this sort of food. The insects they keep as cows are the tiny *aphids* that swarm on flowers in the summer like a bunch of whitish-green pinheads. When these aphids are taken over by a group of ants, they are kept in regular herds either above ground or underground. If they are kept above ground there are always a few ants on hand to guard them and keep them from straying. Underground, the aphids may be kept in tiny rooms.

The aphids feed on plants. Above ground they eat tiny pieces of leaves and flowers. Underground they take some of the liquid out of plant roots. In both cases they make a sweet syrup inside their bodies. The ants know just how to get them to release this syrup, usually by sticking them in just a certain way. The ants line up and take drops of the syrup from the aphids, the way dairy farmers take milk from cows.

TERRIBLE HUNTERS

The ants that hunt for their food are the most terrible ants of all.

In Africa, Asia, and Latin America, there is a large ant, almost an inch long in some cases. It is called the *army ant*. It hunts for its food and is one of the most vicious animals on earth. Army ants thrive on the meat of animals—*any* animal, and even humans. They are equipped with powerful jaws to tear with. But the most terrible thing about the army ants is that they travel in great numbers. That is why they are called army ants.

Millions and millions of these ants, forming a line so long that it stretches out of sight, march together as they go hunting for food. The line they travel in may be only a few inches wide, but it may stretch for miles. One such column was reported as taking two weeks to pass a given point.

The army ants always march, except for occasional pauses of a few days when the queens in the column lay thousands of eggs. Then the army marches on, seeking new food.

In Africa, army ants have been reported as coming upon a sleeping elephant and swarming over the great beast. Even as the elephant awakened and tried to get away, millions of the ants swarmed on him, clogging his breathing and blinding his eyes. More millions of ants climbed on. Before long the elephant was dead and millions of ants had a royal feast.

Like most animals that are strong in one way, army ants are weak in other ways. Some of them, for instance, cannot stand bright sunlight. It kills them almost immediately. When they travel they go through grass high enough to protect them or even make shallow tunnels under the earth.

Sometimes when these ants come to a clearing, instead of tunneling or going around it, they send hundreds of thousands of their number out ahead to climb up on one another and form a tunnel of ants. These ants die almost immediately, but their activities allow the other ants to march through their tunnel without being exposed to the deadly sunlight.

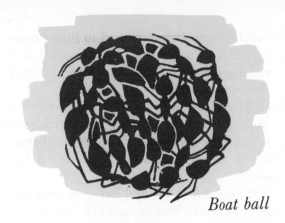

Boat ball

BOAT BALLS

When these remarkable ants come to water, another sort of sacrifice takes place. The ants all march together and form a gigantic ball, many feet in diameter. By moving their bodies they make the ball roll into the water. The ants on the outside are drowned but the ones inside stay alive and the whole huge ball of ants floats with the current until it hits another shore and then the ants climb out and continue their march across the land.

Fortunately, most of the ants are not nearly so fierce. They do not have to kill and plunder as army ants do. For most ants, life is fairly peaceful and they stay close to their nests.

HONEY AND HIVES

Of all the nests that insects make, the beehive is perhaps the most familiar and certainly the most useful to humans. From it we get delicious honey and also the very fine wax called beeswax.

The honey comes from inside the honeycomb that is inside the hive, and the wax is made from the honeycomb itself.

The honeycomb, with all its tiny six-sided compartments, is used to store honey for the bees to eat, and it is also used as a resting-place for the larvae and pupae of the bee.

There are many jobs to be done in a honey-bee hive—keeping the hive clean, laying eggs, taking care of the young, bringing in and storing away food, and other chores.

The work is divided between two different kinds of bees in each hive: the queen and the workers. The queen, who is much bigger and longer than the workers, is the most important bee in the hive. She sometimes lays as many as a million eggs altogether, for a healthy bee colony has between fifty and eighty thousand bees in it at honey-making time.

The workers, who are female bees, perform all the other tasks, but they are never too busy to take good care of the queen. A few of them always go around with her in the hive to feed her and keep her clean.

The worker bees are so careful of the eggs and of the larvae that they even control the temperature inside the hive. Along the corridors of the hive, there are worker bees that do nothing but whirr their wings and bring fresh air into the hive, to keep it at the temperature that is best for the young.

The drones are a third kind of bee in each hive. They are fat and lazy and do no work at all. They are the male bees. They can't gather nectar from flowers to make honey because their tongues are not shaped right, and they have no pollen bags for gathering pollen. They do not even have stings, so they cannot work as guards for the hive. They are noisy, always buzzing and tumbling about and getting in the way. Sometimes the worker bees even put them out of the hive to get rid of them.

"CROWNING" NEW QUEENS

When the bees in a particular hive have got a good store of honey in the combs and there are plenty of healthy bees and eggs and larvae and pupae around, they feel it is time to start another colony some place else. First of all, the bees bring up some new queens to lay eggs. They do this by taking

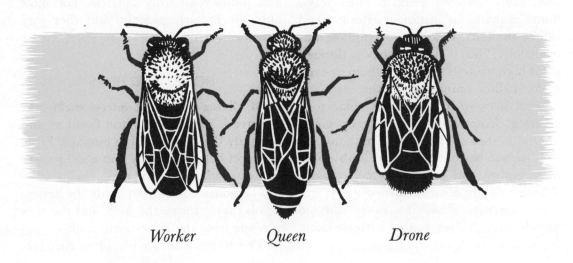

Worker   *Queen*   *Drone*

154

special care of some of the larvae and by feeding the larvae certain food that makes them turn into queen bees. While this is going on, the worker bees in the hive fill themselves up on honey from the stored up supplies. Then they take the old queen and fly away to find a new spot for building a new hive and a new colony or city.

Back in the old hive, the first larva to turn into a pupa and then into a queen becomes the new queen of the hive. The new queen flies out of the hive and into the air where all the drones follow her but she mates with the swiftest and strongest one. The queen then returns to the hive and starts a life of egg-laying. So although the drones take no part in the work of the hive they really are necessary to the life of the whole colony.

ROYAL ROOMS

In the tunnels and caverns where termites live there is a slightly different way of keeping a colony going. The queen termite keeps a male termite with her—a sort of king termite—as she lays her eggs. This pair of termites are given a special cave to live in. The queen, inside this cave, grows so big from laying so many thousands of eggs that often she cannot get out of the door again. Other termites bring her food.

Wasps and hornets also have special nests for the production of eggs and the raising of the young.

MUD HOUSES

Potter wasps, with bands of yellow around their bodies, build nests of mud around the twigs of trees and plants. One kind builds little round vase-shaped nests that just hold

Wasp building mud nest

the larvae of a single family. Others build larger nests that are like rounded cakes of mud on a branch with holes for several families to put their eggs inside.

Most people are familiar with the nests of the bluish *mud daubers.* They make mud nests that look like a series of long baskets stuck together. These nests are usually made under the rafters of old houses or porches or barns. The mud daubers stock these nests with paralyzed insects so that when the wasp eggs hatch inside, the larvae will have food.

PAPER PALACES

The *paper wasp* chews up wood and makes a sort of rough gray paper material that it puts together to make a nest. These nests are round and made of the same sort of six-sided compartments as you find in a honey-comb. From the center of the nest a stem is made and this is attached to a tree branch under rafters so that the nest hangs like an upside-down flower.

The *hornet,* another of the wasp-like insects, builds big paper nests that are shaped something like a football with an opening in the bottom. The nest is usually built around a tree branch and is the one that most people steer clear of for fear that if

155

they disturb it the hornets will swarm out and sting them in order to protect the eggs and larvae inside.

So far we have talked about insects that live on the land. There are many that live in and even under the water. In other cases there are land-living insects that have started life under the water.

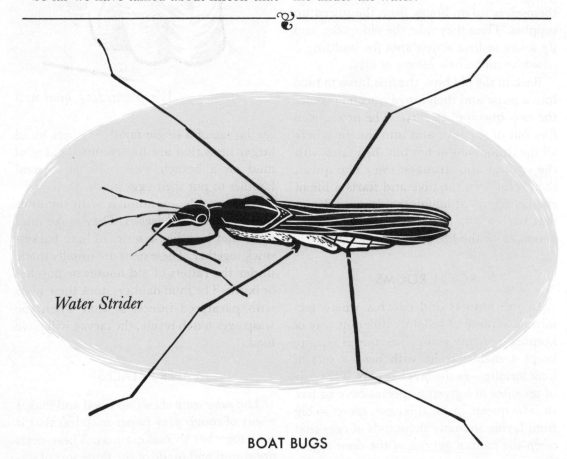

Water Strider

BOAT BUGS

One water insect that many people have seen is the funny little *water strider*. This is the insect with the long body and such very long legs that he almost looks like a little boat with long thin oars stretching out from the side. Only four of his six legs are long like this. Those legs, however, hold the water strider right up on the surface of the water and by using them he can actually run across the water. When he does it looks like a little boat with the oars going very fast.

The reason that the water strider doesn't sink is that its underside is covered with tiny oily hair that the water can't soak. The long legs of the water strider don't go into the water either but for a different reason.

The surface of the water, all water, has what amounts to an invisible film on it. It is caused by *surface tension*. When you put your hands in water you can't even notice it. But it *is* strong enough so that if you carefully place a small sewing needle on the

156

water in a glass, so that the needle doesn't break the surface of the water, the surface tension will make it float. The water strider uses that invisible film as a surface for its long legs to scoot across.

SUBMARINES TOO

When insects live under the water they have a problem of where to get air. A few have been able to develop so that they can take oxygen out of the water the way a fish does. But many others have to have air just as any land animal does.

An insect, by the way, doesn't breathe through a nose or even through an opening in its head. Insects breathe through tiny holes in their sides. These holes are called *spiracles.*

BUBBLE BATHER

One sort of water insect called a *back swimmer* catches air bubbles in a mat of hair underneath its body. It breathes these bubbles as it swims under the water. But, because the air is light, it makes the little insect turn over and it has to swim on its back. That is how it gets its name.

Other water insects carry bubbles of air under their wings when they dive under the surface. Another sort of insect that carries air with it when it dives is the *whirligig* beetle. These are the very tiny insects you see on the water sometimes rushing around in zigzag paths very fast and as though they didn't know *where* they wanted to go.

Dozens of these insects usually live together on the surface of the water, diving from time to time to look for food when there is none on the surface. They move so

fast and so strangely that it almost looks as though the water suddenly had come alive and was making jiggly patterns on its surface just to amuse itself.

TUBE TO BREATHE

One of the water insects has a gadget that humans have only recently learned to copy. It is a *snorkel* or underwater breathing tube. Submarines and divers both use these tubes to get air without coming all the way up to the surface. The *water scorpion,* a long, greenish insect that looks a bit like a praying mantis, has used a snorkel all along.

The water scorpion waits for its food — other insects and even small fish — while standing about an inch below the surface of the water. From its stomach section a long thin tube goes right up to the top of the water and lets the insect draw in air.

Some other young insects have a snorkel while the adults of the same family do not. The larvae or maggots of the *drone fly* are like that. The drone fly puts its eggs into the mud alongside a stream or pond. When the wriggly little larvae hatch out, they stay in the mud. To get air they have a long tail-like tube that they stick up through the mud and water. Sometimes these snorkel tails are as much as three inches long.

Perhaps the most familiar case of a young insect living in the water while the full grown ones do not is that of the *mosquito,* one of man's worst enemies.

RAFT OF TROUBLE

Mosquito eggs are laid in bunches like tiny rafts on the surface of any still water —even on the water in a rain barrel or on a pan left full of water outside a house.

When the eggs hatch, they produce worm-like larvae called wrigglers that hang from the top of the water until they are ready to become pupae and then emerge as full grown mosquitoes.

Because of this the control of mosquitoes depends largely on making sure that all still or stagnant water where the eggs can be laid is treated so that the larvae cannot live. Spraying water with oil puts a film over the water and kills the larvae there. Draining the water out altogether is another good way.

Many groups of boys and girls have aided in this sort of work, either helping grown-ups to spray pools where mosquitoes may breed or digging trenches to drain the pools. They can also help by making sure that old cans or pans of water are not left lying long outdoors as places where mosquitoes may lay their eggs.

INSECT HOBBY

Because insects are everywhere and because they are so interesting, collecting them has become a very important hobby with boys and girls who are interested in natural science—which is the study of nature.

Nets made out of loosely knit cloth, even cheesecloth, are handy for catching insects. Long handled nets to catch butterflies are sold by scientific supply stores. Insects on the ground can be caught in a little jar. But most of the insects that children catch will not have anything to eat if they are caught and kept in a jar. If you catch plant-eating insects it is a good idea to include whatever leaf or flower they are eating. If the insect that is caught eats other insects, then the problem is harder.

Ant colony in jar

ANT WATCHING

One of the best ways to catch and watch insects at work is carefully to dig up an ant colony, or as much of it as can be fitted into a large jar. After digging up the earth and the ants in it, put the dirt and ants all together into a large jar.

Then, instead of putting the lid back on, take some cheesecloth, and put it across the mouth of the jar, holding it in place with a rubber band. Food such as a moist piece of bread will keep some ants alive. In other cases you will have to look very closely at the colony that you have dug up and try to find out what they are eating and then supply that. If you have dug up a colony that lives from the syrup made by aphids, it may be hard to provide the plants that the aphids need. But even if you keep the ants for just a couple of days without food you will see some amazing things in the jar. They will begin to make long tunnels down into the earth and some of the tunnels probably will be made right along the side of the jar so that you will be able to see the ants scurrying up and down through them.

158

The Wonderful Spinners— The Spiders

IN THE balance of nature, the spider may be one of mankind's best friends. Although many people say they are frightened of spiders, these creatures do very little harm to humans. In fact, if it were not for the great service spiders do for people, there might not be any people on earth at all!

How can that be? The reason is that spiders are the number one means of controlling the insect population of the world. If there were no spiders to eat insects, insects might breed and multiply until there wasn't room for any other sort of life on earth except, perhaps, in places so icy that neither insects nor humans want to live in them. As it is, and as we have said before, there are already more insects than any other non-microscopic form of animal life.

Wherever there are grasses or other plants in the world, there are spiders and insects. There may be two or three million spiders in the space of an acre. Every one of those spiders lives by killing insects. All spiders get their food by draining the fluids from the bodies of insects.

Each one of the millions of spiders in a single acre will kill hundreds of insects every year. So, on every acre where there are insects and spiders, hundreds of millions of insects are killed each year—by the spiders.

One of the finest writers on the subject of spiders, an Englishman named John Crompton, has estimated that if all the insects killed in Great Britain each year by spiders were lumped together, they would weigh more than the entire human population of the country. Knowing how light an insect is, you can imagine the staggering number of insects that are killed each year by man's tiny friend, the spider. If it weren't for the spiders, all those insects might have lived, many feeding on man's food supply and causing a serious threat to human life. Spiders are no such threat at all, even though some have poisonous stings.

KNOW MORE, FEAR LESS

So, instead of being afraid of spiders, it might be a better idea to get to know more about them. They are very fierce-looking, but they have some surprisingly nice things about them too.

First of all, why is a spider not an insect? People call them all *bugs*. But *bug* isn't a very good scientific name. Technically it just refers to one kind of insect, a group called *Hemiptera* that have jointed snouts for sucking the liquid out of plants.

Insect is what you should call the "bugs" with six legs. *Spider* is what you should call the "bugs" with eight legs.

Besides having eight legs, instead of six, the spiders differ from insects in other ways.

Insects have three major body portions, a head, thorax (chest) and abdomen (stomach part). Spiders have only two body sections, a thorax and head in one and abdomen or stomach section in the other.

Insects have antennae or feelers stretch-ing from their heads. Spiders have no antennae.

Insects have both simple eyes, with single lenses, and compound eyes, with many lenses. Spiders have only simple eyes, although they may have several pairs.

Insects include creatures that eat plants and those that eat animal matter. Spiders all eat the same food, the juices taken from inside the bodies of insects.

The family of spiders is called Arachnida, a name that comes from a very ancient story. Here is one version of that story.

WHY SPIDERS WERE NAMED FOR ARACHNE

Arachne was the daughter of a merchant in a city of ancient Greece. She spent her days weaving exquisite fabrics and tapestries, making beautiful pictures out of the threads she sewed into the cloth. She got so good at this sort of thing that she decided she could weave even better than the goddess Athena, the daughter of the all-powerful Zeus. The Greeks worshipped Zeus as a god and his daughter Athena, the goddess, was very angry. She came down to earth to look at the tapestry woven by Arachne. It was so very beautiful that it made Athena jealous and she tore it up. This made Arachne so unhappy that she hanged herself. And that, in turn, made Athena unhappy.

To make up for what she had done, Athena took the rope that had hanged Arachne and turned it into a beautiful web, and then she brought Arachne back to life —not as a girl, though, but as a spider. And to the spider, Athena gave the power to do the most beautiful weaving in the world.

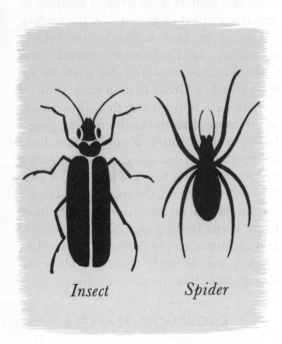

Insect   *Spider*

160

SPIDER WEBS

That is how the class of animals to which spiders belong came to be known as *Arachnida,* after Arachne. They deserve the name because the webs they weave are something very special. There is nothing quite like them and some of them are among the most beautiful objects in all nature.

Not all spiders weave webs, though. Some spiders use other sorts of traps to catch their foods—traps that are, in their way, as amazing as webs. Yes, that's right, the webs of spiders are used as traps. They are important weapons in the age-old struggle of spiders against the insects, a struggle from which mankind benefits very much indeed.

In meeting the spiders we will start with the weaver of webs.

The least attractive of all spider-webs is the shapeless tangle of webs, like a bunch of loose cotton, that we find in split places in trees, under windows, over doors and under stones, and in many cracks and crevices both outdoors and indoors.

The spiders that make that sort of web aren't being careless or showing that they just don't know how to make a good web. Instead they make that sort of web because it is the most effective sort of trap for the particular places where they live.

Another fairly jumbled sort of web is the kind you find in bushes and underneath them. These webs look as though the spider had just crisscrossed a lot of lines without any design at all. The webs go every which way. The weavers of these webs are members of a spider group called *Theridion.* These webs may look clumsy too, but they aren't really. They serve the special purposes that these particular spiders want.

161

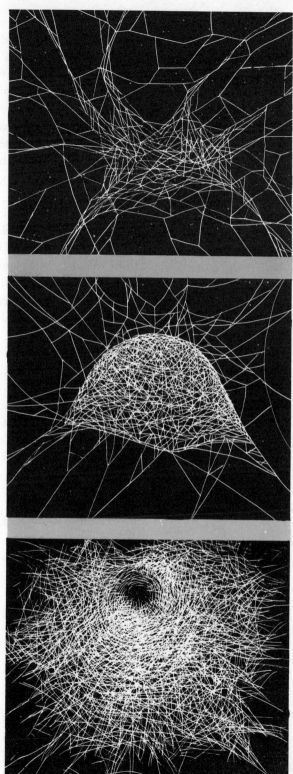

Also in bushes and hedges you can see the strange web of a group of spiders called *Linyphia*. These webs are like silky hammocks hanging between the twigs of the bush and they too serve as the best kind of trap for these special spiders.

On the ground or between stones we find the webs of spiders called *Agelena*. These webs look like a piece of gray cloth but with a hole in the middle—rather like a torn, dirty handkerchief.

The most beautiful of all the webs is woven by a group of spiders called *Aranea*. The name reminds us of Arachne, the girl in the story from whom the *Arachnida* get their name. It is right that we should be reminded of a great weaver, for these spiders weave the beautiful webs most of us think of when spider-webs are mentioned.

The way spiders make the silk for their webs is one of the most surprising processes in all nature.

The silk is made inside the spider and comes out as a milky liquid. But just as soon as it gets into the air, it begins to harden and, within the wink of an eye, it is tough enough to make a web.

SILK "PUMPS"

Spiders have from four to six little lumps on their bodies from which silk is let out. Each of those lumps is called a spinneret. Each one has six hundred tiny openings in it, openings so tiny that even a very powerful microscope can hardly bring them into sight.

Each of those six hundred openings, amazingly enough, connects with a separate gland in the spider's body. These glands

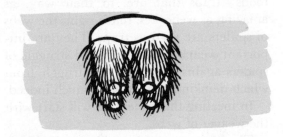

control what goes into the silk. With this sort of control all spiders can make at least three separate kinds of silk: one for webs, one for ropes, and one for tying up their food or for other jobs that we'll learn about later. Altogether seven really different kinds of silk have been found among the spiders. Spiders control not only what goes through each of the six hundred tiny openings in their four to six spinnerets, but also how fast the silk comes out, how thick it is, and so on. By moving the spinnerets, the spider can make threads flow together or separate. And while all this is going on, remember, the spider is controlling several thousand glands that feed the spinnerets.

TOUGH BUT TINY

It is hard for us to imagine the strength of the silk a spider spins for its webs because it is spun in threads far thinner than the

162

threads spun by silkworms, which give us silk for our clothes.

The silk of the spider-web is so fine, in fact, that it is used to make the cross-hairs in telescopic rifle sights where no man-made wires have been found to be as satisfactory or as perfect.

Thin as it is, spider-web silk is the strongest thread on earth. That is, for its size, it can stand more pull than any other thread. There is only one material of any sort on the earth that has greater power when pulled and that is a material made of melted rock called fused quartz.

If a strand of steel could be made as thin as spider's silk, the spider's silk would be *many* times stronger. If you have ever watched a spider-web standing firm and unbroken as a strong wind and a driving rain tear at it, you will have an idea of how strong it is.

Now let us see how the best weaver of all, one of the Aranea spiders, actually goes about weaving a beautiful web. Because of its round shape, scientists call this sort of web an *orb web*.

CROWN SPINNER

The spider we'll look at is the common garden spider—one of the kind that goes by the scientific name of *Aranea diadema*. That last name comes from the word diadem, which means a crown, and so this spider is a sort of royal figure.

The first thing the spider makes is a framework. Usually the framework is a square of silk lines, connected at the corners. (If a man were to make a framework like this, in the same scale to *his* size as the web is to the spider, it would mean that he

would have to make a square about 400 yards on each side.)

Let us suppose that the spider we are watching has chosen to make a square framework. The square is built upright, like a picture frame. Next, the spider runs back to the center of the top line of the square. Another line of silk is dropped down from there. The spider runs down to the bottom of the square and fastens the line there, with a sort of silky glue it lets out.

Now the spider runs out on this cross-piece and fastens a piece of silk in the midde of *it*. The spider takes the free end of that new piece of silk and walks along the cross-piece to the top again. The spider turns and goes along the top. After a few steps, the new piece of silk is fastened to the top. The web now looks like this:

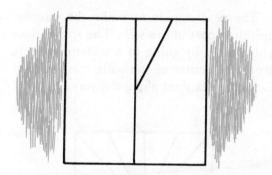

Now the spider runs back down the cross-piece and fastens another piece of silk. Then the same thing happens as before, except that this time the spider fastens the new piece to one of the sides of the web. The web then looks like this:

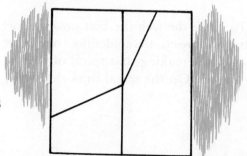

From that point on, the process is repeated over and over until the web looks like the spokes of a square wheel. It looks like this although actually such a web usually has about thirty spokes instead of the few you see here:

The next step is to make the circular spiraling part of the web. The spider does this simply by going in a widening circle from the center of the web, trailing and fastening silk lines along the way.

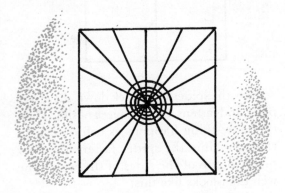

To make the web the best possible sort of trap for insects, the spider does one other thing while making that spiral of web on the spokes. On the spiral lines the spider puts a glue also made inside of the spider's body. This glue can make an insect stick to the web so that the spider can take his time about eating it.

THE SPIDER'S GLUE TRICK

For many years scientists wondered how the spiders got that glue on the web the way they did. The puzzling thing was that the glue was put on in tiny dots and each of those dots was exactly the same distance apart. When scientists say "exactly," they do not mean "sort of" or "nearly." They mean *exactly*. And in this case the scientists measured and found that the drops were so exactly spaced that they would have had a hard time to duplicate the exactness even with their best scientific equipment. How then, they wondered, could a tiny spider do the job without even thinking about it?

When they found out, it turned out to be wonderfully simple. If you take a string, say the string of a violin, that is stretched tight, and put water on it, the water just covers the string. But if you twang the string and make it vibrate, then the vibrations—that is, the super-fast movements of the string along its entire length—will make the water separate into tiny drops. And all the drops will be exactly the same distance apart because they are all twanging on the string at the same rate.

The spider does exactly that sort of thing to make the glue form dots on the web. First the spider smears glue on the line between two spokes of the web. Then the spider backs off, stands on the spoke, and twangs the part of the spiral line it has just smeared. The twanging line makes the glue separate into drops that are *exactly* the same distance apart.

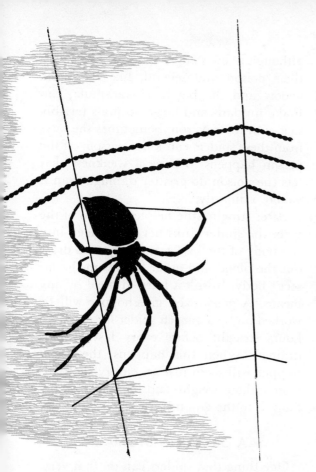

The weaver herself, the spider, has been lurking off to one side. As soon as the grasshopper hits the web the spider knows that dinner has arrived. The movement of the grasshopper makes the lines of the web hum and wiggle. It is almost as though the spider were receiving a message over a telegraph wire.

The spider runs out onto the web to see what has been caught on the glue she dotted along the lines. Seeing that it is a grasshopper, an insect with powerful legs, the spider will realize that she has to work fast, for the grasshopper may be able to kick loose from the web. If the insect on the web were just a plain fly or a moth, for instance, the spider might take her time, knowing that the insect couldn't get away. But a powerful kicker like the grasshopper must be handled at once.

Quickly the spider runs along the web. *She* doesn't get stuck on the glue because there is an oil on her eight legs that keeps her from sticking to the glue.

SPINNING A ROPE

When the spider gets near the grasshopper, she turns so that her spinning apparatus faces the grasshopper. Out of the tiny outlets of the spinnerets comes a kind of silk but this is very different from the delicate thin silk of the web. This time the silk comes out in a broad band, like a bandage. The spider busily tucks up this broad band of silk with her rear legs, and when she has enough tucked away, she flings the silk band over the struggling grasshopper, the way you might throw a towel over a puppy.

As soon as she has thrown the silk band on the grasshopper, the spider goes even closer and begins to roll the grasshopper

When spiders are very young, both the male and female spiders spin webs equally well. As the males grow up, they lose the ability to do this. They just catch what food they can roaming along the ground or along branches It is the female, then, that sits in the web and snares food. She needs to, for she has the eggs to make and little spiders to raise too. She *needs* all the food she can snare. For an idea of how the spider uses the web as a snare, let's go back to the garden spider and her beautiful orb web. The British writer John Crompton has given us a vivid example of how the spider uses that web to capture a grasshopper.

The grasshopper, jumping up and down through the woods, hops right into the web.

165

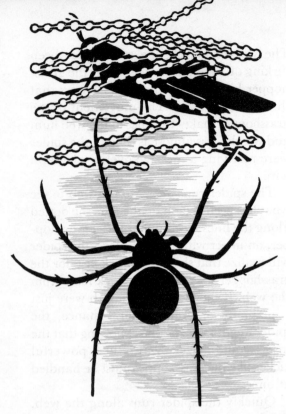

although a few spiders can hurt birds with their poison and several, like the black widow and the big hairy tarantula, can make humans and large animals terribly sick with their poison. Sometimes the bites from these spiders can kill a person—if the person happens to have a weakness that lets the poison do greater damage than it would ordinarily.

After stinging the helpless victim of the web, the spider sinks her fangs deep into the body of the insect and begins to draw out the blood and other liquids in the insect's body. It isn't a hurried meal by any means. A good sized grasshopper will be worked on by a garden spider for about 18 hours straight before every last drop is drained. When this happens, the grasshopper will seem just an empty shell, almost without weight, and the spider simply flings it to the ground.

A GROWING STOMACH

One thing that spiders can do that very few other living things can, is to eat and eat without having to worry about the size of their stomachs. Humans can eat only so much because their stomachs can stretch only so much. Most animals are like that too. But not the spider. There is hardly any limit to how much spiders can hold. They can feast on insect after insect and their very flexible stomachs just swell and swell.

The spiders take full advantage of their special stomachs and cram in as much food as possible at every opportunity. They never know, after all, when the food supply may thin out. Cold weather may keep the insects from flitting about. A lot of things can happen. So the spider stores up.

Because of this, some spiders have been

around, using the same powerful legs that she used to throw the silk band. The spider just rolls the grasshopper up in the silk band that way.

Pretty soon the grasshopper can't struggle any more. He is completely tied up. Now the spider can take her time, saving the grasshopper for a while or not, depending on her mood and whether or not any other insect has come along to add to her pantry supply.

MEALTIME

When the spider is ready to make a meal of the victim caught in the web, she takes one bite to stun or paralyze the insect. All spiders have poison of one sort or another that they inject through tiny fangs. But very few of these poisons are any bother at all to any living thing larger than an insect, known to live for more than a year without any food at all!

NO WASPS WANTED

If when the spider goes to find out what has been caught in the web, there is a wasp there, the spider has no thoughts of food. The wasp, with its needle-like sting and quick flashing wings, is one of the deadliest of all insects. The spiders seem to know this and to fear the wasps.

When a wasp is caught on the web, the spider runs out, but instead of feasting, begins very carefully to bite away the web that is holding the wasp. If that doesn't work to free the wasp, the spider may just go off and hide until the wasp has freed itself.

One of the other webs we have mentioned as a separate example of the spider's weaving art is the one that looks like a flat piece of cloth either flung on the ground or stretched out on some bushes, or even over a crack in a wall. This web is made by a different spider and certainly has a different appearance but it serves the same purpose as the beautiful orb web. It is a trap.

BACK DOOR OUT

When you look at one of these flat webs, with its tightly-woven close-together strands, you can notice that in the center there is a funnel-like hole. Sometimes this funnel is a half-inch or so long. The spider lives at the bottom of this funnel tunnel. And, because this is a very clever sort of spider, these tunnels rarely if ever lead to a hiding place that is altogether closed in. The spider tries to make sure that there is a back way out just in case something super-tough, like a wasp or a tougher spider, might come stalk-ing down the tunnel some day.

There is a particular difference between the way the spider makes this sort of web and the way the orb webs are made. There is no glue on the flat sheet-like web. The only thing the web itself can do to trap an insect is to catch the insect's foot in the tangle of tiny lines the web is made of.

Actually, most insects could free themselves from the web after a moment or two. But very few get the chance. The spider, sometimes waiting right at the top of the funnel in the center or sometimes drowsing down at the end of it, is aroused by the slightest sign of action on the web itself. The spider darts up and onto the web, but stepping carefully so as not to become tangled in it. Even if the insect is a dangerous one, the spider doesn't wait around to work out any special plan of attack but plunges right in and plants her fangs in whatever part of the insect she can reach. At that point the struggle is over. The poison from the spider paralyzes the insect almost immediately and then this spider too can begin to feast.

WEBS IN THE HOUSE

Inside of houses we often find other less tidy sort of webs. These are the webs that are just tangles of lines. But, like all of the other webs, the tangle has just one purpose —to catch insects. And it does, quite well. If you look very closely at one of the tangles, you should be able to see that at one edge of the tangle the web has been spun into a sort of little pipe. The spider who built the web lives in that tiny tube.

WEBS BY NIGHT

Most of the house spiders spin only at night, but they spin steadily, night after night. Perhaps you wonder why they should keep on spinning even after their web has been built up into a tangle that is like a blob of cotton. The reason is that the blob isn't the part that really does the job of catching the food. The part that snares the insects are fresh lines that the spider weaves each night and that stretch above the main tangle of lines rather like a fence of almost invisible wires to trip and tangle anything that flies by.

Because these lines must be kept fresh and flexible, the spider spins away every night, adding new lines on top and letting the old lines just flop down to become part of the ever growing tangle from which she operates.

When mothers become annoyed at spiderwebs because they seem to appear out of nowhere in the corner of a perfectly clean room, they are probably talking about the spinning of the house spider. But perhaps if more mothers knew how many insects the little weaver was taking care of, they might not be quite so annoyed.

OTHER SNARES

Some of the strangest snares used by spiders aren't webs at all. One spider, for instance, practically lassos its victims. Another sets a silken trap that sort of springs shut on the victim. Another sets up an apparatus that actually snatches up insects that are unfortunate enough to walk into it.

ROPE TRICK

The spider with the lasso has long legs and, oddly enough, seems to be very tired. She doesn't move as fast as the other spiders you may see. This isn't because of laziness. This spider uses those slow movements to make insects think they have nothing to fear when she is around. A small insect may stop within a couple of inches of one of these spiders and the spider will just sit there. The insect apparently feels that the spider won't harm it. But that is far from the case. The spider, without moving, shoots a long, thin line of silk onto the insect. This line is made of a very sticky gummy sort of silk. The insect can't shake it off. In a flash, the spider shoots some other lines onto the insect, tying it securely. The spider does this by moving its spinners from side to side as it shoots the lines onto the insect. This tangles the lines all around the insect. When the insect is unable to move with all the silk tied around it, the spider that seemed so lazy scoots over and starts to eat.

SNAPPING THE TRAP

There is a fairly rare spider with the scientific name of *Hyptiotes* that also might appear to be lazy at first glance. This spider spins a web that looks as though it had never been completed. It looks like a pie-slice-shaped part of the rounded orb web of the Aranea spiders. But this isn't an incompleted web at all. It is very complete and very special. From the long end of the triangle formed by the web, the spider weaves a long single line which is carried close to some sort of support, like a nearby twig or branch. There the spider spins another very short line and fixes it to the support. The spider still has been holding the long line that is fixed to the web. Now the spider is like a link in a silken chain. From one side, the spider holds on to the long line that goes to the web. From the other, she holds onto the short line that goes to the support. Now she starts pulling to tighten the long line leading to the web. When the line is really tight, and holding the web itself tight, the spider just settles down to wait.

Sooner or later an insect will fly into the web. The instant this happens, the spider lets the long line go limp. This lets the web fall around the insect. Next, the spider starts shaking the long line to make the web jiggle around and trap the insect all the more. When the insect is good and stuck, the spider lets go of the support and swings over onto the web to have her feast.

A STORAGE SNARE

One of the neatest spiders, when it comes to webs, is a tiny garden spider that lives in Latin America. This spider was once thought not to have any web at all. At least no one had ever seen one. At last, a young boy, the son of a scientist in one of the southern republics, said he would keep watch on one of these spiders for 24 hours straight to see if it did any web-spinning at any time of the day or night.

All day long the spider stayed hidden under some bushes. But the spider was having a feast of insects. How had she caught them? The boy waited and watched some more. Night came. The spider didn't budge. She still wouldn't give up the secret of how she hunted. Finally, just as dawn was breaking, the little spider crept out and onto the bushes. Quickly she began spinning a small web. As soon as it was done, a few tiny insects that are often seen flying in the early morning flew right into the web.

When the sun rose a little higher the spider went to her web, cut it loose from the twigs to which it had been attached and folded it up! Inside, of course, were the insects she had caught. Then, like a shopper carrying a grocery bag, the spider scurried back to her hiding place to enjoy breakfast and lunch and dinner and probably a late supper too—all from the early morning catch in the web that no one had ever seen before the boy kept his 24-hour vigil.

WRAPPER WEBS

Several spiders that live in Australia also have webs that they use to wrap up their victims. But these spiders don't wait for the insects to walk into the web. They stand holding the web and when the insect comes by, they simply throw the web on it, like throwing a blanket on someone. These webs are about the size of a postage stamp.

There is another special web that looks anything but special at first. It appears to be simply a series of lines stretched from a twig or other support right down to the ground, like a set of tiny silken strings. But this web is one of the most deadly of all. Each of the lines that stretches down to the ground is stuck fast there so that the spider can pull it very tight.

When an insect comes walking along and hits one of the lines, it gets stuck. It struggles, of course, and pretty soon breaks the line. Does that mean it gets away? Not at all. That is just the way the spider wanted it to happen. The instant the insect breaks the line, it is snatched right up into the air where it is helpless and the spider can then feast on it. The reason is that the line was stretched *so* tight that when it was broken, the long top part just twanged up in the air, carrying the insect, the way any string that is stretched tight will jump when cut.

HUNTERS AND DOOR-SLAMMERS

Next let's see the sort of spiders that don't use any webs at all. Some are hunting spiders. They go out to find and kill their prey. They would rather do that than wait to trap their victims. Others still use traps, but their traps aren't always webs. Some of these traps are like trap-doors. The spiders that use them are called trap-door spiders.

In many ways what they build is as remarkable as the beautiful orb web of the spinning spider.

With the same fangs that are used to bite the insects that she feeds upon, the trap-door spider digs a hole in the ground. It is just a bit larger around than the spider herself, but it is as much as a foot deep. The spider

lines this hole with silk like the silk used in webs.

At the top of the hole the spider builds a door. It is shaped like a cork. The spider also puts a hinge of silk on one edge of the cork so that it can always be used as a door.

The cork-like door is made out of dirt sandwiched between layers of silk. On the top of the door, the spider puts bits of grass or moss or leaves or whatever will best serve to camouflage the door. It is very hard for the keenest eyes to spot a trap-door spider's door.

But what does the spider do with this elaborate tunnel and door? Does she just use it for a home? Some trap-door spiders do. They live in the holes, safe behind the trap-door, and leave only to set up small webs nearby to catch a meal. But others use the trap-doors for traps!

A spider who does that will open the door slightly, keeping it propped open with her front legs. When an insect walks by, not noticing what is lurking behind the crack

170

in the ground, the spider darts her legs out, grabs the insect, pulls it inside, and begins to eat in the blink of an eye.

TUNNEL AND TUBE

Another of these trap-door spiders builds a silken tube that sticks up beyond the entrance to her tunnel. At first glance at one of these tubes it would seem that the spider had made some sort of mistake and sealed herself into the tunnel, for there is no door in the tube. There isn't supposed to be, for this is one of the spider world's most clever traps. The spider that builds it waits inside the tube, safe from attack by larger creatures who could hardly guess that a spider was inside the little tube sticking up out of the ground.

Sooner or later, though, an insect will come by the tube and touch it. Then the spider, waiting inside, plunges her fangs right through the silken wall of the tube and into the insect, which is paralyzed immediately. Then the spider tears a little hole in the tube and pulls her meal inside. But before she settles down to eat, she carefully mends the hole in the tube.

WOLVES AND CRABS

Among the spiders that go out and hunt, there are two main kinds. One is the *wolf spider,* in whose family are found some of the spiders that are most dangerous to larger animals. These spiders prowl about stalking their prey. They do not wait for the prey to blunder into a trap. With speed and with powerful poison fangs, these spiders are very deadly hunters—but remember that many of the insects they hunt are pests that humans are very glad to have kept under control.

Another kind of hunter is the *crab spider.* There are many different kinds but most of them have the same deadly habit. They curl up inside a flower and await their prey there. When an insect that is used to eating the flower comes up for a meal, the spider leaps into action, sinks its fangs into the insect, and has a meal. Some of these spiders

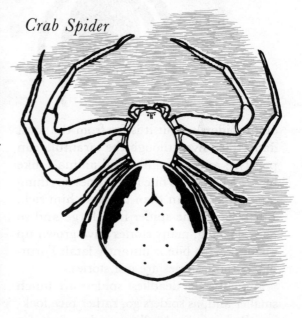

Crab Spider

specialize in killing bees that are coming to flowers for pollen. When they do that, they kill one of mankind's best insect friends. That is one of the bad things spiders do, but on the whole they perform many more useful and helpful tasks for us.

TARANTULAS

Most unpleasant, however, are the few spiders that are dangerous to larger animals and even to men. The largest of all spiders is one of these. It is the *tarantula,* a big hairy spider with a body as large as a frog's. This is perhaps the most frightening

171

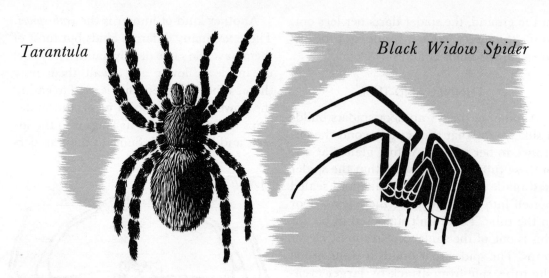

of all spiders — but it is far from the most dangerous. Even though the tarantula can paralyze and even kill small animals, like birds and mice, its bite rarely does anything more to a human than to make him sick. But because the spider is so large and so fierce looking, many stories have grown up about how its bite is instantly fatal. Fortunately those stories are just stories.

Actually, the deadliest spiders are much smaller and, as spiders go, rather nice looking. Perhaps the deadliest spider of all, for instance, is a spider found commonly in America. Although there are quite poisonous spiders in most parts of the world, many scientists feel that none are worse than the *black widow*. This is a jet black spider with, fortunately, very bright red warning marks on the bottom of her body. In some kinds of black widow spiders these red marks are like dots. In others they are like stripes across the body. In one kind the red

mark is shaped rather like an hour-glass.

Any black spider with red markings would be a good one to stay away from. But the bite of this spider and other poisonous spiders is still not as deadly as some people say. In most cases, the person bitten just gets very sick and swells up at the bitten place. But every now and then—and possibly not more than once out of fifty or a hundred times—a person bitten by a black widow or other poisonous spider will die. And, because of that, all spiders frighten a lot of people.

Remember, though, that even though some spiders are frightening, and some are dangerous, the vast majority of them are just about the best friends that humans have—for these eight-legged creatures, with their traps and poisons and beautiful webs, are the number one guardian against the spread of the largest family of living creatures of all, the six-legged insects.

The Kingdom of the Plants

IF YOU divided all living things on earth into just two parts, you could divide them into an animal part and a plant part. You could put everything alive into one of those two parts. Scientists have made just that sort of breakdown of living things. They call the parts "kingdoms" — the animal kingdom and the plant or vegetable kingdom.

HOW PLANTS
DIFFER FROM ANIMALS

Let's run down the differences between the things in the animal kingdom and the things in the plant kingdom.

Plants can make their own food from the things they take from the soil and from the air.

Animals cannot make their own food from raw materials but must eat plants (vegetables and fruits and such) or animals that have fed on plants (cows, pigs, and such) or the things made by animals that have fed on plants (eggs, milk, and such).

Plants have a green coloring material in them that is called *chlorophyll*. This mysterious material is what lets the plants make food out of air and soil.

Animals do not have chlorophyll.

Plants are mostly made of cells with tough stiff walls.

Animals are mostly made of cells with flexible walls.

Animal taking nourishment from plants

*Plant taking nourishment
from air and soil*

173

Plants are stationary, they stay in one place.

Animals move about.

HOW PLANTS AND ANIMALS ARE ALIKE

Plants are *like* animals, however, in that they are built of the same basic things: cells. But, because the plant cells have hard walls, there is a special thing we notice

tough threads. Cotton is one such plant. From these plant fibers we get cloth and rope. Other plant fibers are crushed up to make paper, like the paper for the page you are reading right now.

Plant cells, like animal cells, are usually very tiny. A single leaf may have forty or fifty *million* tiny cells in it.

And, just as there are tiny members of the animal kingdom which have only one cell, and which we can see under the mi-

Algae floating in water

about plants. Many of them, with their hard-walled cells, build hard materials that last even after the plant itself has died. Wood is a good example of this. After the tree is cut down, the tough cell walls of the wood are just as tough as ever. They can be sawed up into lumber or made into models or chairs or anything else.

You may remember, from when we were talking about cells earlier in this book, that the first idea of things being built with cells came when a scientist examined a piece of cork and saw the pockets inside it made by the hard walls of the cells.

Some plant cells form long fibers, like

croscope, there also are tiny members of the plant kingdom which have only one cell as their entire body.

ALGAE—PLANTS THAT FLOAT

The best known of these simplest tiniest members of the plant kingdom are called *algae*. Perhaps you can remember seeing water on a pond covered with a greenish or even a reddish scum. That scum probably was formed of millions of the tiny one-celled algae plants. Although these tiny plants have only one cell apiece they live together in great numbers, each cell attached to the other so that they are like a living carpet spread across the water. Algae, floating like that, can be found on water everywhere in the world, on fresh water and on the salt water of the oceans. Many creatures in the sea live by eating algae. A few types of algae can even be found on dry land. They too are included in the oldest form of plant life that we know anything about. Long before the first animals started roaming across the earth, scientists figure, there were algae on the waters of the earth.

Astronomers, checking on the possibility of life on other planets, have come to believe that if there is any life on, say, Mars, the life there is probably a form of algae or other simple plants.

FUNGI—PLANTS WITHOUT GREEN

Next up the ladder in the plant kingdom are the sorts of plants called *fungi*. That word may be familiar because some people call mushrooms fungi or fungous plants. One mushroom would be called a fungus. And that is just what they are. But there are many more types of fungi than just mushrooms.

Fungi are plants that do not have chlorophyll in them. They have to live off other plants. They are *parasites*. A *parasite* is a living thing that lives off something else.

The tiniest of the fungi are one-celled plants called bacteria—another familiar word because so many people talk about bacteria as a cause of sickness. Actually bacteria are the cause of many things other than sickness. Cheese and alcohol and vinegar and many other useful things are made by the bacteria that go to work feeding on

and changing other plant materials.

BACTERIA—GOOD AND BAD

The most important thing done by bacteria is to make the soil good for growing other plants. One type of bacteria that grows in the soil (and like the others is so tiny that a microscope would be needed to see them) breaks down animal wastes and bodies that are left on or in the ground. They turn animal materials into important materials called *ammonia compounds* which

Mistletoe on tree

are needed in the soil if other plants are to grow there.

When that is done another type of bacteria takes those ammonia compounds and breaks them down into other chemicals needed for plant growth. And remember that if there were no plants there could be no food, for *only plants* can make the mate-

175

rials that animals need to build their own healthy cells and make them grow.

Perhaps the most important of the bacteria in the soil, however, are called nitrogen-fixing bacteria. This means that these bacteria fix or hold nitrogen in the soil. Without those bacteria the soil would have no way of holding nitrogen, which is the main part of air. Without nitrogen in the soil nothing could grow.

On the bad side, though, there are the diseases caused by other bacteria. Tuberculosis, pneumonia, some very bad fevers, lockjaw, in humans, and many diseases of plants are caused by bacteria too. Bacteria also are what cause foods to spoil. Because bacteria have a hard time growing and spreading in very cold temperatures, keeping food in cold places like a refrigerator is one way to stop the food from going bad.

MOLDS

Next in the fungi family are the molds. You may remember seeing food that has spoiled and become covered with a furry substance of different colors. That is mold. It is caused by thousands of tiny fungi growing together and feeding off the spoiled food.

Perhaps you may think that this sort of plant life is quite like the greenish algae that floats on the water. But remember the very important thing about all of the fungi. Fungi do not have chlorophyll to make food from air and from other materials. Fungi have to feed off plants that do have chlorophyll or off animals. Even though a scum of algae sometimes looks like a mold on the water, algae *do* have chlorophyll and can make food from air and sunlight and water.

MUSHROOMS AND TOADSTOOLS

The largest and most complicated of the fungi are the mushrooms and toadstools. Because they are so familiar to anyone who has walked through the woods or seen them served as part of a dinner, mushrooms are often thought of as some special sort of fungi not at all like molds or others. Actually, though, they are very similar. For the real fungus part of a mushroom isn't the part that grows above the ground. The most important part of the mushroom is below the ground and is really just a mass of little roots which, like all fungi, feed off other plant life. The part above the ground, the part we call the mushroom, is just a growth that is sent up to distribute the spores or

Mold found on decaying wood

One variety of mushroom

176

seeds from which other mushrooms will grow. Toadstools are poisonous and so are some mushrooms.

LICHENS AND MOSSES

The next step in the plant kingdom takes us to the *lichens*. These are tiny plant forms which are quite like algae in many ways except that they grow on rocks and trees on the dry land. When you see a tree in the woods that seems covered with a greenish paint on one side of its trunk, you probably are looking at a tree covered with lichen. Right after the lichens, going up the scale of plants come the mosses. Moss is a greenish growth like a very fine, short grass. Sometimes when you feel moss growing on a rock in the woods it feels almost like green fur.

TREES AND FLOWERS

Now we are ready to come to the largest grouping of the plant kingdom. Scientists have a hard name for it: *Pteropsida*. But even if the name is hard it shouldn't be hard to remember what plants are grouped under that name. Just about all the plants we think of *as plants* are in this group: everything from tiny flowers to great trees. All of them have regular roots, rather than just living on water like algae or clinging to rock like moss. They have stems or trunks and they have leaves. Another thing about them is that, except for the ferns, which are a special part of the group, they all produce seeds. It is from the seeds that new plants grow.

Most of us are familiar with the seeds flowers grow from and the seeds foods like wheat grow from. But some seeds are quite

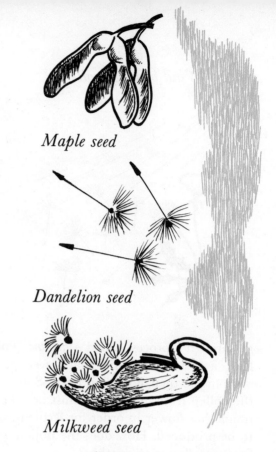

Maple seed

Dandelion seed

Milkweed seed

different. The seeds of oak trees, for instance, are in acorns. The seeds of pine trees are parts of the cones that grow on the branches of these trees. Maple trees have seeds that come in little pods that look like airplane propellers, and when these fall from the trees they whirl through the air. The dandelion's seeds are the tiny white parachutes that scatter when you blow on a dandelion that has lost its yellow petals.

Some plants have another sort of problem with their seeds. To produce the seeds, and so to produce new plants, flowers must

177

Wind blowing pollen

Wasp on one variety of fig tree

go through a process called *pollination*. Pollen is a dust-like material that flowers produce inside their flowering parts. Some of the pollen from one flower must be taken to another flower in order for fertile seeds to be produced. How does the pollen get from one flower to another?

There are two main ways. One way is to let the wind blow it from one flower to the other. The other way is for insects to carry it from one flower to another. Bees, as they go from flower to flower gathering the pollen they need to make honey, carry pollen with them on their feet from one plant to another. They are most important insects when it comes to helping flowers grow, though some other insects do the same thing.

Some fruit trees have an even tougher time. Some need special insects to carry pollen from one tree to another tree in order to produce their fruits. Fruit, by the way, is just a special part of certain plants where those plants grow their seeds. Actually an apple and an acorn are for the same pur-

pose so far as the trees are concerned. They are parts of the seed system. But, while acorns are good for squirrels to eat, the apple and other fruits are good for people to eat. One kind of fig tree can have its pollen carried only by a particular wasp. If that kind of wasp doesn't live near the tree there can be no figs, which is the fruit where that tree keeps its seeds.

MAGIC GREEN

As remarkable as the seeds of plants may be, it is in their green leaves that the most remarkable thing of all takes place. This is the manufacture of the materials on which all life depends.

We have already mentioned that it is the green chlorophyll in plants that makes the plants able to manufacture food. The way that the chlorophyll does this is called *photosynthesis*. That word is made up of two

Greek words. One, *photos,* means light. The other, *synthesis,* means putting together. So the word photosynthesis really means "putting together out of light." Amazingly enough, that is just what the chlorophyll does. It takes the light of the sun and uses the energy from that light to make food. Here is how it happens, although scientists have no idea of just *why* it does:

From the roots of the plant, water is drawn up into the leaves. At the same time, the leaf itself is drawing in carbon dioxide from the air. Carbon dioxide is what animals breathe *out* after they have taken in all the healthful parts of the air. The water and the carbon dioxide are brought together with the green matter, the chlorophyll in the plants.

Before we go any farther, it would be wise to remember that although chlorophyll itself is green, and plants having chlorophyll are called green plants, some of them may have other colors in their leaves. Some seaweed, for instance, looks absolutely brown even though it has plenty of green chlorophyll inside.

The chlorophyll, while the water and carbon dioxide is being brought to it, has been very busy itself storing up energy from the rays of the sun. How it does this is a mystery of science. But it does. Then, with the energy it has taken from the sun, it breaks down the water and carbon dioxide and puts what it takes from them back together again in an entirely new form—as sugar! The sorts of sugar that plants make is not at all like the sugar you put on your breakfast cereal. The important thing about the sugar that the plants make is that it can be used to provide the energy that will build the bodies of other living things. This sugar, made by the plants, is the material that keeps all life on earth going and growing.

But there is another wonderful thing that happens while the plant is making this material in which energy is passed on. When the chlorophyll causes the carbon dioxide and water to break down, it does not use all of the oxygen that is released. So, the leaves that breathe in the carbon dioxide breathe out pure oxygen.

The amount each leaf breathes is so tiny that the most delicate instruments are

Sun

Sun's energy forms sugar to nourish plant

179

needed to measure it. But since all the leaves on all the plants in the world do this throughout the sunlight hours, the air of the earth is continually being purified so that other living things may breathe pure air.

PLANT "MINES"

Although we cannot say exactly how much of the air is purified each day by the plants, scientists have figured pretty closely just how much energy-producing food materials are made by plants each year. They estimate that the energy stored up in plants each year is *100 times greater* than all the energy released by all the coal that is mined in the whole world in a year. When you know that the United States *alone* mines *seven hundred million tons* of coal each year, you have an idea of the enormous store of energy that plants possess to pass along to other living things.

Along with the leafy parts that store the energy sugar, plants also make many other things that men and animals need in order to live. Starches and proteins are among those important things.

To give an idea of just how much of this plant life energy is put to use by men each year, you have to look at the farms which are where men raise plants to be eaten for their food values. More than six billion bushels of wheat are grown each year. If all those bushels were put into separate baskets, they would go around the center of the earth about sixty times! And very nearly the same amounts of rice and corn are produced too. Sugar taken from plants amounts to some thirty-seven million tons each year. Every ounce of all that food depends absolutely on chlorophyll, the "green

Plants store energy 100 times greater than all coal used in a year

magic" in plants with which the plant kingdom makes food for living things.

WOOD—THE TRUNKS OF TREES

Another very useful part of plants with which we are all familiar is wood. We know, of course, that wood for making lumber comes from the trunks of big trees. But have you stopped to think that in many ways the trunk of a great tree really is the stem of the tree. Just as in the stem of a flower, the trunk of a tree is the part of the plant that holds up the leaves and through which water is brought up from the soil.

In a flower and many other plants the stem is pulpy and soft. In a tree it is hard. Wood is just the hard part of the great stems of trees.

The trunk or stem of a tree is formed like this: First there is the skin or bark on the outside. Just as the skin of a human being protects the human's inner body, so does the bark protect the inner parts of the tree trunk.

Just inside the bark is an inner layer of living material that carries the food prepared in the leaves down to every part of the tree. It goes down to the very roots, to keep them healthy and strong and to enable them to grow and spread in their search to find and suck up water in the ground. The roots also keep the plant firmly tied down in the soil.

When bark is peeled from a tree, you can see that the inside of the bark is wet and smooth. This is the layer that carries the food from the leaves. That is why it is so harmful to a tree to cut into the bark. You might remember that if someone ever tells you that sticking a knife into a tree won't hurt the tree. It will, by injuring the important food-carrying inner bark.

Inside the inner bark comes a layer of plant cells that can be seen only with a microscope. This layer is called the *cambium* and it is where the trunk or stem builds new cells in order to increase in size. This is the growing layer of the trunk or stem.

Inside that layer is a thicker layer of moist live woody material called *sapwood*. Just as its name says, it carries sap. What

is sap? We talk about it a lot but we don't always understand what it really means. We know, usually, that the sap of a tree is the thick liquid that comes out of places where the tree has been cut.

Actually, the sap is water and other materials that are sucked up from the ground by the roots. The sap is thick and oozy because the roots, when they draw up water, also draw up tiny amounts of minerals and other parts of the soil to mix with it.

This sap always travels upward toward the leaves of the tree where, as we have said, it becomes part of the process of making food in the leaves.

Along with the nourishment carried down by the inner bark, the sap makes up what could be called the blood of the tree. So you can see that when someone thoughtlessly cuts a tree and lets the sap ooze out, that tree is being hurt in just the way *you* are hurt when you are cut and blood oozes out of the wound.

Inside of the sapwood of a tree is the hardest wood of all. It is called the *heartwood* of the tree. This is part of the trunk that is no longer used in carrying nourishment and instead provides the main strength to support the tree. Inside of this heartwood and in twigs and branches, there is another softer layer called *pith*.

As you can guess any time you walk through a forest or a garden, there are ever so many more plants than there is room to talk about in a single book. Altogether there are some 340,000 separate kinds of plants.

KINDS OF TREES

Because trees are the largest of the plants, and the ones we usually see most and recognize best, let's separate them into some family groups.

All around the world, if you were to count up different varieties of trees, you would find you had counted more kinds of oak-tree than any other kind.

roll a spruce-tree needle between your fingers, it feels as if it had four edges rather than being just flat, like the fir.

The needles of the cone-bearing trees, by the way, are actually the leaves of those trees. They are where the green chlorophyll

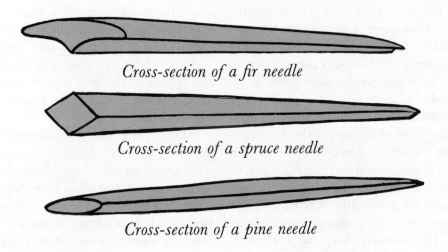

Cross-section of a fir needle

Cross-section of a spruce needle

Cross-section of a pine needle

The best way to recognize an oak-tree is by its acorns. Every oak has acorns of some sort. They are the fruit of the oak, the place where the seeds are grown.

Another kind of tree with a very noticeable and special place to grow its seeds is called a *conifer*. Conifers are trees that have cones; such as the pines and firs, and spruces.

At Christmas-time, when these cone-bearing trees become very popular as decorations, you may wonder just what kind of Christmas-tree is being trimmed with bright ornaments. Here are some easy rules to remember. Pines have pins. That is, pine-trees have long pin-like needles. Firs are flat. That is, fir-tree needles are shorter and flattened. Spruce is square. That is, if you

is stored and where the food is made. Unlike trees that shed their leaves and sort of go to sleep in winter, the cone-bearing trees keep their needles and stay green all year round. That is why they are also called *evergreens*.

Two trees of this kind are special for another reason—they are the largest trees in the world. They are the *redwood* trees and the *bigtrees,* also called the *giant Sequoias.* These trees live on the West Coast of the United States. One redwood has been measured as 364 feet high, higher than a thirty-story office building. Of course it takes a very long time for anything to grow that big. One of the bigtrees, one that is 273 feet high, is more than three thousand years old.

You may wonder what clues we have as to how old a tree is: There is a way to tell that is very exact. It tells us not only exactly how old a tree is but also how the weather was during each year it has grown. The clue to a tree's age is inside the trunk. Each season, as the tree builds a new layer of wood to make the trunk thicker, that layer is marked by a ring we can plainly see. When the tree is cut down, these rings can be counted. Each year produces one ring. When the tree has had a good year with good weather, the ring will be thick. When the tree hasn't grown much, then the ring will be thin. In that way scientists can figure out what the weather was like every year for many years back.

Fortunately, we don't have to chop down trees, like the giant bigtrees, to figure out their age. If just one of the trees is cut down and its rings counted, then the age of other trees of the same kind can be guessed by the size of the trunk itself.

The maple is another tree that, like the conifers, can be spotted by the container for the seeds. Just as the pines and firs and other trees like that keep their seeds in cones, the maple keeps its seeds inside of a winged pod. This is the pod we mentioned before as looking like an airplane propeller. Even though there are many different kinds of maples, all have these winged seed-pods.

The elm is one of the trees people usually tell by its leaves. The shape of the elm leaf is shown in the illustration. But notice particularly that the part of the leaf is quite lopsided as it comes from the stem. That lopsidedness is a sure sign of the elm.

Because the shapes of the leaves are so important in identifying many trees whose seeds or fruits aren't a clear enough clue, here is a picture list of leaves.

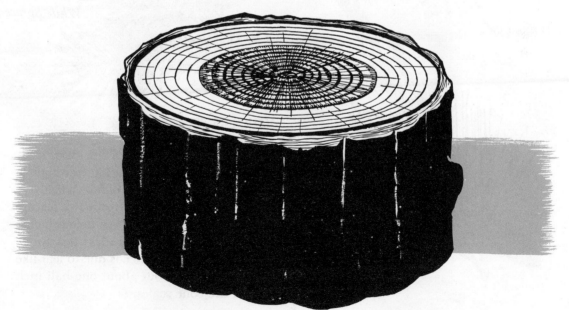

One ring is added each year the tree grows. Thick rings are the tree's healthiest years

Knowing the Trees

PINES

WHITE PINE

The *white pine* may be recognized easily. It is the only evergreen tree native to eastern North America which has its soft, flexible and bluish-green needles arranged in *clusters of five*.

Only a few traces of untouched white pine remain in the world. A trip to these remaining samples of nature's supreme accomplishment in tree development is well worth while.

The white pine is the most important forest tree in eastern North America, and probably in the world. It adapts itself to a great variety of soils, grows rapidly, produces valuable wood, and is beautiful. It grows as tall as 125 feet.

WHITE SPRUCE

If one examines its branches closely, this tree, the *white spruce,* may be separated readily from the red spruce and the black spruce, for its twigs are smooth, that is, hairs are entirely lacking upon them, while those of the red spruce and the black spruce are thickly covered with short hairs. It may also be told apart by the fact that its leaves when bruised have an unpleasant odor, which has given it the name of skunk spruce and cat spruce. Its cones are also larger than those of the black and red spruce.

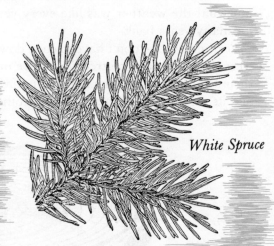

White Spruce

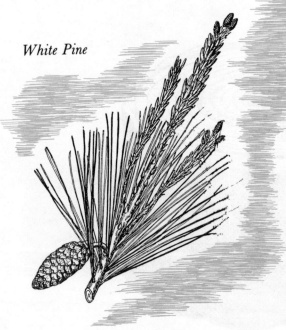

White Pine

DOUGLAS FIR

The *Douglas fir* is one of the giant trees. The tallest on record was 380 feet high. A few trees reach a diameter of fifteen feet.

The cones are the most distinctive feature of the tree. They are from two to four inches long and have a feathered appearance. This unusual appearance is due to leaf-like growths that stick out about one-half inch beyond the cone scales.

In winter the buds identify the Douglas fir. They are sharp-pointed, conical, and covered with numerous bright reddish-brown scales. The buds located at the ends of the twigs are approximately one-fourth of an inch long. The numerous buds found along the side of the twigs are somewhat shorter and blunter.

The bark is a helpful means of identification at all seasons of the year. It is dark-brown on the outside and reddish-brown within. Sometimes the bark becomes eighteen inches thick, and is roughened by deep furrows running up and down along the trunk.

The wood is heavy, hard, strong, coarse-grained, and rather difficult to work. It is sent from the forests of North America to every country in the world.

HEMLOCK

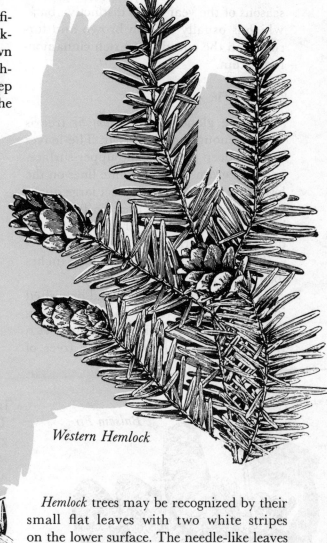

Douglas Fir

Western Hemlock

Hemlock trees may be recognized by their small flat leaves with two white stripes on the lower surface. The needle-like leaves are jointed to short woody stalks, and are arranged in two flat rows alongside the twigs.

185

The cones are about three-quarters of an inch long. The wood is hard, weak, brittle, liable to splinter, and difficult to work. It is used chiefly for rough construction work, coarse lumber, paper pulp, boxes, crates, and laths.

The hemlock can be told apart from other members of the pine family at all seasons of the year by its distinctive bark, which is usually reddish brown and furrowed on the outside, and rich cinnamon-red within.

BALSAM FIR

A mere glance at a *balsam fir* tree is usually enough to identify it. The leaves are flat, deep green on the upper surface, and pale green with two white lines on the lower side. Some people collect large quantities of leaves and use them in filling pillows and cushions, for the leaves, when dried, are very fragrant.

The cones are from two to four inches long and stand erect on the twigs.

Most people who have lived or visited in the regions where the balsam fir grows have a lasting idea of its appearance. It is the king among the Christmas trees of North America.

Balsam Fir

REDWOOD

Redwood

Every feature of the *redwood* is interesting. Its only close relative is the *big tree*. The redwood and the big tree make up the group of trees known by the scientific name *sequoia*. These two American forest trees are among the chief natural wonders of the world. Some are well over 300 feet high. Some have a diameter of more than fifteen feet. The age of the oldest specimen known is about 4000 years. The sequoia gets its name from a Cherokee Indian chief who invented an alphabet and a written lan-

186

guage for his people. These great trees are protected by law. The trunk of the largest sequoia is about one hundred feet around. There is enough wood in a single tree to make several houses. Since the big tree is the only other living relative of the redwood we may compare their chief features.

Redwood:
Found only near the Pacific coast of North America.
Reaches the greater height.
Leaves, usually spreading and of two forms, lance-like and scale-like.
Cones usually less than one inch long.
Buds covered with scales.
Bark cinnamon-brown.

Big tree:
Found chiefly in the Sierras of North America.
Reaches the greater diameter.
Leaves all scale-like.
Cones usually over two inches long.
Buds not covered with scales.
Bark reddish-brown.

RED CEDAR OR JUNIPER

The *junipers* are the most widely distributed group of trees on the North American continent.

The common *red cedar* is the only native species of juniper of any commercial importance belonging to this group. Its berry-like fruit is well known. The berries are about the size of a small pea, dark blue in color and often covered with a white bloom. These berries are eaten by birds.

Western Juniper

OTHER PINES

Other members of the pine family are the *short-leaf pine* with its 3 to 5-inch needles, the *long-leaf pine* with its 8 to 12-inch needles, the *yellow pine,* the *larch* trees with needles that are sometimes three-edged rather than just round like other pines.

Then there are other spruce members of the pine family like the *airplane spruce* with a whirly seed shaped like half a wing and a flat rather than four-sided needle like other spruces.

There are other fir trees in the pine family too, like the *Alpine fir,* the 150 to 200-foot *grand fir.* There are also the cedar trees with their scale-like leaves wrapped around the twigs. One of the cedar trees has the special name of *arbor vitae*, and some people are very familiar with it without ever knowing that it is a cedar and that cedars, in turn, are members of the pine family.

WILLOWS

WHITE WILLOW

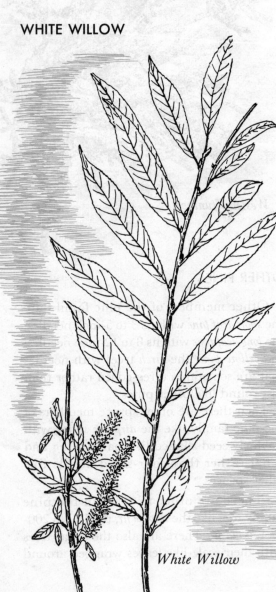

White Willow

The *white willow* is a native of Europe, but it now grows in other parts of the world as well. The white willow is seen along the banks of streams and other wet places. Its chief beauty is its dancing leaves, which are silky and pale on the lower surface. Whenever the slightest breeze blows, the silvery-white lower surface of the leaf stands in strong contrast with the dark-green upper surface, like a light shining.

Most of the large willows we see were introduced from other lands. Three of the commonest willows are *white willow, weeping willow,* and *crack willow.* The weeping willow, the favorite tree of the Orient, has been planted extensively in the eastern United States, and may be recognized by its long, drooping branches.

The crack willow usually is along the banks of streams or in other wet places, and may be recognized by its branches, which crack off very easily. After a storm one usually finds the ground beneath a crack willow covered with broken branches.

TREMBLING ASPEN

Trembling Aspen

If trees had human characteristics, the *aspens* would be the pioneers of the forest community, for they open the way for other trees. Like a mighty army they march along and cover the bare soil left in the wake of destructive forest fires, or other things that strip the land.

The *trembling aspen* has the widest range of any trees native to North America.

The trembling leaves are the most noticeable thing about the tree. The leaves tremble because their delicate stems let even the slightest breeze blow them about.

SILVER POPLAR

The *poplar* is native to both Europe and Asia. It is now also growing widely throughout the eastern United States.

The most striking thing about the *silver poplar* is the marked difference in color between the lower and the upper surfaces of its leaves. The upper side is very dark green and glossy, while the lower surface is a glistening white, which shows up clearly when the wind blows hard and shakes the leaves.

The silver poplar, just as all other poplars, produces its pollen-bearing and seed-producing flowers on separate trees. The flowers emerge from the large flower buds very early in spring, and develop into drooping tassels. The cottony seeds grow in several weeks, and are then scattered far and wide by the wind, because of their light weight and the many hairs attached to them.

OTHER WILLOWS

Other members of the willow family are the *black willow* with its long, narrow leaves, the shining or *glossy willow* with its shiny brown or yellowish twigs, the *large-toothed aspen* with leaves like the trembling aspen but with deeper notches along the edges, the *cottonwood* with heart-shaped leaves, and many different kinds of *poplar* trees.

Silver Poplar

WALNUTS

BLACK WALNUT

The *black walnut* bears little resemblance to any other forest tree except the *butternut*. These two trees may be told apart from other forest trees by their rough nuts, covered with a non-splitting husk. Every available piece of this wood is collected and manufactured into some useful commodity.

Black Walnut

PECAN

The *pecan* is the most important nut-bearing tree native to the United States.

A glance at a pecan tree is enough to show its relationship to common hickories. The most striking thing about the pecan is its fruit. It occurs in compact clusters of 3 to 11 nuts, each nut with a thin husk. The kernel of the nut is large and sweet.

OTHER WALNUTS

Other members of the walnut family are the *butternut,* with its tasty nut inside a fuzzy egg-shaped case, the *pignut hickory* with its bitter kernel-like nut, and the *white hickory* with its fine clear wood for furniture.

BIRCHES

PAPER BIRCH

The *paper birch,* also known as *canoe birch* and *white birch,* is a northern tree.

It is very abundant in the great forest region of Canada and the northern United States, where it is seen on the banks of lakes and rivers and is regarded as one of the most beautiful trees.

Every school-child knows that the bark of this tree was used in the building of canoes by the Indians and early settlers of North America, and everyone who has had the privilege of roaming through the American Northwoods will forever remember its chalky to creamy white bark that peels off in thin film-like layers.

OTHER BIRCHES

Besides the many different kinds of trees actually called birches, there are other members of the birch family called *hazelnuts, hop hornbeams, hornbeams,* and *alders.*

SHAG-BARK HICKORY

The *shag-bark* is the largest of the true *hickories.* It has highly prized wood, shaggy bark, and delicious nuts.

During all seasons of the year the trees may be recognized by the bark of the trunk, which has given the tree its name. The leaves grow in pairs on long stems, are shaped like spearheads, and have a fragrant odor when they are crushed. Its blossoms are yellow. Hickory wood makes good fuel. Bacon, hams and turkeys are often cured in hickory smoke.

Canoe Birch

The family of trees that has been given the overall name of the beech family is so large that to use it in talking about trees might mix us up. Actually, the *beech* family includes all the chestnut trees and all the oaks. So, to keep things straight in everyday talk about trees we usually separate chestnuts and oaks into families of their

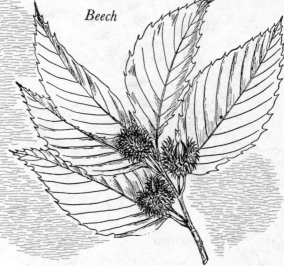

Beech

BEECHES

There is only one *beech* native to America. Its features are so striking and so different from other trees that it may be recognized very easily, and when once known will not be forgotten. One distinctive thing is present throughout the entire year and may be relied upon under all conditions of growth, namely, the close-fitting, and smooth bark, on which people often cut initials and other outline carvings.

The stiff leaves are also distinctive. The wood produced by the beech is by no means the best, but it is probably used more in the manufacture of different articles used in the household than any other wood. It also produces a nut that squirrels, bluejays, and many other animals and birds enjoy.

own and use beech mainly to describe the trees around the world that actually have beech in their name.

CHESTNUT

The *chestnut* is one of the best known and most valuable trees. It is not difficult to distinguish at any season of the year. The ashy-gray, deeply-furrowed bark on old chestnut trees is very plain.

In summer the leaves, which are about six to eight inches long, sharp-pointed, and notched, give us a good way of spotting the tree.

In the early part of May the chestnut tree bursts forth in cream-colored blossoms, and

191

becomes the most noticeable part of the landscape.

The nuts of the chestnut tree are prized highly by man and by many wild animals. The nuts are enclosed in a prickly bur,

Chestnut

which is nature's way of protecting them until ripe.

Altogether, there are five kinds of chestnut trees around the world. Four of these reach tree-size and one remains the size of a shrub.

OAKS

WHITE OAK

The *white oak* is the most important timber tree in eastern North America. Its wood is the most valuable of all the oaks. It is ashy-gray in color, close-grained, hard,

tough, and has a wide range of uses.

In summer the white oak can be told readily by its loose, scaly, grayish-white bark, and by its leaves. In winter this tree can be distinguished by its rather small reddish-brown and blunt-pointed buds. The

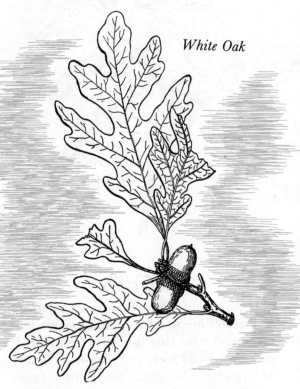

White Oak

swamp white oak has slender reddish to grayish twigs and dark loose-peeling flakes of bark on the branches; the *post oak* has greenish rusty twigs. The *bur oak* has corky winged projections on the bark of the small branches, and the cups of the acorns are fringed.

RED OAK

The *red oak* is one of the most distinctive of the oaks, and may be recognized by its large dull-green leaves. The bark on old

192

trunks has smooth and shiny plates between deep furrows.

The red oak is an important timber tree.
It surpasses other oaks in height, diameter,
and growth. It is the most highly prized of
all the American oaks introduced into
Europe, where it has been planted extensively in Belgium, England, and Germany
since 1740.

BLACK OAK

The name *black oak* calls attention to the
color of the outer bark on old trunks of
black oak trees, sometimes also called *yellow
oak* on account of the yellow *inner* bark which
is always present.

Before we had modern dyes the yellow
inner bark of black oak was used for yellow
dye.

The leaves of black oak probably vary
more widely in size and form than those
of any other oak. The normal leaves grow
to from 4 to 6 inches in length, but some
become 12 to 16 inches long.

In autumn the small acorns with the cup
covering one-half of the nut, and the scales
forming a loose fringe about the edge of the
cup, help us to tell this tree from other oaks.
The large buds, covered over with pale
hairs, set it apart in the winter.

OTHER OAKS

Other members of the oak family are the
*post oak, bur oak, chestnut oak, pin oak, laurel
oak,* and *live oak.*

ELMS

AMERICAN ELM

This attractive and graceful tree, the
American elm, may be recognized at all sea-

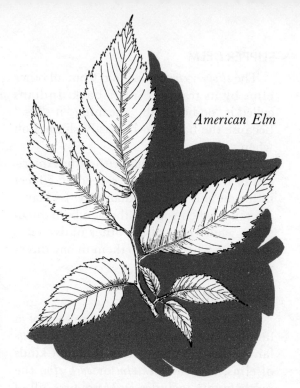

American Elm

sons of the year by its form. Its trunk separates a short distance from the ground to
form several branches. This often gives it
the shape of a slender vase. In winter it has
slender drooping reddish-brown twigs bearing small reddish-brown buds. In spring,
long before the leaves, the flowers come in
small drooping green clusters. The fruit,
which appears shortly after the flowers, has
a small seed, surrounded on all sides by a
tissue-like wing. The bark, brown and
rough, contains a fiber that the Indians
wove into rope. The wood is strong and
can be made into handles for garden tools
and axes. The leaves are oval-shaped, with
saw-toothed edges and have sharp points.

The long and slender twigs do not stand
out stiffly as those of other trees do. Instead, they dangle and sway with the
breezes. The elm makes a beautiful shade
tree, and will make a leafy archway if
planted on both sides of a road.

SLIPPERY ELM

The *slippery elm* can be told from all other elms by its fragrant inner bark. Indians called it "oo-hoosh-ah," meaning "it slips," because the bark can be easily slipped off when cut.

It is a smaller tree than either the American or the *rock elm,* rarely exceeding 50 feet in height and 2 feet in diameter. Its leaves are rough when you rub them in both directions, while those of the other native elms are rough when you rub them in one direction only.

OTHER ELMS

The elms are actually members of a family of trees and shrubs called the *nettle* family. Besides many other different kinds of elms, like the *rock elm* or *cork elm,* the nettle family includes *hackberry trees,* all of the *mulberry trees,* and the *Osage orange tree,* which is native to America and has a big orange-like fruit where its seeds are grown.

MAGNOLIAS

TULIP TREE

The *tulip tree* is one of the most stately and magnificent trees of the forests of eastern North America. It grows to a great size, and frequently reaches a height of 80 to 120 feet, and a diameter of 6 to 8 feet. One specimen was found in western North Carolina which was 16 feet thick. Many of these large trees are 300 to 350 years old.

The tulip tree can be recognized by its straight and clean trunk, with a very deep-furrowed bark and its broad blunt-pointed leaves.

In spring and early summer there are

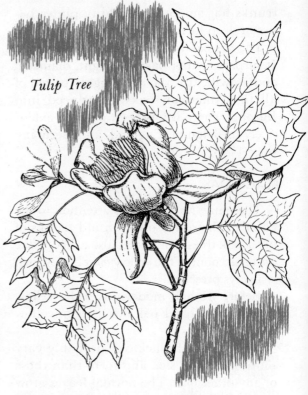

Tulip Tree

tulip-like flowers, and in fall and winter there is a cone-like fruit.

LAUREL

SASSAFRAS

The *sassafras,* which is one of the most interesting trees of the laurel family, was one of the first American plants which became widely known in Europe. The Indians told the early settlers about it. Roots of sassafras were a part of the first cargo ever shipped from Massachusetts.

The taste of the bark, roots, and wood, and the pleasant odor, tell the tree apart from any other. If one breaks off a brittle twig of green-barked sassafras, there is a pleasant odor immediately; and if one

194

chews it, the flavor of the inner bark is very delicious.

The leaves take on several forms. The oval form is commonest. In the mitten form the leaf has one large thumb-like projection, which may be either on the right or left side.

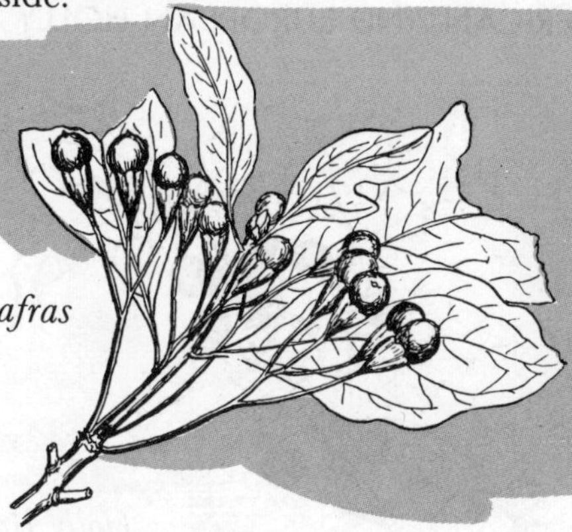

Sassafras

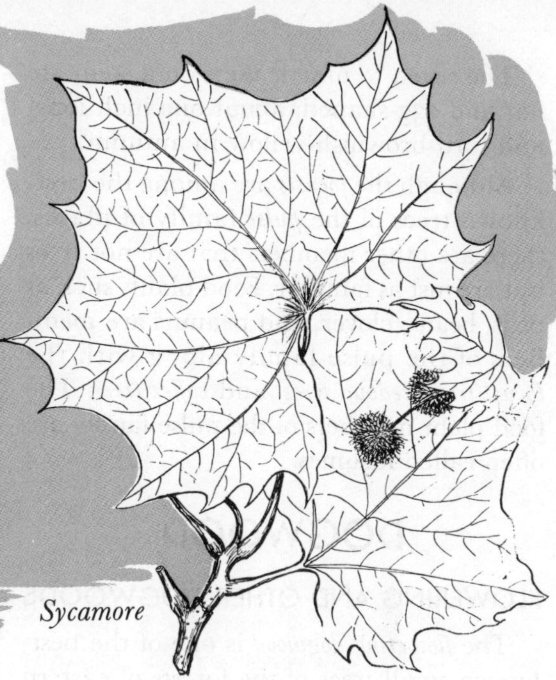

Sycamore

The fruit is a dark-blue berry which furnishes excellent food for birds.

Besides the sassafras, there are about 1,000 different members of the *laurel* family in the world. Many of them are shrubs instead of tall trees, growing like big bushes everywhere from the sides of northern mountains to green-covered hills in the tropics.

In ancient times the leaves of certain kinds of laurel trees were woven into wreaths and crowns and given to people in honor of great achievements.

In Europe, laurel trees are often called *bay trees*.

PLANE TREES

SYCAMORE

Sycamores may reach a height of over 150 feet and 10 feet in diameter. The bark, which peels off, is so unusual that it will never be forgotten if seen but once. It con-

sists of a crazy patchwork of white, green, yellow, gray, and brown. In winter, white is the predominating color.

The sycamore has large leaves somewhat like those of the maple, and ball-like fruit packed with fluffy seeds that come out when a bird pecks them.

Altogether there are six varieties of *plane tree*. All of them have nice broad leaves like the *sycamore*, which is sometimes called the *American plane tree* or *buttonwood*.

The *Oriental plane tree*, with a big, rounded top, is one of the trees often found in parks because it gives lots of cool shade.

PULSE TREES

BLACK LOCUST

At all seasons of the year the *black locust* may be identified by deeply furrowed dark-brown bark on the old trunks, and greenish to reddish-brown brittle twigs armed with short spikes.

The seven to nine leaflets on a stem are flat and egg-shaped, about one inch long, and turn brownish-yellow in autumn.

Although the *locusts* are among the best-known trees of the *pulse* family of plants, there are other members that are not trees but are just as familiar. Food plants such as peas, beans, clover, and peanuts are members of the pulse family along with the *locust trees, redbud trees,* and *coffee trees.* The food plant members of the pulse family are often called legumes.

DOGWOOD

FLOWERING AND OTHER DOGWOODS

The *flowering dogwood* is one of the best-known small trees of the forests of eastern North America. In spring this tree is often so covered with pretty white flowers that it appears like an enormous bouquet. In summer it has dense and deep green foliage, while in autumn it has small clusters of scarlet berries and dark red leaves.

Dogwood Blossoms

Besides the beautiful flowering dogwood there are forty other kinds of trees and shrubs in the dogwood family. Some of these trees are known as *gum trees.*

HOLLY

AMERICAN AND EUROPEAN HOLLY

Holly Branch

Many people are familiar with the leaves and fruit of the American or Christmas *holly,* but few know that they grow on trees.

The holly wreath is attractive and popular but unfortunately the method of collecting the branches is very destructive. In many instances the tops of trees are stripped completely, leaving nothing but bare trunk.

A similar holly that grows in Europe, and is called simply *European holly,* has been raised for decorations for so long that more than 150 distinct varieties, with different kinds of leaves and berries, have been produced.

MAPLES

SUGAR MAPLE

The *sugar maple* is one of the best known hardwood trees native to North America.

The brown bark on old trunks is roughened by shallow furrows, and the slender brown twigs are marked wtih pale dots.

The sugar maple produces great numbers of seeds. It is from the sweet sap of this tree that delicious maple sugar is made!

RED MAPLE

The *red maple* never forgets its name. At all seasons of the year some part of it is distinctly red. Early in spring red clusters of flowers appear on it. In summer there is a tinge of red on the leaves, and in autumn the whole tree stands out among its neighbors as a flaming torch of color.

In winter the red maple is bare of foliage but it has bright red twigs loaded heavily with winter buds. In winter it is often difficult to distinguish the red maple from the *silver maple*. The silver maple, however, lacks the red twigs, and if the twigs of the silver maple are broken they give off a sharp odor not found in the red maple.

In the United States alone there are 13 different kinds of maple trees. Beside the ones we have described, there are such other maples as the *ash-leaf maples* that are seen growing near river-bottoms, the *striped maples* in mountain forests, and the *mountain maples* clinging to bare rocky places high on mountainsides. One of the most common shade trees in many cities is the *Norway maple*.

Red Maple

The Beautiful Flowers

WHEN we talk about flowers, we usually mean flowers in bloom in a garden or field or even in a flower pot inside a house. That, certainly, is the most pleasant place to start with flowers: watching petals of brilliant colors or soft glowing warmth unfold and open to the brightness of the day, sending their lovely perfumed scents into the spring and summer air.

But that is actually the *middle* of the flower's life. Just a bit later it will send seeds into the ground to make new flowers. Then, as fall comes, the old flowers wither. Some die; others sleep until another spring and summer roll around.

So we shall begin our story of these beautiful plants, the flowering plants, not when they are in full bloom but when they are just seeds.

SEEDS ARE THE START

Just what happens to a seed when it is planted in the soil? How does it grow? Where does it get its food?

When you plant a seed, you really plant stored-up food, because the seed has within itself the energy (that is, the strength or force) for growth. When it is first placed in the soil, the seed takes in water equal to half its weight. As it begins to grow, the seed uses the food that is stored inside it. And the soil helps in the growth of the young seedling by supplying minerals and water.

As the seed grows, the roots develop. The stem and leaves break through the soil, and the young plant is soon able to take care of itself.

ROOT FOOD

How does the plant get this food from the soil? Tiny hairs, called root hairs, grow from the finest roots when they are beginning to sprout. These root hairs grow into the soil and take in food that has been dissolved in water. They have no holes or openings, so solids cannot enter. But liquid food can pass through the very thin tissue. From the root hair, the food is carried inside the plant.

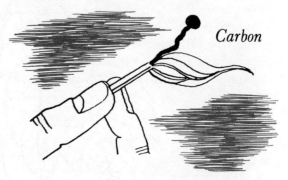

Carbon

Root hairs do not grow on the larger coarser roots, so the large roots do not take in food for the plant. It is their job to carry the food up into the plant after it has been taken in by the root hairs.

Plants get their food from the air as well as from the soil. If you burn a match, you will see that it turns black. This black product into which the match changes is carbon. Every part of the plant contains carbon, and this is very important to it.

LEAF LUNGS

Leaves supply the plant with carbon and oxygen by taking them in from gases in the air. Green plants build these elements into plant foods, and they can use them only in sunlight. The green color in a plant leaf is like a machine, and the power to keep the machine running comes from the sunlight. The plant makes starch and sugar from the carbon and other elements it takes in.

Besides starch and sugar, plants make juices, gums, woody fiber, oils, and proteins. Sometimes plants use their foods right away, and other times they store them. When the food is used, two tube-like passageways carry it to all parts of that plant. One tube carries the liquid up, and the other carries it down. Plants use some of these products as energy for growth. Other products are stored up in the seed, to be used later.

Where do plants come from? All plants grow from either a seed or a bud. Every plant that has a seed produces a flower, though it may not look like one. For instance, the ear and tassel bear the blossoms on a corn plant.

SEED SYSTEMS

Look at a flower closely. See the green leaves on the outside? These are the *sepals,* and they protected the flower while it was a bud. Next on the inside is a row of colored leaves or *petals.* The shapes and colors of the petals are very different in each kind of plant.

Arranged inside the petals are thread-like parts with a knob on the end of each. These slender, erect threads are called *stamens.* Do you see the fine powder on the knob of a stamen? These tiny specks are *pollen,* and without them there would be no

seeds. At the center of the flower and inside the circle of the stamens is the *pistil.* The swollen tip of the pistil is called the *stigma,* and the swollen base is the *ovary.* In the ovary are young seeds called *ovules.*

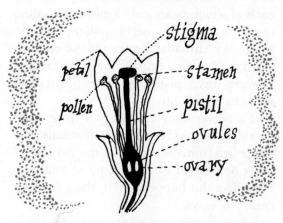

The flowers on some plants have within them all the parts they need to form a seed. That is, in certain plants these necessary parts, the stamens and pistils, are within one flower. Some of the other plants also have these two parts, but they are not con-

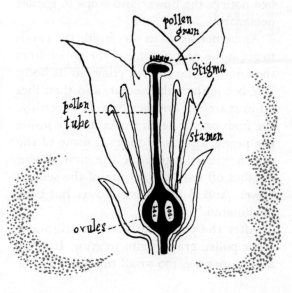

tained in one flower. Instead, the stamens are in one flower and the pistils in another, all on the same plants. For example, the tassel of a corn plant is a cluster of many flowers, each bearing only stamens. The ear of corn is also a cluster of many flowers, each of which bears only a pistil. The dust that falls from the tassel is pollen, and the long silky threads or silks on the ear are stigmas. There is a third kind of plant whose flowers have pistils on one plant and stamens on the other.

If a flower does not have all these parts necessary for producing seeds, it means that the pollen from one flower of the same kind must be carried to the stigma of another. How does this happen? Well, there are two common ways.

Sometimes the pollen from one flower is blown by the wind to the stigma of another. Sometimes bees carry pollen from one flower to another as they fly about in search of nectar, from which they make honey. Mother Nature has provided flowers with attractive colors and perfumes so that the bee notices the flower and stops to gather nectar from it.

As the bee works its way inside the petals to get at the nectar, some of the pollen from the knob on the stamen clings to its body. The bee gathers the nectar, and then flies off in search of another flower. When the bee finds one, it again works its way inside the petals and as it does so, some of the pollen picked up from the first flower brushes off onto the stigma of the second flower. And so this second flower has been "pollinated."

After the pollen falls on the stigma, a single pollen grain begins to grow. It forms a tiny opening, too small to see with your eye, all the way down through the stigma into the ovary. This tiny opening reaches down into the ovary, and a process known as "fertilization" takes place. Now this partly-formed seed grows and forms the seed such as you sow in your garden to form a new plant.

New plants may be grown from buds as well as from seeds. A bud may form a new plant in various ways. A branch bearing buds may be bent to the ground and covered with soil. This is called *layering*. Or the bud may be cut away from the branch and put in the soil to grow by itself. When the bud is cut away from the plant like this, it is called *cutting*. The third and last method is *budding*. Budding means that a bud is cut from the branch of one plant and is placed on the branch of another plant to grow.

Now that we have learned about the first part of the flower's life, the seed part, we can pass on to the flowers as we know them, blooming and beautiful. Here are some that you may see.

Knowing the Wild Flowers

Yellow Flowers

MEADOW BUTTERCUP

THE *meadow buttercup* grows in meadows and pastures and almost any place where it can get enough water. It blooms in the spring and early summer, and sometimes the bright yellow flowers make the fields look like a great golden sea. Each plant has several flowers and each flower has five glossy yellow petals that open out almost flat.

The leaves of the meadow buttercup are dark green and are covered with soft hairs. Each leaf is divided into three, five, or seven parts, and these parts are deeply cut around the edges. The leaves have short stalks which clasp the stem where they are attached to it. The stem of the plant is round and hollow, and is usually slightly hairy. The plant grows from one to two feet high.

DANDELION

The *dandelion* is one of the first wild flowers you will find in the spring, and one of the last you will see in the autumn. It blooms almost every month in the year, and often appears in sunny places even when there is snow on the ground.

Each flower-head grows singly at the end of a long green stalk. The stalks are hollow, and when they are broken a white milky juice oozes out. Just below the flower-head is a green cup made of narrow pointed leaves. Some of these leaves curve backward toward the stalk. At night, or in rainy weather, the leaves of the green cup fold over and cover the yellow flowers.

When the flowers have withered, the round disk is covered with tiny seeds—each seed in a slender stalk which has a beautiful tuft of short white hairs at its tip. This ball of hairy down is one of the most beauti-

ful things in the flower-world. If you blow upon it, the seeds will be carried far away by the wind.

The leaves of the dandelion are smooth and green. The edges are cut into large teeth which are said to resemble the teeth of a lion. This is how the plant gets its name —*dent de lion* being French for lion's tooth.

GOLDENROD

The pretty *goldenrod* grows nearly everywhere, and in the late summer and autumn its flowers often make the fields and pastures yellow.

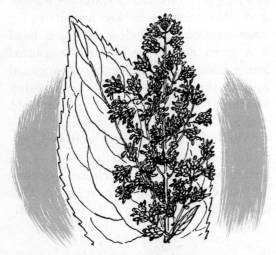

Each goldenrod plant has many heads of yellow flowers arranged in clusters at the top of the branching stem. There are about ten flowers in each head.

Surrounding each head of flowers is a large number of very small green pointed leaves. Their edges overlap and they form a cup in which the flower-head is placed. Each head has a short stalk, and there is often a leaf where the stalk joins the stem.

There are many different kinds of goldenrod and they have leaves of different shapes.

The edges of the leaves usually have sharp teeth. If you rub the upper side of a leaf you will often find it very rough.

The stems of the goldenrod are sometimes rough and hairy and have tiny furrows running up from the base.

One kind of goldenrod that grows in the woods has white flowers, and is sometimes called *silver-rod,* but all of the others have yellow flowers.

EVENING PRIMROSE

One tall wild plant that grows nearly everywhere, along roadsides and in waste places, is the *evening primrose.* It is so named because the flowers usually unfold toward evening and wither on the following day. Several flowers grow together near the top of the plant, and where each flower-stalk joins the stem, a leaf is also attached. The blossoms are pale yellow in color and are large and showy.

Each flower has four broad yellow petals, and each petal has a broad notch in its outer edge.

The flower appears to have a long stalk, but if you split this stalk open you will find that it is hollow, and in the center is a green thread. If you follow this green thread down to its lower end you will find that it is attached to a seed holder.

The leaves of the evening primrose are coarse and not very pretty. They usually have no stalks, and the edges are slightly toothed. The whole plant is often covered with coarse hairs, which are sometimes sticky and catch the dust.

BLACK-EYED SUSAN

The *black-eyed Susan* has large yellow daisy flowers and is often found in fields and meadows.

There is usually one large head of flowers at the top of the plant. The flowers on the outside of the head are much different from those in the center.

The center of the flower-head is shaped like a thimble. The purple or brown flowers which form this thimble are so small that they do not look much like flowers. But by looking closely you may see that each of these tiny flowers has a brown tube with five small teeth at the top.

The plant is called the black-eyed Susan because yellow ray-flowers surrounding the head of dark tube-flowers make us think of a black eye fringed by lashes. Just below the flower-head, and attached to the end of the stem, are several very small leaves which are pressed close against the yellow rays.

Most of the leaves of the black-eyed Susan are near the base of the plant. These have slender stalks, but the small leaves near the top of the plant have no stalks. The edges of the leaves are usually smooth, but sometimes they have blunt teeth. The whole plant is rough and hairy.

TANSY

The *tansy* is found growing in dense patches along roadsides and on the borders of old fields and yards. It is a tall, bushy plant, sometimes two or three feet high, and it flowers in late summer and autumn.

The tansy plant has a green stem rising stiff and straight from the root, and this stem branches toward the top into three or four forks. Each of these forks divides again into several smaller branches, and at the end of each of these smaller branches is a yellow flower-head which looks somewhat like a button.

If you pull one of the flower-heads to pieces you will find that it is made up of very many yellow tubes, each having a little green holder at its base. Each yellow tube is really a flower, and they are attached to a round disk. At the back of this disk is a double row of small, pointed, green leaves which form a cup behind the yellow heads.

The leaves of the tansy are dark green and fernlike. They are shaped somewhat

the place where it is attached. In this tube is a drop of nectar, and that is why bees so often visit these flowers.

Each flower is on a slender hairy stalk which is attached to the main stem just above a leaf. There may be as many as five flowers on a single plant. The leaves are rounded.

YELLOW LADY'S SLIPPER

like a feather, and the parts into which they are divided are toothed around the edges. The whole plant has a bitter taste and a spicy odor. The odor is more noticeable when the stalks or leaves are crushed.

EARLY YELLOW VIOLET

The *yellow violet* is found on woody banks and in swampy places early in the spring. If you pull the flower to pieces you will see that it is much like other violets.

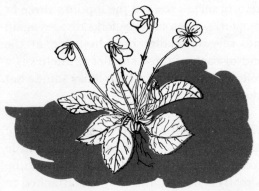

In the parts where these flowers are found many people know them so well that they call them by their scientific name, which means *Venus' Shoe*. From Venus' Shoe we have *lady's slipper*.

The two yellow kinds—that is, the smaller and larger yellow lady's slipper — are common, the last being found chiefly in the woods, and the smaller one is usually a plant of the bogs and swamps.

Sticking out, one on either side, are longish, narrow and twisted brown curls, each of which is a petal. The third petal is transformed to make the "slipper" or inflated sac of the flower. This is about two inches long and open at the top.

Each flower has five yellow petals with tiny purple or brown lines on them. The two upper petals are alike, and the two side petals are like each other, but the large lower petal is swollen into a short tube near

The lady's slipper is found under evergreens and among withered leaves that lie under birch, beech, poplar, and maple. The time of flowering for both varieties is early in the summer.

White Flowers

FALSE LILY-OF-THE-VALLEY

THIS plant does not look like the *lily-of-the-valley,* but we call it *false-lily-of-the-valley* because it is closely related to the true. It is found very commonly growing at the bases of trees and in wet places in the woods.

The tiny flowers of the false lily-of-the-valley are white but are not shaped like those of the real lily-of-the-valley. Each flower has four white parts which spread flat out. Standing straight up in the center of the

flower is the seed-holder. It is shaped somewhat like a bottle. Each tiny blossom has a short stalk of its own which is attached to the main stalk.

You can easily learn to recognize the false lily-of-the-valley because it usually has two leaves attached on opposite sides of the stem, one slightly above the other.

If in the summer or autumn you visit a place where you have seen the false lily-of-the-valley blooming in the spring, you will find that each seed-holder has become a round pale red berry, speckled all over.

COMMON CHICKWEED

The *common chickweed* is found almost everywhere. It grows in fields and gardens and in waste ground, and you may find its flowers and green leaves nearly every month in the year. It is a feeble creeping plant and forms green masses near the ground. It does not grow well in dry stony places. But in untidy gardens where there is good soil, the plants are larger and have many white flowers and green leaves.

The white flowers are small, and each has five tiny petals which are deeply notched at their outer edges.

Each flower grows at the end of a stalk which rises between a leaf and the main stem. If you look at the stem closely, you will see a line of fine hairs running down one side, and if you break the stem you will find that there is a green thread inside which is more difficult to break than the soft green covering. The stems are usually branched.

The chickweed leaves are oval in shape, and they have smooth edges. They grow in pairs and are attached to the stem by short stalks. The birds and chickens like to eat the fresh green leaves of the plant, as well as the tiny brown seeds.

WAKE-ROBIN OR TRILLIUM

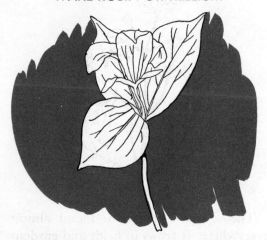

This well-known plant is found growing in woods and fields where the ground is moist. Sometimes it is so abundant that you can gather all that you can hold in your arms, but often you will find a single plant growing alone. The flowers are large and beautiful, and are white, red, or pink in color.

Each flower has three large petals which are pointed at the tips and there are many veins running from the base to the tip of each petal.

You can easily know a *wake-robin* when you see it because of the leaves. Each plant always has three leaves, and these are arranged in a ring or circle around the stem just beneath the large flower. Each leaf is

broad and rounded with a pointed tip, and usually has no stalk. The edges are smooth, and numerous veins may be seen running all through the leaf.

WHITE WATER-LILY

Instead of growing on the land as most plants do, the *white water-lily* chooses its home in ponds and small lakes. It is our prettiest water-loving flower, as it sits floating on the surface of the water among its broad green leaves. The flowers are prettier growing, but if you can get one you will find that it is very interesting to study.

In the center is the large round green seed-vessel. It has many small openings through which the seeds come out when they are ripe. You may not be able to find the seeds, for they are always under the surface of the water. Each seed is in a tiny bag which opens at the top.

Hidden along with the seeds are very small sacks containing nectar with a sweet scent. This is why the bees visit the flowers so often.

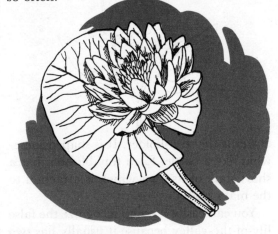

The stem of the white water-lily is round and hollow and is not strong enough to hold the flower straight up. Each plant has several leaves which rest on the surface of the water just as the flowers do. The leaves are like flat plates, and are purple on their under sides. The leaf-stalk is attached at about the center of the leaf.

WILD STRAWBERRY

The *wild strawberry* is common in fields and meadows, along roadsides, and in woods and fence-corners. This pretty plant is related to the wild rose, and has white flowers arranged in loose clusters.

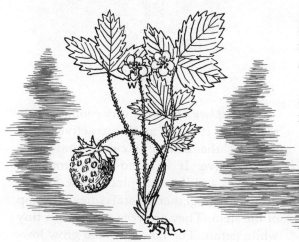

The flower has five white petals, which are broader and often notched at the outer edge.

When the flower has withered, the cup below the seeds in the center begins to grow, and swells into a beautiful bright red berry. You can see the tiny yellow seeds still clinging to the juicy berry.

The dark green leaves of the wild strawberry are beautiful. They are slightly crinkled, and the edges are cut into large teeth with soft hairs upon them.

The plant sends out long green shoots which lie close to the ground. Wherever a tuft of leaves rises from one of these shoots a little cluster of white roots grows down into the ground, and these help to keep the plant steady.

YARROW OR MILFOIL

In pastures, fields, and lawns you will find the *milfoil* growing in dense patches. The straight stiff stem grows about a foot or two high and branches at the top. The plant blooms in summer and autumn.

The flowers of the milfoil resemble small daisies, and there are a dozen or more growing together at the top of the main stem. Each daisy flower has a slender, hairy stalk of its own.

Underneath the small flower-head stands a circle of tiny green pointed leaves. These fit closely against each other and form a cup

which protects the tiny head while the flowers are in bud.

The leaves of the milfoil are very pretty. They are very finely cut so as to look like a plume or a very fine fern leaf. They are hairy, and if you crush them they will give a strong and somewhat unpleasant odor. Most of the leaves are near the ground, but there are a few on the upright stem which bears the cluster of flower-heads.

INDIAN PIPE

You can never mistake the *Indian pipe,* for it is unlike any other plant. The whole plant is white, including the flowers, stem, and leaves. It is usually found in the woods near the base of trees.

The single stem rises about six inches above the ground and bends over at the top. At the end is a large white nodding flower. Scattered along the stem are several thin scale-like leaves. These tiny leaves are pointed at the tips and have no stalks. They are almost transparent.

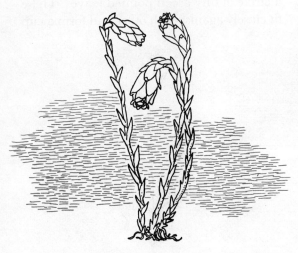

When the petals have withered and fallen off, the seed-holder stands straight up. If you break it open you will find that it is divided into four or five parts inside, and each part is filled with tiny seeds.

When the plant is old, it is no longer

white and beautiful, but appears black and dried. If you pull it up you will find at the base a mass of tangled fibers.

SHEPHERD'S PURSE

The *shepherd's purse* is a very common little plant, but it is not at all attractive, for it has not the beautiful colors that most flowers have. It is found all summer by roadsides and in waste places. The flowers grow close together on stalks near the top of the stem. They are very small, with tiny white petals. The flowers which grow lowest on the stem open first, and the green buds are in a cluster at the tip.

After the flower has withered, the seed-holder, which still clings to the end of the stalk, grows larger. It looks like a small green heart with a hard knot in the center. You will easily recognize the shepherd's purse by these seed-holders which are far more noticeable than the flowers.

The plant has two kinds of leaves. Those near the ground have short stalks and are long and narrow, and their edges are deeply cut, nearly to the center vein.

The leaves which grow further up the flower-stem are shaped like the head of an arrow, and their bases clasp the stem closely.

MAY APPLE

This is one of the wild plants that you can easily learn to know. It grows in the woods and on shady banks and sometimes in open fields. Many plants usually grow near together, their broad leaves almost covering the ground. The leaves are not near the ground, but are often a foot or more above it.

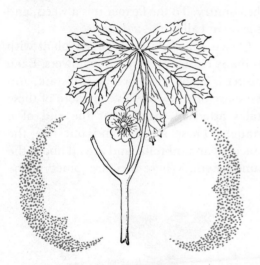

The *May apple* leaves are rounded, and the edges are deeply cut.

You may find two kinds of plants. One kind has just one large leaf, with the stout hollow stalk attached to the middle of the leaf on the under side. This plant bears no flowers.

The other kind of plant has the stem forked a little more than halfway up from the ground, and each fork bears a large one-sided leaf. Where the stem forks you will find a large white showy flower placed on a long slender curved stalk.

The flower has six or more large white petals, and each petal is hollowed so that the flower is like a deep saucer. In the center of the flower is the fat green seedholder.

After the flower has withered, the seedholder grows into a yellow fleshy egg-shaped May apple, with many seeds inside. It is not really an apple. It is more like a tomato, and it may be eaten.

FIELD DAISY

You will find the flowers of the *field daisy* from summer until the autumn, sometimes making the fields a mass of white. It is a pretty plant, but the farmer calls it a weed because it spreads rapidly in fields and pastures and keeps the grass from growing.

The flower-heads are large and one large flower-head grows at the end of each branch of the plant. At the top of the green flower-stalk is a double ring of green pointed leaves which will be seen as you turn the flower over. When the flowers are in bud, the head looks like a thick green button with a yellow spot in the middle, as these small

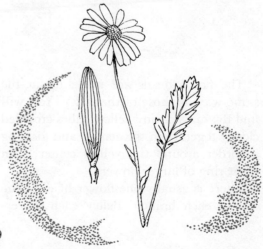

green leaves are tightly folded in a circle around the flat yellow center.

The leaves of the field daisy are feather-shaped, with their edges cut up into many blunt points. They usually have no stalks but spring from the main stem. The stem is tall and stiff and has many ridges running from the top to the bottom.

MAYWEED

Mayweed may be found in meadows and waste places, and along roadsides, often forming large patches. It is much branched and bushy and often grows close to the ground, but sometimes it is a foot or more high. The stems are tough and quite smooth, with fine ridges running up them.

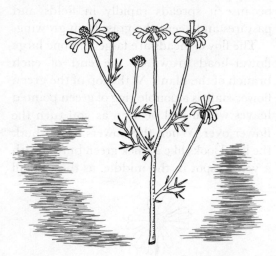

The flower-heads are made up in the same way as those of the daisy. You will find the mass of tiny yellow tubes crowded closely together in the center, and forming a border around this yellow center is an outer ring of larger flowers.

There is usually one flower-head at the end of each branch. Below each flower-

head is a double ring of small green leaves which fit closely together to form a cup. The tips of these leaves are sometimes tinged with pink.

The leaves of the mayweed are divided into very narrow parts. They are somewhat feathery and very beautiful. If you pick one of these leaves and crush it you will find that it has a strong disagreeable odor.

QUEEN ANNE'S LACE

Queen Anne's lace is a very common plant that grows in fields and pastures, in waste places, and along roadsides in most parts of the country. To the farmer it is a weed, and it is often called the *wild carrot*.

Queen Anne's lace is a pretty plant with its many clusters of tiny white flowers. Each cluster is at the end of a long stiff stalk, and there are often twenty-five or more of these stalks attached together at the end of a branch. These stalks stand out like the braces of an umbrella, and are all about the same length. Where they are joined to the

end of the branch there are several very narrow, deeply cut leaves with tapering tips.

Each flower is very small. There are five white petals, but they are not all the same size. One is much larger than the others. The tips of the petals are folded over, and are sometimes tinged with pink.

The seed-holder is beneath the petals, and has ridges upon it. When it grows to its full size the ridges are covered with tiny prickles. These prickles stick tightly to your clothing, and help to scatter the seeds. When the flowers have all withered, the clusters on the outside fold over toward the center, and all together form a little cup which looks somewhat like a bird's nest.

The leaves of the Queen Anne's lace are cut up into many very narrow parts. There are many leaves close to the ground and they are covered with hairs.

POKE WEED

One of the best places to find *poke weed* growing is where the woods have been burned over by fire, but you will also find it by the fences along the roads in the country. Maybe, too, in other places, but not nearly so often. You cannot miss it, for it may grow to be ten feet high. It has a stout branching stem, pithy inside. The leaves are narrow and pointed at both ends, and the small flowers, in bunches, do not specially catch your eye in the summer. You will notice them more when their places are taken by the rather large green berries, and when nearly all the parts of the plant begin to turn a bright red late in the summer. The long clusters of berries are then very dark red and very juicy. You will see the robins, cat-birds, brown-thrashers, and other birds feeding on them. Some people get the berries to make red ink with, others gather and eat the tender shoots in the spring after boiling them. The root is poisonous and should never be eaten by anyone.

Do you wonder why the poke weed is nearly all red when its berries are ripe at the end of the summer — stem, leaves, berries, and all? Now, a big bush, such as a poke weed, when bright red in the early fall, can be seen much more easily by the birds than a green one; and when it is red the birds know that its fine, juicy berries are ripe and ready to eat. Many birds flock to the poke weed bushes to feed on the berries, of which they are so fond. When they have eaten all they can these birds fly away to many different places; and if you could find their droppings, you would be sure to find poke weed seeds in them. These seeds are pretty sure to sprout, and poke weed bushes grow up from them, and so more plants of the kind grow up in a great many places.

Pink and Pink-Purple Flowers

WILD PINK

The *wild pink,* with its beautiful bright flowers, is found very commonly in rocky woods in the springtime. The plant spreads out on the ground and often forms a small mat. There are usually several flowers growing together at the end of each branch, but only one or two unfold at the same time.

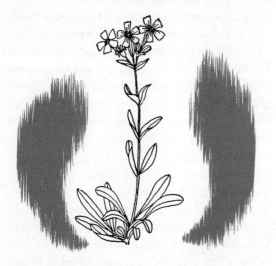

Each flower has five bright pink petals which spread flat out. They are rounded at the tips and sometimes notched. Between the petals you may see five small green points. These are the teeth of the calyx.

The petals are not attached near the top of the calyx as in many flowers, but if you split the calyx-tube open you will see that the petals are very narrow at the bottom and attached to a slender green stalk which extends up into the middle of the calyx-tube.

You may not see the stamens until you have pulled off the petals of the flower. The yellow stamen-heads are very small and are attached to slender stalks. In the very center of the flower is the long seed-holder. It is just above the place where the petals and stamens are attached.

The leaves of the wild pink are arranged in pairs on opposite sides of the stem. Their edges are smooth. The plant is covered with sticky hairs.

WILD GERANIUM

The *wild geranium* is one of the most beautiful wild flowers. In the late spring it often covers the wooded fields with its delicate pink or lavender blossoms. It is related to the geranium which is cultivated in gardens and as a house plant.

The flower has five large thin petals. The outer edge of each petal is notched and there are darker-colored veins running from the base to the outer edge.

The petals soon wither and fall off, and the long spike of the seed-holder, with a

small star at the end, can be seen extending out from among the sepals. This spike has five seeds clustered around its base, and when the seeds are ripe the spike splits into five thin strips. Each strip curls. Then the seeds are blown away by the wind.

The flowers of the wild geranium grow few together toward the top of the plant. Each flower has a slender stalk of its own.

The leaves are very pretty. Each is shaped like a hand with the fingers spread out. These five parts or fingers are deeply notched all around the edges. Some leaves grow from the ground and have long stalks, while those higher up on the plant have very short stalks. Both the stem and the leaves are covered with long white hairs.

singly at the ends of tiny stalks. The five petals are beautiful pale pink or purple with darker-colored veins. Each petal is narrow at the base, and the edges do not meet closely where the petals are attached.

The mallow has pretty rounded dark-green leaves with wavy edges. Each leaf has a short stalk. If you pull up the plant you will find it has a long straight root like a carrot running down into the ground, with several tiny white roots attached to it.

FIREWEED

This plant is found abundantly in fields, especially in places that have been newly cleared and burned over. For this reason it

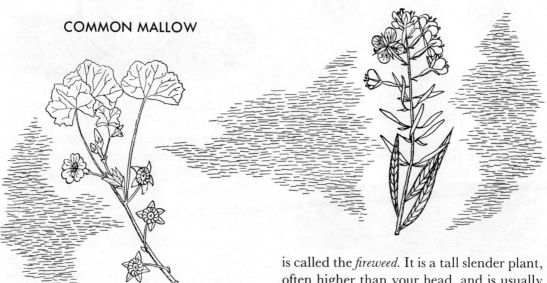

COMMON MALLOW

The *common mallow* is a spreading plant which grows close to the ground and may be found by roadsides and in waste places throughout the summer and autumn. It is often called a weed.

The flowers are rather small and grow

is called the *fireweed*. It is a tall slender plant, often higher than your head, and is usually branched at the top.

The fireweed has rather small purple or pale-pink flowers with four petals, each of which has a V-shaped notch in its outer edge.

The flowers grow in clusters near the top of the stem, and those lowest down open first. As the stem grows longer, those nearer the top unfold, while the ones below wither.

The leaves of the fireweed are oval with pointed tips and sharply toothed edges. The stem of the plant is quite smooth, and is red on the side that gets the most sunshine.

TRAILING ARBUTUS

The *trailing arbutus* is a favorite flower of early spring because it is so fragrant and because the blossoms do not wither for so long after they are gathered. The plant often grows in large patches in sandy or rocky woods, especially under evergreen trees.

The leaves of the trailing arbutus are thick and remain green throughout the winter. They have smooth edges and are rounded at the outer end, with a very short point at the tip. Each leaf has a short hairy stalk. The stem of the plant grows from ten to fifteen inches long and creeps along the ground. It is covered with short brown hairs.

PITCHER PLANT

Unless someone had already told you why these strange plants are called *pitcher plants,* you might think their beautiful flowers were shaped something like a pitcher. But no. It is their curiously shaped leaves that tell the story.

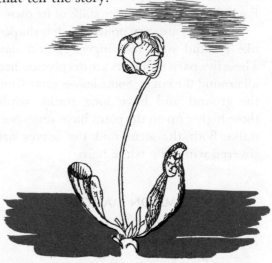

In some places these plants may be seen growing in plenty; in others, where in the past they were common, there are none. People picked too many of them on account of their showy flowers and curious leaves.

The places where pitcher plants grow are in boggy marshes, skirted by different kinds of trees or under the shade of still other water-loving trees, as they grow in some big mire or mossy swamp. Where the plants are to be found, you will meet with them in all their glory, generally growing a few in one place, or single plants standing far apart from the others. The scene is one that you are not likely to forget; everything about the place is most beautiful, and is lovely in all kinds of weather.

The pitcher plant has a big nodding

flower fully two inches across and of a deep purple color, sometimes with a reddish, pinkish, or even a greenish tinge. It blooms at the top of a stout straight green stem, which may be from one to two feet tall. The petals lap over each other, and there are five of them.

The curiously formed leaves, from four to ten inches long, are hollow and shaped like little trumpets, with the stem at the mouthpiece end, bending inward, to be attached to the base of the plant. There may be a dozen or more of these strange leaves, and they grow about the stem in a circle, with their open ends upward. Each perfect leaf is winged, and the whole is beautifully colored, being of various shades of green, streaked and lined with purple. Generally, each perfect leaf is nearly full of water, and in it you will find many different kinds of little insects. This plant is most common in the eastern United States.

Blue and Blue-Purple Flowers

BITTERSWEET

THE *bittersweet* is a common wild plant that is found in moist places and in thickets climbing on banks and walls and among the bushes. The stem of the plant often twines around other plants. It is branched and is sometimes covered with fine hairs.

There are several flowers near together, but only two or three are open at the same time. In the center of each flower is a yellow cone. Coming out through the top of this yellow cone is the green top of the seed-holder.

The five blue petals form a ring around the base of the yellow cone. They are pointed, and lie flat out. There are two yellow spots on each petal near the place where it is attached. If you try to pull off a petal you will find that the five petals are joined together at the base.

Even when the flowers are in bloom you may find upon the plant bright red or orange berries which are smooth and shining, and very pretty. These are the ripe seed-holders of flowers that have withered and fallen off.

GROUND IVY

The *ground ivy* bears little resemblance to the common ivy that you know so well. It is a creeping plant with a square stem which is very hairy and is usually tinged with pink. It is common along roadsides and in waste places, and blooms all summer.

215

The flowers have no stalks, they grow in circles close to the stem where the leaves spring from it. There are usually six or more flowers in a circle.

Each flower is a blue or purple tube prettily divided at the mouth into two rounded lips. The lower lip is marked with white and dark purple blotches.

From each side of the stem, close among the flowers, two leaves grow on short stalks. These leaves are round and their edges are beautifully scalloped. Each leaf is covered with a network of veins and is sometimes hairy on both sides, as well as around the edge.

The circles of leaves and flowers grow at intervals all the way up the stem, with a few inches between each circle. The flowers in the lower circle open first.

THISTLE

The *thistle* is a very common plant and is found almost everywhere that plants can grow. The stem of the thistle is stiff, and stands straight up. It is sometimes white and wooly.

The flowers are purple and grow in a dense head, forty or fifty of them packed closely together. If you pull one of these heads to pieces you will find that each flower is a tiny purple tube with five small teeth at the top. The base of each tube is surrounded by a covering of white down.

When the seeds have fully formed, and the flowers have withered and fallen off, the flower-head will appear like a ball of white wool. If you blow upon this ball, the tiny seeds with their numerous white hairs will be carried away in the breeze.

Just outside and below the flower-head are dozens of tiny narrow green leaves, close together. Each leaf ends in a sharp point, and it is this prickly green covering that makes the flowers difficult to gather.

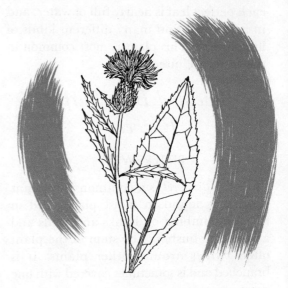

The leaves of the thistle have very sharp spines on their edges. They are dark green and are thinly covered with gray down. The young leaves are white and wooly when they first unfold.

WILD ASTER

You can scarcely go out into the fields in the late summer or autumn without finding the beautiful flowers of the *wild aster*. The fields are often blue or white with these daisy-like blossoms. The flowers grow on short stalks which branch from the upper part of the main stem.

Each flower-head is made up of many tiny flowers and these are of two kinds. In the center is a crowded mass of tiny tube-flowers which are evenly notched around the mouth. They are yellow or purplish in color. Outside these tube-flowers is arranged

a ring of larger flowers. Each of these larger flowers has a short tube which spreads out into a broad strap at one side. These blue or white straps stand out like a frill around the center bouquet of tube-flowers. Each flower-head is placed in a green cup made up of several rows of small green pointed leaves laid closely one above another like the scales of a fish.

After the flowers have withered and fallen off, the seeds still cling to the end of the stalk, and each seed is winged with a tuft of dingy white cotton down, as in the thistle. When the seeds are ripe the wind blows them away from the plant.

There are many different kinds of asters. Some have broad leaves with toothed edges, while others have narrow leaves with smooth edges. Sometimes the leaves are stalked, and sometimes there are no stalks. The flowers are usually blue, purple, lavender, or white.

BLUE FLAG

The *blue flag*, with its iris flowers and sword-like leaves, is found in summer by the side of ditches, marshes, and ponds. The flowers are large and showy, and grow one or two together at the top of the stalk.

Rising in the center of the flower you will see what you may think are three pale-blue petals with fringed ends which curl upward. These are really the three branches of the slender column which rises from the center of the seed-holder. The seed-holder is below the flower-tube. It becomes very large after the flower has withered, and bursts into

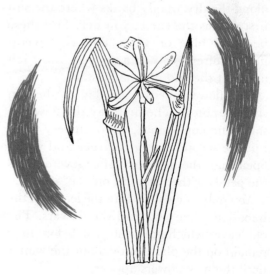

217

three parts showing the rows of dark brown seeds tightly packed together inside.

The smooth pale green leaves are sword-shaped, with long lines running from base to tip.

HEPATICA

BLUE VIOLET

The *blue violet* begins to bloom early in spring. There are many kinds of blue violets, and one or more of them may be found in woods and pastures and along the banks of streams. Sometimes there are so many together that they form a great mass of blue.

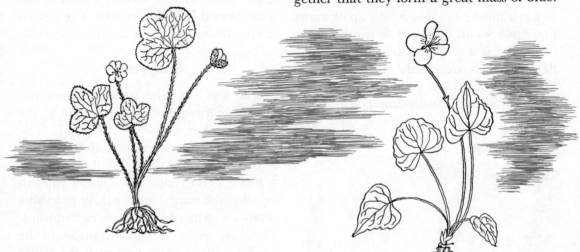

The *hepatica* may be the very first flower you will find in the woods in spring. Just after the snow is gone, if you look carefully along the dry woody banks where the sun first warms the earth, you may find these beautiful blue or white flowers. Several flowers often grow in a cluster, and each one is at the end of a hairy stalk.

The flower opens each day as the sun shines upon it. The first day the flower is small and cup-shaped, not open very wide, but the second day it is larger and wider open than the first day. After several days the petals wither and fall off.

You may not always find the leaves of the hepatica when you find the flowers. The old leaves which grew the year before may remain on the plant throughout the winter until the new flowers appear.

The leaves of the blue violet are usually heartshaped with toothed edges, but sometimes they are cut up into many lobes. Sometimes the leaves have long stalks, but often the stalks are very short.

You may also find white violets with blue veins. These are usually smaller than the blue violet.

FORGET-ME-NOT

Most people know the dainty, pale-blue flowers of the *forget-me-not*. The plant is found growing in ditches and in wet places by the sides of brooks, and sometimes it is cultivated in flower-gardens, where it forms great mats of tiny blue flowers. It is a straggling, slender plant, sometimes a foot high.

Each flower has five small rounded blue petals which lie almost flat open like a wheel, and in the center is a bright yellow eye.

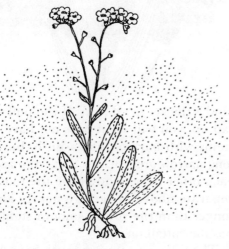

Each flower has a short stalk and these stalks are arranged along the stems above the leaves. The flowers lowest on the stem blossom first, and the pink buds are always at the very top of the branch. The top of the stem is often curved over until the buds are ready to open.

The dark-green, hairy leaves of the forget-me-not are long and narrow, with blue points and smooth edges. They have no stalks, but often clasp the stem. They are very smooth and glossy.

The slender stem is four-sided and hairy, and it creeps along the mud before it rises to bear the leaves and flowers.

FRINGED GENTIAN

One of the most beautiful flowers that bloom in the later summer and autumn is the *fringed gentian*. You will find the bright blue blossoms in moist woods and meadows and in marshy places. There is usually one large flower at the end of each branch.

The flower has a large tube which spreads out at the top into four lobes, and these lobes are fringed all around with beautiful blue threads. This is why it is called fringed gentian. The four stamens are inside the tube, and their white stalks are attached to the corolla near the bottom of the flower. In the center of the tube is the long seed-holder with a large knob at the top. This knob often stands up higher than the stamen-heads. Outside the corolla is the green calyx-tube with four pointed lobes which reach almost up to the fringed lobes.

The stem of the fringed gentian is round and smooth and grows from one to two feet high. It has several branches which are usually curved before the flowers open.

The leaves are placed opposite each other in pairs. They are pointed at the tips, but are much broader toward the base.

Before the flower unfolds the lobes of the corolla are folded around each other very tightly, and the fringes make the bud look like a little brush. If you pick a flower the corolla-lobes will soon fold up, and will never open again as those of some flowers do.

219

JACK-IN-THE-PULPIT

When you walk in the woods in the springtime the *Jack-in-the-pulpit* is one of the interesting plants that you will find.

You will perhaps notice first the broad green sheath with its purple stripes. It is split down one side and has a pointed flap which projects over the opening of the tube.

When you turn back the flap and look inside you will see a pencil-like spike standing straight up in the middle. This spike is green or sometimes purple and is rounded at the tip.

If you fold back the edges of the tube where it is slit down on the side, you will find at the bottom of the spike a dense cluster of tiny green flowers.

If you pull up a Jack-in-the-pulpit you will find that it has a turnip-like root, and for this reason the plant is sometimes called the *Indian turnip*. There are several thread-like roots extending from the main root.

CATTAILS

Cattails are found in marshes all over the United States.

There are two kinds of cattails. It is not very hard to tell them apart, for the leaves in one are very long and narrow, while the part you call the "tail" is much slimmer; and there are other differences. This kind we call the narrow-leaved cattail. The other kind is thicker in all ways. If you pull a cattail up, you will see it does not have hard stems with bark on like a bush, but only long narrow green leaves that wrap around each other below and above the root, but separate above. They are nearly always longer than the round smooth stem that has the cattail on.

These leaves commence to show themselves very early in the spring, being very beautiful and green as they sprout up in the marsh among the old dead cattail leaves of the summer before. Along in August and September, when hundreds of other plants have bloomed and are gone, the fine big brown cattails are seen waving in the wind among their long and narrow leaves. Still later, they swell and burst like puffs of yellowish cotton. These carry the seed, and are blown far and wide by the fall breezes, to land in other marshes and swamps, thus producing cattails where there were none.

Cattail flowers are very simple and of two kinds—the tail being made up of the seed-producing flowers, while the light-colored part above supplies the pollen. If you take a cattail in the fall and tap on the stem below it, you will see that the pollen falls from the flowers of the spike above it, and dusts over the big brown part that is waiting to receive it.

The Important Job of Saving our Natural Resources

From THE FIRST BOOK OF CONSERVATION
By F. C. Smith

THOUSANDS of kinds of plants, insects, birds, fish, reptiles, and animals, and over two billion human beings inhabit this earth. Each kind is in many ways different from every other kind. Yet they are all living things and they all depend on the work of other living things in order to stay alive. Every single one takes something from other living things and from some non-living things, too. And every single one gives something, also.

THE GIVE AND TAKE OF GROWING THINGS

All growing green plants take minerals from the soil. Many of these minerals actually came to the soil from decayed plants and animals. For when wild plants and animals die, they give something back to the earth.

Without green plants nothing else could survive. People can build great cities but they cannot use nature's raw materials to make their own food inside their bodies. Only green plants can do this. They make not only their own food but food for every other living thing on earth. Many forms of life, like cattle and rabbits, are plant-eaters. Others, like foxes and hawks, eat the flesh of plant-eaters. People depend on the flesh of plant-eaters for meat.

Plants also drop leaves, which make a sponge-like surface on the ground. This soaks up rain water which might otherwise run off. Roots also help hold the soil so that it does not wash away in heavy rains.

There is a giving and taking also between green plants and some of the non-green plants called "fungi" and "bacteria." In taking their food from old and dead plant and animal matter, bacteria and fungi cause decay. This means that they constantly change the plant and animal matter, on which they live, into simpler and simpler chemicals. Gradually the chemicals go back into the air in the form of carbon dioxide and other gases or into the soil in forms which living green plants can use to make food for the world.

WILD CREATURES THAT DO SPECIAL JOBS

Some wild creatures do very special jobs. Those which eat up dead and decaying matter, called "carrion," serve as a clean-up crew. In the United States these animals include vultures or buzzards, carrion beetles, and such part-time carrion-eaters as eagles, crows, coyotes, and bears.

The beaver is an important specialist. He is an engineer who lives and works in streams. He swims to shore, waddles to a

small tree, turns his head to one side and starts whittling big chips from the tree with his chisel-like front teeth. When the tree is cut down, he and his family drag pieces of it to the water and use them, together with stones and sticks and mud, to build a dam which holds back water and makes a pond.

In the middle of the pond, or in the dam, the beavers build a house of sticks and mud. They store many logs in the bottom of the pond for their winter's supply of food, which is bark from trees. The pond makes a safe home for the beaver family. It provides homes, too, for other wild creatures such as muskrats, fish, ducks, and geese.

Beaver ponds help prevent floods, too. For when waters from spring rains and melting snows rush downstream, beaver dams slow them up and make them spread out. This gives time for the soil carried along by the flood-waters to settle to the bottom of the pond and for the water to soak deep into nature's underground water-storage places.

The earthworm is also a specialist. Earthworms take their main food supply from leaves and other plant matter on top of the ground. They usually feed at night, when some of them are caught as "nightcrawlers" for fish bait. But the important work of the earthworm is soil cultivation. To make its home, an earthworm burrows in the ground and swallows the soil as it digs. It digests some food from the soil and passes the rest through its body, leaving it at the top of its burrow. This soil, ground fine by going through the worm's body, is made rich by body juices. The burrowing

222

of worms also lets necessary air and water into the ground.

HOW WE DEPEND ON OUR NATURAL RESOURCES

People have not always realized how much they depend on the natural working of all living things. In the United States we have always used our forests, grass, animals, and the soil and water which support them. We think of them as our "natural resources." For years it seemed as if we would always have all we wanted of them.

Until recently we have not paid much attention to the "give and take" of all natural things. We have *taken* what we needed, but we have forgotten that every living thing, including human beings, must also *give* in order to survive.

The actions of people have important effects on other people and on all forms of nature. Scientists have begun to study these effects. They realize that people have damaged the earth so badly that we must work to save our natural resources. They are thinking about the way our country used to be and the way it is now. They know that some things in nature have changed for the worse, and they know why. But they are finding that it is often hard to make these things better again.

If you had been an Indian boy or girl in the days before white men came to North America, you would have seen a land far different from that of today. Almost all of the Eastern part of the country, as well as much of the vast mountain region of the West, was covered with great forests where a carpet of dead leaves lay always on the ground. The largest trees were very old, but between some of the great trees sunlight sifted down to where young trees grew crowded together as they reached upward for light.

The animals and plants that lived in these untouched forests, or in the open spaces at their edges, furnished food for each other. Each had its place in nature's scheme, from the insects up to the deer that ate away the bushes and low branches and in that way helped saplings and seedlings to get the air and sunshine they needed.

When an old tree began to die, insects and woodpeckers bored holes in it so that rain water and air hastened its breakdown. Fungi and bacteria continued their work till the softened wood crumbled into the soil. In this way the dead trees returned to the soil and air the chemicals which they had taken while growing. In turn, the enriched soil gave food and life to new seedlings.

This way of life had gone on for thousands of years. In the Great Plains, stretching from the Mississippi Valley to the Rockies, there was a different kind of land. There were few trees, but the vast prairies were covered with thick grass. Here, as in the forest, plants and animals furnished food for one another.

In the forests and grasslands, the streams ran pure and clear. The Indians were spread so widely over the vast forests and prairies that what they took from the plants and animals each year was usually replaced by the following year's natural growth.

Beginning with the latter part of the sixteenth century, white men settled in North America. In about three hundred years they made more changes than there had been for perhaps thousands of years before. With their axes and plows they felled thousands of acres of forest trees and plowed up the green lands to plant crops of wheat and corn. The crops covered the soil for only a few months of the year, and between growing seasons the ground was simply left bare.

Of course they made some of these changes so they could survive. But often they cut down hundreds of forests and plowed up thousands of acres of grasslands unnecessarily. On the remaining lands there were often too many sheep and cattle grazing, and where there was not enough food for them all, they cropped the grass and bushes too close. When this happened, the earth was left without its natural blanket of plants, oalled its "plant cover."

Often, when their land had been worn away or "eroded," by wind and water, the farmers did nothing to repair the damage. They just moved westward to new acres, until much of the empty territory was occupied.

As cities grew up, there was great need for lumber. Sometimes lumbermen greedy for money, cut all the trees in a forest, leaving no way of providing seeds for new

growth. Sometimes careless men allowed forest fires to start and they wiped out thousands of acres of trees that had taken years to grow.

In destroying the forests and plowing up the grass, men removed too much plant cover from the "watersheds" of the country. A watershed is any ridge and its slopes down which rain water or melting snow can run into a stream or a pond, a marsh or lake. A natural watershed may be a little thing like the sides of a ditch or brook, or it may be as large as the slopes of the Continental Divide in the Rocky Mountains, in some places over 14,000 feet high.

Trees and grass, with their thick roots and their leaves, help water to soak into the ground where it is needed, instead of running off rapidly and taking soil with it. Perhaps you remember rain storms so hard that they washed the dirt from the flower bed or driveway into the street. But where the grass was thick on the lawn the dirt did not wash away. Or you have walked through the woods after a rain and have seen how every dead leaf on the ground was a tiny cup that held a few drops of rain. Plant covers were working there.

DANGERS

As more and more grass and trees were removed from our country's watersheds, there was not enough natural plant cover to slow up the runoff of water on the slopes. Even on level ground, crops like corn and wheat and cotton, covering the earth for only part of the year, did not protect the land as well as the forest trees and the grass had done.

Gradually floods became more frequent and damaging. And in the former grasslands of the Midwest, great dust storms came in times of little rain. Sometimes the air was so thick with dust that day seemed as dark as night. The rich topsoil was blowing off the fields.

Garbage and sewage from the rapidly growing cities were often dumped into the streams. This made the water unfit for fish, animals, or people to use.

Gradually what the white man had done in settling North America was to upset the natural relationships of living things and change their natural surroundings or environment.

Even though many kinds of animals and plants range widely over several regions, others can live in only one kind of environment. A heavily furred polar bear could not live in the jungle or a warmth-loving alligator on the Arctic ice. Plants of the cactus family need dry desert air because their hard wax surfaces prevent the sun from evaporating their moisture. Marsh plants have masses of long roots which hold them in the watery soil they grow best in.

When an environment is changed, that affects the living things within it. If the moist soil of a certain place is made dry, as it might be if a man drains water from a marsh, the plants that grow in wet soil can no longer live there, nor can the birds and animals, such as ducks and muskrats, that depend on the water plants for food and protection. If for some reason the trees and shrubs that are the homes of insect-eating birds are cut down and the birds have no shelter, they must go elsewhere. Then the insects in that place may grow too numerous and become pests.

Upsetting the relationships of nature has had most serious effects, sometimes direct and sometimes indirect, on our natural resources of soil, water and plant and animal life.

WE MUST ALL BE CONSERVATIONISTS

When scientists began to realize that careless, wasteful methods of farming and industry were changing the natural environment too rapidly and were destroying our resources, they went to work to renew our soil, our forests and grasslands and our wildlife. The work of *managing* these and our mineral resources wisely is called "conservation." People who help conservation are "conservationists." Everyone can and should be a conservationist. A boy or girl who plants a needed tree, puts out bird houses, or saves a useful plant or animal is a conservationist.

There are, however, conservation *specialists* who are trying to find out just what each natural environment is best suited for.

They have learned that in some regions of scant rainfall and thin soil, like parts of our Western states, it is wise to leave the land in grass as food for the right number of beef cattle rather than to plow up the grass and plant grain. They know also that a marsh is not necessarily waste land simply because corn and wheat and cotton will not grow on it. A marsh can be a valuable soil-builder and water-holder, important to the country's water supply.

HOW CONSERVATION CAN HELP FARMERS

A conservationist can help farmers in a way like this: He takes samples of soil from various parts of a farm and sends them to a laboratory. There experts find out what soil chemicals the samples contain. Then the conservation specialist makes a sketch of the whole farm, showing the different kinds of slopes, hills, flatlands, and soil. Together he and the farmer make a "land-use-map" and decide what the various parts of the farm are best suited for and how they should be used.

Then the farmer goes to work. Some fields are suited only for pasture. These the farmer leaves in grass. Others he cultivates in special ways to protect the land and also to restore valuable chemicals to the worn-out soil. This is done by rotating crops— that is, by planting crops like clover or soy beans which restore nitrogen to the soil, then plowing them under and planting grain which needs the nitrogen.

In his cornfield, the conservationist advises the farmer to plow his furrows across the slope instead of down it. This plowing to follow the natural curves or "contours" of the land makes each furrow into a little dam which holds back the water and keeps it from washing away the rich topsoil. On some slopes the farmer makes terraces to hold the water. On others he leaves strips of sod between the plowed sections. Where deep gullies have been worn he builds little dams, and in the smaller ditches he plants grass. The conservationist advises planting trees and shrubs along muddy creek banks and in fence rows he suggests hedges as homes for insect-eating birds and game animals.

After a while the farmer has nature working *with* him on his farm. He has helped to control floods. His study of conservation has paid off in better crops and valuable wild life.

Men are learning how to help nature correct the damage done to our forests, too. When lumber is cut, whether in a farmer's woodlot or in a great forest, enough trees are now left standing to provide seed for new trees, and to protect young seedlings from strong sun and wind and from weeds. In our national forests trees are now cut this way. In areas where too many trees have been cut or burned away, young trees must be transplanted from a nursery. Many of the state governments, the national government and some private companies have tree nurseries where the seeds are planted. Seedlings are cared for until they are strong enough to be transplanted to a natural environment. Foresters, farmers, school children, or anyone interested can buy seedling trees for a few cents and plant them where they are needed.

IT IS UP TO ALL OF US TO KEEP OUR FORESTS FROM BURNING

Each year fire is the greatest destroyer of the remaining national forests. Forest fires destroy not only the trees themselves but often burn and scorch the soil so that seeds may not be able to grow for five or six years, or perhaps ever again.

The United States Forest Service makes these suggestions for preventing forest fires:

BE SURE your match is out. Break it in two before you throw it away.

BE SURE that pipe ashes, cigarettes, or cigars are dead before they are thrown away.

BUILD A SAFE CAMPFIRE. Scrape away all leaves, grass or pine needles from a spot five feet wide. Keep your fire small. NEVER build it against a tree or log or near a bush.

DO NOT LEAVE A FIRE UNTENDED.

PUT OUT YOUR FIRE COMPLETELY when you leave. Soak the coals with water. Turn small sticks and drench both sides. Wet the ground around the fire. Be sure the last spark is dead.

KNOW THE FIRE LAWS in your state. Learn the areas where campfire building is allowed, and get a fire building permit if necessary.

NEVER BURN LEAVES OR BRUSH IN WINDY WEATHER or when there is the slightest danger that the fire will get away.

REPORT ANY FIRE YOU DISCOVER. Go to the nearest telephone and ask for the local Fire Warden or Forest Ranger.

227

The Earth and How It Came to Be

*Earth clock would take
3,000,000,000 years to
go around once*

One "second" would equal 69,000 years

"HOW old is the earth?" It is hard even to explain how very old the earth is. Scientists who have studied the subject figure that the earth has been here somewhere between three billion and five-and-a-half billion years. We'll see, later, how they figured that out. But now let's just try to see how much time we are really talking about when we say three billion years.

Suppose you started counting right now, and you counted one number every single second, without stopping to eat or sleep or for anything else. By the end of a day (that is, in 12 hours) you would have counted to 43,200. That may seem like a lot to you. But it is hardly more than a start toward

228

counting the number of years the earth has been here. And, remember, you have been counting *seconds,* not years. And there are thirty-one million, five hundred and thirty-six thousand seconds in every year.

Maybe we can make it plainer by putting it another way: Suppose we had a clock that went all the way around just once every three billion years instead of once every twelve hours. Every time such a clock ticked off just one second, 69,000 years would have gone by. And all the counting you could do in twelve hours— counting one number every single second of that time—would make up about one-half of a second on our three-billion-year clock.

In other words, it would take you *over a hundred years* of doing nothing but counting one number every second just to *count* to three billion. And that would be just three billion *seconds*. Three billion *years* would be 3,000,000,000 multiplied by 31,536,000 (the number of seconds in a year). So we can hardly imagine what a very long time three billion years really is. And we are not sure that the earth may not be almost *twice* that old (five-and-a-half billion years).

HOW DO WE KNOW HOW OLD THE EARTH IS?

Of course, nobody has been sitting around counting up the age of the earth. We have found its age in a very interesting way. It is almost like a detective story.

The detective work really started a couple of hundred years ago when a scientist said he had figured how to tell the age of the earth in a way that was certain to be correct.

This is how he did it! First he figured out that ocean water contains salt because the rivers feeding the oceans are always carrying tiny bits of salty chemicals into them. Next he tried to figure out how long it would take the rivers to carry enough salty chemicals to make the oceans as salty as they were. Unfortunately, he just couldn't work it out. But even so, for the first time someone had tried a special and scientific way of figuring out the earth's age.

Up until then it had been mostly guesswork, and all the guesswork added up to was a fairly wide belief that the earth was only four or five thousand years old. Today we know that that is just the tiniest fraction of how old the world really is.

But, at any rate, people had really begun to search for the age of the earth, and they were on their way to finding it.

River flowing into the sea

Next came men called geologists. They realized that the rocks and stones of the earth and the layers of rock under the ground must have taken many times four thousand years to form. Other geologists figured out that where oceans are today, there once had been dry land; and where dry land is today, there once had been water. They knew that those changes must have taken millions of years. They were getting closer, but still there was no answer that the scientists really could trust.

Finally, and not very many years ago, the scientists made a truly exciting discovery. The discovery was possible because of some strange metals that men didn't even know the existence of a hundred years ago. These are not metals like iron ores that lie in great hunks on and under the earth. These metals are found as particles in the ground and in rocks, and they have what the scientists call radioactivity. That means that they are always letting off energy, the way a light bulb lets off light. You'll learn how they do that in another part of this book. The important thing here is that these radioactive metals slowly change as they let off their energy. Slowly, in this case, really means slowly — and that is over millions of years. These radioactive metals keep giving off their energy and changing and changing. At the end they have changed into plain lead.

Scientists finally used those facts to track down the age of the earth like this: They would find places in the earth where these radioactive metals are plentiful even though all mixed up in rocks and earth. In these places, also, they would find lead that once had been radioactive.

Scientists have delicate instruments that can measure just how fast radioactive elements give off energy. Then they can get out their adding machines and figure out how many millions of years it would take for *all* of the energy to be given off and for the radioactive material to become lead.

Next, the scientists look around at the rest of the rocks and earth in the area and find out how much radioactive material *hasn't* worn out. They put all the facts together and come up with an answer of how old the whole area must be just the way you might look at a supply of pencils in school and say, "Well, it took one week to wear one pencil down to the eraser. There are three pencils left. So, I'd say that was a one month's supply of pencils."

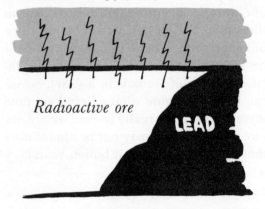

Radioactive ore

LEAD

In some places, as in Colorado, geologists discovered deposits of lead and radioactive metals that, they found out, were fifty-eight million years old. But it seemed to them that the earth must be even older than that. So they looked farther. Finally, in parts of Africa, they found deposits that they figured must have been there without anyone or anything disturbing them for nearly THREE BILLION YEARS. Then, because those deposits were themselves on top of rocks that might have been even older, the scientists made a final calculation. They figured that the earth was *at least* three billion years old and that it might be as old as five-and-a-half billion years.

WHAT HAS THE EARTH BEEN DOING ALL THIS TIME?

While scientists were discovering the age of the earth, they also were busy discovering what the earth had been doing all that time. Ordinarily we wouldn't think of the earth *doing* anything at all. It just seems to be there. It doesn't move like an animal. It doesn't grow like a tree. It doesn't roar and have waves like an ocean, and it doesn't run along like a river. Or at least it doesn't *seem* to do those things. Actually it does all of them. But it takes the earth many, many thousands of years to do most of those things. Only in a few special cases

can you see the earth doing anything.

Perhaps it would be interesting to start our look at what the earth does by examining those very special cases when the earth does something we can see with our eyes, things that happen right here and now and don't take thousands of years.

The two main things like this are earthquakes and volcanoes. In both of those things the earth does something in days or hours, sometimes in seconds, rather than in thousands of years.

WHAT IS AN EARTHQUAKE?

Earthquakes happen frequently. During an earthquake, certain parts of the earth shake and quake, the way a bowl of jelly would if it had been hit with a hand. In the case of an earthquake, though, this shaking can be very powerful. It can be powerful enough to knock great buildings down. Sometimes it causes the earth itself to split open, leaving a deep thin valley or chasm. One earthquake that happened in the year

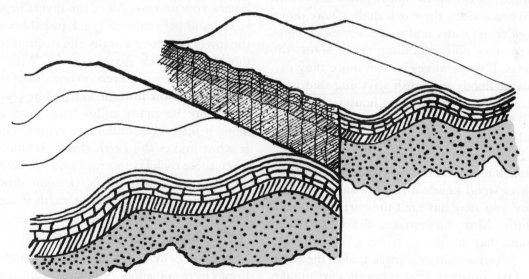

When rocks are formed like this, earthquakes are a possibility

231

Actual cracks in the earth's surface

1906 was so powerful that it shook the city of San Francisco so that most of the buildings were knocked down and set on fire. Thousands of people were hurt and left without a place to live.

Sometimes an earthquake will happen in a part of the earth that is under an ocean. When it does, the earth shakes 'way down under the water and makes waves as big as ten-story office buildings crash across the seas. If these waves hit the shore they can cause floods and crush anything that is on the shore, even piers and houses.

But even though an earthquake *can* do all of those things, it usually doesn't. It just shakes the ground about as much as a heavy truck might do in passing by. If you have ever stood beside a place where trains go by, you may have felt the earth tremble a little. Most earthquakes shake the earth only that much.

When a train or a truck makes the earth shake, however, that is not an earthquake. Here is how earthquakes do happen.

Underneath the ground, everywhere on the earth, there are layers of rock, like the layers in a chocolate cake. Sometimes these rock layers are 'way, 'way down under the ground so that even if you dug a hole big enough to put a battleship into, you wouldn't hit the rock layer. At other places this rock layer is just a few feet down. In some places it comes right up on the surface in the form of rock hills, the kind that are so much fun to climb on.

Sometimes one of these layers of rocks begins to sag, as one of those layers in the chocolate cake would sag if you took a big bite out of the bottom of the cake and left the top part hanging there like a bridge. Something like this can happen in the earth.

Whatever part of the earth is underneath part of one of these layers of rock may settle down a bit or even cave in. Then the rock layer itself starts to sag, then bend, and finally it is ready to crack. The rock layer that is ready to crack may be just a couple of feet thick. But piled on it are other rock layers, row on row. All of the layers begin to sag and get ready to crack just the way the lower one does. Finally the strain is too much. The rock layers crack. With a rumble, all the rock layers on one side of the crack sink lower into the earth. The crack itself may be many miles long. And all along it the rock rumbles and grinds. That is what makes the earth shake. It shakes when those rock layers crack and the layers all along one side of the crack boom down into a new position. Then the earth shakes, and that is an earthquake.

WHAT IS A VOLCANO?

Another way earthquakes can happen brings us to volcanoes. Volcanoes can cause earthquakes too.

232

Volcano erupting

To understand a volcano you would have to look down below even those layers of rocks that cracked and caused the earthquake. You have to go to a place so deep inside the earth that everything there is terribly hot. It is hot because of all the billions of tons of earth and rock and oceans and buildings and people that are pressing down on the inside of the earth, for when weight as great as that keeps pressing down, heat is formed. And the farther down you go, the more weight there is on top, and so the hotter it gets. In fact, down deep in the earth it is so hot that even the rocks melt. It is 'way down there that we have to start the story of the volcano.

The melted rocks form a white-hot liquid called *magma*. Most of the time this ocean of melted rock under the earth is held in place by all the solid rock layers above it. But sometimes cracks start in those solid layers holding down the melted rocks. Some of the melted rock, the white hot magma, forces

its way into the crack. It makes the crack wider and longer. On and on the white hot magma forces itself. It may even reach up to the surface of the earth. If it does, and even though it loses a lot of its white-hot heat as it forces its way up, it is still at least red-hot. It crashes up through the last layer of rock and then crashes right on through the surface of the earth spurting up into the air like water shooting out of a broken hose.

When that happens, a really big volcano is beginning. The melted rock that now shoots up through the earth is called *lava*. As it rushes up, or erupts, it carries dirt and stones with it and piles them up around the hole it has blasted in the ground. All of this and the lava boiling up inside the earth can cause the earth to quake.

Gradually the pile starts forming a hill, and finally it may grow into a mountain. Some of the greatest mountains in the world today were formed by just that sort of volcanic eruption. Scientists call them

233

mountains of accumulation because the lava rushing out "accumulates" or collects a pile and finally a whole mountain of stone and earth. Most of them are very nicely shaped, with cone-like peaks, and most of them stand alone towering over everything in sight.

Unfortunately, when a big volcano erupts it can cause terrible damage for hundreds of miles. The red hot lava can be shot through the air for great distances. If it fell on a town or a forest it would start fires. Even when the lava doesn't get shot off as if it came from a giant's cannon, it can flow across the countryside like a red-hot river, burning up everything it comes to. There have been volcanoes in many lands that have done just that. But now it seems that the melted rock down in the earth might have found just about all the cracks through which it could escape, for there are now very few eruptions of volcanoes.

Ancient astronomer at work

234

Earth and Its Neighbors in the Sky

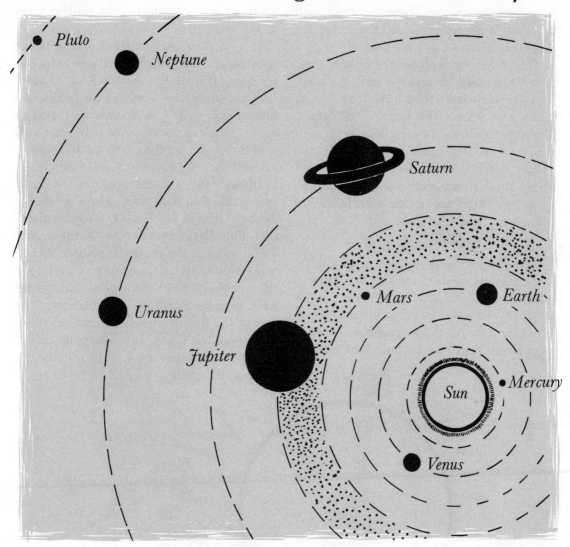

Earth and planets in relation to the sun

WHEN we look up into a clear star-filled sky at night it often looks like a dark velvet curtain with tiny pin-holes letting brilliant white lights filter through. Many of those pin-pricks of light are hundreds of times larger than Earth! They are giant suns gleaming and burning billions and trillions of miles from Earth. We call them stars. Every one of the stars is like our Sun, a blazing burning ball of molten metals and rocks.

Others of those pin-pricks are called planets. They are round worlds like the world we call Earth—except that some are red-hot, some are ice-cold, some are small, and some are large. And it is said that there are no people living on any of them.

The planets have no heat or light of their own. They swing around the suns, the stars, and get what heat they have from them. They also reflect the light of the stars. There are millions of suns besides *the* Sun that we know and other planets besides the planet Earth that we live on. We'll learn about them in another part of this book. First let's learn about our own family of planets in the sky and our own Sun.

A TRIP TO THE SUN

The Sun that we know, the great golden, sometimes red, ball in the sky that gives us warmth and light, is actually a star, and it is 93,000,000 miles away from Earth. Yet it is nearer to Earth than any other star. The next closest star, which would look like our Sun if we were close enough to it, is 25,000,-000,000,000 (twenty-five trillion) miles away, or about a quarter-of-a million times as far away as our Sun!

It is hard to imagine what distances like that mean. But maybe this will help you see how far away the Sun is—not to mention showing how very far away the *next* closest star is. If you wanted to travel as far on Earth as the distance between Earth and Sun you would have to go all the way around the world almost 4,000 times!

It is not only the distance from the Earth to the Sun that is so great. The Sun itself— *our* Sun, that is—is 864,000 miles in diameter. Our Earth, on the other hand, is only 7,900 miles in diameter. It is about 25,000 miles around its circumference. That means that the Sun is more than one hundred times as large as the Earth in every direction. The size of the Sun is about one million times the size of the Earth. It is a flaming ball of gas with a temperature of 40 million degrees at its center.

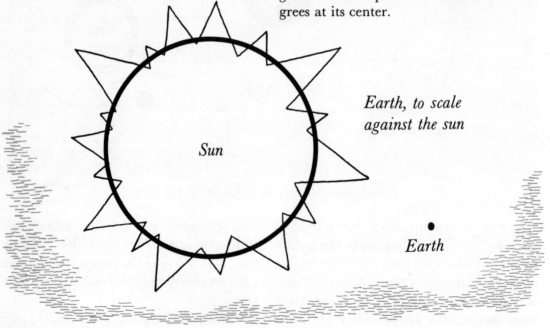

Sun

Earth, to scale
against the sun

Earth

236

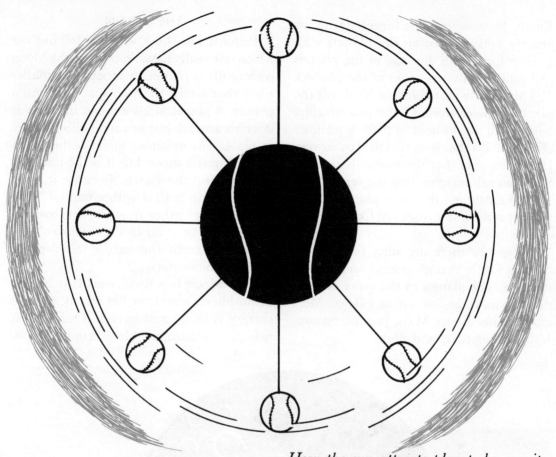

How the sun attracts planets by gravity

SOLAR SYSTEMS

Around the Sun are the planets of what we call our *solar system*. "Solar" is the word for something that has to do with the sun. A group of planets around any sun is called a solar system.

There are many many millions of solar systems throughout the reaches of outer space. Yet, so far as anyone knows today, only on the planet we call Earth are there living things, like human beings and animals and birds and fish and plants and trees and all the things we know as life.

GRAVITY HOLDS THE PLANETS

The planets of a solar system all stay in place, as they spin around a sun, because of gravity. This is the same unexplained invisible force that holds all of us on Earth and causes things to drop to the ground instead of dropping up into the air.

The force of gravity, scientists have learned, works so that objects in space always attract other objects. Well, the Sun is the largest thing, by far, within millions of miles of the Earth and within millions of miles of *all* the planets near the

237

Earth. Because it is the largest thing, its gravity pulls against all the planets with greater force than any one of the planets can pull against any other of the planets.

This means that the Sun holds all the planets in place around it just as a whirling basket-ball would hold in place a number of tennis balls that were tied to it by strings. If you imagine that the basket-ball is the Sun, you can imagine that the tennis balls are the Earth and the other planets of this solar system. The strings are like the force of gravity.

Altogether there are nine planets, including Earth, that go around and around the Sun. The planets in the order of their distance from the Sun are as follows: Mercury, Venus, Earth, Mars, Jupiter, Saturn, Uranus, Neptune, and Pluto.

THE MOON

Perhaps you think we have left out the Moon. We really haven't, because the Moon isn't really a planet. A moon is a smaller body that whirls through space around a planet. A planet holds a moon in place as it whirls around, just as a sun holds a planet in place. The moon we know as the Moon is really just *a* moon but it is the one that goes around the Earth. Because it is *our* moon we can spell it with a capital "M." But there are other moons going around other planets, even though we can't see them all except through a telescope or powerful binoculars.

The Moon is a dead world. It has no atmosphere, water, or life of any sort. Its surface is rocky and barren. Our nearest neighbor in space, the Moon is only 239,000

The moon with its craters

238

miles away. No doubt the Moon will be the first station visited when people become space travelers. The Moon looks large because it is so near the Earth. Actually it is much smaller than the stars, which are much farther away. It is ball-shaped, and the distance through its center, its diameter, is 2,160 miles. This is a little over one fourth the diameter of the Earth.

The beautiful light that comes from the Moon is not all its own. The Moon shines by reflecting some of the light it receives from the Sun.

Now, starting with the planet that is closest to the Sun, let's visit the Earth's neighbors in space, the other members of our solar system.

MERCURY

Besides being the planet that is closest to the Sun, Mercury is also the smallest planet of our solar system. Its diameter is only 3,000 miles which is less than half that of the Earth's. And, instead of being 93,000,000 miles away from the Sun, like Earth, Mercury is only 36,000,000 miles away. Being so (comparatively) close to the Sun means that the strength of the sunlight on Mercury is nine times as great as the strength of the sunlight on Earth. Some metals, like lead, would melt just sitting out in the open on Mercury, it is so hot there.

VENUS

Nothing except the Sun and Moon shine as brightly in the sky as does Venus. On a dark night when the Moon is not showing in the sky, the light from Venus alone is sometimes enough to cast a faint shadow of a person or a tree or something else. Even in the daytime, at certain times, Venus can be seen shining faintly although the light of

Mercury

Venus

Earth

Mars

Jupiter

Saturn

Uranus

Neptune

Pluto

The planets in relative size to each other

the Sun is bright enough to hide all the other lights in the sky. Venus is often called the *Morning* or *Evening Star*.

This doesn't mean that Venus has some sort of light of its own. It hasn't. No planet, remember, has any light or heat of its own. Only stars, which are really suns, give off light and heat of their own. Planets seem to shine because they *reflect* the light of the nearest star or sun. The reason Venus seems so bright is that it is just between the Sun and the Earth and has many clouds around it that reflect the sunlight. Venus is the second planet away from the Sun. In size, Venus is just about the same as the Earth. It is 67,000,000 miles from the Sun.

EARTH

Just to keep things straight, let's put the Earth right here, where it belongs, 93,000,-000 miles from the Sun. It is the third planet away from the Sun.

If you could see it from a spaceship, the Earth would look like a green-colored globe, almost three-quarters of its surface covered with water. What we call a "year," is the length of time it takes the Earth to complete one journey around the sun.

The Earth is a very special planet in many ways. First of all it is the only place in all the heavens, so far as we know, where there is any intelligent life. Scientists think that there may be very simple plants growing on some other planets, but nothing more.

One of the reasons Earth can have living things on it is that the Earth, as it travels through the skies, carries with it a deep ocean of air. On other planets, the atmosphere that surrounds them may be anything from boiling poisonous gases to air that is so thin it hardly can be said to exist.

Perhaps the best way to sum up the wonder of this planet of ours, the Earth, is to remember the simplest and most beautiful thing we can say about it. It is our home.

MARS

This is the planet people talk most about. For centuries people have wondered if there might be any living things on Mars. Perhaps the reason they have wondered this about Mars more than about other planets is that Mars is close to Earth. But unlike the even closer Venus with its thick covering of clouds, the surface of Mars can be clearly seen from the Earth through a telescope.

Mars, the fourth planet from the Sun, looks orange-red. Because of its color, it is easy to identify. When Mars comes nearest to us, it is about thirty-five million miles away. It comes that close only once every 17 years. The year on Mars is nearly twice as long as ours.

Mars is a cold planet because of its distance from the Sun. It receives less than half as much light and heat as the Earth does.

The red color of Mars may be due to vast sandy deserts. There are no mountains on Mars. If there were, their shadows would show. Nor are there any oceans. If any bodies of water exist, they must be shallow pools that dry up soon after they form.

A white cap covers each pole of Mars during its winter season. Probably the cap is made of snow and ice. It shrinks in summers and at the same time bluish-green splotches of color appear in places near Mars' equator. Scientists believe these show that Mars has changing seasons such as we have.

240

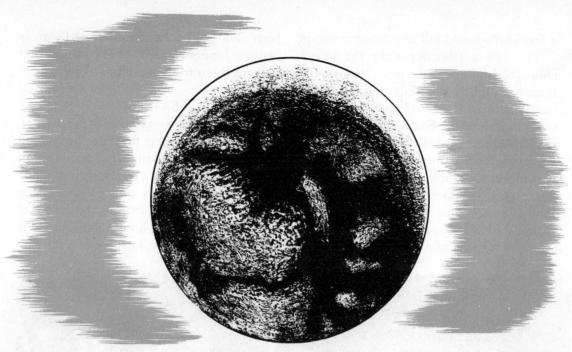

Mars with its canals

Although no oxygen has been found in the air around Mars, scientists think certain plants such as lichens might be able to grow on Mars, and that possibly fields near the equator are covered with them. But if there are any living things on the planet, our telescopes have found no trace of them.

Mars has two tiny moons that spin around it. They really are tiny, too. One is only about 10 miles around and the other about 15 miles. Mars itself is only half as large as the Earth in diameter and one-eighth in volume.

JUPITER

After Mars, in the solar system, comes the giant of all the planets, Jupiter. This great planet is 1,300 times as large as the Earth! If all the other planets in the solar system were lumped together, Jupiter would still be two-and-a-half times as large as all of them rolled into one.

Jupiter is a giant in other ways too. It also has a giant's share of moons spinning around it. It has twelve moons! Four of those moons are larger than the Earth. But there is one thing Jupiter has extremely little of, and that is heat. In fact, you might say it doesn't have any—although scientists tell us that even when things get ice-cold they do have *some* heat because they could be still *colder*. Jupiter's *highest* temperature is 216 degrees *below* zero on a Fahrenheit thermometer, and it gets even colder. Brrrr!

Scientists believe Jupiter has a small rocky core surrounded by a thick shell of ice that never melts. Above this ice lies an atmosphere of hydrogen that extends thousands of miles out into space. In this atmosphere float clouds of two gases so poisonous that a few whiffs would kill any living creature.

Through a telescope only the poison clouds of Jupiter can be seen, looking like bands of slightly different colors. On one band there is a big red spot, more than twice as wide as the Earth. This spot is due, perhaps, to hot gases that shoot up from volcanoes buried under the ice. This red spot makes it possible to tell how fast Jupiter rotates. It makes a whole turn in less than 10 hours. This is a terrific speed for it means that at its equator Jupiter's surface whirls at a speed of about 27,000 miles an hour. The poisonous gases cannot fly away because Jupiter's gravity is so powerful that it keeps them from escaping.

SATURN

When artists draw pictures of the planets, Saturn is one of their favorites because of the strange circle or ring that goes around it. This ring really is a series of rings made up of small particles of rock and other materials that circle around the center of Saturn as a thin flat hoop might look if it were put around a balloon. Besides the ring

242   *Jupiter with its moons*

Saturn with its rings

around it, Saturn has nine moons that circle it in space.

Saturn is the sixth planet from the Sun and shines brightly because of its size. It is almost as large as Jupiter and has almost as much gravity. Since the planet is so far from the Sun, it is a world of eternal cold. Saturn's year, the time it takes to make its journey around the Sun, is 29 of our years.

URANUS

Even though the planet Uranus is more than four times as large as the Earth, it wasn't even noticed by scientists until the year 1781. One reason for this is that Uranus is more than one-and-a-half *billion* miles away from the Earth. That makes it mighty hard to see. We know now that Uranus has five moons—but scientists didn't discover the fifth moon until 1948!

Uranus has a diameter four times larger than the Earth's. It takes 84 of our years to travel around the Sun.

NEPTUNE

Although it is slightly larger than Uranus, the planet Neptune is more than *two*-and-a-half billion miles away from the Earth and takes about 165 of our years to go around the Sun. Back in the 1800's, as a matter of fact, no one even knew that Neptune existed. The story of how Neptune was discovered is a sort of scientific detective yarn.

After the discovery of Uranus, the planet we learned about just before this, scientists set to work figuring out just where and when Uranus could be seen best in the night skies. When they got their figures all neatly laid out, something went wrong. Uranus just wasn't showing up in the right place in the sky at the right time.

What was wrong? The best answer seemed to be that another planet, way out in the darkness of space, was tugging at Uranus as the two passed each other and that that was making Uranus bobble a bit on its course. That prevented it from keeping the sort of time-table the scientists had figured on. That answer seemed good enough, but it wasn't until 1846 that a man with a telescope finally spotted the mysterious other planet. It was named Neptune and for quite a few years scientists were sure that it was the *last* of the planets in the solar system.

PLUTO

In 1930, scientists finally spotted another member of the solar system, Pluto. It is a planet about half the size of the Earth and *three-and-a-half billion* miles away from the Sun. Being so far away from the Sun, Pluto hardly gets any of the Sun's light. That is how its name was chosen, for Pluto is the name of the ancient Roman god of darkness.

Some scientists think that Pluto was once a moon of Neptune and somehow escaped. Are there other planets beyond Pluto? Perhaps, but if so they have not yet been discovered. Some day scientists may find them.

A BELT OF ASTEROIDS

In between the paths that Mars and Jupiter travel around the Sun, there are a number of small rounded chunks that seem like miniature planets. Scientists who study the skies (and they are called astronomers) call them *asteroids* or *planetoids,* which means little planets.

Until 1801 scientists didn't know these asteroids existed. It took telescopes powerful enough to spot them, and astronomers wise enough to figure out what they were, to discover the "asteroid belt," as it is called, between Mars and Jupiter. About 1,000 asteroids have been spotted and their courses charted so far. Unlike moons, which swing around a planet, the asteroids have courses or orbits of their own. Like the big planets themselves, the asteroids are held in those orbits by the pull of the Sun.

The largest of the asteroids is only about 500 miles in diameter and many of them are less than 10 miles in diameter.

DIFFERENT DAYS AND NIGHTS

No matter how large or small a planet or planetoid is, it has one thing that the Earth has too — day and night. Besides spinning in a great circle around the Sun, as the Earth does, the planets also spin like a top as they go along. The Earth, of course, does this too. It is this spinning like a top that causes our days and nights, as has been described in the part of this book about how years and days are figured.

Day is when the planet has spun so that a part faces the Sun and is lighted. Night is the darkness that comes to the part of the planet that is *not* facing the Sun. That is why it is night on one side of a planet while it is day on the opposite side.

Because all the planets spin at different speeds, the lengths of the days and nights are bound to be different on each of the planets.

To give you an idea of how different the length of days can be, let us consider Jupiter, the largest of the planets. This planet spins so fast that instead of a 24-hour day, like the kind we have on Earth, Jupiter goes from sunrise to sunrise in only 9 hours and 50 minutes.

Saturn, the planet with the ring around it, has a day that is only 10 hours long.

Not only the days are different lengths on the different planets, however. The time it takes to make a year go by differs even

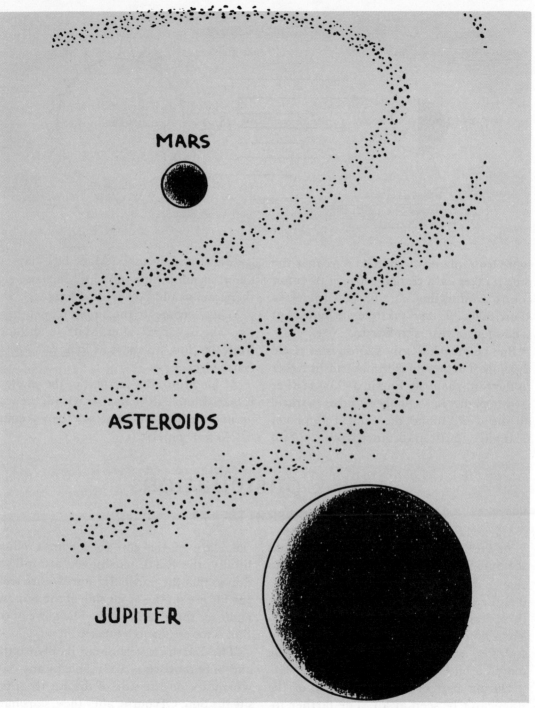

MARS

ASTEROIDS

JUPITER

Belt of asteroids between Mars and Jupiter

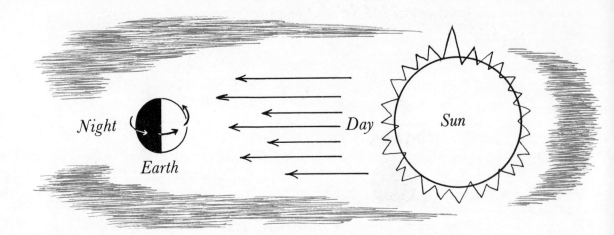

Night — Earth — Day — Sun

more from planet to planet. A year is the time it takes for a planet to travel its entire course around the Sun. The Earth, as we know, takes 365 days to circle the Sun. That is how long a year is on Earth.

But Venus takes only 225 days to circle the Sun. The reason is that Venus is closer to the Sun than the Earth is. The farther away a planet is, the longer it takes to travel all the way around the Sun. The planet next after Earth in distance from the Sun is Mars, and it takes Mars 687 days to travel around the Sun. The Martian year, therefore, would be 687 days long.

When it comes to the largest planet, Jupiter, which is next after Mars in distance from the Sun, a year is as long as *twelve* of Earth's years.

As for Pluto, the farthest of the planets, it takes Pluto 248 years to travel all the way around the Sun. So a *single year* there is equal to *248 years* on Earth.

The Constellations

PICTURES IN THE SKY

As the Earth makes its journey around the Sun each year, the stars seem to us to change their positions in the skies. Actually it is the way the Earth moves that makes them seem to be in different places at different times. The movement of the Earth is such that each night the stars seem to have moved a bit farther west in the sky.

During part of the year many of the stars can't be seen at all. The farther toward the west they appear, the closer to the glare of the sun they come. When, finally, the Earth has moved around the Sun so that the particular stars we are looking for are on the other side of the Sun, we can't see those stars at all. The glare of the Sun is too strong to let us see them.

The Earth travels along its own path, and only those stars are visible at any date which are on the side of the Earth opposite the Sun. Of course, after these stars have been passed, they remain unseen until the

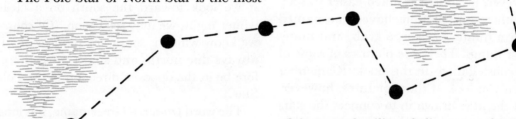

same time of the following year, when the Earth has again reached that particular point in its path. So you will see that we have the stars of spring and of summer, of autumn and of winter.

Although most of the constellations may be seen only at certain times of each year, some stars are visible all the year round. The reason for this is that they lie nearer to either the North Pole or the South Pole than the horizon is, so that in their apparent rotation, caused by the spinning of the Earth on its axis, they never dip below the horizon, and are visible all night, every night of the year.

Some stars, like the North Star, which is also called the Pole Star, stay in sight every night all year around. This is because they are in the skies above the top of the Earth, and the Sun never comes between them and the Earth.

The Pole Star or North Star is the most useful of stars. By noting its direction, travelers are able to find which way north is. Knowing that, they can keep track of the other points of the compass too. Sailors, long before they had maps and instruments to guide them, used the Pole Star as a beacon to tell them the right directions in crossing the seas.

One of the best ways to find the North Star is to use a group of stars called the Big Dipper as a guide. The Big Dipper is one

of the most familiar of all groups of stars in the northern skies. (Down in the lands far below the equator, such stars as those can't be seen at all. Instead, there are other groups of stars that are visible only there— *they* can't be seen from countries *above* the equator.)

The Big Dipper is made up of seven stars. Three of them form a bent handle. The other four form the bowl of the dipper.

Now, to find the North Star, you look along the two stars that form the part of the dipper farthest from the handle—the part that would be the far edge of the cup of the dipper. Then you pretend there is an imaginary line leading upward from these stars.

Out along this imaginary line, pretty much all by itself in the sky, is the North Star. When stars are seen together in groups that look like pictures of something, we call that group of stars a *constellation.*

There are constellations that have reminded people of ever so many things. Names have been given to the groups of stars because of those things. The Big Dipper, of course, was easy to name. The position of the seven stars is just like the outline of a dipper made up of seven dots of light.

There is a Little Dipper also. And, as a matter of fact, the North Star is the first star in the handle of *that* Dipper. We use the Big Dipper to find the North Star, however, because it is much easier to spot.

Other constellations have been named after a hunter, a bear, a crab, and many other things. There are pictures of some of the constellations in this book. Remember when you look at those pictures, however, that the lines drawn in to connect the stars and show the shape they are supposed to represent are all imaginary. When you look for the constellations in the sky you will just see the dots of light. Your imagination has to supply the rest of the picture.

THE CONSTELLATION OF ORION

Of all the star-figures, one of the most interesting and beautiful is *Orion,* the Huntsman. This is the largest of all the constellations, and it can be seen only during the months of late autumn, winter, and early spring. In the northern half of the world,

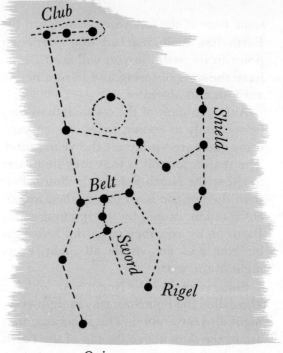

Orion

if we look toward the south on a clear winter night, we may see Orion. (Of course we know which is south, for the *Pole Star* is always due north, and south must therefore be in the opposite direction to the Pole Star.)

The word *Orion* is a Greek name, but long ago the English people used to call him "Orwandle." The brightest star of the constellation they called "Orwandle's Toe," but it is now known as Rigel.

If we look carefully at the stars forming this constellation, we can make out the shape of a man marked by the stars. The two bright stars at the top show the place of Orion's shoulders, while two other stars, lower down, mark his knees. Three smaller stars in a line mark the place of his belt. Below that are some more stars representing the jeweled handle of his hunting-knife.

248

Orion is swinging a great club high in his right hand, while with his left he holds up a shield. Orion is one of the star-pictures in which we can easily imagine the figure of what it was intended to represent when the people of long ago gave it the name.

Orion was supposed to be a mighty hunter, but he did some wicked deed, and the gods put him in the sky to be a warning to men for all time.

They also put his two dogs near him, and if you look a little to the left, and lower down than Orion, you will see the Big Dog, or *Canis Major,* as it is called by astronomers. *Sirius,* the brightest star in the whole of our skies, can be seen in this contellation, and because it is the chief star in the Big Dog, it is often referred to as the *Dog-Star.*

Near by, but higher up, is *Canis Minor,* or the Little Dog; while the chief star in this group, though not so bright as Sirius, is a beautiful object called *Procyon.*

There is another star-picture besides the dogs connected with Orion: *Taurus the Bull.* It is this animal that Orion is supposed to be hunting through the heavens. There is not the full figure of a bull in the sky, only its head.

It is charging down on Orion, and he is holding out his shield with his left hand to protect himself, while with his right he is about to use his great club upon the head of the oncoming Bull.

Higher up than the Little Dog we can see two bright stars known to astronomers as *Gemini,* the *Twins,* but called by some the *Giant's Eyes.*

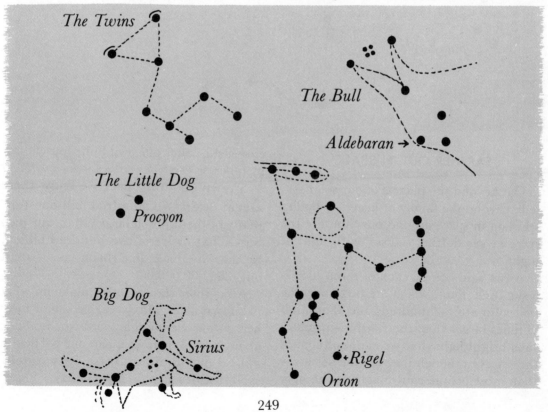

249

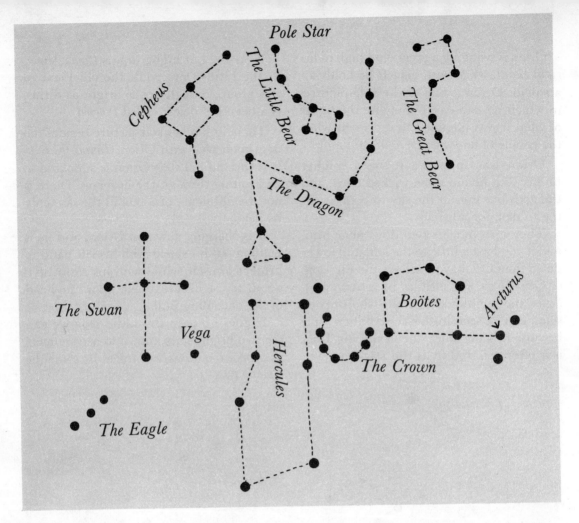

Pole Star · Cepheus · The Little Bear · The Great Bear · The Dragon · The Swan · Vega · Hercules · Boötes · Arcturus · The Crown · The Eagle

FARTHER OUT IN SPACE

Out beyond the planets of our solar system, beyond the family of heavenly bodies whirling in space around our Sun, are the stars we see dotting the sky with light at night.

As we said before, each of those stars is a sun itself. Suns, which are huge burning balls of matter—hundreds and thousands of times larger than the Earth — produce such bright light that we can see them in the sky even though they are farther away than most people can imagine. The very

closest star, after our own Sun, you will remember, is *twenty-five trillion miles away.*

Strewn about in space we know there are at least two hundred billion stars, many of them much larger than our own Sun. That figure of two hundred billion, by the way, looks like this if you write it out: 200,000,000,000.

All of those stars together make up what is known as a galaxy. Perhaps you have heard someone use that word when talking about stars. When we mean our particular galaxy or "island universe," we usually spell it with a capital G—Galaxy.

250

LIGHT A YEAR LONG

The stars of our Galaxy whirl together in space in a gigantic spiral so vast that our ordinary words for measuring hugeness can't describe it. Miles or even billions of miles just wouldn't be enough. Scientists describe the size of the Galaxy by using a measurement known as a *light year*.

Light year means just what it sounds like. It means a distance so great that it would take a beam of light a whole year to get from one end to the other. To get an idea of what a great distance that is, we must start with the way we usually measure the speed of light.

Light travels 186,300 miles in a single second, in just one tick of a clock. That is, in one second light can travel farther than seven times around the Earth.

That is a long long distance — isn't it? Yet what we are talking about is only the distance that light travels in a second. Try to imagine how far it travels in a whole year. That distance is about six trillion 6,000,000,000,000-miles. That is what we mean by a light year.

But wait a moment. We're not through yet in measuring our Galaxy just because we know that *one* light year equals six trillion miles. No indeed. Our Galaxy is two hundred thousand times that size. It has been figured by scientists that our Galaxy of stars is 200,000 light years across. It would take a beam of light 200,000 years to go all the way across the Galaxy. In miles that distance is 200,000 times 6,000,000,-000,000 miles or 1,200,000,000,000,000,000, miles altogether.

Because of the great distances in space, light plays some funny tricks. Suppose that a star 1,000 light years away blew up. It could happen, because as stars grow older they sometimes do blow up and turn into nothing but a seething blast of heat and scattering pieces of matter.

Well, if that star 1,000 light years away blew up, we wouldn't even know about it —not for 1,000 years because the star is so far away. If it blew up, the brilliant light from the explosion would immediately start traveling out through space. But it would take that brilliant light 1,000 years to reach Earth.

When we look into one part of the night sky, we can see many of the stars that are on the edge of the Galaxy like our Sun and its planets. When we look into another part of the night sky, on a clear night, we can look toward the center of the Galaxy. There we can see the most stars of all, arching across the sky like a band of diamonds. We call this part of the heavens the Milky Way. Sometimes, when we look at it, it seems less like millions of separate stars than like a cloud of milk-white light glowing in the sky.

THE BIG MILKY WAY

Inside of the Milky Way part of the Galaxy that we see there are probably one hundred billion stars. Around each of those bright shining stars planets revolve—we do not know exactly how many. But you can see how very full our Galaxy is.

Just as the planets revolve around the suns, so does everything in the Galaxy revolve like grains of dust blowing in a circle, slowly around and around the center of the Galaxy.

To get an idea of how slowly the Galaxy turns around its own center, we must think about how the Earth and its Sun travel. Back in the times of the dinosaurs, our

Earth and Sun were on the other side of the Galaxy from where they are in modern times. In about two hundred million more years the Earth and Sun will have turned about that far again.

Perhaps all of the great distances involved in learning about our Galaxy of stars has made you a bit dizzy. As a matter of fact, thinking about such vast spaces is difficult even for scientists. They know all of the numbers for the distances all right, but when it comes to realizing just how huge space is and how tiny the Earth is, everyone has some trouble.

The Milky Way

OUTER SPACE

But the bigness of space doesn't stop with our Galaxy by any means. Out beyond our Galaxy there are other galaxies—other vast clusters of stars. Scientists didn't even suspect that they existed until 1776, the time of the American Revolution. About that time, scientists had built telescopes powerful enough to see quite a few more stars than the 2,000 or so that could be seen with the unaided eye on a clear night.

Through these telescopes could be seen patches of bright light that some scientists thought must be out far beyond the familiar stars. Their telescopes just weren't powerful enough to really let them prove this, however. For another hundred years, men peered through telescopes and wondered about these patches of light. Other men, meantime, built bigger and better telescopes and, finally, some were built that could bring in light very clearly even from those distant patches in the sky. Then, when they were investigated more clearly, it was discovered that these patches of light were indeed galaxies of stars, all turning in great wheel-like circles just like our own Galaxy but so far away that merely *thinking* of such vast distances made people's heads swim.

One of the first of these clusters of stars beyond our own Milky Way is believed to

Modern telescope

253

be about *one-and-a-half million* light years away!

In other words, the light that left the stars in that cluster a million and a half years ago is just *now* reaching the Earth!

Because light travels at the same speed as radio waves, you might think about the distance this way. If there were someone alive in that cluster of stars beyond our Milky Way, and if that someone sent a radio message, it would take it one and a half million years to reach our Earth. Quite a long time to wait for a message, don't you think?

Now, with the help of the powerful telescopes that have been built, scientists are

discovering that there are many many clusters of stars even farther away in the vastness of space. Giant telescopes have picked up the light from clusters of stars that are *two billion* light years away from Earth.

Even out at such a tremendous distance in space, scientists have noticed an awe-inspiring thing. The stars are just as thick. So far as anyone can tell, they keep on and on and on. No matter how far we look, there are still more stars.

In all the vast ocean of space with all of its billions and trillions of stars and planets, our Earth and the people on it may seem terribly small. And they are. But there is this to remember: In all that vastness, so far as anyone has been able to discover, there is no life like the life on Earth. The Earth may be a very tiny dot in the universe, but to us who live here that dot is a very special dot indeed.

Not everything in the sky moves quite as steadily as the planets and the stars do. Every now and then, for instance, blazing bright objects called *comets* may be seen in the sky. (Comets are different from shooting stars, as we'll see in a moment.)

A comet, it is believed, is formed of millions of bits of matter all jammed together and apparently blazing. The blazing brightness of the comet makes it appear as a great ball of fire in the skies.

Then it has one thing that sets it apart from everything else. It has a long blazing streamer of fire, like a tail, curving behind it. The comet itself may be the size of the Earth, but the long flaming tail may stretch for a hundred million miles. This tail of the comet is formed as the comet swings closest to the Sun.

Comets travel around the Sun just as the

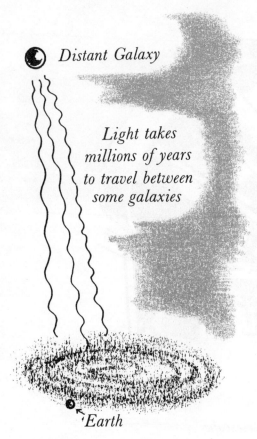

Distant Galaxy

Light takes millions of years to travel between some galaxies

Earth

Halley's Comet

planets do, except that they have elongated paths that take them far out beyond the planets where they cannot usually be seen.

One of the most famous comets, Halley's comet, can be seen from the Earth about every 75 or 76 years. We should be able to see it next sometime in the 1980's.

So far, scientists have not been able to explain just where the comets come from, or exactly what their blazing bodies and flaming tails are made of.

SHOOTING STARS

We know much more about "shooting stars." They aren't really stars at all—we just call them that because, when we see them streaking across the sky like a sudden white flame in the heavens, they do look like tiny stars shooting down toward the Earth. Actually, the name for these "shooting stars" is either *meteor* or *meteorite*.

Here is the difference between those two names: Both meteors and meteorites are pieces of matter, often huge hunks of rough metals, torn off a comet or some other object in space. Those that come close enough to Earth, are pulled down by the force of gravity. As the big chunk of metal enters the air surrounding the Earth, it starts getting red-hot and then white-hot because it is traveling so fast that even the air rushing against it makes it heat up. Most of the time the whole thing burns up before it

255

Meteorite

reaches the surface of the Earth. As it burns it makes the streak in the sky that we call a shooting star.

Now then, these falling things that *do not* reach the surface of the Earth are called meteors.

Others, however, are large enough so that they do not burn up entirely before hitting the surface of the Earth. These, the ones that do hit the surface of the Earth, are called meteorites.

Most of the meteorites are no larger than pebbles, and many are just the size of grains of dust when they hit the Earth. But every now and then a very much larger one crashes on to the Earth. One of the largest of these hit the Earth long ago right in the United States, out on the plains of Arizona. The meteorite was so large and hit so hard that it made a hole in the Earth nearly a mile across and hundreds of feet deep.

****

Now, when you look into the star-filled night you will have several things to do. First you can try to imagine all the vast distances of space and the amazing numbers of stars in it—and then you can try to find the pictures in the sky. You may find that the sky is a far more interesting screen, with far more interesting pictures than you can see on a mere movie or television screen. Some people say that the pictures in the sky are like pictures put on a screen for us by God. That is how wonderful they are.

256

The Seasons, the Tides,
and the Weather

THE day and the night, the shape of the moon, and the coming of winter and summer all depend on the way the earth moves around the sun.

WHAT MAKES DAY AND NIGHT?

The most noticeable thing that the earth does when it moves around the sun is to cause the day and night to come and go over the earth. As the earth travels around the sun, the earth itself is spinning. It spins around once every 23 hours, 56 minutes and four and nine-tenths seconds. We think of it as 24 hours. But that is because when people first figured on the earth's movement as a way to divide time into different parts, they dealt in round numbers. So they said the earth spins completely around once every 24 hours. We call those 24 hours a day. It means that during those 24 hours the spot on the earth where you live faces the sun, then turns away from it, spins all the way around, and then comes back to face the sun.

But while the earth is spinning, like a top made out of a ping pong ball, it is also moving in a circle around the sun — as though the spinning ping pong ball were going in a circle around a basket ball.

It takes the earth 365 days *and* 5 hours, 48 minutes, and 45½ seconds (and another 1/100 of a second to boot) to make one complete circle around the sun. We call

that complete circle around the sun a *year*. But, as you can probably guess right away, we can't very well divide our calendar up to include those five extra hours and the extra seconds as well. We just say a year is 365 days.

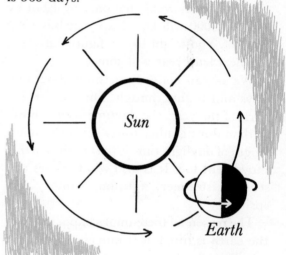

To take care of the extra hours, we just save them up! That is, every fourth year, which we call a leap year, we add a whole extra day to the year, making it 366 days long. This gets us all even again with the time. If we didn't do something like that, our calendars would just keep getting farther and farther behind and, after a few hundred years, we would start having December where November should be.

The extra day we add every fourth year is February the 29th. If you look on your calendar and find that February has only 28 days, then you will know that it is not a leap year. If you see it has 29 days, you will know it *is* a leap year.

(If you are very good at arithmetic there is another way to tell when leap years are coming. Every year that can be exactly divided by four, without anything left over, like 1812, for instance, or 1916 or 1956, is a leap year. There is one exception, though. If you are figuring the years that mark the turn of a century, like 1900 or 2000, for them to be leap years you have to be able to divide them evenly not only by 4 but by 400. So 2000 will be a leap year but 1900 was not. You might like to figure out when the next leap year will come).

We all can notice something about our days and nights though. During certain parts of the year, the daytime seems shorter than during other times. This changing length of daylight time is part of the earth's movement too. It is also what causes the seasons: summer, autumn, winter, and spring.

The reason all these things happen is that the earth is tilted as it moves around the sun. Think back to our saying that the earth is like a spinning ping pong ball going around a basket ball. Let's say that the ping pong ball is spinning around a long nail stuck right through its center. But instead of spinning like a top with the nail straight up and down, imagine the ping pong ball spinning at a tilted angle.

The earth is like that as it turns around the sun. It is tilted on its axis, which is an imaginary line straight through the earth from the North Pole to the South Pole— like the nail through the ping pong ball. As the earth turns around the sun, the angle of this tilt changes in relation to the sun.

WHY SUMMER? WHY WINTER? CLIMATE

When winter begins, the part of the world that America and England and Europe and China are on is tilted away from the sun. The closer to the North Pole any place is, the *less* sunlight it gets. The days seem shorter. In places very close to the North Pole, the lands where the Eskimos live in their ice igloos, there just isn't any sun at all while the earth is tilted this way. For many weeks it is night in those lands.

Even in the other parts of the world, where there is some sun during this time, the sun's rays come down at a slanting angle, instead of beating straight down as they do in summer. Because of the short days and the slanting rays of the sun, it is cold during this time of the year. We call it winter.

In winter you will notice that the sun seems to move across the sky much closer to the horizon than it does in the summer when it seems to go in a great curve overhead. In winter the sun appears much closer to the southern part of the horizon than any other time of the year, because of the way the earth is tilted away from the sun.

As the earth turns around the sun during the rest of the year, it tilts differently at different angles.

Toward the end of winter it begins to tilt so that the North Pole slants more in the direction of the sun instead of away from it. As this happens, of course, the southern part of the world begins to tilt away from the sun and it starts getting cooler there.

258

The seasons in the southern part of the world are just the opposite of those in the northern part. The line that divides the northern and southern parts is called the Equator. It goes through the center of Africa and across the top of South America. Of course there is no real line there. It is just an imaginary line used by mapmakers. All parts of the United States are north of this line. But, in the places closer to the line, the tilting of the earth is never great enough to make the climate as cold or the daylight as short as in places farther away. Along the Equator itself, there is very little change in the length of the daylight.

WHERE THEY HAVE NIGHT ALL DAY

After the earth starts to tilt the North Pole toward the sun, things begin to warm up in the places where it was cold, and the daylight begins to stay longer.

Up near the North Pole itself, instead of having night all the time, the days get longer and longer until finally, for a few weeks, the sun may be seen in the sky 24 hours a day. People sometimes call this part of the world "the Land of the Midnight Sun" because during the summer the sun shines even at midnight. If you lived there, with the Eskimos, during the summer months you would see the sun merely making a circle in the sky instead of rising and setting.

The thing that makes the weather warmer during these months, besides the length of the days, is that the sun's rays come down on the earth quite straight. Instead of rising and setting close to the southern horizon, the sun seems to climb much higher and straighter across the sky even though, in our part of the world, it is always at least

In summer the North Pole tilts towards the sun

a little closer to the southern than to the northern horizon.

Of course, as you have probably noticed for yourself, there is one thing about the sun that just doesn't change no matter what time of year it is. In the morning the sun is always in the east and in the evening it is always in the west.

We say that the sun rises in the east and sets in the west. What we really mean is that the earth spins so that the eastern horizon turns toward the sun first and then moves so that the western horizon passes by it.

Perhaps the easiest way to remember which way this happens is to remember that the sun finishes its day in the west. The sun's rest is in the west. Rest, west. It rhymes. Just remember that and you will remember the way the sun sets.

While the earth is spinning and tilting around the sun, the moon and the earth are doing some special turning of their own.

The moon, as you learned in an earlier part of this book, is a satellite of earth. This means that it turns around the earth in about the way that the earth turns around the sun. That is, the earth is the center of the moon's movement, the way the sun is the center of the earth's.

MOONRISE AND MOONSET

Like the sun, the moon is said to rise and set. But, as with the sun, it is the spinning of the earth that is the real reason for the rising and the setting. Like the sun, too, the moon is said to rise in the east and set in the west. But there are a lot of differences.

In the first place, unlike the sun the moon has a turning motion of its own. It circles around the earth. It takes the moon about four weeks to go all the way around the earth.

The fact that the moon itself moves while the earth is turning means that each day it appears above the horizon about 50 minutes later than it did the day before. For half of the time during a month this means that the moon appears during daylight hours and sets during nighttime hours. Some nights, too, you have probably noticed that the moon just seems to stay in the sky for a few minutes before it sets. When it does that, we know that it first appeared sometime during the day, so that by early evening it is setting. Some nights, of course, when the moon appears early in the evening, you can see it practically all night long and right up to dawn.

The thing about the moon that you probably notice most, though, is that it seems to change shape regularly throughout the month. At least the lighted part of the moon appears to have a different size or shape during the different nights.

The reason the moon looks different on different nights is that it has no light of its own. The light we *call* moonlight is actually sunlight that is reflected from the moon. The moon acts like a big mirror in reflecting sunlight to the earth.

But, as we have learned, the earth and moon are both moving around the sun. And the moon makes a separate circle around the earth as well.

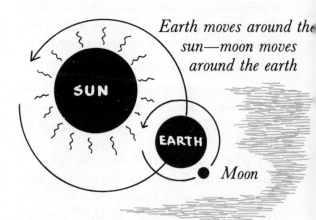

Earth moves around the sun—moon moves around the earth

When the moon and the earth have moved so that the moon is directly between the earth and the sun, we have what we call the time of the new moon. This means that we can't see any moon at all. The reason is that the sunlight is shining on the side of the moon nearest the sun. The side of the moon facing the earth is dark. It is between the earth and the sun and cannot reflect any sunlight to the earth.

After the moon and the earth have changed position a little, though, the moon reflects sunlight from its edge. Then we see what we call the crescent moon, like a backwards letter C in the sky. The sunlight reflecting from the edge of the moon is what

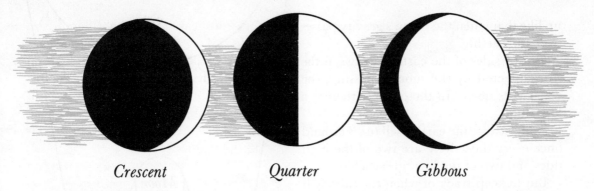

Crescent   *Quarter*   *Gibbous*

causes that bright crescent sliver of light.

After the moon has moved to a certain point in its trip around the earth, it faces the sun so that we can see light reflecting from half of the moon. When this happens, we say that the moon is in its "first quarter." We mean that the moon has moved a quarter of the way on its trip around the earth. As it moves on, more and more of the surface of the moon that faces the earth reflects light from the sun. Now it looks like an almost full circle of light, except for just its rim that is dark. When the moon is between a half and a full moon it is called a gibbous moon. (The word *gibbous* means hunched or humpbacked, and that is how the moon looks at this stage).

Next comes the full moon. This is when the moon has gone halfway around in its circle of the earth and faces the sun fully. Now the entire surface facing the earth reflects light for us to see. The moon is full. It is full and round as a bright ball in the sky.

Then the moon starts moving around the earth for the other half of its trip, or orbit. It starts reflecting less and less light toward the earth until finally it is back again in its "new moon" position, directly between the earth and the sun. Now, once again, we have no moonlight.

The trip of the moon from one such position to the next takes twenty-nine and one-half days.

HOW THE MOON CAUSES THE TIDES IN THE OCEAN

There is one particular job that the moon does that has nothing to do with reflecting light onto the earth. The moon is the cause of the rising and falling of the water in the oceans that we call the tides.

As the moon moves past parts of the earth covered by oceans, there is a pull of gravity. Gravity is the force that keeps all the planets in their proper courses around the sun. It is the force that keeps the moon moving in its course around the earth.

As the moon moves over the oceans, the force of gravity affects the ocean waters. It causes the water to rise. This same force of gravity tugs at the earth itself in such a way that the oceans on the opposite side of the world also have a high tide. Those oceans have a high tide because gravity actually has pulled the earth a little away from the ocean. It is like a glass of water when you suddenly lower it. The water in it will splash upwards. The ocean on the side of the earth opposite the moon moves

261

up like that when the moon's gravity passes over the earth.

On the sides of the earth in between the sides affected by the moon's passing, the water goes down. In those places there is a low tide.

And because the earth itself turns around once every day, there are two of the high tides and two of the low tides each day.

But to keep track of when the tides will be high and when they will be low, you have to remember what we said earlier about the moon rising about 50 minutes later each day. This means that the moon will pass over any particular spot on the earth 50 minutes later every day. So, each day the tide comes 50 minutes later.

SPECIAL TIDES

There are special tides during the month that are caused when the sun's gravity adds force to the moon's pull on the waters. When the moon and the sun are in a straight line with the earth, when there is a "new moon," the tides are especially high and are called "spring tides." The same thing happens when the moon is on the opposite side of the earth from the sun, during a full moon. Then, too, there is a spring tide.

When the moon is at its halfway spot around the earth, things are just the opposite. This is the time of the half moon when the moon and the sun work against each other, rather than with each other, in pulling against the water. At that time the tides are not as high as usual. They are called "neap tides."

Just how high the moon and the sun will cause the tides to rise depends on the shape of the shore around the water. In narrow bays, where the shore holds the water in tightly, the tides are very high. When the water rises there is no room for it to spread out as there is in the open sea; so it rises way up.

In one bay, the Bay of Fundy in Canada, the water is held within a narrow, 145-mile long shoreline. The tides in that narrow bay rise as much as 50 feet, or as high as a four or five story building.

Now that we have seen the sun and moon at work making the seasons of the year, and pulling the waters, we can move off the earth a little bit and look into the world of the air that surrounds our earth. In that world we will find out about weather.

There is an ocean of air all around the earth, like water around a stone.

On the ground, where we walk around, this air is taken for granted. We don't ask where it came from or where it goes. We just breathe it. We also fly airplanes in it. So we know that the ocean of air goes far, far up. We see clouds high in the sky. We know that they are held there in the air, floating in it the way snow floats on water.

HOW MUCH AIR IS THE EARTH WRAPPED IN?

Does the air go on and on forever? Does it go as far as the moon? *No,* is the answer to both those questions. The air that is around our earth goes only to a certain point. It is like an envelope around the earth. In comparison to the size of the earth, this layer of air that is around the earth would seem quite thin. If you could see this layer of air from somewhere far off the earth, the layer of air wouldn't seem any thicker compared to the earth than a wrapping of tissue paper would seem compared to an orange.

Yet, within the wrapping of air around the earth many amazing things happen. It is there that weather is formed, that clouds are born and grow, that thunder crashes

and lightning flashes, and that rain and snow collect. Even though we can't see the air that surrounds our earth, we can learn a lot about it.

First, let's just see exactly how this layer of air around the earth is formed, and what sort of an "ocean" it really is.

Most important to us most of the time is that part of the air-ocean that lies fairly close to the earth and gives us the air we breathe. Scientists call this important first section of our ocean of air the *troposphere.* It goes up to about ten miles above the surface of the earth. Most of the air is in this layer.

HOW MUCH DOES THE AIR WEIGH

Actually, though you may never think of air weighing anything at all, the way scientists measure air is by its weight, or pressure. All the air in the first layer, the troposphere, actually weighs *five quadrillion tons!*

Five quadrillions is such a tremendous number that it would take a person counting continuously 150,000,000 years even to count it. And don't forget that each ton has 2,000 pounds in it. That number, five quadrillion, looks like this if you write it out: 5,000,000,000,000,000.

That's how many *tons* the air weighs. It presses down and around on everything on earth with the weight of one ton for every square foot. You may wonder why everything isn't crushed by all this weight. The reason why it isn't is really very simple.

WHY WE AREN'T CRUSHED BY ALL THIS WEIGHT

Suppose we think of this in terms of an eggshell. Eggshells are so fragile that it would take ever so much less than a ton of weight to crush one. But the weight of the

Earth with layer of air around it

air, don't forget, is everywhere. It means that the eggshell has as much air weight around it from the top as from the bottom and from the sides, from everywhere. So, all that weight of air just balances itself out. It is the same with your body. It has air *in* it and *around* it. The weight of the air can't even be felt because it is evenly distributed everywhere, inside and outside. If you had an eggshell without any air inside it, the air outside would crush it immediately.

Three-fourths of all the air weight is in that ten-mile first layer we call the troposphere. From there on up for many many miles, the remainder of the air is stretched, getting thinner and rarer the higher it goes.

THE STRATOSPHERE

After the ten-mile first layer, there is another layer of air that is very much thinned out. It is called the *stratosphere*. There is just enough air in the stratosphere to support giant balloons used to explore this high part of the air. Airplanes that use propellers, can't fly there because there isn't enough air for the propellers to bite into. A propeller of an airplane, 'way up there, would be like the propeller of an ocean liner taken out of the water: it would just spin but wouldn't be able to provide any power. Farther on in this book you will learn how rockets can go up through this thin layer of air because they don't depend on air to hold them or provide something against which to shove or pull.

One way of figuring how the air thins out as you go higher is to find where there isn't enough air for you to breathe. That point comes at about six miles above the earth. There you could not get enough air to keep you alive. Even a mile before that there would be so little air that you would pass out. Nothing can burn without oxygen. At twelve miles above the earth there wouldn't be enough oxygen even to let a tiny match burn.

Now that we have mentioned oxygen, you may remember that you have heard people speak of air as being oxygen. A lot of air is. About one-fifth of air is oxygen. But almost all of the remaining four-fifths is nitrogen. You learned about the importance of nitrogen in the part of this book that told about plants. You may remember also that if it weren't for plants, which release oxygen, our air would not remain breathable and nothing on earth could remain alive.

The tiny part of the air that isn't oxygen and nitrogen is made up of other gases like neon—the sort that is used in bright, blinking lights—and hydrogen and rarer gases like helium and xenon.

OZONE

There is one other word you may have heard when people speak of air. It is *ozone*. If you have ever been around when a light bulb broke, you may have heard someone sniff and say "Smell the ozone."

Ozone usually is air through which electrical charges have passed. In the upper layer of air we called the stratosphere, there is a 15-or-so-mile-thick blanket of ozone. This doesn't happen to be caused by electrical charges, but by certain rays from the sun which do the same job.

Ozone is just the same as air except that, because of the changes the electrical charge or sun rays make in it, it cannot be breathed by living things. It is poisonous to them.

264

HOW HIGH DOES THE AIR GO?

Now that we know what is in air and how it covers the earth, there is only one question left before we get on to the weather, and that is the most amazing part of the ocean of air. That question is: How high up *does* the air go? How high up could we find some trace of air, no matter how thin? Scientists do not agree about this. They hope that the rockets they are sending hundreds of miles above the earth may be able to scoop up samples of what they find there and so help to answer the question.

So far, however, some scientists feel that the ocean of air ends about 400 miles above the earth with all but the very tiniest traces of air gone by the time the 250-mile mark is passed.

The highest boundary any scientist has suggested for any trace of the air is 6,000 miles.

When some people think of the "top" of the air around the earth, they think of it as the "sky." It is easy to think of the sky as sort of a ceiling above the earth. But it is really not a ceiling in any way at all. In fact, what we think of as the blue sky is just part of the air around the earth. It is a part where the light from the sun is scattered by the air.

WHY THE SKY LOOKS BLUE

The color of the sky is caused by the air itself. The air happens to be made of just the right things to reflect most of the blue light that comes along with all other colors of light from the sun. At a point about 12 miles above the earth, the air is just right to scatter this blue light.

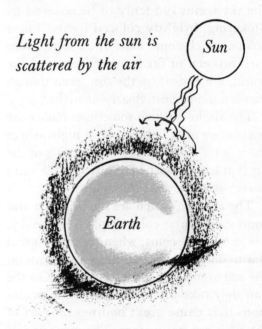

Light from the sun is scattered by the air

Earth showing layer of air thinning out to nothing but tiny particles after 250 miles

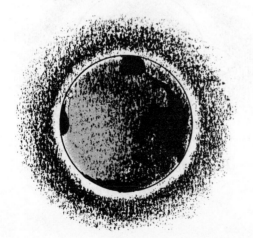

Most of the sunlight, of course, goes right on down to the earth. But the air does scatter just enough of the blue part so that, when you look up, it seems as though there is a ceiling of blue. If you were able to fly above the point where the blue light is spread to form the sky color, you would find that the air beyond would be filled

265

with a sort of violet light. Then, up at the top of the stratosphere, about twenty miles above the earth, where the air thins out to practically nothing, you would see only the bright stars, shining in deep black outer space.

The other colors that appear in the sky, the reddish colors of sunrise and sunset for instance, are caused by water particles and dust in the air.

AIRGLOW AND THE AURORAS

There are also some very special colors, known as "airglow" and the auroras, when the sky seems suddenly to be covered by flickering, brightly colored lights. These colors, which come most of all in the very far northern or far southern parts of the world, are caused by the sun, even though you see them most clearly at night.

The airglow, which sometimes makes the horizon seem to light up on a night where there is no moon, is caused by parts of the air that have absorbed so much of the sun's energy that they actually glow.

The auroras, which are the brightest and most spectacular color displays in the sky, are caused, it seems, when there are great storms on the surface of the sun. Storms on the sun aren't like storms on earth. On the sun they take the form of gigantic explosions that cause great boilings on part of the sun's red-hot surface. The gigantic sun storms, that easily can cause waves of melted matter and flames bigger than the entire earth, send vast quantities of energy charges shooting down onto the earth. This surge of energy is believed to be what makes part of the skies glow.

The reason auroras occur in the areas relatively close to the North and South Poles

is that these are the centers of what scientists call the magnetic field of earth. That means that energy flows toward them. A compass points to the North Pole because of that invisible flow of energy. And the sun's energy, that causes the auroras, also tends to hit hardest near the top and the bottom of the globe.

WHAT IS WEATHER?

Everything we call weather takes place in the lowest layer of the air that is wrapped around the earth. This part of the air, which scientists call the zone of weather, is not a perfectly even layer all around the earth. It is thinner at the two poles, the North Pole and the South Pole, and thicker around the sides of the earth. This is because the earth spins. Anything that spins will throw things away from itself as it whirls—the way a merry-go-round seems to be pushing you toward the outside when it goes very fast or the way a penny will slide off a record if you put it on while the record is spinning.

The earth as it spins throws air out more at the sides where the spinning is very fast than at the top and bottom where there is

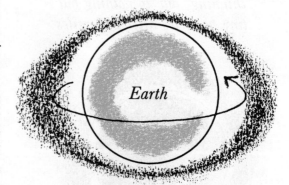

Earth spinning and showing how the air bulges out

266

hardly any motion at all. This means that the air bulges out more around the sides of the earth than at the top and bottom.

The thickness of the zone of weather is about 25,000 feet at the North and South Poles and about 60,000 feet around the middle of the earth—or around the line we call the Equator which is the imaginary marking, like an imaginary belt, of the middle of the earth.

Halfway between the Poles and the Equator, the thickness of the weather zone is about 36,000 feet. The United States, part way between the Equator and the North Pole, has a weather zone that generally goes up to about 36,000 feet.

In the summer when the air gets warmer, it expands. This means that the weather zone may grow by a few thousand feet.

In winter when the cold makes the air shrink in size, the weather zone may drop a bit.

You can make an experiment that shows how air expands and contracts if you can find a very, very thin piece of rubber sheet to put over the mouth of an empty bottle. You'll have to make it cover the bottle very tightly so that no air can get in or out. Strapping it on firmly with rubber bands should work.

Now, when you put the bottle in a warmer place, the air inside will expand and puff the rubber out some.

If you put the bottle in the ice-box for a while, it will shrink or contract and the rubber will go flat again, or even push down inside the neck of the bottle a little bit.

WHY THE AIR EXPANDS
AND SHRINKS

The air around us, of course, expands

and shrinks because of the heat of the rays of the sun, and it absorbs much of that heat. If there were no air around the earth, there would be nothing to take in all that heat from the sun or hold it on and in the earth. During the daytime, the temperature on the earth would go up to 230 degrees Fahrenheit, more than hot enough to boil water.

When we use that word Fahrenheit with temperatures we mean that we are reading temperature on what is known as the

Boy blowing breath out on a cold day

Fahrenheit scale. On that scale, water boils at 212 degrees and freezes at 32 degrees. The other scale that is often used for temperatures is the Centigrade. On that scale, water freezes at zero and boils at 100 degrees. (Many countries in Europe use the Centigrade scale).

The air around the earth does more than just absorb the heat. It also stores up the heat and lets the earth store up heat too, so that, when the sun is not shining on a particular part of the earth, there will still be some heat left. If there were no air, it has been figured that as soon as the sun set the temperature would start falling and would go as low as 300 degrees below zero Fahrenheit before the sun came to warm the air up again.

We know about this because of the moon. There is no air around the moon and the temperatures on the moon go through just this sort of boiling and freezing every day.

WHAT THE WATER IN THE AIR HAS TO DO WITH WEATHER

Inside of the air there are three most important things that happen to make weather. The first thing is that the air always holds different amounts of water vapor. You can see the sort of water vapor the air holds when you let your breath out in the winter time. Your breath turns into a whitish puff in the cold air. That is because your breath is moist. It has tiny water particles in it. In the cold air these tiny water particles freeze or condense and cause the whitish little clouds our breath makes in the winter.

Well, everywhere in the air there are tiny water particles like that. But not all of them

are condensed in the form of mist or frozen droplets or snow or rain. Most of the time, the water particles are in the form of a vapor. They are so tiny and so light that they just hang in the air and are invisible.

The air you are breathing now has water vapor in it, but probably not enough to see or feel. The only time you can *see* the water vapor in your breath is when you breathe in cold weather. Clouds also are water vapor that you can see. So is fog. In hot weather there may be a lot of water vapor in the air and it makes everything feel "muggy" or damp. But still you can't see it.

The reasons why water vapor condenses into mists or fog or snow or rain or sleet or clouds are very important parts of the making of the weather. The reason the water vapor in your breath condenses to form a white mist while the rest of the air, which also has water vapor in it, stays clear is one of the weather stories we will read about now.

How much water vapor is present in the air at any given time is one of the first things that causes different kinds of weather. Most of the water vapor comes from the water in oceans, rivers, and lakes. A lot of it comes from rain and snow—which is just water vapor that has collected in the air and condensed into something more solid than vapor. Other water vapor is given off by plants and, of course, in the breath of animals.

Where there are large areas of water, large amounts of water vapor are given off as the water evaporates. Water evaporation is what happens when you leave a little bowl of water overnight in a warm room. Next morning you see that there isn't as much water in the bowl. Some of the water has disappeared because it evaporated—because it turned into water vapor and the water vapor went into the air.

Places where there are large forests and jungles also put a lot of water vapor into the air. In the summer, when the air is warmer, much more water vapor is given off and taken into the air.

The amount of water vapor in the air is what people mean when they talk about "humidity." Humidity means the amount of water vapor in the air.

The amount of water vapor the air will hold at any given time is very much like the amount of sugar a glass of water will dissolve and hold. You can put sugar into the glass of water and it will dissolve. It will just melt into the water. You keep putting more and more sugar in. Suddenly, at a certain point, the water just can't dissolve any more sugar. It has all the sugar in it that it can hold. The next sugar you put in will just sink to the bottom of the glass but it will not dissolve or melt into the water.

When the glass of water just won't dissolve any more sugar, we say the water has reached the saturation point. It is saturated with sugar. It can't hold any more.

But, wait a moment! If you *heat* the water, it *will* be able to dissolve more sugar. That means that when water is heated its saturation point is raised. It can dissolve more sugar before it becomes saturated.

Air is just like that glass of water when it comes to holding water vapor. When the air has been filled with all the water vapor it can hold, it has reached its saturation point. But when air is heated, it can hold more water vapor than when it is cooler.

When you breathe out in the winter time, your breath is warmer than the air outside. That means that your breath can hold more water vapor than the air outside. But when the puff of breath gets outside, it is cooled off very quickly. It can't hold as much water vapor as it did when it was warm. So, some of the water vapor condenses and you have the whitish mist. But after a second, the air in your breath is all mixed with the other air and so is the water vapor. As it spreads out like this, the water vapor can be taken into the surrounding air. Then the whitish mist from your breath disappears.

HOW TEMPERATURE AFFECTS WEATHER

The second of the three important parts of the weather is temperature. You can see already that whether or not the air is hot or cold means a lot when it comes to how much water vapor the air holds.

As the temperature of air changes, so does the weather. When warm air with a water vapor in it cools off, some of the water vapor will condense. The air will then not be able to hold as much water vapor. Its saturation point drops down. The water vapor can then condense into such things as fog or rain or snow.

Changing temperature in the air can also cause the air to move. Warm air moves upward and cool air drops down. When some air starts going up and other air starts moving down, we get breezes and winds. Sometimes we get storms. We'll hear about them later.

Practically all of the heat that affects the air close to the earth comes from the earth itself. That doesn't mean that the earth *makes* the heat. This heat is *reflected* by the

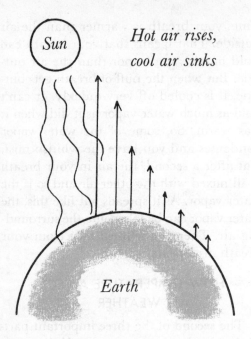

Hot air rises,
cool air sinks

Sun

Earth

earth. The heat comes from the rays of the sun. Those rays warm the air a little bit. But most of the heat from the sun's rays goes into the earth, into stones and water and the land itself. And this heat goes into the air that passes over the earth.

The higher you go into the air, in the weather zone, the less air there is that has had a chance to be warmed by being very close to the earth. The temperature begins to drop. The air is cooler. Generally speaking, at every thousand feet up, the air is cooler by five-and-a-half degrees Fahrenheit.

THE DEWPOINT

The temperature at which a given part of the air is saturated with water is called the *dewpoint*. It means that if the air is cooled any more, some of the water vapor will have to condense. *Dewpoint* is a good name because when you find dew on the grass, you know that the air outside cooled off just enough during the night to make a little of the water vapor condense into little droplets. It covers the grass and makes most things outdoors feel wet until the sun heats the air up enough for the water to evaporate and go back into the warmed-up air.

The dewpoint of the air in your own home may be found by a simple experiment. Take a thin metal pitcher partly filled with water and put a thermometer in it. Then, start adding small pieces of ice. When the water and the pitcher have been cooled to the dewpoint, small drops of water will form on the outside of the pitcher.

The temperature on the thermometer when those drops begin to form is the dewpoint in that room. It means that if all the air in the room were cooled to the temperature shown on the thermometer, some of the water in the air would have to condense out in the form of water and you would have dew right in your room.

WHAT RELATIVE HUMIDITY MEANS

One other important measurement used in talking about the amount of water vapor in the air is called *relative humidity*. If we hear someone say "The relative humidity is 50 per cent," it means that the air is holding just 50 per cent of the water vapor it

270

could hold under the air's pressure and temperature at that particular time.

WEATHER DEPENDS ON THE WEIGHT OF THE AIR TOO

The third and last major part of weather has to do with the weight of the air. You remember that air does weigh something and that it presses on every square foot of everything on earth with a weight of about a ton. This means that on every square inch of you and the earth and everything else, there is a little less than 15 pounds of air weight, or pressure.

But this pressure changes depending on where it is measured and at what temperature. Usually, at sea level, it stays pretty close to the 15 pounds per square inch that we mentioned. On top of a mountain, however, the weight is less because the air gets thinner higher up.

The pressure of the air can change, too, because of temperature. As air gets warm its weight changes. Warm air has less weight than cold air. This is because, as the air warms up, it spreads out and gets thinner. You remember the experiment with the bottle of air? The air warmed up and expanded, spread out.

When air gets cold it gets heavier. The cool heavier air tries to sink down. The warm lighter air tries to rise up. At sea level, the warm air moves up and cool air comes down until it reaches the steady point where it again has a pressure or weight of close to 15 pounds per square inch. It will stay like that until it warms or cools again and the air begins to move up and down again. It is this air, moving up and down, that causes airplanes to have bumpy rides. When people talk about "air pockets" that bounce airplanes around, they really mean that the airplane is bounced up by an area of rising air and then comes to an area of cool air that is going down. When that happens the airplane feels as if it is dropping straight down like an elevator.

WHAT "PREVAILING WINDS" ARE AND WHAT THEY DO

On a larger scale, it is the different temperatures of air that cause the winds that are always blowing around the world. These winds are called *prevailing winds* because they prevail—that is, they keep going all the time. Sometimes they don't move very fast or blow very hard but they always move at least a little bit.

These winds are caused by warm air that is always present in the hot parts of the world around the center of the earth and by the cold air that is always present at the earth's poles.

The warm air rises and moves toward the poles. The cold air pours down to fill in where the warm air used to be. Of course, on the way, the cool air warms up and the warm air cools off. This flow from the equator to the poles sets air in motion all over the world.

The world actually can be divided into six major sections of these prevailing winds. We'll describe the three sections of the Northern Hemisphere. This includes all the world north of the equator and takes in such places as the United States, England, Europe, China, and even the top half of Africa. The three sections of the Southern Hemisphere are *exactly the reverse* of the Northern Hemisphere when it comes to prevailing winds.

The first wind area is from the equator up to a point about even with the top of

Mexico, or the city of El Paso, Texas.

In this zone there is a belt of very calm, fairly light air called the *doldrums*. The air movement in this area is not very fast or very great.

When sailors used to say that their ship was "in the doldrums," they meant that it just couldn't find enough wind to fill its sails. Today people say they are "in the doldrums" when they don't feel like moving.

The top edge of this first zone of air we are discussing is a belt of fairly heavy air known as the *horse latitudes*.

Because the air of the top boundary is heavy, it tends to move down toward the lighter air in the doldrums. While it is moving, however, the spinning of the earth has an effect on it. The earth spins from west to east. Facing north, this means that the earth is spinning to the right.

The heavier air that starts moving down from the horse latitudes is affected by this. Instead of moving straight down from the

north, it moves at an angle as though it were blowing from the right—that is, the northeast.

All winds, by the way, are named after the direction they come *from*—not the direction they are blowing *toward*. So, when the winds move from the horse latitudes down to the doldrums, they are called northeasterly winds. And because sailors used to be able to depend on this movement of air to help move their trading vessels, they called it a *trade wind*. It became known as the Northeasterly Trade Wind.

Below the equator, remember, everything is just the opposite from the way it is above the equator; so that in the first zone there are southeasterly trade winds.

The second zone of winds, in the Western Hemisphere, stretches up to the middle of Canada. In Europe that would bring it to about the bottom tip of Norway and in Asia to the northern part of Russia.

The bottom boundary of this second zone is the horse latitudes with its fairly heavy

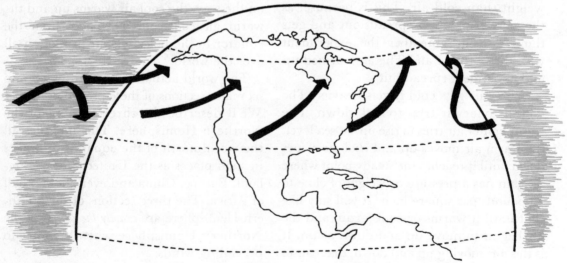

Prevailing westerly winds

272

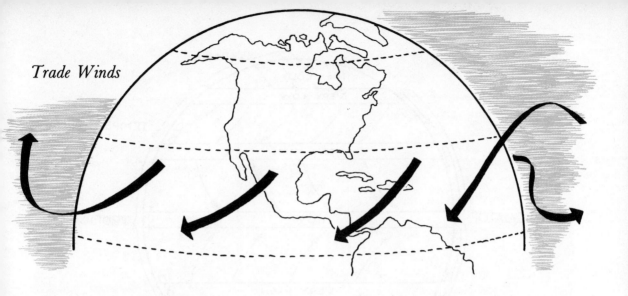

Trade Winds

air. At the top of the zone, even though it is in an area of very cold air, there is a very stormy belt of light air that streams around the world. This means that air from the horse latitudes, besides flowing down to the low pressure area of the doldrums, also can flow toward the low pressure to the north. This flow also is influenced by the

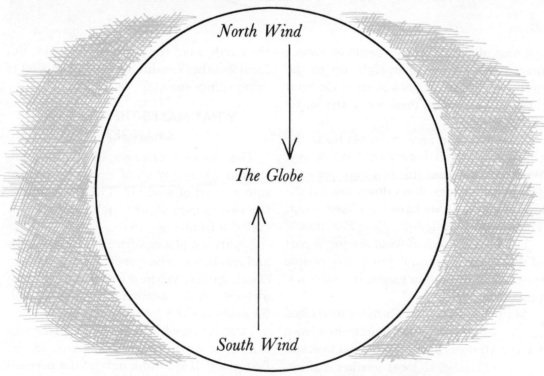

North Wind

The Globe

South Wind

Winds are named for direction from which they blow

273

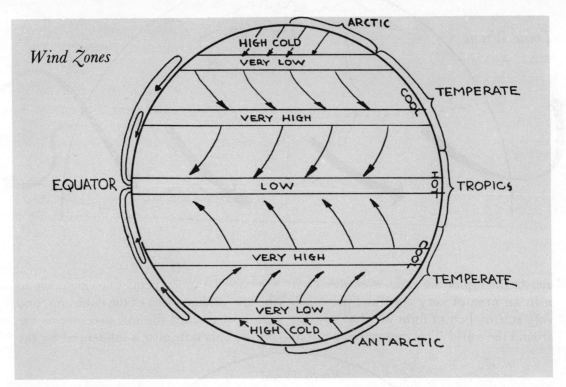

Wind Zones

ARCTIC

HIGH COLD

VERY LOW

TEMPERATE

COOL

VERY HIGH

EQUATOR

LOW

HOT

TROPICS

VERY HIGH

COOL

TEMPERATE

VERY LOW

HIGH COLD

ANTARCTIC

spinning of the earth and becomes, rather than a wind blowing straight up to the north, a wind that blows at an angle from the west. Sailors call these winds the *Stormy Westerlies.*

The next wind zone stretches up to the pole where the air is very cold and heavy. We would say that this is a high pressure area. This air, too, flows down toward the low pressure area we have just talked about. The winds are called the *Polar Easterlies.*

Those great zones of wind are just a part of the weather picture. For many people they certainly wouldn't seem the most important part either.

Most people are much more interested in the weather right around their own homes. All they care about is local weather.

Now, of course, all local weather is affected by the larger movements of air around the earth, as in the zones of the wind; but local weather conditions depend on a lot of other things too.

WHAT MAKES THE WEATHER CHANGE?

The greatest changes in weather are caused when a mass of warm air bumps into a mass of cool air. The place where the two masses of air touch each other is called a front.

Fronts are places where storms are born and winds rise, where snow forms, and rain clouds gather. When it comes to predicting a change in the weather, the places to look for clues are the fronts.

First, let's see how a mass of cold air and a mass of warm can flow together in the first place. If we think only of the prevailing winds, we might think that all the

274

movement of air is very orderly and shouldn't change much from day to day.

Actually, there are millions of reasons why the flow of air around the world cannot be so smooth and orderly.

One of the important reasons is that the amount of heat reflected into the air from the earth changes from day to day, as the earth tilts toward and away from the sun. This means that more warm air will flow from the equator one day, and less the next, or just the other way around. Air in one part of the world may be warmed and cooled quite differently one day as compared to the next. That is why the moving air is always different everywhere in the world—every day. The general *directions* of the prevailing winds remain the same all right, but not the temperatures or speeds of the winds.

HOW WARM AND COLD "FRONTS" AFFECT WEATHER

Now we can take a close look at the fronts that cause our big weather changes.

The fronts we hear most about are warm fronts and cold fronts. A cold front is formed when a lot of cold air suddenly pushes into an area of warm air.

A warm front is formed when a lot of warm air is pushed into cold air.

The first front we'll look at closely is the warm front.

Imagine that somewhere in the South there have been some especially hot days and a great mass of warm air has built up and is pushing out against some cooler air that is lying to the north. The area where the two masses of air are meeting will stretch for at least a couple of hundred miles. In some cases it might stretch for a thousand or two thousand miles.

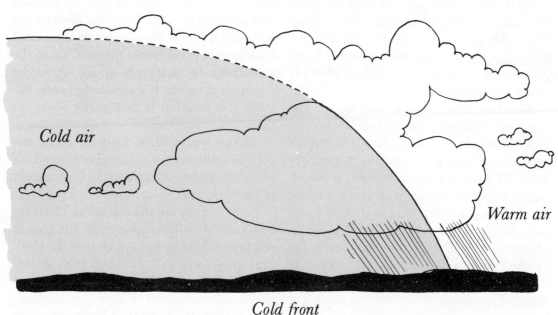

Cold air

Warm air

Cold front

275

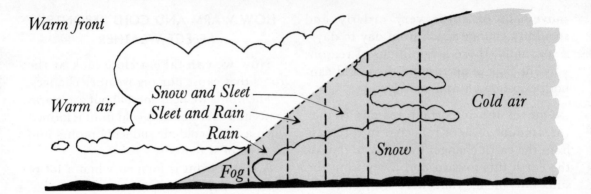

Warm front

Warm air

Snow and Sleet
Sleet and Rain
Rain

Fog

Snow

Cold air

The warm air, being the air that is doing the moving in this case, begins to push right over the cold air. Because the cold air stays closest to the ground, this means that the warm air can't push the cold air back in a straight line like a wall. It sort of bends it back at an angle until the cold air is just like a wedge lying on the ground, with the warm air going over it at a slant. This slant, or slope, of the front is a very gradual one. It rises just one mile for every 150 miles of ground covered. That means that if the wedge of cool air goes back for 300 miles, it will only be two miles high. The warm air will have pushed that far along the cold air.

All along this sloping line where the warm air is pushing the cool air, things are happening to the weather. As the warm air touches the cool air, it begins to get cool itself. This means it can't hold as much water vapor as before and thick stormy clouds form. Out of these clouds may come rain, sleet, or snow. The clouds in some places may be so thick that they touch the ground. When clouds are right down at the surface of the earth, we call the weather foggy. The clouds touching the earth are fog.

Most of the time, when a warm front is on its way, long streaky clouds called *cirrus clouds* form very high in the sky in advance of the warm front.

The most important clouds of the warm front, however, are the thick, bad weather clouds called *nimbostratus*. These clouds are the greatest sources of rain. We'll describe all the different kinds of clouds later.

Now we come to the cold front. This front starts with a mass of cool air pushing away from the polar regions toward the warmer air near the center of the earth. Unlike the warm front, the cool air of the cold front doesn't push up on top of the warm air it meets. It slides underneath, because it is heavier. It pushes the warm air up.

As the warm air is pushed up by the cold air, the warm air begins to cool off and a lot of the water vapor in it condenses to form clouds.

If the warm air that is being lifted up has a lot of water vapor in it, the clouds will probably stretch down close to the earth and grow very tall. It is inside of clouds like this that great thunderstorms form and also sudden showers of rain.

If the warm air doesn't have too much

276

water vapor in it, the clouds will be formed high in the air and there won't be any rain.

The slope along the meeting of the warm and cold air is much steeper than it was with the warm front, about four times as steep.

All along this cold front there may be individual storms called *squalls*. These squalls are about the worst of the ordinary wind and rain storms.

Strangely enough, however, there may be parts of the front that are fairly clear. These are parts where the warm air didn't have much water vapor in it.

One of the big differences between the warm and the cold front is that the cold front is usually not nearly as wide as the warm. Usually a cold front is only about 50 miles wide—100 miles is about as wide as any of them get, though it may be as much as 2000 miles long. That is, the effects of the meeting of the cold and warm air may be felt for as many as 2000 miles back from the point where the two air masses actually meet.

When a warm front is coming, as we have learned, long wispy clouds high in the air may come before it.

There is something that comes before a cold front develops too. The first thing you would notice in this part of the world when a cold front is forming is that a south wind is blowing. Then clouds start showing up on the west and northwesterly horizons. This all happens faster than the forming of a warm front. The temperature suddenly drops a few degrees. Instruments that check the weight or pressure of the air suddenly show that the pressure is rising. The instruments that measure the pressure are called *barometers*.

Then the wind shifts from a southerly to a northeasterly direction and the clouds begin to come together to form larger clouds. Some of these clouds may be responsible for violent thunderstorms. Winds may shift and blow hard within the area of the front. Rains, from drizzles to downpours, may happen all along the edges of the front.

Sooner or later, of course, as the air seeks to get back to its old balance, the fronts move on and the air temperature in them evens out so that calm and clear weather comes back again.

THUNDERSTORMS

From thunderstorms we have had we can surely remember the lightning we have seen flashing and the thunder we have heard booming.

Thunder and lightning are born in clouds that are making rain. The cloud itself is formed of water vapor that is condensing out of air that has cooled and thus lowered its saturation point. When this happens some of the water vapor that used to be "dissolved" in the air (as we "dissolved" the sugar in the glass of water) has to come out.

The next step is that the tiny water particles in the water vapor gather around pieces of dust from the earth, or grains of salt from the oceans, and form drops of rain. These drops of rain, as they form high in the air, have very tiny charges of electrical energy in them. This energy is produced by the great movements of air that come before a thunderstorm. The particles of air rushing past each other and tumbling about form the energy. You can form a similar sort of electrical energy in cold weather by walking across a thick rug and rubbing it with your shoes. You probably know what happens when you touch metal after doing that. You get a little electrical shock.

The thundercloud, however, builds up this electrical energy in tremendous quantities. The electric lights in your home probably take a little more than 100 volts of electrical energy to operate. A thundercloud can build up charges of up to 100,000,000 volts. (A volt is a measurement of electrical force just as an inch is a measurement of distance).

Thundercloud and lightning

The cloud becomes so heavily charged with this electrical energy that it has to get rid of it somewhere. Sometimes it does it right within the cloud, sending a great bolt of lighning, which is electrical energy, flashing from one side of the cloud to another.

Other times, though, the earth is the target. Then the cloud lets the electrical energy flash down to the earth. Actually, when this happens, the earth lets some of the electricity it has collected travel back up into the cloud. (The cloud sends down electrical charges called negative charges. The earth

sends back positive charges). This means that each flash of lightning, actually, is a double stroke of blazing electrical energy. In fact, many scientists believe that the brightest flashes that we can see are the parts that travel up toward the cloud rather than the parts traveling down toward the earth.

The danger about lightning is that if a house happens to be in the place where the earth and cloud are exchanging electricity, the lightning bolt can smash the house to smithereens. Lightning rods help guard against this by providing rods and wires for the electricity to travel through into the ground. That way the house is usually saved.

After each flash of lightning there comes the thunder. The noise we call thunder happens this way: As each flash takes place, it heats the air it travels through. The heat is so great and so sudden that the air sort of boils. The heated air expands very fast, the way air expands in a hot bottle—fast enough to pop a cork out of the bottle. The heated air, as it expands, makes the rumbling crashing noise we call thunder. Since the thunder always comes *after* the lightning, you can be sure you haven't been hurt if you hear the thunder. It *sounds* loud, but it is a sign that a flash of lightning has passed.

Besides the thunderstorms that form in fronts, there are two other kinds of thunderstorms. One can happen just about anywhere. It begins with the sun heating part of the land. This causes a rising mass of air. If the air has the right amount of water vapor in it as it rises into the cooler air, it will form clouds. If the rising air is strong enough and the clouds that form are big enough, a thunderstorm can build up. But,

Raincloud and mountain

when it does so in this way, it is usually over by evening when the sun goes down and the heated land cools off and the rising air settles down.

The other kind of thunderstorm is one that forms over mountains. Here the rising air that is needed to get a thunderstorm started is caused by winds pushing up the slope of the mountain. The mountain acts like a sliding board for the air to rush up rather than down. This creates a rush of air shooting high up over the top of the mountain. As it pushes up into cooler air, the air that rises can form clouds and thunderstorms can be born, as in the other cases.

If we are lucky, thunderstorms are about the worst sort of weather we have in our neighborhood. But there are far worse sorts of weather that people sometimes have to put up with.

TROPICAL HURRICANES

The worst sort of storm that happens on the earth is called a tropical hurricane. These terrible storms begin very quietly in the warm band of air near the equator, the zone we called the doldrums.

It all begins after the sun has been shining brightly for many days on a part of the ocean that is very calm. The water in the ocean gets warmer and warmer. It begins to heat the air. This air rises. As it does, other air moves in to replace it. A hurricane begins when this new air moving in and the warm air rising up begin to turn around

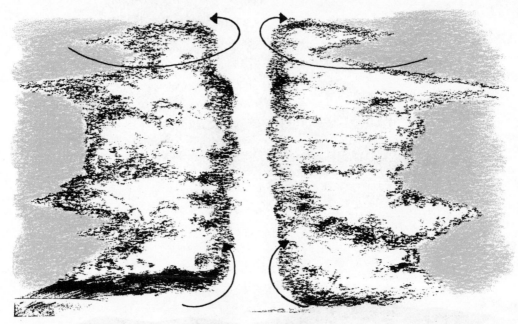

Inside a hurricane

together like the stripes on a barber pole. Soon the warm air has formed dark clouds overhead. But, still, the air is moving around and around. The dark clouds begin to pour rain down, and lightning flashes. The air begins to go around and around even faster. Soon, in the center of the stormy area, there is an "eye" (that's what scientists call the center of a hurricane) where the winds swirl around as fast as 150 miles an hour.

Now that the hurricane has formed it begins to move. The whole whirling mass of air, with the storms around it, starts to move slowly—sometimes not much faster than a walk.

When it moves across the land it can knock down houses and blow away trees. As it moves over the water it makes huge waves and these waves can cause great damage along the shore. It disturbs water in rivers and lakes too and sends torrents of rain pouring into them so that when a hurricane hits floods may come.

CYCLONES

Another name for hurricane is cyclone. Scientists often say hurricane when they mean any wind with a speed of 75 miles per hour. They use cyclone as the name for the whirling winds we have just described. Newspapers, however, almost always say *hurricane* when they report on these storms. Weather bureaus, each year, give names to the different hurricanes that form over the tropical waters. The names each start with a new letter of the alphabet and usually are the names of girls, like Hurricane Carol. Fortunately, not all of the hurricanes—and there may be a dozen or so a year — pass over any areas where they do damage.

TORNADOES

Another very bad sort of weather is called a tornado. In some parts of the world, this word is used to name a windy storm blowing along after a thunderstorm from a cold front. In America, tornado has another meaning. It means a whirlwind. If you have read *The Wizard of Oz,* you may remember that Dorothy and her house were supposed to have been blown away by a whirlwind. This was a tornado.

Tornadoes are one sort of weather that you can see very plainly and never mistake for any other kind. A tornado is a tall black funnel that twists and turns across the earth. In America, tornadoes happen, most of the time, east of the Rocky Mountains in the middle part of the country where hot dry air coming up from the Gulf of Mexico sometimes meets cold dry air from the North. The two air masses meet and start swirling together, sometimes like the hurricane except that it all happens very much faster.

The tornado looks like a black funnel because of all the dirt it swirls around with it. The winds inside the funnel of wind go as fast as 200 miles an hour.

The whole funnel moves along, knocking down buildings, ripping up trees, blowing away cars. It moves along as fast as 40 miles an hour. Fortunately, tornadoes usually die out after an hour or even a half hour.

Tornado

FLYING WEATHER

One sort of weather talk that we hear a lot about is flying weather.

We have heard that aviators have had trouble because "the ceiling was zero." Or they have had a good flight because the ceiling was unlimited. The *ceiling* is the distance in feet from the ground to the base of the lowest clouds covering more than four-tenths of the sky. If there are no clouds covering four-tenths of the sky below 10,000 feet, the ceiling is said to be unlimited. The ceiling is also called unlimited if less than

281

half the sky is covered by clouds below 10,000 feet.

When the ceiling is described as zero, it means that the weather conditions have made it impossible to see ahead as much as 50 feet.

ALL KINDS OF CLOUDS

Finally, let's look closer at the clouds we see in the sky.

The lowest hanging clouds are usually *cumulus* and *stratus* clouds. The cumulus clouds are big, scattered clouds with flat bottoms and rounded tops. You quite often see them during very fine weather.

Stratus clouds, that usually come between 2,000 and 7,000 feet, are often the clouds that make a winter day seem so wintry by keeping you from seeing the sun. These clouds just cover the sky in a layer.

Plane flying above layer of clouds

When the stratus cloud brings rain or snow it usually is called a *nimbostratus cloud.*

When a layer of clouds covers the sky fairly low down and seems to sort of be in ripples or waves, then it is called *stratocumulus.*

Another cloud that usually forms fairly low in the sky is the *cumulonimbus,* the great big bulging giant of a cloud that produces thunderstorms. In good weather you may see these clouds too. But then they float separately like great mountains of white wool. When they begin to move close together and start growing upwards in size— bad weather usually follows.

At middle altitudes in the sky we find *altocumulus* and *altostratus* clouds.

Altocumulus clouds cover the sky in what look like woolly tufts. Sometimes when these clouds form, people say the sky is a *mackerel sky,* because it looks to them like the pattern on a mackerel's back. Such a sky often comes with storms.

Altostratus clouds are fairly high, layer-like clouds that sometimes are thin enough for the sun to light up in parts as its rays pass by. These clouds are formed mostly of ice and water, and rain or snow may be expected when they appear.

The highest clouds in the sky are *cirrus, cirrostratus,* and *cirrocumulus.* Because they form so high in the air, they are always made up of ice crystals. When you see them, it is often a sign that bad weather is on its way. They form from 20,000 to 40,000 feet up in the air.

Cirrus are filmy, white clouds that look sort of like white feathers tossed around every which way in the sky.

Cirrostratus clouds are darker than cirrus and they are not as scattered. They are be-

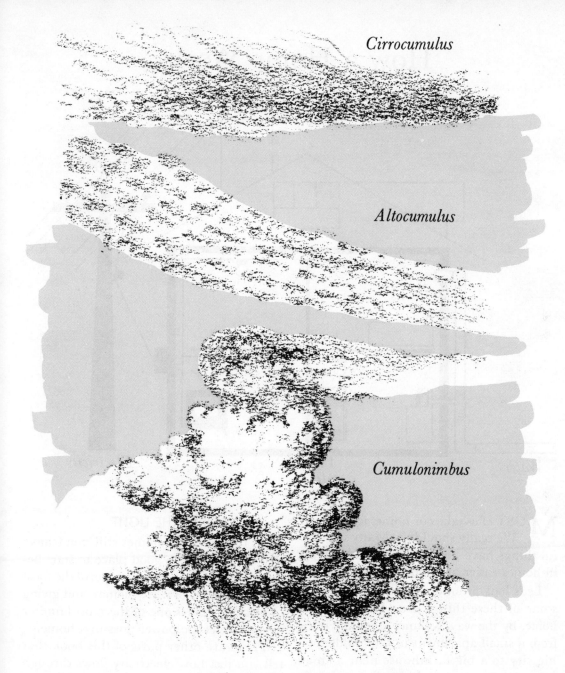

Cirrocumulus

Altocumulus

Cumulonimbus

Various kinds of cloud formations

ginning to form into closer streaks. They often appear like wispy lines. They are the clouds that come before a warm front.

Cirrocumulus clouds form a layer of rounded tufts like the altocumulus clouds but higher up in the air. But, because they look alike, these clouds too are said to form a mackerel sky.

283

How a Home Works

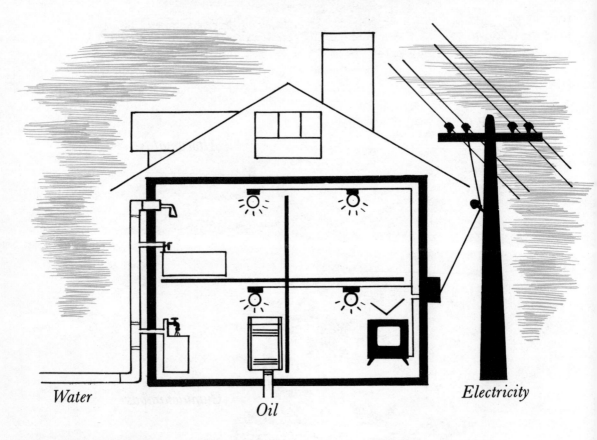

Water

Oil

Electricity

M OST of us take our homes for granted. We really shouldn't. Many wonderful things have been done to make living in homes easier and more comfortable.

Let's look around a home and see what some of these things are. When we say home, by the way, we may mean anything from a small apartment in the middle of a big city to a big farmhouse near a small town. We mean any place where a family lives, for it is the family inside the house that makes it a home and not just another building.

Let's start by turning on an electric light.

FIRST THE LIGHT

Even though some homes still don't have electric lights, it's a good place to start because electricity has become one of the most important parts of many homes, and giving us electric light is one of the most familiar jobs that electric power does in a home.

There are other parts of this book that tell you just how electricity flows through wires, how it is produced, and how it makes things work. Here, without going into those details of how and why, we'll just watch it at work around the house.

We wanted to start by clicking a switch

for the electric light. Click! There, the light goes on. But much more has happened, too. If this house is supplied by power made at one of the great power plants that use the force of falling water to make electricity, this is what happens when you click the switch:

POWER OVER MANY MILES

The power starts many—sometimes hundreds—of miles away, with a big river and a waterfall.

On some rivers nature has carved out great steps, hundreds of feet high, where the water crashes down in a waterfall. At places like that when men decide to build a power plant, the water is ready to help them. If the men put great water-wheels in the falls, the dropping water will make the wheels turn. Actually, at such places, the water-wheels are often built inside of huge tunnels so the water can pour through them as it comes down the falls.

In rivers where there is no natural waterfall, men have to create one. They do this by building dams. A dam can hold back millions of gallons of the water. When the water behind the dam gets very high, it can drop through openings in the dam and pour down just like a regular waterfall. In the dam there are the same sort of tunnels or channels for this falling water as there would be at a power plant beside a natural waterfall.

At both kinds of waterfall, the falling water does the same job. When it turns the big water-wheels, those wheels turn big machines called generators or dynamos. These machines *make* electricity.

FROM WATER TO WIRES

As the electricity is made it flows into big wires, some as big as water pipes. These wires are called high tension wires because they carry the electricity at its full or highest strength. From the power plants at the

Power Dam

285

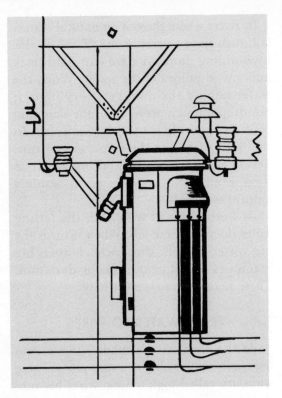

Transformer

less power so that it may be used by ordinary machines and lights.

Sometimes these transformers can be seen from the road. The largest ones look like mysterious devices with tall porcelain insulators sticking out of them like antennae. The insulators are there to keep the wires from touching metal as they go into the transformers. Because of the terrific amount of power that circulates inside these devices, transformer stations like this are often kept behind high fences with warning signs on them. Perhaps you will see some when you take a walk or go for a drive.

As the wires bring the electricity closer to homes and other places that use it, smaller transformers (either built like boxes on the poles that carry the wires above ground or set beside the wires that go underground) change the current, for the last time, into just the right power for use in the home.

UNDER THE MANHOLE COVERS

If you live in a city, the wires and the transformers we just mentioned are reached through certain special manholes whose covers you see in the streets. If you live in a smaller place or in the country, the wires may go to your house from a high pole—the same kind of pole that carries telephone wires and even, in some cases, the very same pole. You can see where the wires come from the pole to your house and perhaps you can even locate the transformers that tame the power of the electricity so that you can use it.

Now, back again to the switch that we clicked to make the light go on. The power that was made back at the great dam or waterfall in the river has moved for many

river, the wires may stretch across tall towers that march across the desert to a distant city. The wires may wind and curve across high mountains, across other rivers, or through deep forests to wherever the electricity is needed.

As the wires travel, sometimes they divide into wires going in separate directions, for these great power stations produce enough electricity for many places. As the wires get close to the town or city or farm lands where the electricity is to be used by homes and factories and farms, they hook into strange-looking big metal boxes called transformers. These start to change the super-powerful electricity into current of

Electrical appliances used in the home

miles through great wires and small wires, through different transformers and above the ground and under the ground, across water, and across hills and mountains or plains and prairies. When you click the switch it is as though you opened a tiny gate in the switch. It lets electricity pass through the switch and on into the light— or whatever else is controlled by the switch.

Think of that when next you turn on a

light—of the great, rushing waters and the tall towers and poles with their wires—and you will begin to appreciate how truly wonderful are the workings of a modern house.

AN ELECTRIC LIST

You might look, too, at the wires coming from the pole to your house, or imagine the wires coming into the house or apartment underground, and think of just how many wonderful things are run by the power that comes from those wires. What have you in your house or apartment that uses this power? Toasters, radio, television, heaters, stoves, lights, power tools, elevators, cooking equipment, irons, electric blankets?

As you find the things that use electric power, remember one very important thing though—electricity can harm as well as help us. Wires that are old or that have cracked coverings may let electricity flash from the wire and start a fire or shock someone. Plugs that have too many things plugged into them may get hot from all the power that is coming through the wires. Sometimes the wires in a plug that is serving too many things may get hot enough to melt and start a fire. Open plugs, and sockets too, can be dangerous. If someone sticks a finger or a piece of metal in one, the electricity can leap out to burn or shock.

In a moment we'll learn one of the ways a home is protected against the damage that electricity can do. But first we should not leave our light switch without doing something very important—turn off the light when you are not using it. To leave it on when you don't need it wastes precious power. When men have gone to all the trouble of building great dams or harnessing waterfalls to bring you that power, you certainly don't want to use it up needlessly.

MAKING ELECTRICITY SAFE

Now let's find out how we protect homes against the dangerous part of electricity, the fires that can be caused by it when it gets out of control.

You will remember that sometimes the covering of wires—the insulation—gets worn or broken. That insulation does more than just keep the wires covered on the outside. It keeps them covered on the inside too.

Each electric cord or wire really has two separate strands of wire inside of it. The insulation keeps those strands apart. The reason is that if they touch, the electricity won't be able to go on to the light or whatever it is supposed to make work. Instead, it will flow together at the place where the wires touch. When electricity flows together like that, it causes sparks and great heat. We call it a short circuit. The reason for that name is a very good one. It means just what it says.

End of electric cord showing open strands

WHAT A CIRCUIT IS

The way in which electricity flows in order to work anything is called a circuit. Circuit means something like a circle. It means that electricity flows in a sort of circle. It goes through one of the two strands in a wire to the light or machine it is supposed to work. The electricity flows through the light or machine to work it and then flows back out through the other wire. Only when electricity flows through two wires in this way can it do any work at all. And that is a regular circuit.

A *short* circuit occurs when the electricity flows together *short* of where it is supposed to do its work, like when the wires touch through the worn out or cracked insulation.

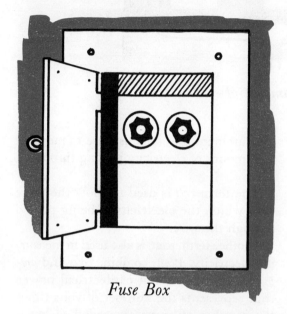

Fuse Box

When there is a short circuit, the electricity turns the wires red hot, as we have said, and fire may be caused.

How do we protect our homes against electric fires? We use fuses.

HOW FUSES FIGHT FIRES

The fuse is the most important safety device for electricity. Fuses are used in your home and in great factories as well as in airplanes and automobiles. The job of the fuse is to stop the electricity whenever a short circuit happens or whenever too much electricity is being pulled through any particular wires, heating them and making them dangerous.

Perhaps the fuses in your house are in a square metal box in the basement. If you live in an apartment or a house without a basement, maybe the fuse-box is on a wall somewhere. A fuse looks rather like the bottom of an electric light bulb, the part that screws into the lamp.

Fuses sometimes have little windows in the front. Through this window you can see a flat silvery wire stretched across the inside of the fuse. In order to get to any place in the home, the electricity must flow through this flat silvery wire in the fuse. The fuse wire is made so that it will melt if the electricity flows through it at a greater rate than it is supposed to.

Now suppose that the wires *have* touched and so caused a short circuit. The electricity through the wire will suddenly start causing sparks and heat and much more electricity is pouring through the wire than an electric light or appliance would need.

Back at the fuse, this sudden spurt of power rushes across the flat silvery wire inside the fuse. The wire melts. As soon as it does, the circuit is broken. No electricity can flow anywhere in the wires to which the fuse was connected. The place where the short circuit happened is left without any power, and so a possibly serious fire has been avoided.

The same thing happens inside the fuse when someone plugs too many things into a single place and in that way makes more electricity than is safe come through the wires.

Well insulated thick wire can safely handle more electrical current than lightly insulated thin wires. The thicker the wire, the less the electric current heats it up and the more electricity the wire can safely carry.

In many houses there are parts of the wir-

Amperage is the amount of electricity

ing in the house that can stand more current than any other parts. This means that there have to be different fuses to take care of those different amounts of current. So, in one fuse socket, there may be a fuse that would melt when a toaster, two lights, and an electric heater are trying to take electricity from a single set of wires. If all those things needed more electricity than the amount the fuse had been made to carry, the fuse wire would melt and the current would be turned off. But then, another set of wires might be able to handle all the electricity needed to run the toaster, the heater, and the lights, and a washing machine or an electric train as well. In that case, a fuse would be put in that could stand more current than the first fuse.

Fuses are marked according to the amount of current they will carry across the fuse wire without burning. They are marked in terms of *amperes*. Amperes are the units of

measurement that scientists use to measure the amount of electricity passing through a wire.

The term *volt* is used to show the force with which the electricity is being passed through the wire.

Another term, *watt*, is also used in measuring electricity. *Watts* combine *volts* and *amperes*. A watt is a unit of electrical power that represents the number of volts times the number of amperes needed to get a particular job done.

When a bulb is marked as being a 100

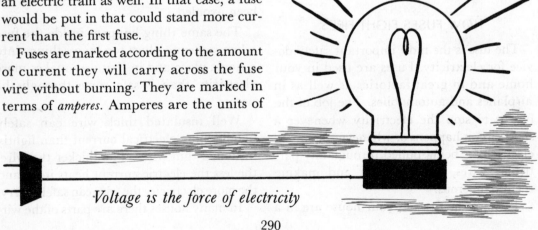

Voltage is the force of electricity

watt bulb it means that it takes the energy equal to 10 amperes of electricity times 10 volts of force, or 1 ampere times 100 volts —any multiplication of volts and amperes that equals 100 would do the job.

From those units of measurement we can figure out just how much current a fuse will let pass by. Suppose the fuse is made so that it will melt if 20 amperes of power go through the fuse wire at one time. Now suppose that the electricity in the house has a force of 110 volts. This means that 20, the number of amperes, times 110 volts will give us the most amount of watts that can be used. That amount, in this case, is 2200 watts. Now that would take care of plenty of 100 watt bulbs all right. But something like a radio might take up 300 or 400 watts all by itself and an electric heater might take more than 1000 watts.

Safe homes have safe fuses in them. Maybe you will be interested to go along next time someone in your house goes to the fuse-box, now that you know how they help keep you and your home free from fire.

A.C. AND D.C.

There is still another thing that may puzzle you about the electricity in your home. Some homes have a sort of electrical power called *direct current,* or *d.c.* for short. Other homes have a sort called *alternating current,* or *a.c.* for short. The difference between the two is this: The direct current, just as its name says, flows in a direct path through one wire to a light or machine and then out the other wire. Alternating current goes back and forth. Alternate means to change back and forth regularly. This sort of current flows through the wires in one direction for a split second and then in the

other direction the next split second. It does this as often as 50 or 60 times a second in many homes.

One of the reasons alternating current is so widely used is that engineers have found it the best kind of current for wires that have to carry electricity for many miles. The reason is that the power of alternating current can be very easily changed in transformers such as we have described. That means that the current can be sent at great power through the big wires from the power plant and then changed to lower power for use in the smaller wires in homes. Direct current can't be changed this way and would all have to be sent all the way at the same power.

In that case each home using direct current would have to be connected directly to the power plant that made the electricity. This is all right if the power plant happens to be very near by, but it wouldn't be very practical to connect hundreds of homes to a power plant hundreds of miles away.

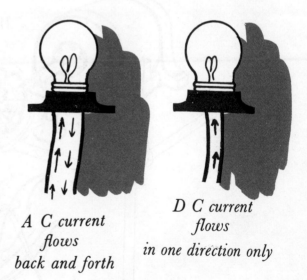

A C current flows back and forth

D C current flows in one direction only

291

A CYCLE OF ELECTRICITY

If your home has the a.c. kind of electricity, you'll know now, every time you turn on the electricity, that inside the wires, each second, the electricity is flowing back and forth, back and forth, 50 or 60 times a second. If you are told how many "cycles" your electricity is, you will know just how fast it *is* flowing back and forth. For the number of cycles are just the number of times a second the a.c. electricity flows back and forth.

For something you *can't* see, electricity is certainly an active force in the home, isn't it?

There are other ways of producing electricity for homes besides the use of rushing water which we learned about earlier. One of the other ways, in fact, is often a better way. That is, it costs less in time and trouble and money. This other way is to make electricity from coal!

POWER FROM COAL

When you look at a lump of coal, you would hardly think it might be used to make electricity. But it is. And for many places it is the best way. Water power is the best when there are tremendous demands from giant factories as well as big cities and farmlands for power in an area. But when a single town or just a part of a city needs

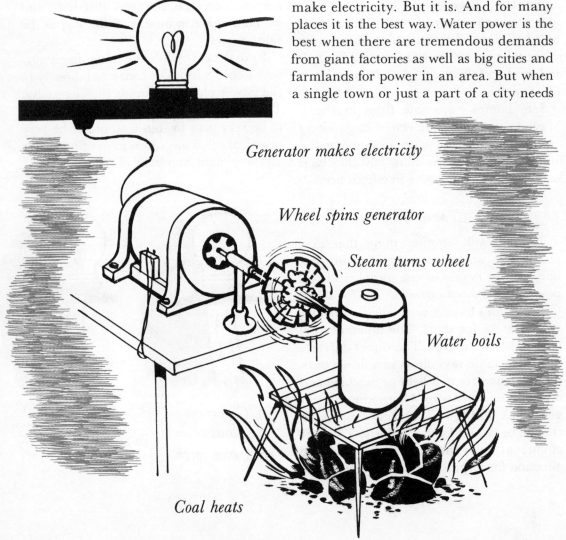

Generator makes electricity

Wheel spins generator

Steam turns wheel

Water boils

Coal heats

power, coal often turns out to be the best means of producing it.

Coal, you know, burns very well. When coal is burned, it releases heat energy and a lot of it. This is how that energy is turned into electricity: The coal is burned to make heat. The heat is used to boil water. The boiling water makes steam. The steam is sent rushing through great pipes and is used to turn wheels. The wheels turn generators. And the generators make electricity. This electricity comes through wires to your home just the same way as the sort of electricity made by water power.

There is another interesting way that electricity can be made from water besides using a waterfall. In places where the tides —the rising and falling of the ocean—are very great, tunnels can be drilled under the ocean and the pressure of the water as it rises and falls can be used to turn wheels to drive generators.

POWER FROM AIR AND SUN

Even the sun and air may be used to make the electricity for homes. Perhaps you have seen farm homes with windmills near them. Some windmills, like the big ones in Holland that you see so often in pictures, are used to turn machinery to grind grain and do other jobs. Other windmills, though, are smaller and may be seen at many farmhouses. Some of these windmills turn machinery that works pumps to bring water to the farmhouse or to the fields. But others may be used to drive generators and make electricity.

Scientists have built special batteries that can make electricity for homes just from sunlight. When the sunlight falls on the battery it causes the chemicals in it to make

electricity. There are also several chemicals which can produce electricity when brought together with other chemicals, but they usually wear out just the way the battery in a flashlight wears out. In the sun batteries, the chemicals aren't used up. Instead they just change sun energy to electric energy.

Some places use gasoline to make electricity. Little motors that operate just the

Windmill

293

Hot water heater and stove

way a motor in an automobile does can be used to turn generators and make electricity. Power plants like that are sometimes used by people camping, by explorers, and by soldiers, and by people who live too far away from regular power sources for regular electricity. How is the electricity for *your* home made?

GAS FOR SOME HOMES

Electricity, however, is not the only form of energy that is used in homes.

One other important form of energy that helps make many homes work is gas. Some houses use gas to make the fire for the stove, some to heat water. Others use it to heat the whole house.

Gas is like electricity in one way. It takes a great deal of work and many wonderful things have to happen before the gas can get to the home to be used.

One kind of gas used in some homes is made from coal. Just as you might not think of electricity coming from a lump of coal, you might not think of gas coming from it either. But it does, like this:

In great plants or factories coal is heated to very high temperatures in large iron containers. As the coal gets hot, almost hot enough to burn, some of the chemicals in it melt and then turn to gas.

From the big hot containers the gas goes through big pipes to a huge round tower where it is stored.

A ROOF THAT SLIDES

As the gas goes into the towers an amazing thing happens. The roof of the tower begins to rise! This is because the tower is built like part of a telescope, in two sections, with one section fitting inside the other. As the tower is filled up, the roof section can slide up to make room for more gas.

This sliding roof does more than just make room for more gas, though. Because it presses down on the gas, the gas is always under pressure in the tower. Because of that pressure it can be sent rushing through big pipes in the ground.

These pipes spread through the city or town where the gas plant is located. As the pipes pass houses that use gas, smaller pipes lead off and take as much gas as is needed into the houses.

Inside a house, let's suppose, someone is turning on a gas stove. Gas from the big pipe that comes from the big tower pours into the smaller pipe and into the pipes of the stove. Up through the burner comes the gas. Someone lights the stove. It is ready to cook supper!

Just as electricity is dangerous as well as helpful, so is gas. If the gas is turned on and

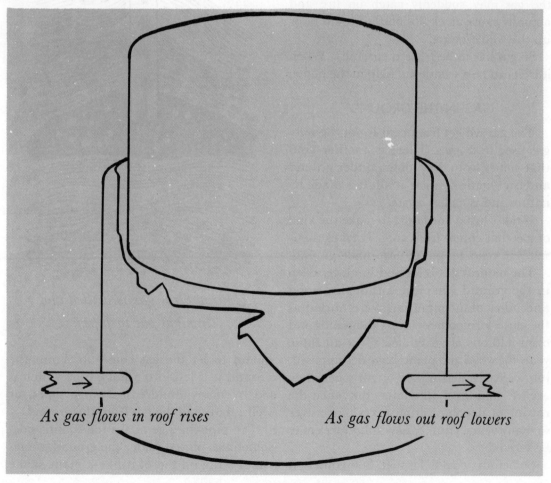

As gas flows in roof rises   *As gas flows out roof lowers*

not lighted, it can fill the home. Humans and animals cannot live if they breathe much unlighted gas. So you can see how important it is to light the gas as soon as it is turned on.

There is another terrible danger. If gas leaks out into a closed oven, for instance, it may fill the entire oven. When someone lights the oven, all that gas will flash into flame at once and possibly cause bad burns. If gas leaks out of a burner on the stove, it may even fill up a whole room. Then, if someone lights a match or even causes a spark by turning on an electrical switch, all the gas may suddenly catch on fire and actually cause an explosion that could blow up the whole house.

So gas has to be treated carefully. When it is, it can be a wonderful help in the home.

GAS IN THE GROUND

The gas we get from coal is not the only gas used in homes. There is another kind that comes from deep down under ground and isn't made by men at all. It is made by nature and is called *natural gas*.

It takes just a few hours to make the kind of gas that comes from coal. It takes thousands of years for gas to form underground.

The natural gas is formed in places deep in the ground where, it is thought, wood and other plant materials were buried as the earth formed new layers thousands and even millions of years ago. Over all those years the wood and plants have decomposed, just as leaves decompose or rot when they are left on a lawn all winter. But when the rotting or decomposition takes place over so many years, entirely new substances may be formed.

Sometimes coal is formed. Sometimes oil

is formed. Sometimes gas is formed. To reach the natural gas, men drill holes just as they drill them to reach oil. When they reach a place where the gas is, a pipe is

How natural gas is drilled and brought out in pipes

put in to let the gas come up. From the ground it is led into a huge pipe which is fed by many hundreds of these pipes, or wells, that take the gas from the ground.

The pipe-lines go across the countryside, sometimes buried under the ground, sometimes lying on top of it like a giant snake curving across the land. It is from great pipe-lines like that, that the gas is brought to homes.

Imagine, if natural gas is used in your home, what this means. When you turn on the gas you are using a substance that may have been forming when the dinosaurs roamed the earth, possibly millions of years ago. The gas that comes out of the stove or that heats the water in the home once lay deep in the earth as the land changed from ice-covered plains to valley-lined hills long before man had begun to live here.

For homes that cannot have gas brought to them through pipes, there still is a way to have gas. Sometimes you may see houses with metal tanks four or five feet tall nearby. Those tanks may hold gas. This is sometimes called "bottled gas" because trucks bring fresh supplies of it in big metal bottles or tanks. The tanks outside the house are filled from the tanks brought by the truck.

The bottled gas is made by heating oil and turning part of it into gas. The metal tanks in which it is stored are very strong so that great amounts of gas can be squeezed in to last weeks or even months.

If gas is used in your house, you can ask which kind of gas it is, where it comes from, and what it does in the house. It will be interesting to find the things that use gas in your house and see just how the gas is used in each of them.

It will be good to know about these things for another reason, too. When you know where the gas is used, you can be careful never to play with those things or touch them without permission for you might let unlighted gas into the house and by now you know how dangerous that can be.

COAL AND OIL

The other forms of energy used in homes are those we get from coal and oil. Coal is used in furnaces and stoves to provide heat. And each lump, don't forget, was made

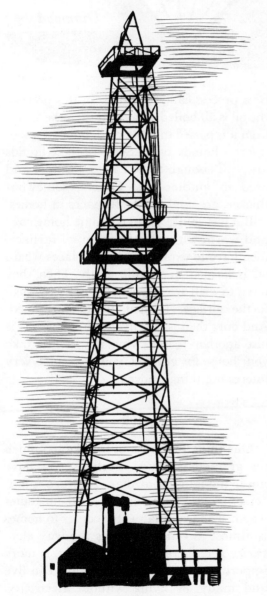

Oil Well

Coal

Diamond

from wood and plants that—like the natural gas—were on the earth hundreds of thousands or millions of years ago. Perhaps the coal that goes in the furnace in your home, or in the home of someone you know, came from a tree that was knocked down by a dinosaur!

Coal, by the way, is a close relative to something that looks less like coal than perhaps anything you could find. Coal is pure carbon, one of the main chemicals in woody material. Carbon is what charcoal is made of, for instance. Charcoal is the black part of wood that has been partly burned or around great heat.

Another thing that is pure carbon is a diamond! Diamonds are formed when carbon under the earth is subjected to tremendous pressure and great heat. But, except for the changes made by heat and pressure, *diamonds and coal are just the same thing.* So, when next you see a lump of coal go into a furnace in a home, remember that except for pressure and heat under the earth, that lump of coal could be a shining diamond!

Oil is also used for heating in homes. Oil is formed deep in the earth too. When it comes out of the earth it is thick and black. It is too thick, in fact, to be used in most furnaces or motors. It has to be thinned out

by a process called refining. In this process, the oil is all boiled away and then the steam from it is passed through colder places where it forms liquids again. Some of these liquids are thin enough to be called gasoline and used in automobiles. Others, somewhat thicker, are used for the furnaces in homes.

But just think! To make some home cozy and warm with heat from an oil furnace, men have to explore and find places where oil is formed under the earth. Then they have to drill way down to let the oil rush to the surface. Then it has to be refined. And only then is it delivered to homes. It is just another reason why, if you just take your house for granted, you miss some very interesting things indeed.

WATER

One thing that most of us take too much for granted is water. Perhaps you have never thought about that. You turn a faucet, or move a pump handle, and out comes water. The way that water comes to homes is almost as remarkable as the way electricity gets there. Water, actually, is more important than electricity. People can live and many *are* living without electricity. They can be happy, healthy, and wise without electricity. But people *cannot* live without water.

WATER FROM A WELL

The easiest way to get water is to dig a hole in the ground. If you are lucky, water will appear in the bottom of that hole after you have dug down a few feet. On the other hand, there are many places where you could dig a thousand such holes and there would be no water. Holes like that, dug for water, are shallow wells. They are called "dug" wells because you just dig them.

When a digger doesn't find water in a well like that, another kind is tried. This is the drilled well. It is bored by a big drill that makes a hole deep down into the ground, sometimes hundreds of feet deep. In these wells men try to drill down till they find layers of earth that are soaked with water or layers of rock that also are soaked with water deep down beneath the surface of the earth.

The water in these layers of ground or rock comes from rain that seeps into the earth and is stored there. Sometimes, if it stays near the surface, the dug wells can reach it. But when it flows way down into the deep earth or rocks a drilled well has to be made in order to reach it.

With the simple dug well, all you would need would be a bucket to get the water. With the deep drilled well, a pump is needed.

Sometimes the pump is worked by hand to suck the water up. Sometimes it is worked by an electric motor that is turned on when someone in the house turns on a faucet.

Sometimes pumps like that are worked by windmills.

WATER FOR BIG CITIES

City people usually get their water in another way. Cities use so much water that wells usually can't supply enough, even if those wells, as in some cities, are huge ones from which thousands of gallons of water can be pumped. Lakes and rivers are often used to provide the main supply of water

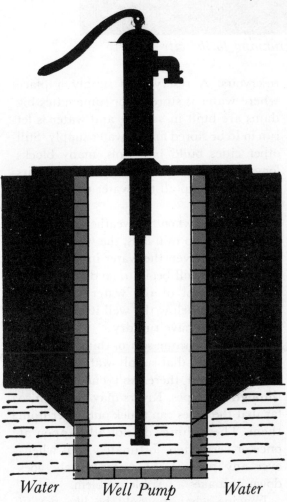

How a well pump brings water up through rock and earth

299

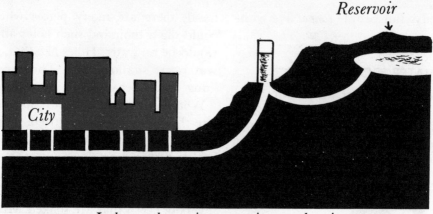

Lake or dam pipes running to the city

for a city. Big pipes carry the water from the lakes and rivers into the cities.

If those pipes have to climb over mountains to carry the water, pumps are put in the pipes along the way to help push the water along. Some of these pumps are so big that several houses are built along the pipeline just to shelter the pumps.

HOW WATER IS CLEANED

When water comes from a lake or a river, it isn't as clean as the water that has sunk down through the earth to the places where it is taken out by a well. Before the water from lakes or rivers is put into the pipes that will carry it finally into the houses of the city, it usually is specially cleaned. Sometimes this is done by letting it run through sand and earth that can clean it. Sometimes it is sprayed up into the air from giant fountains to be purified and cleaned, just as rain drops are cleaned as they fall by the air and sun. Other times special chemicals are put in the water to kill any germs that might be in it.

When a city sets aside certain lakes for its water supply, those lakes are often called reservoirs. A reservoir is simply a place where water is stored. For some cities big dams are built in valleys, and water is let run in to be stored for the water supply. Still other cities build big pools, many blocks long and very deep, to be used as reservoirs to help store up all the water the city will need.

Sometimes, when the weather is very hot and dry and no rain falls, the water supply will get low. Even the water in the underground wells will begin to go down. Sometimes the level of the water under the ground sinks below the well itself and the well is said to have run dry.

In cities the same sort of thing can happen. The lakes that supply water may sink and sink until there isn't enough to go through the pipes. Rivers may go down so far that the pipes can't suck out water from them. These things do not all happen at once or very often, fortunately. But whenever any part of the water supply goes down, it makes a terrible problem.

Imagine what it would be like not to have water for anything for even one day! Think about how many times you use water every day! Think of how it is used for cooking, for washing, for drinking—for so many things in the home. When you think of that, you may not ever want to let water run when you aren't really using it. Saving water is one of the best habits you can get into in any home. If all the people in all the homes remembered where water came from, and *how precious* it is, they wouldn't let leaky faucets waste this wonderful treasure of nature.

The great pipe-lines drawing the water from many miles away for great cities and rich farmlands and the wells boring down deep into the dark cool earth should all remind us of the importance of water every time we turn a faucet or use a pump. We ought to think of how we get our water, and use it wisely.

When you think of things like that — of how the things in your house work and how the wonders of the home come to pass — you will stop taking your home for granted and you will appreciate more than ever the things that go on around you.

But we must also remember that the machinery in the house — the things that make it go—are not the things that make it a good home. Those things just make it what some people call a good "machine for living." They aren't what make it a happy home.

The most important things in any house are the people who live in it. The most important things are the people who click the switches and turn the faucets and do the things that machinery can never do — like laughing and singing, and even crying, and loving and being happy.

Electricity

From MORE POWER TO YOU
By Herman and Nina Schneider

ELECTRICITY does many jobs for us. Electricity rings the bell, spins the mixer, whirls the fan, turns the hands of a clock, runs the radio, the TV, the refrigerator, and maybe the stove. Electricity does these jobs quietly, without a fuss, without fire or fuel or smoky gas to bother about.

What is electricity and how does it do so many different kinds of things?

Perhaps you have wondered about this. So have scientists, for there are many things about electricity that are still not known. Let's see what we do know, or what we are fairly sure about.

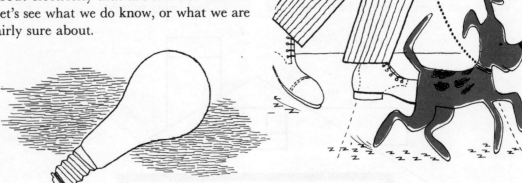

WHAT WE DO KNOW ABOUT ELECTRICITY

Scientists are sure that electricity has something to do with *electrons*. Electrons are very tiny things, much too small to see with even the most powerful microscope. Electrons are in everything—in wood, in metal, in air, in you. The tiniest grain of sand has billions of electrons in it.

Electrons usually stay put, and we don't notice them. However, they can be made to move. When they do, they flow along in a sort of stream or current. We call it an electron current, or *electric current*.

How do we make electrons move? We push them! You do it all the time. As you walk along, you push the electrons of the sidewalk with the electrons of your shoes.

You leave a trail of little electric currents as you go, but they are too tiny for you to notice. In cold dry weather, if you shuffle along a rug, you may stir up a larger electric current—enough to give somebody a slight "shock" when you touch them.

You make electric currents in other ways, too. When you comb your hair, you push electrons from your hair on to the comb. When a great many electrons have piled up on the comb, some of them jump back to your hair. That's the crackle you hear.

302

If you comb your hair in a dark room, you can sometimes see the flash made by the tiny stream of electrons as they jump.

A flash and a crackle—does that make you think of lightning and thunder? If it does, you are right. Lightning is made by an enormous stream of electrons jumping back and forth between two clouds, or between a cloud and the earth. Thunder is the very, very loud crackle that the jumping electrons make.

ELECTRIC GENERATORS

However, the electric current in your house was not made by somebody combing his hair, or by stringing a wire up in the sky to bring lightning from the clouds. The electric current in your house is made by a *generator*. Let's see what a generator is and how it works.

People discovered that if you move a magnet back and forth near some electrons, you cause them to flow back and forth. The magnet pushes electrons. This makes a current of electrons, or an electric current.

A generator is a machine for pushing electrons. The magnet in a generator doesn't look just like a little toy magnet. It's a much bigger and more powerful kind, called an electric magnet, or *electromagnet*. But it can do the same thing. It can push electrons. The electrons it pushes are in a coil of wire right next to the electromagnet.

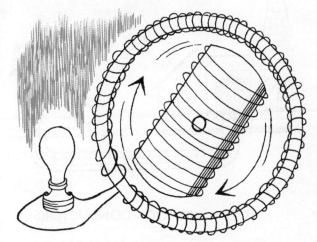

The electromagnet is built so that it can turn. As the electromagnet turns, it pushes the electrons in the coil of wire. It causes the electrons to flow out of the coil and through the glowing wires of the bulb in your desk lamp, or the electric motor in your electric train, or the heating wires in your electric toaster.

The flowing electrons cause the lamp to give off light, the train to run, and the toaster to heat.

As long as the electromagnet keeps turning, it keeps pushing electrons out of the coil. The electrons go through a wire that goes to something that uses electricity. Then they go through another wire right back to the coil to be pushed again!

You could say that the electrons keep flowing in a sort of circle, around, and around, and around. They flow out of the generator, through the light bulb or motor or heating coil, and then back to the generator again. We call this flow of electricity a *complete circuit*.

gling through materials such as wood, rubber, plastic, and glass.

Some materials are called *good conductors* of electricity. We use them where we want the electrons to flow.

Some materials are called *poor conductors*, or *insulators*. Electricity does not flow easily through these materials.

Look at a piece of wire. You will see that the inside is made of copper. Copper is a good conductor, so the electrons flow through it easily. That's just what we want.

The copper is covered with rubber, cloth, or plastic. These are poor conductors, so the electrons in the copper are kept from flowing out through the cover. And that's just what we want, too.

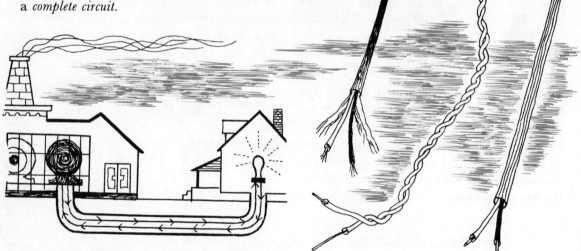

GOOD AND POOR CONDUCTORS

By experimenting, people found that electrons flow more easily through some materials than through others. They found that electrons flow very easily through metals. However, electrons have a hard time strug-

You know how electrons are made to flow by the turning of an electromagnet. You know, too, that they flow more easily through some materials than through others. Now let's see how these flowing electrons can be made to work for you.

304

Electrons do all kinds of jobs that seem very different from each other. They run clocks, lights, toasters, bells, telephones, and hundreds of other machines. But, no matter how different all these jobs seem, flowing electrons are only doing one of two things. They are making heat or they are causing motion.

First let's see how they make heat.

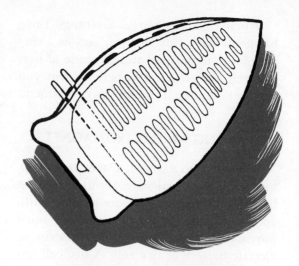

ELECTRICITY MAKES HEAT

The flow of electrons is something like the flow of traffic. When the road is narrow or bumpy, the traffic becomes crowded. The cars are squeezed together and can only crawl along. With only a little room between cars, they scrape and bump into each other.

When electrons are shoved through a narrow wire or a poor conductor, they bump and scrape and bang and rub into each other. This rubbing and bumping makes the wire hot. If the wire becomes hot enough, it glows and gives off light.

The wires in a toaster, an electric iron, or an electric light bulb are all rather thin. And they are made of a metal that is a fairly poor conductor. The electrons have to crowd and push and bump their way through the wire. The wire gets hot, and gives off heat and light where we want it.

ELECTRICITY MOVES THINGS

Flowing electrons can work for us in another way. They can make something move. They can move the hands of an electric clock. They can move the clapper of a doorbell back and forth. They can make the speaker in your radio vibrate back and forth to make sound. They can make the blades of an electric fan whirl around. All these motions are made by moving electrons. Let's see how.

305

When electrons move, a strange thing happens. Each tiny electron acts as a tiny magnet that can pull things made of iron or steel. This is hard to believe, but you can see it happen if you do this experiment.

MAKING AN ELECTROMAGNET

You will need a pencil, a steel paper clip, and a piece of bell wire about three feet long. (Bell wire is copper wire wrapped with cotton thread.) You will also need some moving electrons. You can get these in an electric battery or dry cell. A dry cell has billions of electrons stored up inside it, all ready to move. They will start moving as soon as we give them a path to move through.

First unwind an inch of cotton thread from each end of the wire. Wind the wire around the pencil, to make a coil like this. Then pull out the pencil.

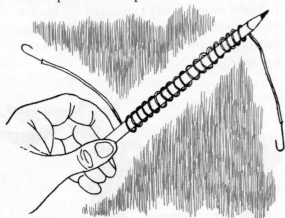

Now we're ready to see whether moving electrons act as magnets. If they do, they may be able to pull the steel paper clip toward them. Let's send the electrons through the coil of wire. You do this by fastening the two bare ends of the wire to the two screws on the dry cell. Then touch the paper clip to the wire. Does it stay on or fall off?

If your dry cell is fresh, with plenty of electrons to send through the coil, you will see the paper clip stay on. The moving electrons flowing through the coil act as magnets. They pull the steel paper clips and keep it from falling off.

What will happen if the electrons stop moving? You can find out by disconnecting the coil from the dry cell. Does the paper clip stay on? You will find that it does not. Electrons do not act as magnets unless they are moving along.

MOVING ELECTRONS AT WORK

Now let's see how the magnetism of moving electrons can be put to work. Let's see how their magnetism can ring a bell.

Imagine a coil of wire and a dry cell, like

those you used in your experiment. But in place of a paper clip we have a strip of iron with a little round clapper at one end. The clapper is right next to a gong. When the clapper strikes the gong it will ring. How can we get the clapper to strike the gong?

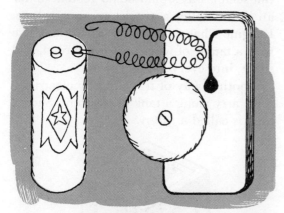

Moving electrons will do it for us. We attach the ends of the coil to the dry cell. Electrons rush through the coil. Moving electrons act as magnets. They pull the strip of iron toward the coil. As the iron moves, the clapper strikes the gong and makes a "bong." We have used the magnetism of moving electrons to do a bit of work.

ELECTRIC MOTORS

An electric motor works in almost the same way. Here, too, there is a coil of wire, with an electric current flowing through it.

The electrons in the current act as tiny magnets that can pull something made of iron or steel. But the pull in a motor is different from the pull in a bell. In a bell, the pull makes a strip of iron move in a straight line. But a motor is built so that the pull makes something go round and round.

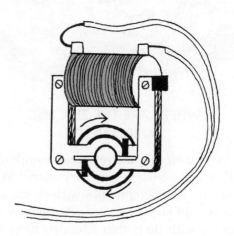

Here is a very simple kind of electric motor. This is the motor in an electric clock. You can see the coil through which the electrons flow. The little metal wheel is like the iron strip in the bell. It is pulled around by magnetism from the electrons moving through the coil.

Most electric motors do not look quite like this one. They are bigger and they have other parts or different shapes. But they all work in the same way, by the magnetic pull of millions of tiny moving electrons.

Today, we use electric motors more than any other kind of motor. In your home, for example, you may have a fan, a clock, a mixer, and a refrigerator, all run by electric motors.

Imagine what a nuisance it would be to run these machines by a water wheel, a

307

steam turbine, or a gasoline engine! An electric motor needs no stream of water, no furnace or boiler, or fuel, and it is quiet.

WHERE ARE THE ELECTRIC AIRPLANES?

Well, if electric motors are so wonderful, why don't we use them everywhere? Why don't we run automobiles with them, and trucks, and airplanes? Because there is one trouble with them that scientists have not yet been able to clear up. Let's see what it is.

Electric motors run by electricity, of course. In a house or a factory, the electricity comes through wires from a generator. But how do we send electricity to something that travels? There are two ways, but neither is very good.

One way is to have an overhead wire that supplies electricity. That is how an electric locomotive gets the electricity that drives its motor. There is an electric wire that goes everywhere the train tracks go. But such a way would be no good at all for an automobile, a truck, or an airplane. Imagine what this country would look like with a tangle of wires over every road, and street, into every garage!

Another way of traveling by electricity is to carry along a tank of electrons. Such a tank is called a *battery*.

You know that small batteries are used in ordinary cars and trucks. But such batteries do not turn the wheels. Their main job is to supply the electricity for the electric starter that starts the gasoline engine. The power that makes the wheels turn comes from the burning of gasoline in the engine, not from a battery. Then why not use a bigger battery to run an electric motor that would make the wheels turn? That way has been tried, and batteries are still being used to run some kinds of trucks.

Here is a 1906 electric automobile that was run by a big battery. And here is a modern electric truck, with its battery box underneath.

Such cars and trucks are much cheaper to build and easier to run than those run by

So we need an invention. We need a battery that weighs very little and yet can supply lots of electricity. Such an invention could make a wonderful change in our ways of travel. And maybe some day it will be discovered.

Cars, trucks, and airplanes would glide along silently, driven by electric motors that cost much less to build than gasoline engines. With no gasoline to carry, and no fumes to give off, our travel machines would be safer and healthier for everyone.

gasoline engines. Then why don't you see more of the electric kind? Because they can't travel far enough.

POWER FOR GENERATORS

Even if we haven't yet found a good way to take electricity traveling with us, we have many uses for it. Every day we use electricity to do a tremendous number of big and little jobs for us at home. Where does all this electricity come from?

The electricity in your house comes from a generator. You know that a generator is a kind of pump that pushes electrons. But a pump doesn't just work by itself. Some form of power is needed to make it work.

Any form of power can be used to work a generator. Anything that spins the electromagnet in a generator will cause electrons to flow. Let's look at some generators to see what makes them spin.

The battery that runs an electric car or truck is quite heavy. Yet it can supply only enough electricity for about thirty miles of travel. Then the battery has to be charged with more electricity. That takes an hour or more. A battery that could store up enough electricity for a hundred-mile trip would be enormous. It would weigh more than the car itself!

WIND-POWERED GENERATORS

Perhaps you live on a farm, far away from electric lines. Then you may get electricity from a wind-powered generator, like this one.

The wind turns a windmill, and the windmill turns a generator. The generator pumps electrons into a battery. In this way, whenever the wind blows, it turns the generator which sends electricity to a storage battery.

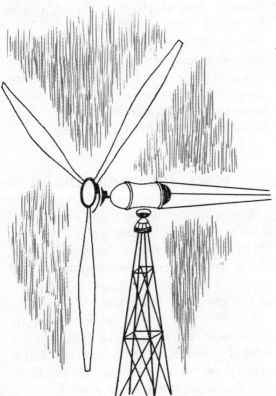

The electricity in the battery flows through wires and lights the electric lights, heats the toast, and milks the cows that give the cream that turns into ice-cream in an electric freezing machine. The wind does it all!

A generator that is worked by the wind is called a *wind-powered generator*. A better name, however, would be a sun-powered generator, for you know that wind is only moving air that moves because it was heated by the sun.

WATER-POWERED GENERATORS

In many places, water power is used to drive a generator. Here you see how flowing water spins an electric generator.

Water from a dam or lake flows against a huge water wheel. This kind of wheel is called a *water turbine*. The force of the falling water turns the huge water wheel. As the wheel turns, it turns a shaft. This turns an electric generator.

The generator sends out electricity through wires. The wires lead to nearby farms and faraway cities. The electricity is used to light lamps and run electric motors. The electric motors run all kinds of machines.

310

sun's heat to light their lights, to run their radios and television sets and electric trains. Even the ice cubes in their refrigerators were frozen by the sun!

Falling water spins generators that supply electricity to millions of homes and factories in this country. But water power is really sun power because the water was lifted by the sun's heat. So, it is really the power of the sun that drives the huge electric generators. The people who get their electricity from water turbines are using the

STEAM-DRIVEN GENERATORS

In many places steam power is used to spin a generator. Powerful steam hits the blades of a turbine and makes it spin. The spinning turbine whirls a generator. The whirling generator sends out electricity through wires that you see stretched across the country on tall towers. Some of these wires lead to cities where you can't see them any more. But they are there just the same, buried in the ground.

Perhaps the electricity in your house or school comes from a generator driven by a steam turbine. If that is so, then you are really using fire to light the electric lights in your home. Fire, made by the burning of a fuel, is used to boil the water to make the

311

steam that spins the turbine that whirls the generator that sends electricity to your home.

A generator run by the power of steam is called a *steam-driven generator*. It could really also be called a sun-driven generator, because the heat for boiling the water into steam comes from burning coal or oil. And where do coal and oil get their energy? That's right, from the sun.

So, you see that your electric lights, your vacuum cleaner, and your refrigerator *are* run by a windmill, a water wheel, or a steam engine after all. But the water wheel or steam engine are not at your house. They are far away in a huge power house that makes power for many people. Electricity running through wires brings the power of falling water or of steam to you from the far-off power house. Electricity is a way of bringing power from where it can be made most easily to where it is needed.

How the Telephone Works

WHAT happens when your telephone rings? First of course, you pick it up and answer it. But how do the voices carry through miles, sometimes hundreds and thousands of miles, of wire? How is it that you can hear even traffic noises, doors slamming, and things being dropped, through the wires of the telephone?

The answer begins with noise and sound itself. All sounds are vibrations in the air. Vibration simply means the sort of motion you get when a tight string is twanged or when a spring is let fly. All sounds are caused by such vibrations. When you drop a rock on the floor, the thud it causes comes from vibrations in the air set in motion by the bump of the rock on the floor. When you talk, the sounds you make are caused

by vibrations in the air that are set in motion by slender cords of tight muscles in your throat, cords that vibrate and are called vocal (or voice) cords.

Vibrations in the air mean movements of the tiny particles that make up air. These are molecules of air—so small that not even microscopes can show them to us. When the vibrating air particles reach the ear they strike a stretched tight part inside the ear that we call the ear-drum. We call it a "drum" because it has a surface that is stretched tight exactly like the top of a drum. The sound waves, striking this, are what we "hear" with our ears.

Perhaps you have heard a noise so loud that it actually seemed to shake you or made things rattle around you. That was because the vibrations set up by such a loud sound are strong enough to vibrate and move things heavier than your eardrum. Some sounds that scientists can produce are so loud and vibrate so powerfully that they can actually crack strong pieces of metal or rock.

Now let's follow some of these sound waves or vibrations as they go into the mouthpiece of a telephone.

Inside the telephone mouthpiece there is a thin circular piece of metal, arranged so that it will vibrate whenever sounds hit it. Behind this metal circle there is a compartment filled with tiny and very specially prepared grains of carbon, like the carbon left from scorched wood or coal. Through this little compartment of carbon and through the wires of the telephone flows an electric current.

When no sound waves are hitting the thin metal in front of the carbon grains, those grains are not tightly packed. When sound does strike the mouthpiece, however, the thin piece of metal bends—though so slightly you wouldn't notice it at all.

As the sound waves make this metal vibrate, the metal pushes with varying pressure against the grains of carbon. And, as it pushes, it packs the grains more closely together. When the pressure is less, or as the sound stops, the grains are permitted to go back to their loose state again. (Here too you wouldn't be able to notice any difference in the grains with your naked eye. You would need an extremely powerful

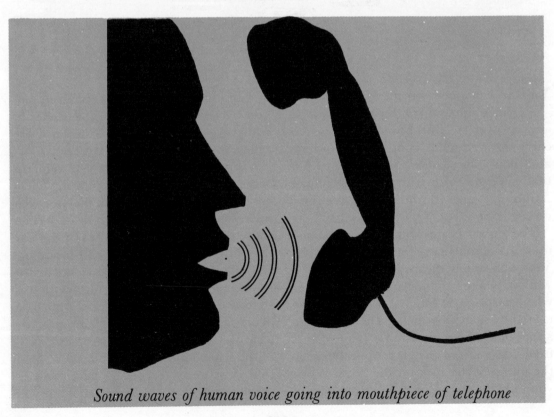

Sound waves of human voice going into mouthpiece of telephone

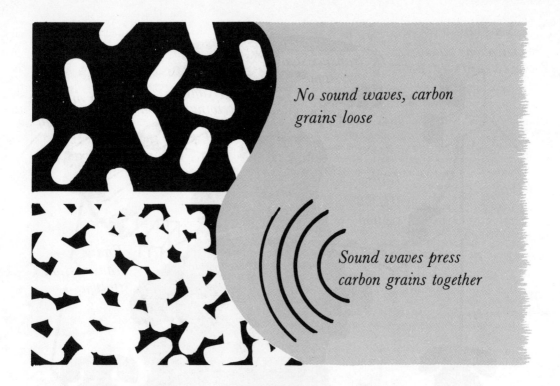

No sound waves, carbon grains loose

Sound waves press carbon grains together

microscope and the fastest camera in the world, one that could take a picture in a millionth of a second, to notice any differences.)

When the grains of carbon are pressed together, the electricity in the telephone wires can pass through the carbon more easily. You might imagine it like this: suppose a group of men are trying to cross a river on floating blocks of ice. When the wind blows the ice blocks closer together, it is easier for the men to get from one to another. When the wind dies down and the blocks drift farther apart, it is harder for the men to cross the river on them. That's the way the electricity finds the grains of carbon. They are easier to pass through when vibrations have packed them close, harder when they are packed loosely.

The changes in the electrical current going through the carbon grains in the mouthpiece of the telephone mean that there are also changes in the electrical current going through the wires of the telephone. This changing electrical current goes along the wires until it reaches the receiver of another phone.

In the receiver of a telephone there is a thin metal disc just as there is in the mouthpiece. But the receiver does not have the little compartment of carbon grains. Instead, there is a magnet that is worked by the electricity coming through the wires. The more electricity there is coming through, the more powerful the magnet becomes.

This magnet in the receiver of the telephone pulls on the thin metal disc and

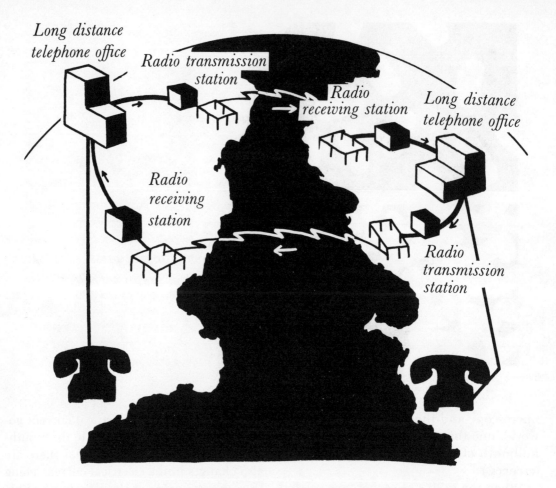

Long distance telephone office

Radio transmission station

Radio receiving station

Long distance telephone office

Radio receiving station

Radio transmission station

makes it vibrate—in exactly the same way that a voice makes a thin metal disc in the mouthpiece vibrate. The result is that the disc in the receiver makes sounds which are exactly like the sounds that cause the disc to vibrate in the mouthpiece.

HOW THE WORDS YOU SPEAK CAN BE HEARD ACROSS ANY DISTANCE

In other words this is what happens:
You speak.
Your voice causes vibrations in the metal disc of the mouthpiece.
Vibrations in the metal disc cause dif-

ferent amounts of electricity to pass through the phone wires.

The electrical current works on a magnet in the ear-piece of the telephone of the person to whom you are speaking.

The magnet causes a metal disc in the receiver to vibrate in exactly the same way as the disc in the mouthpiece does.

When the disc vibrates in just that way it causes the same vibrations in the air that a voice does.

The ear of the listener picks up these vibrations. His ear picks up the same sound as that made by you as you speak.

316

So, really, it is not sound that travels through the wonderful wires of our telephones; it is electricity, traveling in bursts and spurts.

In every country where there are telephones there must be special networks of wires to link those telephones so that people can talk to one another. Then there are special parts of the network to connect the phones of one country to the phones of another country, even though oceans and mountains must be spanned to do it. Sometimes the great distances are covered by bundles of wires bound together into great cables. Sometimes, instead of wires, the phone networks include radio networks to carry words spoken in a telephone all around the world.

Many miles of the wire used to link telephones together can be seen above the ground. Those wires are strung from tall poles that are a familiar sight beside roads and highways. Other wires, however, are under the ground. Some go under deep rivers and even span the oceans.

If all telephone conversations were held between people at short distances from each other, there would be very few problems. But, nowadays, people can speak to one another across any distance. To make that possible many problems have had to be solved.

One of the most important involves the strength of the electricity that makes the telephone work in the first place.

If you speak into a telephone that is just a few miles away from the telephone you are calling, this what happens: The force of the electrical current is changed at the mouthpiece of your telephone by the vibrations of your voice and the pressure on the tiny bits of carbon in the mouthpiece. The electrons or particles of electricity at the mouthpiece start bouncing against the other electrons that form the electrical current in the wire. (All this happens so fast that an electrical current in a telephone wire could flash all the way around the world in less than one-seventh of a second!)

When the electrons at one end of the line start to pass the current along, they

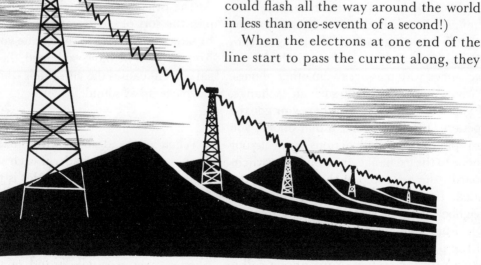

Electricity carrying sound waves through telephone wires

317

are very strong. The farther the current has to travel, however, the less power is left at the end. If the telephone line were very long the current wouldn't be strong enough to do its job at the other end. Wherever telephone wires have to travel long distances, therefore, there are special stations along the wire highways of the telephone networks. These stations are called "repeaters." As an electrical current comes along the wires, if it has been traveling a long distance, the repeaters send in additional power, proportional in amount to the pulses of current carrying the conversation. This means that the tiny changes in current caused at one end of a phone conversation may be carried thousands of miles, in the twinkling of an eye, and the words will come out loudly and clearly on the distant phone.

It would be very clumsy, of course, to have actually to link every single phone together with every other phone in the world. Instead of doing that, the telephone companies of the world link the phones in each neighborhood or area to a central "exchange." It is called an exchange because it is the building in which messages from phones in that area can be switched to or exchanged with messages from other phones.

Your phone wires go to such an exchange. If you want to call a number, you get the operator. Or, if you have a dial phone, you just spin the dial. Both actions connect your phone to the exchange. In it, on huge switchboards, the next step of the journey is decided. If you want a phone right in the neighborhood, the switchboard lets the current from your phone pass on to the wires of the phone you are calling. It is rather like a railroad system. Your phone call is like a train. It goes to a switching yard.

The switch is thrown to decide in which direction it is to go next.

If you have a dial phone this is all done automatically. If you do not have a dial phone, an operator in the exchange takes a plug from your line and puts it into a hole in the switchboard that will connect it with the other phone you want.

If the phone is very far away, the exchange in your neighborhoood or area switches your line onto a line that leads out to other exchanges. Your call is switched from one to another until you reach the exchange that handles the phone you want. That exchange, then, connects you. All this happens so fast that a call may take just a few seconds to get through to a phone thousands of miles away.

If the phone call has to go across oceans or vast mountains it is usually easier to let radio do the job rather than to have wires crossing those long and difficult distances. When this is done, the electrical current from your phone is just changed into radio waves and flashed across the vast distance. At the other end a receiver turns it back into the sort of electrical current that can be sent along a wire to the phone you want. And there, as we have explained, the electrical current causes the vibrations which your ear picks up as sound.

TELEPHONE WIRES

When you read about wires linking telephones, you many wonder if each wire you see held up by telephone poles is the wire for just one telephone. The answer is no, it is not.

Telephone wires are designed so that they carry many messages, from many telephones, over a single strand of wire. In some places, the same wires that carry elec-

318

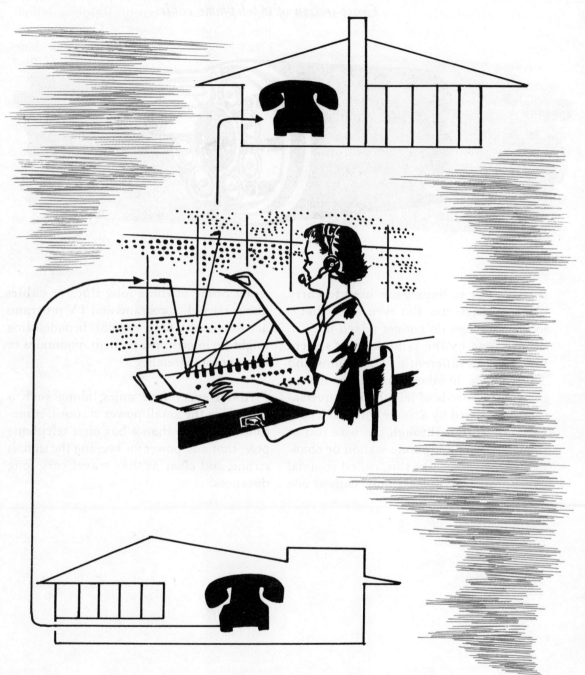

How your phone call gets from one phone to another

319

Cross-section of a telephone cable.

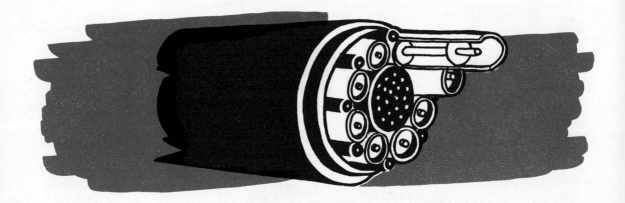

trical power to houses are used to carry phone messages too. But even when that is so, the messages do not get mixed up.

It is done by the same kind of system that gives us different radio stations and TV channels. In other words, when dozens or even hundreds of telephone conversations are carried by a single wire, each conversation travels through the wire just as though it were a separate station or channel. Large cables like this, called co-axial cables, can carry 5,400 phone calls at one time. Some of these long lines or cables also carry radio programs and TV programs across areas where regular broadcasting might be interrupted by high mountains or large empty stretches.

About every four miles, along such a cable, are the small power stations, sometimes no larger than a box on a telephone pole, that add power for keeping the signals strong and clear as they travel very long distances.

320

How the Television
Picture is Made

From TELEVISION WORKS LIKE THIS

By Jeanne and Robert Bendick

THE television picture begins in the camera. There is no film in this camera. Its job is to change the picture it sees into a sort of electrical picture that can be sent through wires and across space.

The heart of the camera is an electron tube. Usually this tube is a special one called the Image Orthicon, and it works like this:

The picture comes in through the camera lens and is focused on a screen that is sensitive to light. The screen is made of thousands of tiny, chemically coated spots. As a ray of light hits each spot, it gives off the microscopic charges of electricity called electrons. The brighter the ray of light, the more electrons the spot sends out.

These electrons shoot along to another screen called the target, hitting it so hard that they knock more electrons out of the target. These displaced electrons are collected, leaving the target hungry for electrons.

At the other end of the tube is an electron gun, shooting out a thin stream of electrons the way a water pistol shoots out water. This stream of electrons moves back and forth across the face of the target, which has light sensitive spots too.

As it moves, each spot grabs electrons back from the stream to replace the ones that were knocked out of it.

Finally the stream bounces back to an electron collection plate. When it leaves the

gun, the stream is of a constant strength, but when it bounces back from the target it varies because of the electrons it has lost.

LIGHT ENTERS LENS

① RELEASING ELECTRONS

③

④ WHICH FLOW TO TARGET

⑤ ELECTRON GUN "SCANS" TARGET

321

The stream varies just as the light and dark varied in the picture that came into the camera lens.

The stream sweeps back and forth across the target just the way your eyes do when you read a book. It covers every point on the picture. This is called scanning.

After the beam is collected in the plate, it is called the signal, and it is an electrical reproduction of the picture in light that came into the tube. Before it flows out of the tube, this signal is made much stronger.

The electron beam scans so quickly that 30 separate pictures are being sent out every second. This is fast enough to catch and send out whatever action is going on in front of the camera.

The tube that does all this work is only about 17 inches long, but it costs about $1,200. And though the picture on your television screen is much larger, that first picture on the camera tube is seven-eighths of an inch high and one and a quarter inches wide.

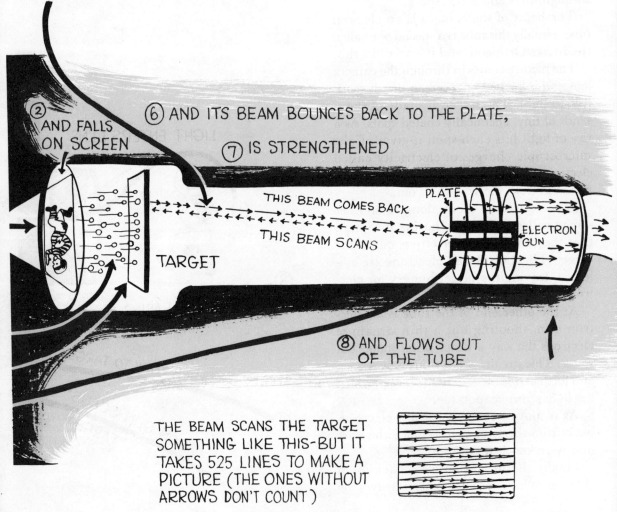

② AND FALLS ON SCREEN

⑥ AND ITS BEAM BOUNCES BACK TO THE PLATE,

⑦ IS STRENGTHENED

THIS BEAM COMES BACK

THIS BEAM SCANS

TARGET

PLATE

ELECTRON GUN

⑧ AND FLOWS OUT OF THE TUBE

THE BEAM SCANS THE TARGET SOMETHING LIKE THIS—BUT IT TAKES 525 LINES TO MAKE A PICTURE (THE ONES WITHOUT ARROWS DON'T COUNT)

Levers, Pulleys and Wheels

From NOW TRY THIS
By Herman and Nina Schneider

CROWBARS AND SEE-SAWS

VERY often people find that they have a big load to lift. A big stone has to be pried up out of the field. A heavy piece of old railroad track must be lifted to make way for a new piece. A truck is stuck in the mud. There are all sorts of lifting and moving jobs.

Even in play, there are lifting jobs. Children who see-saw lift each other. Fat, thin, big, middle-sized, all children can see-saw and lift each other.

You can't see-saw by yourself. If you try you just stay at the bottom.

A heavy person at the other end isn't much use. Then you just stay at the top.

But people do see-saw even though they don't weigh the same.

It's easy to see how a heavy person can make his end of the see-saw go down and

323

lift you up. But how can you make the heavier person go up?

HOW A LIGHT PERSON CAN LIFT A HEAVY PERSON

(Experiment)

YOU WILL NEED: a large and a small drinking glass, a ruler, and a pencil.

If you make a little see-saw of a ruler placed on a pencil, you can try to see-saw things with different weights.

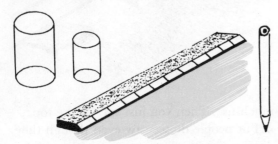

TRY THIS. Place the pencil under the number 6 of the ruler to make a see-saw.

Place the large drinking glass on one end of the ruler. This is your heavy person. Put the small glass on the other end. That's you. *YOU WILL FIND* that the heavier glass keeps the little see-saw tipped up. It's no good for see-sawing.

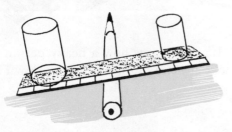

NOW TRY THIS. Move the larger, heavier glass, a little at a time, toward the number 6. You will come to a place where the small glass can lift the large one.

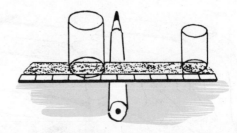

This shows that even though the small glass is lighter, it can lift the heavy one. The light thing farther away from the pencil can lift the heavy thing nearer the pencil.

A ruler, or a pencil, or any stick or bar used to lift something else is called a *lever*.

You have seen that a lever can help a light thing to lift a heavy one.

HOW MUCH LESS PUSH YOU NEED WITH A LEVER TO HELP YOU

(Experiment)

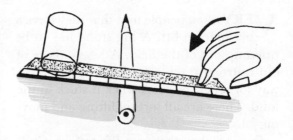

YOU WILL NEED: a large glass, a small glass, a ruler and a pencil.
TRY THIS. Put the large glass at one end of the ruler and push down with your finger at the other end. Feel how much push you need to lift the glass.

Now move the glass close to the pencil and push down with your finger at the other end.

YOU WILL FIND that when your finger is far from the pencil, and the load is near the pencil, the lifting job is made easier.

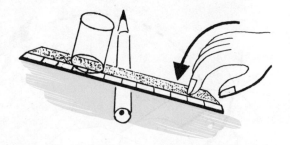

NOW TRY THIS. Make a lever with one part much longer than the other. You can do this by setting the pencil under the number 1 on the ruler. Put the little glass on the short end. Blow hard on the long end. *YOU WILL FIND* with such a lever you may be able to lift the glass just by blowing at the long end (near the 12.)

This shows that when you push on the long end of a lever, much less push is needed.

If your lever is strong enough, *you* can lift a grown-up.

Rest a thick broom handle or plank across a block of wood. Ask the grown-up to stand on the *short* end while you push down on the *long* end. You will find that you can lift him. *NOW YOU KNOW* that levers are simple but very useful machines. They help us to lift, pry, weigh, pull, twist, and push with great force.

• • • • • • • • • • • • • • • • • •

LEVERS AT WORK

Farmers, carpenters and roadmenders often use a lever called a crowbar. Perhaps you've seen workmen prying loose a curbstone, or moving a steel rail by using a crowbar.

A heavily loaded truck or a house can be lifted by one man using a very long lever.

When you use the claw of a hammer to pull out nails, you are using the hammer as a lever, with a curve in it.

A pump handle is a bent lever. You push down on the handle and you lift the heavy weight of water in the pump.

Big scales for weighing heavily loaded coal trucks are really long levers with the truck at the short end and a little two-pound weight at the long end. A two-pound weight can balance a truck weighing 20,000 pounds.

Scientists' scales are built so carefully and accurately that they can weigh the ink on this dot.

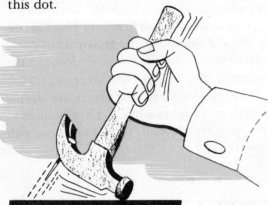

Pliers are two levers criss-crossed. Mechanics and electricians use them to hold or squeeze or twist bolts or wires with more force than they can with their bare hands.

Tin shears are two levers criss-crossed. Tin-smiths use them to cut heavy metal. Pruning shears are criss-crossed levers with long handles. They can cut a branch an inch thick with one snip.

THE LONG WAY IS EASIER

Heave-ho! Up you go! Working people are always busy lifting things. From the ground up to trucks or freight cars, from docks up to ships, from one floor of a factory to another, lots of lifting is always going on.

It's easier to load a ship by carrying things up a gangplank than by climbing straight up a ladder with the load.

It's easier to climb a high mountain up a long slope than straight up a steep side.

It's shorter straight up the ladder than up a gangplank. It's shorter up the steep side of the mountain than up the long slope. Still people usually take the long way up.

TRY THIS. Tie a string to the wagon or skate and make a loop on the end.

Put your little finger through the loop of the string and try to lift the skate straight up from the floor as high as the first rung of the chair. You can do it, but your finger will hurt because the skate feels so heavy.

NOW TRY THIS. Place the board with one end on the floor and the other on the chair rung. Put your finger through the loop of the string and pull the skate from the floor, along the board road up to the chair rung.

WHY PEOPLE FIND IT EASIER TO TAKE THE LONG WAY

(Experiment)

If we make a road out of a slanting board and try to get a load up it, we can find out why the long way is easier.

YOU WILL FIND that it's much easier now, even though you had to move the wagon a longer distance to get to the same place.

This shows that it is easier to lift something along a slant than straight up.

But a big heavy thing like a piano stays big and heavy no matter how you move it! How does a slanting road make a lifting job easier?

HOW A SLANT HELPS US TO LIFT THINGS

(Experiment)

YOU WILL NEED the same things you just used and a rubber band.

YOU WILL NEED: a skate (or a toy wagon), a board, a chair, and a string.

327

TRY THIS. Attach a thin rubber band, instead of the string, to the skate or wagon.

Attach the other end of the rubber band to a tack at the end of the board.

Hold the board flat. The rubber band is loose. The whole weight of the skate is held by the board.

Now, tip the board a little. Watch the rubber band tighten. Some of the weight of the skate is held by the rubber band, instead of all by the board.

Now tip the board more and more. More of the skate's weight is held by the rubber band and less by the board.

When the board is straight up, all of the weight is held by the rubber band and none of it by the board.

This shows that it is a lot harder to pull something up a very steep hill. The gentler the slope, the easier it is to move the load. The steeper the slope, the harder it is to move a load.

You pull the load with your muscles like the rubber band pulls the skates. On a steep hill *you* are holding more of the weight and the road is holding less. When the hill is not steep, the load rests mostly on the road.

A hill, a sloping road, a plank placed on a slant, these are called *inclined planes*. Inclined planes are of great help in moving things.

Inclined planes make lifting and moving jobs easier in millions of different ways. Sometimes they are hard to recognize because they have lots of different shapes. For instance, mountain roads are inclined planes.

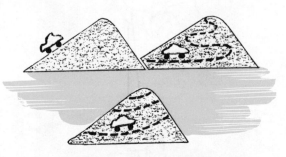

The first hill is a simple inclined plane. It is too steep for a car to climb. The road on the second hill is really a zig-zag inclined plane. It's easier to climb because the slant is not as steep.

Here is another way of building a gently sloping road on a steep hill. The road goes around like a corkscrew.

Every day you use inclined planes that go around and around like corkscrews. You can find them in the clamps on your skates, in piano stools and office chairs, in many of your toys. They are called screws, and they are a special kind of inclined plane.

HOW A SCREW
IS AN INCLINED PLANE

(Experiment)

YOU WILL NEED: a round pencil, and a sheet of paper.

TRY THIS. Tear the sheet of paper into this shape.

It looks like an inclined plane. Now roll the paper around the pencil like this:

When you are finished it will look like this:

This shows that a screw is really an inclined plane turned around on a nail.

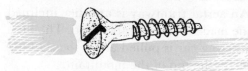

YOU FOUND OUT that an inclined plane is one way of lifting and moving things more easily.

• • • • • • • • • • • •

INCLINED PLANES AT WORK

Heavy loads are pushed or rolled on to trucks and freight cars up slanting planks.

Driveways slant up to gas stations so that cars don't have to jump over the curbs.

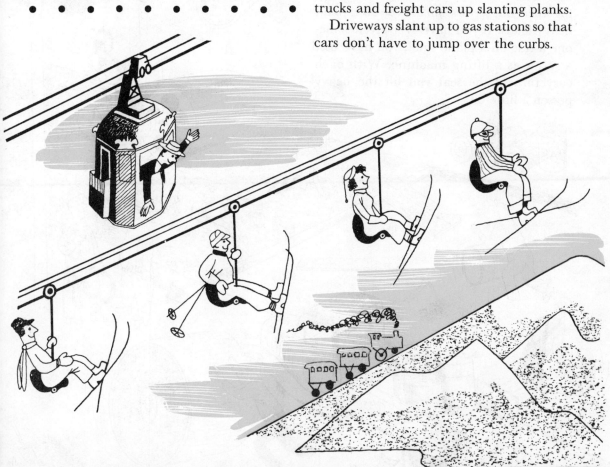

Ramps are slanting roads. You may have seen them in railroad stations, and on piers. Some garages have ramps instead of elevators.

A ski tow is an inclined plane. A steel cable is the road.

An aerial tramway is another inclined plane made of a steel cable road. The little sightseeing car is pulled along the slanting cable to the top of the mountain.

There is another inclined plane used for sightseeing. The passengers and the locomotive remain level while the little train climbs the slope. Ordinary smooth tracks don't give enough friction for the wheels to grip, so there are teeth on the track to fit the teeth on the locomotive wheels. It is called a funicular railroad.

You have used screws for holding things together. But screws can also be used to lift heavy loads. If you have ever given someone a ride on a piano stool, you have used a screw as a lifting machine. With each easy turn of the seat you lift the heavy person a little bit.

House carpenters use screws for lifting things, too. They lift whole houses with something that looks like a large piano stool screw. It is called a jack screw.

ROLLING INSTEAD OF DRAGGING

One of the busiest kinds of moving jobs is building a new road. Of course, the workmen try to make the moving as easy as possible. When they are moving something round, they *roll* it instead of dragging it. The

lumbermen who chop down the trees roll the logs aside. The truckmen roll the logs up into the trucks. The big water pipes (culverts) are rolled into place. Barrels of tar and drums of oil are rolled off the trucks. Big reels of telephone cables are rolled off the telephone truck and rolled into place.

Why do the workmen always try to roll things whenever they can?

WHY ROLLING IS AN EASIER WAY OF MOVING ROUND THINGS

(Experiment)

YOU WILL NEED: a box of salt or fine cereal poured on a clean dish towel, and a round can of food.

TRY THIS. Flatten the salt like a road. Pull the can down the "road" like this.

You will see the piles of salt pushed to each side as the can drags along. The can digs into the road and doesn't move easily this way.

Now *roll* the can down the road. You will see the salt flattened down as the can rolls easily along.

YOU WILL FIND that dragging or pushing on a road means going *through* all the bumps

that rub and grip, even the little ones. Rolling presses the bumps down and the load passes over the road without needing much work.

This shows that it is easier to roll a load than to drag it, because there is much less friction in rolling than in dragging.

Round things roll so easily it would be helpful to use them for carrying heavy things that are not round.

CAN WE USE ROLLERS FOR CARRYING AND MOVING A LOAD THAT IS NOT ROUND?

(Experiment)

YOU WILL NEED: a heavy book, two candles or two round pencils, the table top for a road.

TRY THIS. Slide the book along the table, one short push. See how far the book moves.

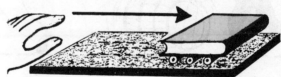

Now put the book on the candles. Push the book as hard as you did the first time. *YOU WILL FIND* that with rollers under it the book will move at a good speed and travel much farther. Without rollers, the rough surface of the book drags over the table. There is a lot of friction, the book goes slowly and stops.

331

This shows that rollers can be put under a load to change a sliding job into a rolling job.

NOW YOU KNOW that moving a load on rollers is easier than dragging it. Less friction makes the job easier.

ROLLERS AT WORK

Barrels are their own rollers. Tar, flour, sugar, tobacco, are packed in barrels.

Houses sometimes are moved long distances on rollers. The house is jacked up and smooth logs are put underneath. A truck pulls the house a short distance. Then the back rollers are picked up and put down in front and the house is moved a short distance again. This is repeated over and over again, until the building is rolled to its new place.

Heavy boats that are too big to be carried are rolled in and out of the water on rollers.

There are rollers on the floor of lumber trucks to make them easy to unload.

In factories, heavy things are moved on rollers set closely together in floors or on frames. The heavy stove or airplane engine is rolled along all over the factory, from one machine to another, where each worker does his part of the job.

Sometimes a wide belt is put on top of a long row of rollers to make a moving road. Such a belt, called a conveyor belt, has many important jobs. Candies, packaged cereals, cookies and skates—most things made in large quantities—are moved on conveyor belts supported on rollers.

Conveyor belts are used in mines as well as in factories. The moving belt brings coal and iron out of deep mines up to the surface.

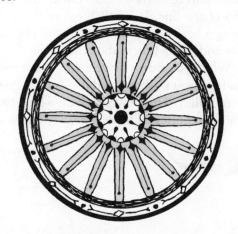

FASTER AND EASIER

Rollers make moving easier. But they are either fixed to stay in one place, or you have to lift them and carry them from the back of the load to the front as the load moves along. This is slow work.

You can take plenty of time to move a big machine off a loading platform, or to move a house. But a fire engine wouldn't be very welcome if it came crawling along on rollers the morning after the fire.

It would be easier and quicker to move things on rollers, if you didn't have to keep picking them up and putting them in front of the load. If the rollers could be attached to the load it would save all this work.

No one knows who invented the wheel. Perhaps this is how it was done. A round smooth tree trunk was cut into thick slices. Holes were bored in the middle of each slice. A long thin pole was put through the hole and the pole was fastened under a box —a wagon. The slices of tree trunk have been made into wheels. The wheels move along with the loaded wagon.

This simple kind of wheel was used long ago, and it is still used today. Of course, we don't use only slices of tree trunk. Now, pieces of wood, metal, plastic, hard rubber, and other materials are used to make wheels.

The simple wheel is one of the most important machines ever invented. It is good for wheelbarrows, kiddie-cars, hay-wagons, oxcarts, slow freight trains, and thousands of other things.

WHEELS AT WORK

You need wheels when you travel by car, plane, train, bicycle, tricycle, skates, scooter, or baby carriage.

You need wheels in the home in vacuum cleaners, carpet sweepers, egg-beaters, clocks, electric fans, oil burners, dial telephones, washing machines, elevators, refrigerators and many more things.

A merry-go-round is only a large wheel. So is a ferris wheel.

A pulley is just a wheel with a rope around it, but it's a great help in making lots of jobs easier to do. You can hoist a flag to the top of a flagpole while you stand on the ground and pull a rope.

With a pulley, a man can stand on the street and hoist buckets of tar up to the man mending the roof.

Sometimes two pulleys work together as in a clothes line. A person can stand at one place and send the clothes out to the other end of the line. It is much easier than carrying a heavy basketful of wet clothing from one end of the line to the other.

When you ride a bicycle you make use of pulleys. You push the pedals which turn the front pulley. This moves a chain which turns the rear pulley. The rear pulley turns the

rear wheel and so the whole bicycle moves.

A clothes line carries people's clothing. An escalator carries people. Of course there's lots of machinery besides, but the main part of an escalator is a long chain that turns around two big pulleys. On the chain are fastened steps for the people to stand on.

An elevator, too, uses pulleys for moving people up and down.

First there is a pair of pulleys like an up and down clothesline. An electric motor turns the bottom pulley, which turns the top pulley.

The elevator car hangs from another pulley like a tar bucket. At the other end of the wire ropes there are heavy iron weights that balance the elevator car.

The motor turns the bottom pulley, the bottom pulley turns the top pulley, the top pulley turns the "tar bucket" pulley, and the elevator moves up and down.

FULL SPEED AHEAD

Of all the ways of making work easier, the wheel has been the most useful. People have used it for thousands of years in all sorts of moving jobs. But useful as it is, there's something wrong about a plain wheel. There's something that needs to be made better.

WHAT'S WRONG WITH THE PLAIN WHEEL

(Experiment)

YOU WILL NEED: a cardboard oatmeal box (or any round container) and a pencil. *TRY THIS.* Make a simple wheel out of the round end. Poke a hole in the center, a little bigger around than your pencil. Put the pencil through the hole and *spin* the wheel.

L.C.Q.X.R.

801

CAPY 200000
LD LMT 205300
LT WT 45700 McKR 337   BLT 837

IL 24 FT 5 IN
CU.FT. 1640

335

YOU WILL FIND that it makes a few turns and stops. Try again and watch the hole. The cardboard rubs and drags against the pencil. There is a lot of rubbing where the cardboard turns around the pencil.

This shows that there is rubbing at the axle of a plain wheel.

A plain wheel on an oxcart rubs around the axle. No matter how large the hole is, or how smooth the wheel and axle are, there is friction as the wheel turns. The hole in the wheel soon gets larger and the wheel rolls crooked. The axle and shaft break from constant rubbing. It isn't safe to ride along quickly in that kind of wagon.

Grease and oil will help keep the axle and the wheel from rubbing, but there will still be some friction. Wheels have to be greased all the time, because the grease pushes to the sides and is squeezed out. Locomotive and railroad car wheels are built with big oil boxes around the axle. The trainmen have to fill these boxes with oil at almost every stop.

So we see that a plain wheel is good in one place and not so good in another. It's good at the place where it touches the ground. It rolls along, and rolling is easier than dragging. But it's not so good at the axle, because that's where it drags instead of rolling. Isn't there some way of making the wheel *roll* around the axle? Can we put something at the axle to change the dragging to rolling? If we can, we will have a wheel that spins more easily than a plain wheel, and lasts much longer.

CAN WE CHANGE THE DRAGGING MOTION INTO A ROLLING MOTION

(Experiment)

YOU WILL NEED: a dozen marbles of the same size, the cover of a round tin coffee can, and a heavy thing like an iron or a teakettle.

TRY THIS. Put the heavy thing on the floor and try to spin it.

Now put the marbles on the floor and the coffee can cover over them with its rim down. (The cover will keep the marbles from rolling away.) Set the iron on the cover and try again to spin it.

YOU WILL FIND that it won't spin very well on the floor. But when the marbles are put between the floor and the iron it takes only a very light push to start the iron going, and it spins for quite a long time.

This shows that we can change a dragging motion to a rolling motion. All we need to do is put marbles (or any round things) between the two surfaces that are rubbing against each other. Then the dragging is changed to rolling.

In the plain wheel, the two rubbing surfaces are the axle and the hole in the wheel. So we make the hole large enough to hold a ring of steel balls between the wheel and the axle. Such a wheel is called a *ballbearing* wheel because the weight of the load bears down on a ring of balls.

336

NOW YOU KNOW that a ballbearing wheel is a really fine wheel for speedy things. It rolls where it touches the ground and it rolls around its axle. There is much less friction than in a plain wheel. It spins easily and lasts a long time.

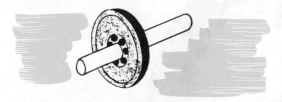

YOU FOUND OUT that of all the work savers, wheels are the most useful. They work for us dozens of times a day in all kinds of ways. Ballbearing wheels have made it possible for us to do many jobs speedily and easily.

BALLBEARINGS AT WORK

Ballbearing wheels are in almost every speedy machine. Bicycles, scooters, motorcycles, autos, and airplanes all have ballbearings. And so do malted milk beaters, washing machines, elevators, and refrigerators.

The wheel of a dial telephone turns smoothly and easily on ballbearings.

Beginner's skates have plain wheels. Faster skates have ballbearings.

There are some ballbearing wheels that spin so fast that they turn 2500 times while you count quickly from one to five.

Sometimes, when loads are very heavy, rollers are used in wheels instead of balls. Such wheels are called *roller bearing* wheels, but they work just like ballbearings.

Streamlined trains roll on roller bearings. Because there is less friction at the axles of their wheels, they can start and stop smoothly without jerking.

Most new locomotives have roller bearing wheels. They reduce friction so much that two people can easily pull a 400-ton engine along a flat track.

How We Can Fly

MANY people have called this particular time in the world's history the Air Age. They mean that this is the age in which man learned to leave the ground and travel through the air. Learning that has changed man's whole way of life. In the first place, learning to fly has meant that great walls of distance and mountains and oceans no longer keep men from visiting one another —or, unfortunately, from making war on each other either.

If you had been born before the Air Age, you would have thought all the countries of the world across the ocean were strange and far away. Today, even though you may never visit those countries, there are so many people who *do* visit them that people in America sometimes hear more about Paris and London and Berlin than about Cincinnati or Boston. In the same way, a person living in New Zealand may hear as much about Washington as about Auckland.

The ease of traveling by air means that people everywhere have a new and wonderful chance to learn about each other.

THE AIRPLANE IS EASY TO UNDERSTAND

But what about the wonderful machine that has made it all possible? What about the airplane? Most of us have come to accept it, just as we accept radios and automobiles, but not many people understand just what it is that makes the airplane fly. Because this is one of man's most important new tools—a tool that lets him turn distance into hours of flying time rather than thousands of miles—we *should* understand it. And it isn't very difficult to understand. The airplane is really one of the simplest machines no matter how complicated it looks.

Here is how we can fly.

If you have ever looked at the wing of an airplane you may remember its shape. That shape is the first key to understanding how we can fly. The wing is rounded at the front. That is called the *leading edge* of the wing. The wing comes together more sharply at the back. That part is called the *trailing edge.*

The top of the wing is curved. The bottom of the wing is almost a straight line. If you looked at a section of this wing after someone had sliced it off, you would see

that the flat bottom goes to a thick stubby curve at the front, then the curved top slants back so that the back end is very thin.

HOW THE AIRPLANE LIFTS

When this wing moves through the air at fairly high speeds, with the thick curved end first, a very interesting thing happens. The thick front end pushes the air out of its way. Part of the air, of course, goes under the bottom of the wing while part of it goes over the top of the wing. This air that has been pushed apart by the wing goes back together again when it gets to the back end (the trailing edge) of the wing.

But the layers of air that went *over the top* of the wing had to behave differently from the layer of air that went *under* the wing. The air that went under the bottom of the wing had to flow along the straight line that forms the wing's lower part. And a

Full view of plane

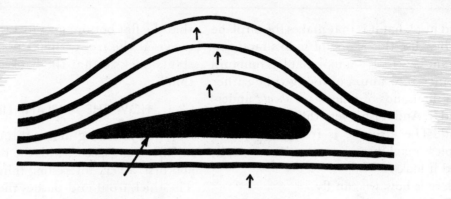

Plane wing moving through air

straight line always is the shortest distance between two points. The air that went over the top part of the wing had to flow along a curve. That curve actually means that the air on top traveled farther than the air that went right along the straight line of the bottom of the wing. In traveling farther, the layer of air on top of the wing thins out.

All along the top of the wing, therefore, there is thin air. All along the bottom of the wing there is a thicker layer of air. It is as though a partial vacuum had been created on top of the wing. With more air under the wing than above it, only one thing can happen. The air underneath pushes the wing upward in the direction of the thinner air.

This is called *lift*. It is what lifts the wing of an aircraft. By changing the sort of curve across the top of the wing, the men who build airplanes can change the amount of lift. They design the wings so that the amount of lift on the wings will be the same as the amount of the weight of the airplane and everything it can carry.

If the plane weighs just a ton, like some small airplanes, then the wings need only have enough lift to hold up that ton plus the weight of the passengers and baggage.

You can look at lift in this way: you may remember, from what you have learned about weather, that air normally has a weight or pressure of about 15 pounds per square inch at sea level. Well, if an airplane wing moved very fast through air like that, the pressure of the air under the wing will stay at 15 pounds. But the pressure on top of the wing where the air thins out may drop down to, say 14 pounds per square inch. So, there is one pound less on top than on the bottom. This means that there is one pound of lift pushing up for every square inch of the wing.

If the wing is 120 inches (ten feet) long and 36 inches (three feet) wide then there are 120 x 36 square inches. That would be 4,320 square inches. For each of those square inches the wing has one pound of lift. So the wing could lift 4,320 pounds. Two wings could lift twice as much, or 8,640 pounds.

The airplane, remember, weighed only a ton, or 2,000 pounds. This means that there are more than 6,000 pounds left that the two wings can lift. And all that weight could be used by baggage and passengers.

That description doesn't fit any particular real airplane but it will show you how lift is figured and how it determines the load that an airplane can carry.

There is a way that you can actually see how this lift works. Take a small board and move it edgeways through the water —at a slight angle to the direction in which you are moving it. If you move the board fast enough you will see that the water moves away to leave a sort of hole at one side of the board. That side is like the top side of an airplane wing. That hole in the water as the board moves through it is like the thinned out area in the air on top of the wing.

You can watch another thing while moving the board through the water. If you slow it down there will be no open part in the water on one side of the board. The water flows all over equally. The same thing happens to an airplane wing. When it slows down to certain speeds, and depending on the exact shape of the wing, the air no longer rushes along the top curve in such a way as to create a partial vacuum. Then the wing can't lift anything and the plane can't fly. Very light, little planes have to go about 60 miles per hour to fly. Some big ones have to go more than 100. After they get into the air, of course, they can go many times faster.

The next question, then, is how do we get the wing of the airplane to move through the air fast enough to cause the lift that is needed to fly?

We do it, in ordinary planes, with the propeller. Jets and rockets do it differently. First let's learn about propellers.

Two views of propeller

Propeller at rest showing shape of blade

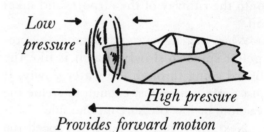

Low pressure

High pressure

Provides forward motion

Propeller spinning to show how air pushes

WHAT PROPELLERS DO

The propeller is shaped very much like the wing of the airplane. It has one fairly flat side and a curved side. The flat side is the side closest to the airplane. The curved side is out on the front.

When the propeller is made to spin by the airplane's engine, the propeller cuts through the air the way a wing does. The air rushes past the flat side without any trouble. But the air going over the curved part has to travel farther and, just as with the wing, thins out. This causes a partial vacuum on the front of the propeller while the air behind it has its regular pressure. You can imagine what happens. The air behind the propeller actually pushes it forward. And, because the propeller is spinning so fast—thousands of revolutions per minute—it is almost as though it is a solid disc for the air to push against. When you look at a spinning propeller you will notice that it seems like a solid blurred circle. You can't see the individual blades at all when it is spinning.

This push on the propeller is lift just like the lift that the wings get. But this lift is in a different direction.

To see how it works, let's watch an airplane as it comes out of its hangar, goes onto the runway of the airport, and takes off.

When the engine starts turning, the propeller spins so slowly that it is like the board going through the water slowly. It just doesn't move fast enough to create the vacuum or low pressure on one side.

Next, however, the pilot will speed the engine up. The propeller spins faster. Now it has some lift. That lift pushes straight ahead against the propeller. As soon as the amount of the push against the propeller equals the weight of the plane, it will make the plane move.

For the time being, the pilot just wants the plane to move slowly along the ground like an automobile. So he doesn't make the propeller go any faster; just fast enough to

make the plane move. This isn't fast enough for the wings to start getting any lift. When the pilot makes the plane move on the ground like this, it is called "taxiing." The pilot taxis the plane out on the runway— the long concrete strip on an airport where planes land and take off.

When the pilot is ready to take off, he lets the engine turn as fast as it can. This spins the propeller very very fast. The push against the propeller becomes very great. The plane starts to move. It moves faster and faster. The air rushes around the wings faster and faster. Suddenly the wing is moving through the air fast enough to have lift of its own. The plane starts rising off the ground. The pilot moves a control that points the plane upward. It climbs up into the sky. When it is high enough, the pilot levels it out and the flight is underway.

TAKING OFF AND LANDING

Perhaps you have heard that airplanes always take off into the wind. Pilots call this "upwind." The direction of the wind is called "downwind." Sometimes, of course, the direction of the wind may be across the runway rather than up or down it. Then the plane has to take off or land "crosswind." Many airports have several runways at different angles to one another so that one of the runways will be close to the

Wind direction

Plane taking off upwind

wind direction no matter which way it is blowing.

The reason that planes both take off *and* land into the wind is this: When a plane is standing still and heading into the wind, it means that the air is moving over the wings, and starting to build up lift, even before the plane is moving. When the plane starts to move, it already has the wind working for it ahead of time and it doesn't have to go as fast before the air is flowing over the wings fast enough to create lift.

When the plane is landing the same sort of thing happens. As the plane slows down and sinks toward the earth, the moving air into which it is heading helps to give it lift right up to the moment the wheels touch the ground. If the plane landed with the wind blowing from behind it, the lift on the wings might be cancelled out too fast and the plane would bump down on the ground and perhaps even be damaged by the drop. Also, with the wind behind it, the plane always would be in danger of being pushed right over on its nose by a sudden gust of air. When the plane is facing the wind, it is in its steadiest position.

USING THE CONTROLS

To land, take off, and fly where the pilot wants, the airplane must have controls to make it move in different directions while in the air. A plane can go straight ahead, dive down, climb up, or turn.

The controls that make the plane climb and dive are called "elevators." The elevators are movable parts of the flat part of the tail of the airplane. The flat part of the tail is called the horizontal stabilizer and is like a small wing built horizontally or crossways into the tail. It is called a sta-

bilizer because it stabilizes the plane, or makes it steady against nosing up or down.

When the pilot does want to go up or down he moves the elevators in the tail. These are flaps in the tail and they can move up or down. When the pilot pulls back on his stick or wheel in the cockpit, the elevator flaps go up. When the air rushing past the airplane hits these raised flaps, the tail is shoved down. When the tail goes down, the nose goes up and the plane starts to climb.

If the pilot wants to dive down, as when he starts to land, he pushes the stick or wheel forward. This makes the elevator flaps go down. The air hits the lowered flaps and shoves the tail up. This makes the nose go down.

In order to turn, the plane needs two controls. One of the controls is the rudder. This is a moveable part of the vertical stabilizer. The vertical stabilizer is the part of the tail that is vertical or straight up. It is like a wing sticking up straight from the tail, and it stabilizes the plane against turning left and right.

But the moveable part of it, the rudder, can *make* the plane turn right or left. When the pilot presses on the right-hand one of two control pedals in the cockpit, the rudder moves to the right. The air rushing alongside the plane hits the rudder and pushes it away. As the tail turns, of course, the nose turns and the plane turns to the right. If the rudder moves left, the plane will turn left.

But if the plane just turned flat like that it would skid in the air, the way an automobile sometimes will skid going around a curve unless the road is tilted or banked to make the car lean. You should know

343

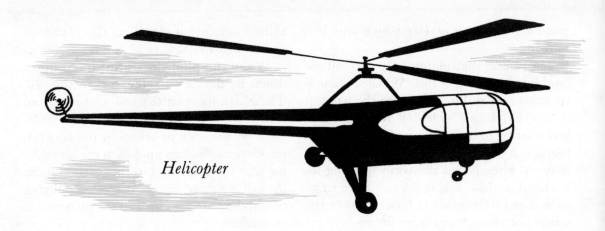

Helicopter

about this from riding a bike or sled. When you turn a corner on either a bike or a sled, you have to lean toward the inside of the curve or you may either skid or fall down.

The airplane has to do something like this too. It has to be tilted toward the direction of the curve. The sharper the curve, the more the plane has to be tilted. In very fast turns of, say, fighter planes, the plane tilts all the way sideways while it turns.

In order to tilt the plane like that, the pilot uses moveable flaps that are in the wings. These flaps are called *ailerons*. There is one out toward the end of each wing, on the trailing or back edge. When the pilot wants the plane to tilt to the right, for a right-hand turn, he uses both the rudder and the ailerons.

He presses on the right-hand pedal in the cockpit to turn the rudder. This swings the tail and turns the nose of the plane to the right. At the same time, the pilot turns the wheel or presses the stick—whichever his plane has—to the right. This makes the aileron on the right wing go up and the aileron on the left wing go down. When the aileron on the right wing goes up, the wind hits it and shoves the wing down-

ward. When the aileron on the left wing goes down the wind hits it too but when the wind shoves against it from below, the left wing is pressed upwards. This all means that the whole plane tilts over to the right, in the direction the plane is turning. The rudder turns it, the ailerons in the wings tilt it, and the plane turns—smoothly and safely. This tilting is called "banking."

FLYING WITHOUT WINGS

Maybe by now you are wondering about things that fly but don't have wings. The helicopter is just that sort of craft. It has no wings but it certainly can fly. In fact, it is the only sort of flying craft, except for a balloon, that can go straight up, just hang suspended in the air, and even go backwards.

Instead of wings, the helicopter has a giant propeller, called a rotor, that turns on top of a post on top of the helicopter. Some have two sets of rotors, in which case they are placed at either end. Because the helicopter can do such strange things—like hovering above a boat while someone is hoisted up to the helicopter in a stretcher to be taken to a hospital—these machines

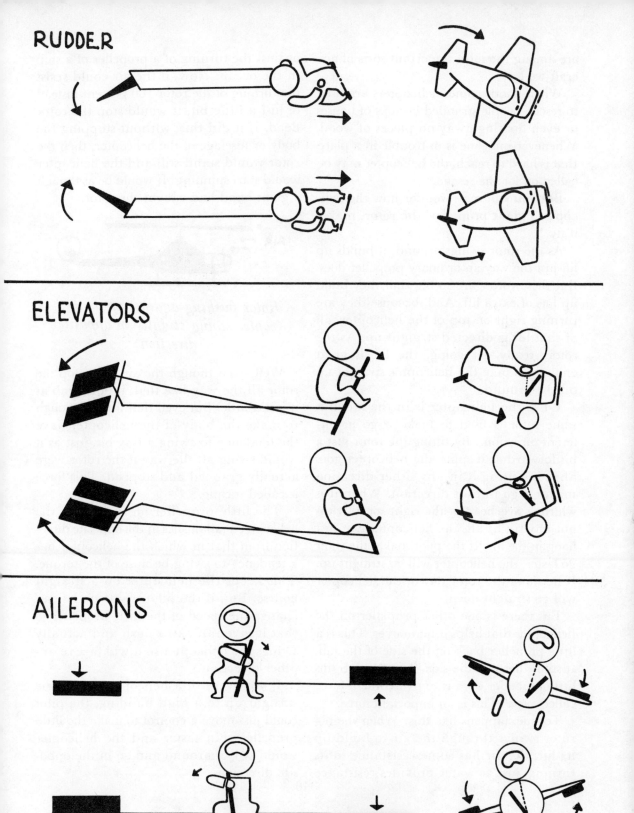

RUDDER

ELEVATORS

AILERONS

are among the most important sorts of aircraft we have.

When floods come, helicopters are used to rescue people stranded on tops of houses or even floating away on pieces of wood. Whenever someone is in trouble in a place that is hard to reach, the helicopter may be called on for the rescue.

But you still may wonder how the helicopter's giant propeller, the rotor, makes it fly.

As the rotor swings around, it builds up lift just the way an ordinary propeller does. But these rotors are so big that they build up lots of extra lift. And, because they are turning right on top of the helicopter, all of that lift is directed straight up. As the rotors really get going, the lift is great enough to take the helicopter straight up off the ground.

Once the helicopter is in the air, this same rotor is used to make it go in different directions. By tilting the rotor just a bit forward as it spins, the helicopter goes ahead. Tilting it in any other direction makes it go in that direction. When it is whirling overhead at the right speed without any tilt at all, the helicopter can just hang in the air. If the pilot makes the rotor go faster, the helicopter will go straight up. If he slows the rotor down, the helicopter will go straight down.

But there is one other propeller on the helicopter that helps it maneuver. This is a little propeller back on the side of the tail. It spins there on the side. The first job this little propeller does is to overcome a force called *torque*. This is an important force.

Torque happens like this: When the big rotor swings through the air to build up its lift, the air has some resistance to its turning, just as water provides resistance against the turning of a propeller of a ship in the ocean. Now, if the air could resist the turning of the rotor 100 percent instead of just a little bit, it would stop the rotor dead. If it did this, without stopping the body or fuselage of the helicopter, then the rotor would stand still and the helicopter would start spinning! It would be as though a giant hand had caught the rotor.

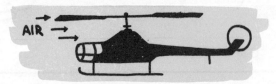

Rotor pushing against air makes 'copter swing slightly in opposite direction

Well, even though the air can't stop the rotor all the way like that, it does grab at it just a little. But even that little is enough to make the body of the helicopter have the tendency to swing a tiny bit, just as it would swing all the way if the rotor were actually grabbed and stopped. This force is called torque.

The little propeller on the side of the helicopter's tail pushes in the opposite direction from that in which the helicopter has a tendency to swing because of the torque. This keeps the helicopter on a straight course. But, if the pilot wants to, he can change the speed of the little propeller so that it gives an extra push and actually swings the helicopter so it will face in another direction.

If you were in a helicopter and came straight up to a high building, the pilot could just move a control to make the little propeller spin faster and the helicopter would swivel around and go in the opposite direction.

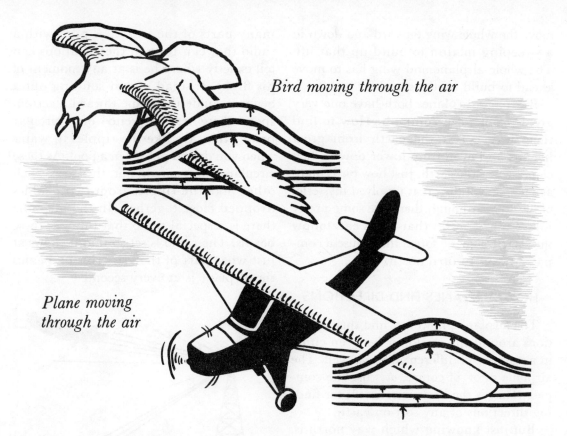

Bird moving through the air

Plane moving through the air

When it comes to jets and rockets, which we will learn about in the next part of this book, there are no propellers. The force to make the plane move, and thus get it going fast enough for the wings to have lift, is provided by a sort of force called *thrust*.

The thrust comes from the hot gases blasting out of the end of the jet or rocket. While these gases are blasting out of one end of the jet or rocket, they are providing thrust, or a giant shove, against the forward end. That is what makes the plane move. Exactly how jets and rockets work is described later in this book. Some helicopters have been built with jets but, in that case, the jets are placed at the ends of the rotors and merely provide the power to spin the rotor.

HOW WINGS WORK

Perhaps you have wondered, as the wings of a plane were described, just how these wings compare to the wings of a bird. In the part of this book that tells about birds, there is a description of how a bird's wings work; but now that you have just come from airplane wings, it might be a good idea to mention the difference again.

The bird wing works on exactly the same principle as the airplane wing. When the bird is in flight, he curves his wing so that air passing over the top of the wing will thin out in comparison to the air underneath. The birds gets lift that way just the way an airplane gets it. But there is this important difference. The bird's muscles move the whole wing forward and down in a sweeping motion to build up that lift. The whole airplane and wing has to move ahead to build up the speed for its lift.

Birds and airplanes both have one very great problem in common: How to find their way across the earth from great heights and even from lower down when clouds cover the earth. Just how birds manage it is one of the great unsolved mysteries of nature—although there are some pretty interesting guesses that birds can follow the same magnetic forces that cause a compass always to turn north.

HOW AIRPLANES FIND DIRECTIONS

The airplanes, however, find their directions around the world, or between cities, in a number of different ways as well. The airplane pilot, of course, *does* use the compass. That is the basic instrument for finding directions of any sort on earth.

But just knowing which way north is, isn't nearly enough for the airplane pilot. He has to know exactly where *he* is and not just where north, south, east, and west are. He has to know this so exactly that he can land at an airport even when he can't see it.

Here are some of the ways he does it:

Radio is a very important way of finding directions, for an airplane pilot. Special radio transmitters are set up, for example, near airports. In the airplane there is a special radio. As the pilot tunes this radio, a dial on it shows directions. When the pilot tunes it in to one of the special stations near an airfield, the dial shows just what direction it is in, so that the pilot can fly straight toward it.

Even better are networks of special radio sending stations that have been set up in many parts of the world. A pilot with a radio that can tune in these stations can tell exactly where he is at any moment of his flight. Instead of just sending out a beam to guide the plane toward a certain spot, these radios send out circular beams that are like the ripples in water when you drop a pebble in a pool. As these circular beams spread out, they cross each other, like the ripples from two pebbles dropped close together. In the airplane there is a special radio that tunes in these beams. The radio is set so that it shows at just what part of the crisscrossing beams the airplane is at every second.

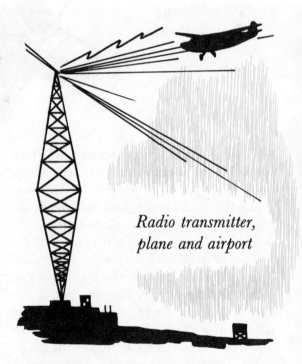

Radio transmitter, plane and airport

Another special way of finding directions for airplanes is the use of radar. Radar sets are special radio sets that send out beams which bounce back as soon as they hit something solid. The radar set, in that way,

348

Operating by radar

can detect any solid object its beams can reach. When the beams bounce back, they even show, roughly, the shape of the solid object they hit.

Radar sets on the ground can keep track of airplanes as they fly in the air. If the pilot of the plane can't see the ground or gets lost, a man at a radar set can spot the plane and then get on a regular radio to tell the pilot just where his plane is. These radar sets are so accurate that they are used to help pilots land airplanes when the weather is so bad that the pilot can't see a foot in front of him. The man at the radar set spots the plane on a special screen. Then he just keeps telling the pilot which way and how to fly until, before you know it, the plane is safely down on the ground at an airport.

Jets and Rockets

Jet Plane

WHEN you see an airplane without propellers or rotors of any sort, you are seeing a jet or rocket plane. Not so long ago, back in the 1940's for instance, when people talked about jet and rocket planes, they usually meant things they thought wouldn't really be used for forty or fifty years or even more. Yet, today, jets and rockets are taken for granted by anyone interested in aviation, and even people who have never flown in a plane, when they hear a certain kind of loud roaring overhead, like an express train, know that a jet airplane is zooming through the sky.

Although it may seem sort of mysterious that jets and rockets can fly without any propellers, there is a way to understand this kind of airplane that is even simpler than trying to understand the propeller-driven airplanes we have talked about before.

To understand the principle of jet and rocket propulsion, all you need is a toy balloon. (That word *propulsion*, by the way, simply means how something is propelled, or how it is made to move).

To understand jets and rockets with your toy balloon, blow the balloon up as fat as it will go. When you have finished blowing it up, hold onto the end tightly so that no air will escape. Now, what you have in the balloon is a lot of air all stored up and under pressure. The rubber skin of the balloon is pressing the air.

You probably know exactly what will happen if you let go of the end of the balloon: The air will come out in a great rush and the balloon will go shooting across the room diving and twisting and dipping and zooming until all the air is out.

People have known about things like

350

that for hundreds of years. But it was not until Sir Isaac Newton first figured out such things as the law of gravity, that anyone figured out a rule to explain *why* such things happen.

Newton's law is that for every action there is an equal and opposite reaction. More exactly: If body A acts on body B, body B acts on body A with an equal and opposite force.

When the toy balloon is closed, the imprisoned air presses on the inside of the balloon in all directions. As a result, the balloon presses on the enclosed air with equal forces and in opposite directions. The balloon does not move because the air presses on the inner surface of the balloon equally in all directions.

But when you let go of the end of the balloon, the stretched balloon forces the air out of the opening. The reaction to this force is a force exerted by the air in the balloon upon the balloon's inner surface. This force is equal to the force pushing the air out, but its *direction* is opposite. That is why the balloon flies off in the direction opposite to that of the stream of air coming out of the balloon.

That is exactly the principle behind jet and rocket aircraft engines. Inside of these engines, just as inside the engine of an automobile, fuel is burned. Inside of an automobile engine the burning fuel makes gases that push the pistons that turn the drive shafts and so forth. But in the jet and rocket, when the fuel burns and makes gases, these hot gases rush out of the back end of the jet or rocket.

Those gases rush out with such terrific force that people can't stand anywhere near the back end of a jet or rocket. Anything or anybody standing as much as a hundred feet behind some jets would be blasted to a crisp by the roaring, rushing gases.

When those gases rush out like that, the jet or rocket gets the same sort of push the balloon did. There is a force pushing ahead in the jet or rocket that is exactly equal to

351

the force of the gases pouring out the back end.

Suppose the gases rush out of the back of the jet rocket with enough force to move something weighing 1,000 pounds. You might say that the engine had a thousand pounds of push or thrust. If the force of the gas coming out the back could move a thousand pounds, then the force of the reaction, which is a force in the opposite direction, also could move a thousand pounds. Actually, the force of the gases from most jet and rocket engines is at least *five times* as powerful as that. That force is what moves the jet plane or the rocket forward.

Once the jet or rocket is moving, of course, and if it has wings, the wings build up lift just the way they do with a propeller-driven aircraft, and the pilot can make the plane do whatever he wants it to.

AIRSHIPS WITHOUT WINGS

There is one thing about jet and rocket power, however, that is of particular interest. The thrust, the power from jet and rocket engines, is so great that scientists have built airships without any wings at all that can be made to fly through the air.

Such airships may carry people or scientific instruments. In war they probably would carry bombs. (See the section on "The Challenge of Outer Space," near the end of this volume.)

The way these wingless craft work is that the rocket or jet engine sends them soaring high into the air. The force of the thrust of these engines is enough to lift the ship off the ground, the way a skyrocket rises off the ground. Once the ship is high enough, automatic controls tilt it a little. Because it doesn't have wings, it can't fly straight across the sky the way a plane does. Instead it just starts curving toward the earth in exactly the same way as the shell from a cannon does. If the people who launched such a ship have figured correctly, it will land just where they want it to. If it is carrying instruments to take a sample of the air very high up, or mail or messages, a parachute will open toward the end of its flight and lower the ship slowly and safely to the ground.

Figuring out the flight directions for one of these wingless craft takes just about the same sort of figuring as is needed to make a cannon shell land on its target. But, unlike the cannon shell, this sort of wingless

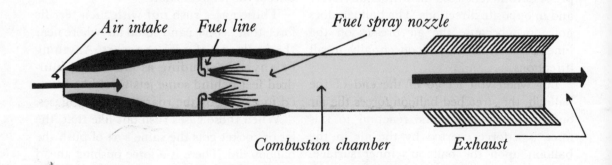

Air intake   *Fuel line*   *Fuel spray nozzle*

Combustion chamber   *Exhaust*

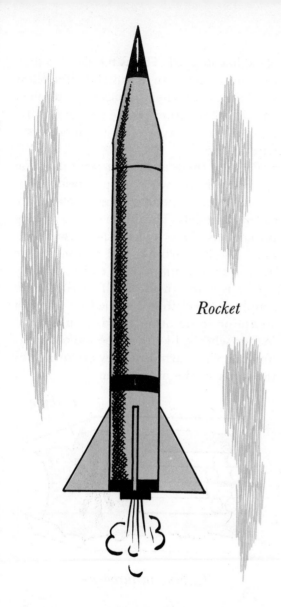

Rocket

HOW A JET DIFFERS
FROM A ROCKET

Let's look at the difference between jets and rockets. Although both of these kinds of power use the same principle—the equal and opposite reaction for every action—they are different in actual operation.

The chief difference is that a rocket carries everything it needs for fuel and power right inside itself. A skyrocket—the kind you see when a holiday is celebrated by setting off fireworks—is a good example of a rocket.

Inside the rocket there are chemicals. When these chemicals are lighted they do not need air to burn. Oxygen to let the chemicals burn comes from inside the chemicals themselves. When this fuel inside a rocket is lighted it produces gases that rush out of the rear of the rocket, and these gases produce the power for propelling the craft or the fireworks.

Inside of some of the larger rockets, the fuel is handled differently. Instead of just a chemical fuel as there is inside the small skyrocket, the big rockets carry great tanks full of different materials. One of the tanks will hold material that can produce great amounts of oxygen. Some rockets even carry their oxygen in liquid form, under great pressures or at very low temperatures. Other tanks inside the rocket carry other materials that will help produce the most powerful rush of gases out of the rear of the rocket and, thus, the powerful reaction to thrust the rocket up into the air.

But the skyrocket and giant rocket are the same in that they carry absolutely everything they need for fuel right inside of themselves. That is why rocket power is the sort of power that scientists are planning to use

rocket or jet can be made to change directions a bit even while it is diving, in a sort of gliding slant, toward the earth. Little jet or rocket outlets on the side of the ship do the steering. If a left-hand jet or rocket on the nose is made to go for a moment, it will shove the rocket over to the right. The right-hand rocket or jet would make the nose point the other way.

for flights into the emptiness of outer space where there isn't any of the oxygen that other sorts of engines would need.

Because it is so completely self-contained, the rocket is closest of all to working like the toy balloon with which we have described the principles of jet and rocket propulsion. In the balloon, all the energy came from the air that was inside the balloon. In the rocket, all the rushing gases, with thousands of pounds of force, come from materials inside the rocket.

The jet is quite different in that respect. The jet depends upon outside air for the oxygen it needs to feed the flames that make the gases that rush out of the back of the jet.

A jet engine takes air in from the front of the plane, or from scoops in the edge of the wings of the plane. This air goes into a series of whirling blades that force the air even faster into a special part of the jet engine. When the air rushes into that part of the jet engine, fuel such as kerosene is spurted into the engine too. The fuel and the air mix and then an electrical spark or flash sets it all on fire. This fire produces the gases that rush out of the jet's tail and provides the thrust that makes the jet fly.

Because the jet depends on taking in air to get the oxygen for its engine, it can be used only inside of the atmosphere of the earth. In outer space, where there is no oxygen, the fuel used in a jet engine couldn't burn and the engine wouldn't work.

Perhaps now that the jet engine has been described, some of the words used by jet pilots will make more sense. Sometimes jet pilots talk about a "flame-out." This simply means that their engine has stopped. The flaming process inside the engine that creates the rushing gases which propel the

plane has stopped. This is the same as stalling the engine of an automobile. Jet pilots sometimes call their planes blow-torches. This is because they create a jet of red-hot gases just the way a blow-torch creates a jet of flame.

Perhaps there is another term that you may have heard when people speak about jet airplanes. Sometimes these airplanes are called turbo-jets. This is the same as saying turbine-jets. *Turbo* is just a short word engineers use for turbine. The reason people use this term is that the jet engine actually uses a turbine inside itself. A turbine is simply a wheel that is turned by water or steam or some other flowing substance. Water-wheels, like those beside old mills, are, in a way, turbines. They are turned by the water of the mill-stream.

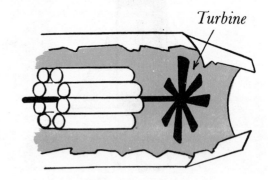

Turbine

Turbine in turbo-jet

The hot expanding gases pass through the turbine. They hit the blades and make the wheel turn. The turning of the turbine makes the compressor turn, forcing more air into the combustion chamber. The fuel and air burn up, rushing out at the back and turning the turbine at the same time. As the gases are forced out by the terrific pressure, they kick back (react) and thrust the jet

354

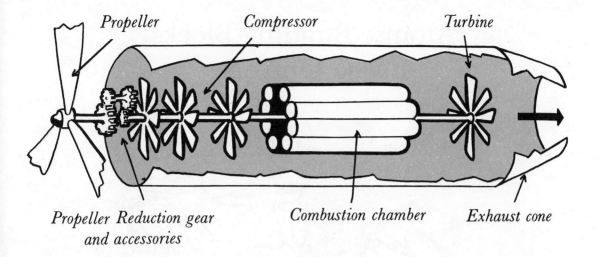

Propeller   Compressor   Turbine

Propeller Reduction gear   Combustion chamber   Exhaust cone
and accessories

Turbo-prop Engine

forward. Because the jet engine uses turbines, it is called a turbine-jet or turbo-jet engine.

The turbo-prop (also called prop-jet) operates like a regular turbo-jet except that in addition to turning the compressor, the turbine also turns a propeller. The propeller is on the front end of the shaft (see diagram above). The propeller pushes air backward. That's an action. The *reaction* pushes the propeller forward, and this pulls the airplane forward. The hot expanding gases forced out of the back of the airplane react to help thrust the airplane forward. At the same time these rushing gases turn the turbines which turn the compressor and the propeller.

One reason for having power-plants like that (and power-plant, by the way, is what airplane makers call engines) is that plain jets haven't yet been found practical for some airline work. There are some jet airliners flying, but they fly great distances, usually over the ocean.

For shorter trips the tremendous speed of the jet isn't needed and, in fact, makes it difficult to plan trips. If you have an airplane that goes 500 miles an hour, everybody has to go to a lot of expense and work just to prepare it for a flight. Then, if that flight is only for a couple of hundred miles, the plane will hardly get up in the air before it has to start coming down. So, for shorter trips, the turbo-prop, which uses a turbine to turn a regular propeller, but turns it with greater power and efficiency than most piston engines, is better than a straight jet—so far. But, because this is the Air Age and because things change so fast in it, tomorrow may be quite different. That makes the Air Age an exciting age, full of surprises, doesn't it?

Atoms: Building Blocks
of the Universe

Democritus conceives the idea of atoms

ATOMIC power is a phrase we all hear. People speak of splitting the atom and releasing forces such as were never dreamed of before. In the atom there seem to lie some of the richest promises of the future—a future in which we will have unlimited power at our command to run machines, to power ships, and even to travel out into the seemingly endless frontiers of space.

But what is this wonderful atom and atomic power? That is a question men have been asking for more than 2,000 years.

EARLY IDEAS ABOUT THE ATOM

In ancient Greece, more than 2,000 years ago, a very wise man named Democritus caused quite a stir with a new idea about all solid things. He felt that a block of metal, a gold ornament, and even the skin of a human being, were not simply solid pieces of matter. He felt that all things, no matter how solid they *seemed*, actually were made of tiny particles that no one could see. Democritus even had a name for his tiny particles. He called them *atoms,* from the Greek word for *indivisible,* which means *cannot be divided.*

It was Democritus' idea that the atoms, of which all matter was made, were the tiniest particles of matter imaginable. He thought that when you divided matter into its tiniest parts—parts that could not be divided into tinier parts—you would have atoms. We'll see just how close he came to understanding the atom as we continue to follow the story of atomic power.

One of the next very important chapters in that story was written by another great thinker of ancient Greece, Aristotle. He said that all the millions of things on earth were actually made up of the same four basic things. He called these things *elements* and said that the four elements were fire, air, earth, and water. He was wrong about the four elements, but he was right about the idea that all things on earth are made up of combinations of certain basic materials.

It was not until 1808 that someone finally made real sense out of Democritus' and Aristotle's ideas. The man who did it was a teacher in England by the name of John Dalton.

HOW SCIENTISTS DISCOVERED THE BASIC ELEMENTS

Dalton had often wondered about the ancient riddle of why no one had been able to turn common metals into precious gold. Finally he concluded it was because gold was a basic element—a piece of material that could not be changed or broken down into other materials. There must be many such basic materials, he reasoned, and he was absolutely correct.

Scientists soon began discovering just what materials could not be broken down and were therefore basic elements.

The way they went about it was something like this. Suppose we start with a piece of rock for an example. First of all, to find out if the rock itself is just a hunk

357

of some basic element, we can smash the rock into many tiny pieces. This is known as breaking it down mechanically.

Then we can look at the tiny pieces. Let us suppose that the tiny pieces of rock have been smashed into bits of many shapes and sizes and colors. One bit might look like a grain of sand. Another might look like a tiny sliver of some sort of glass. Other bits might look like tiny flakes of rust. So, we conclude that the rock was made up of several different basic sorts of things, some of which separated from the rest when we smashed the rock.

Our next step is to pick some of the tiny bits and see if we can break them down into even more basic parts. Suppose we pick the ones that look like tiny flakes of rust. Even when we grind them and pound them into the tiniest particles, each particle still looks like a grain of rust.

Mechanical ways of breaking down the bits of rock, we see, just won't work any more. We'll have to try something else. The next thing, then, is to try breaking them down with chemicals. One way to do that is to put the bits of rock into an acid. As the bits float down, tiny bubbles are released from them. This means that the acid *is* breaking them down. When the bits of rock are put through enough chemical baths like this, we might end with only tiny bits of some dark substance.

No matter what we do, from now on, those tiny particles won't change. When scientists put a substance through enough breaking-down processes like that, they can finally arrive at the basic elements from which anything is made. This is called *chemical analysis*.

In the case of the rust-like flakes from the rock, what we were supposing we had was bits of iron in the rock. The reason they

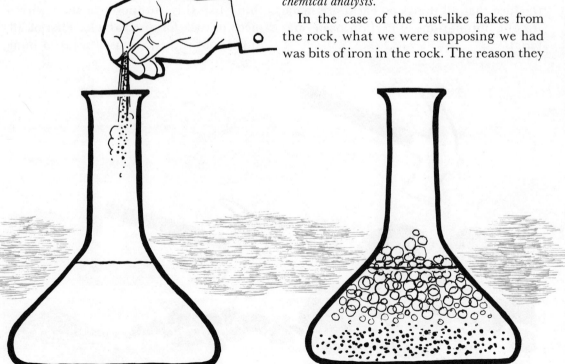

looked rusty was that oxygen from water and from air had combined with the iron to make *iron oxide,* which simply means iron and oxygen. And iron oxide is what we call rust.

When we dropped the rusty flakes into the acid, the oxygen was released from the iron and bubbled away. What was left? Just the iron, of course.

Then, no matter what we might try to do, we could not break those bits of iron down into anything else. Iron, and gold and oxygen and hydrogen and silver and lead (plus nearly a hundred other materials), are known as *elements*—that is, materials that cannot be chemically or mechanically broken down into other materials.

Now that doesn't mean that elements can't be broken down into *anything*.

Even after John Dalton convinced other scientists that he was on the right track with his idea of basic elements, scientists still insisted that even elements must be composed of tiny particles, of atoms, as Democritus had said. But the scientists also figured that the atoms of each element must be different from the atoms of every other element.

They finally arrived at the idea that the tiniest particle of any element would be called an atom of that element. Those atoms, however, are so tiny that not even the most powerful microscope can show them to us. Scientists *know* that there are such tiny particles but they know it only because of experiments they can perform —not because they can see them.

359

ATOMS INTO MOLECULES

As atoms of elements go together to form a substance, there is another special word that scientists use. It is the word *molecule*. A molecule is the tiniest substance that can be formed of atoms. A drop of water will help us to understand this.

If we could keep splitting up a single drop of water into tinier and tinier drops, we would sooner or later get to a point where we couldn't make any smaller drops no matter how hard we tried. Each one of those tiniest drops would be so tiny that it might take thousands of them even to be seen under a super-powerful microscope.

Each one of those tiniest of drops of water would be composed of three atoms. Two of the atoms would be hydrogen atoms. One of the atoms would be an oxygen atom. Hydrogen and oxygen are two gases—like the air we breathe. But when they join together in chemical union in the proportion of two atoms of hydrogen to one atom of oxygen, they form water.

Scientists use special initials for atoms. They call hydrogen H and oxygen O. So, when they write about water they call it H_2O, meaning two hydrogen atoms and one oxygen atom. And the tiniest particle of water, remember, is a molecule, composed of three atoms.

Around the early 1900's, scientists began to go even farther into those tiny building blocks of the universe, the atoms. Even though no one had ever seen an atom, scientists began to figure out what it must be like *inside* an atom!

Imagine, even though, according to the scientists, 36,000,000,000 (thirty-six *billion*) atoms could fit easily on the head of a small pin, they were very curious to find out what went on inside of each separate one of them!

First of all, the scientists figured that each atom of each element must have something about it to make it different from the atoms of all other elements.

AN AMAZING DISCOVERY

Finally, a great English scientist named Sir Ernest Rutherford actually opened up the path to the Atomic Age by coming up with an idea that explained many things that scientists had been wondering about as they studied atoms.

Rutherford figured that atoms are made up of different kinds of electrical charges. His idea was that each atom had a center, or nucleus, of electrical particles called *protons* and *neutrons*. Around this center, he

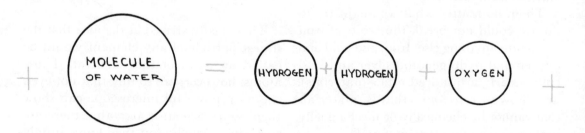

The tiniest drop of water would contain two atoms of hydrogen and one atom of oxygen

360

Diagram of atom showing protons and neutrons in the nucleus, and electrons circulating in the orbits around the nucleus

said, whirl other electrical particles called *electrons*.

By experiments, scientists proved that this idea was an exactly correct explanation of the atom. Then, in more experiments, other scientists checked over each kind of atom and found out just how many protons, neutrons, and electrons were in each different kind. It is the numbers of these electrical particles in the nucleus of an atom that makes one atom different from another.

THE EXTRAORDINARY POWER OF URANIUM AND RADIUM

In an element called uranium—a metal —for instance, there are 92 protons and 146 neutrons in the center or nucleus. Around that center there are 92 electrons.

Sometimes, though, uranium is found with three less neutrons in the center. Now, that doesn't sound like much of a difference, does it? But it is one of the greatest differences known to science. Just that tiny difference in an atom of uranium turns it into a material that can be used to create the greatest explosions known to man, or to send out the greatest amount of energy that man has ever been able to create to run his machines.

One of the first clues to the sort of force that uranium can give off came in the 1890's when a French professor named Antoine Henri Becquerel and, later, a Polish chemist named Marie Curie discovered that the atoms of certain elements keep shooting off some of the electrical particles from inside their centers.

361

One of the elements that do this, they found, is radium. When you see a watch or clock dial that glows in the dark it may be because tiny amounts of radium have been used in the paint on the dials. The atoms of radium, as they shoot off particles from their centers, make the glow that you see. Larger amounts of radium are used to fight certain diseases. The rays the element gives off kill certain diseased cells and stop them from multiplying.

You can actually watch atoms splitting up. All you need is a fairly strong magnifying lens and a watch or clock with a luminous dial. This experiment should be done after dark in a perfectly dark room or closet.

After a few moments your eyes will get used to the dark. Then hold the lens near your eye and look closely at the figures on the dial of the clock or watch. You may have to move the clock back and forth a little until you see the dial sharply. Instead of the even glow of the figures on the dial, you should now see many flickering points of light.

The paint on the dial of your watch or clock has a speck of radium mixed with it. Each little flash of light is caused by a radium atom splitting up, making a tiny spark in the paint material. Thousands of these flashes give the steady glow that you see without the magnifying lens.

Radium-painted dial of clock glowing by the radioactivity of radium

When an element gives off radiation, as radium does, it is bound to change. Each time it shoots off some of the electrical particles from its center, the atoms change and become like some other atoms—atoms with smaller numbers of charges in their center. Radium, for instance, is the element that forms after uranium has given off protons. To create even the tiniest visible amount of it takes hundreds of thousands of years because each atom is so unimaginably tiny and so many billions of them have to change to make even a speck of the new element.

RADIOACTIVE ELEMENTS

When these elements, which we call radioactive, give off enough of their radiation, they end up as lead, an element that is so arranged inside its atoms that it does not send off any charges and just remains the way it is. That is one reason, also, why lead can act as a shield against the rays of radioactive elements. Another reason is that lead is a very dense or compact substance and rather cheap.

When scientists began digging deeper into the secrets of these strange radioactive elements, some amazing new ideas occurred to them. Sir Ernest Rutherford began to wonder what would happen if the charges shot off by such an element as radium were made to hit certain other elements. He knew that a lot of elements not radioactive themselves do have atoms so arranged that a slight nudge might change them.

He thought about nitrogen as a good example. In a nitrogen atom there are seven charges of positive electricity, the particles we call protons. (Electrons are negative charges and neutrons have no charge, they are neutral.) Radioactive elements, in turn, fire off protons. Why not, Rutherford wondered, try to have some of those protons strike atoms of nitrogen—one of the gases in the air—and turn it into an entirely new element? And that is exactly what he did.

With special machinery he bombarded atoms of nitrogen with the protons given off by a piece of radium. It was as though the radium were a cannon firing proton shells into the nitrogen. Some of those protons went straight into the centers of the nitrogen atoms and became part of those centers. Then, instead of having seven protons, the atoms had eight. With eight protons they were no longer nitrogen at all. They had changed, as though by a miracle, into oxygen which is the gas in the air that *does* have eight protons in its center.

Pretty soon scientists made new machinery to do this atomic shooting. The machines had names like *cyclotron* and *synchrotron,* and *betatron*—but they all had the same purpose: to send electrical charges smashing into atoms to change the structure of those atoms. Generally, people just call these machines "atom smashers."

For a time, scientists thought these "atom smashers" would be good for nothing more than to change small quantities of one element into another. Then, in Germany, in 1939, two scientists named Otto Hahn and Fritz Strassman got some interesting new results from a new sort of atomic bombardment.

Instead of shooting protons into the center of atoms, the two scientists were using equipment that shot out neutrons, the particles of an atom's center that are "neutral," having neither a positive nor a negative charge. These neutrons, it was found, would crack into the center of an atom much more easily than protons had ever been able to

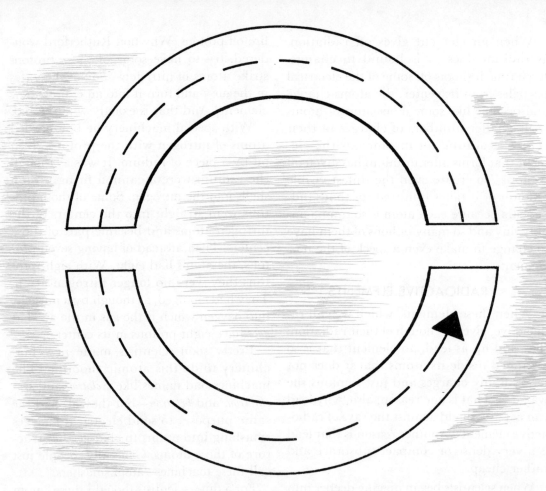

Some atom smashers work by whirling electrons between giant magnets

do. And when the neutrons *did* get inside, the atom changed. Although they did not know it at the time, those two men had just crossed the threshold of the Atomic Age.

SPLITTING THE ATOM

For the atoms they bombarded, instead of changing into a new element by *adding* neutrons, changed into two different kinds of elements by *splitting in two. Uranium* was the element that the scientists chose to bombard because it was known to have the sort of atoms that are subject to change and that give off radiations automatically.

When the uranium was hit by a stream of neutrons, the atoms divided into atoms of two different elements, barium and krypton. But something else happened too, something that the scientists couldn't understand.

If two atoms of the new elements were added together they weighed less than an atom of uranium from which they had been made. What, the scientists wondered, could have happened to the part that was missing? Soon scientists all over the world were asking the same question.

The answer was found in Denmark by a

364

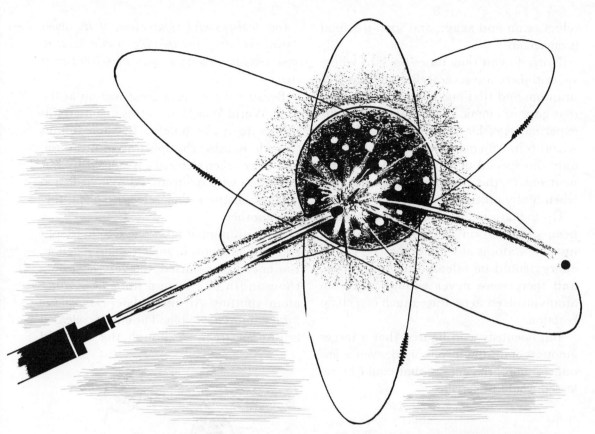

Neutron hitting center of atom, blasts part of it away

woman scientist named Lise Meitner who was working with Niels Bohr, a famous Danish scientist who had made important discoveries about the way atoms are put together. Dr. Meitner remembered a discovery by a German scientist named Albert Einstein that tremendous energy would be released if a small quantity of matter were so completely destroyed that it no longer existed. Einstein's ideas were still only theory. Dr. Meitner turned Einstein's discovery into something practical. She figured that the missing part of the uranium atoms actually had been completely destroyed—had disappeared—and in doing so had been changed into pure energy.

Dr. Niels Bohr added another amazing fact: When the uranium atoms split up into new elements, energy was released and other neutrons sped off just like the ones that had "split" the atom in the first place. This process is called *atomic fission.* Perhaps you can imagine what that thought led to.

If the splitting uranium atom released two neutrons and each of those neutrons hit two other atoms of uranium, then those four atoms also would be split releasing four neutrons, these four caused eight more releases of neutrons—and so on and so on as long as there were uranium atoms nearby to be hit. Scientists call this sort of thing a *chain reaction.* The numbers double them-

365

selves again and again, and soon the total is enormous.

Now, do you remember back to where we said there are several different kinds of uranium and that one of them is the kind that gives us atomic energy? Well, after the experiments of Dr. Bohr and Dr. Meitner scientists in America discovered that it was only this special uranium, with three less neutrons in the center, that would split when hit by other neutrons.

Up to that time, all the experiments had been with such tiny portions of uranium, just a few atoms at a time, that very little energy could be released in the process, and there were never enough uranium atoms involved to produce much of a chain reaction.

But scientists soon figured that if larger amounts of uranium were used, even a few ounces more, the energy that could be released would be terrific.

One tablespoonful of uranium, if its atoms started exploding and splitting, would have the same amount of energy as more than 700 tons of coal!

Because there was a great war on at the time, World War II, scientists first used this energy to make bombs. In such bombs (atomic bombs) the splitting of uranium, and later other elements, is started by hitting them with neutrons. As soon as fission begins, the atoms themselves keep splitting one another.

With uranium it takes one second to split two million atoms in such a chain reaction. But once it has started, the very next one-thousandth of a second finds *forty billion* atoms splitting. An instant later *nine hundred trillion* atoms have split. The energy released is just as great as though the sun had

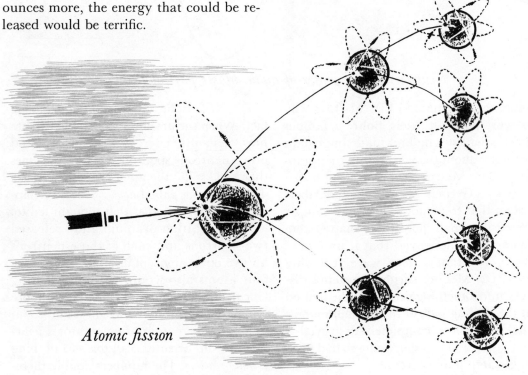

Atomic fission

Atomic bomb explosion

touched the earth for an instant.

Fortunately, there are other ways to release this vast energy than in bombs. Just as water can either slow down a fire, or put it out, so can certain materials slow down chain reactions.

By using these special materials, uranium can be started on a chain reaction, but can be made to do it slowly so that it produces only heat instead of an explosion.

WHAT IS A URANIUM PILE?

When uranium is made to produce this sort of controlled energy, scientists refer to it as a uranium or atomic "pile."

In a "pile" like that, rods made of the kind of uranium whose atoms can be split are put into a block of graphite—the sort of material that is inside pencils. Then, rods of the material that can slow down the atom splitting are put in across the uranium rods.

When the slow-down rods are all the way in, the neutrons that the uranium is sending off are absorbed in the slow-down rods and are not able to split other atoms.

As the slow-down rods are pulled out, however, some of the neutrons can smash through and split other uranium atoms so that energy *is* released. The farther out the rods are pulled the more energy is produced. If the slow-down rods were pulled out all the way, the atoms might split fast enough to cause an explosion, but it is easy to keep that from happening, and to protect the piles.

One of the easiest ways to turn the heat from an atomic pile into energy that is useful to men is to let it make steam by boiling water. The steam can be used to turn generators that make electricity.

Besides making electricity for factories and homes, uranium piles can be used to provide the power for boats, trains, and even airplanes. Atomic power is already running submarines. Rockets that will eventually reach outer space may use atomic power as well.

And, remember, *for each tablespoonful of uranium used in such a pile, man can get the same energy that he would get from more than 700 tons of coal.*

It is not only energy that these atomic piles produce, however.

If other elements are brought close to open parts of an atomic pile, the neutrons that the uranium shoots off make those elements radioactive—that is, those elements start to fire off electrical charges of their own.

Man-made radioactive elements, such as radioactive iron, can be very useful in special ways. If a machine is made with some radioactive iron in it, scientists can trace that radioactive iron to see how and where the machine is wearing out. Or, if some radioactive elements are put into the soil near a growing plant, scientists can tell just how the plants draw up nourishment from the earth.

Other radioactive elements, put into a person's food, can show how the food gives up *its* nourishment. Other man-made radioactive elements are used to help fight diseases in ways that were impossible when radium was the only radioactive element known to doctors.

So far as is known, the power and promise

One tablespoon of uranium can provide the energy of 700 tons of coal

The Atom: Man's opportunity and problem

of atomic energy has only one limit. That limit is man's own judgment—whether he is wise enough to use the energy for the greatest good of man or whether it will be wasted the way mankind has wasted so many of its natural resources in the past.

In this, as in all other fields of science, it is really men who are the measure of what is achieved, not the machines and the power that they have produced.

The Electronic Brain Machine

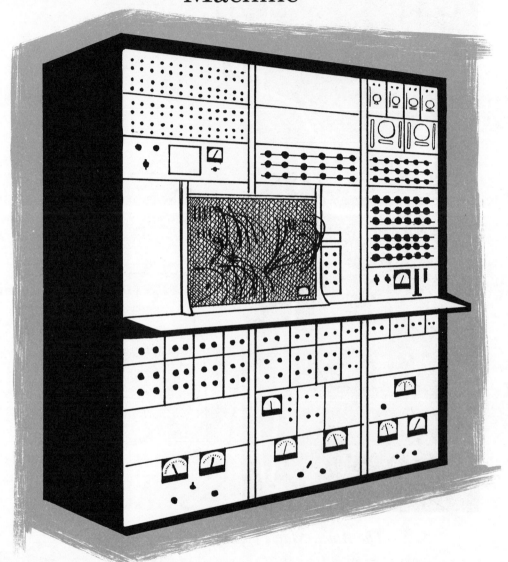

ONE OF THE strangest things we hear about in science these days (and probably for many days to come) is the *electric brain*. Electric brains are also called *electronic computers*. They *are* electronic. They use electronic tubes just as your radio or television does. They are computers too. A computer is something that can figure, or compute, as you do when you figure out a problem in arithmetic.

Now we know what electric brains are. What they *aren't* is very surprising. To begin with, they are *not* "brains." They can't "think." They are, really, giant adding machines. They do all their work by simple arithmetic. But they do it at such amazing speed that they can solve many of our toughest scientific problems in just a few minutes or sometimes seconds.

YOUR BRAIN IS BETTER

In telling the story of these "brains" that aren't really brains, we will also be telling the wonderful story of why it is that *your* brain—even if you are still in school — is really a better brain than the very biggest of the machines that we have come to call electric brains.

In the very first place, an electric brain has only two thoughts in all the thousands of miles of wire and thousands of tubes that may go to make up its "head." Many people, when they hear that, don't believe it. They say that such remarkable machines must have more than two simple thoughts. But the fact is that they haven't. The only two thoughts that an electric brain has are "Off" and "On." In other words, either there *is* or there *isn't* electricity flowing through one of its tubes or wires. In its basic form an electric brain is nothing more than thousands of switches that go either "On" or "Off."

How can anything so simple do work so complicated? Here is how.

Numbers—as we know them in arithmetic—are the basis of all scientific figuring. Anything in science can be put down in numbers, even the description of a puppy dog's tail.

To do that with a puppy dog's tail you would have to make certain numbers mean short tails, other numbers mean long tails, other numbers mean brown or black or shaggy or clipped and so on until you had

Even dogs' tails can be described in numbers

given a number to every part of the puppy's tail, even how many hairs were on it. When you got through, such a number, as for instance, 27590384 might mean "a short, spotted tail ending in a tuft."

So, all the electric brain has to understand is numbers. But there are an endless number of numbers. How can the brain even repeat them if it only goes "On" and "Off?"

A NUMBER SYSTEM FOR LIGHTNING CALCULATION

The answer is in a special kind of number system that scientists use for these giant adding machines. It is called the binary number system. In the binary system every number that can be thought of is written with just two figures—zeroes and ones.

In the number system that you are familiar with, each figure has a value depending on where it happens to be placed in relation to other figures. For example, in the number 36, the 6 stands just for 6. But in the number 67, the 6 stands for 6 X 10 or 60. In the number 624, the 6 stands for 6 X 100 (or 6 X 10 X 10) or 600. That is what we mean when we say our number system is based on 10 and that is why we call it the *decimal number* system. (The word *decimal* coming from the Latin *decimus* meaning tenth.)

In the *binary number system,* (the word *binary* meaning *twice*) the number 2 plays the same part that 10 does in the decimal system. In the decimal system you have a unit's place on the extreme right, then a ten's place to the left of it, then a hundred's (10 X 10) place, then a thousand's (10 X 10 X 10) place. In the binary system, you also have a unit's place on the extreme right, a two's (2) place to the left of it, then a four's (2 X 2) place, then an eight's (2 X 2 X 2) place, etc.

Let's take some examples:

DECIMAL SYSTEM	BINARY SYSTEM EQUIVALENT
1	1
2	10 $(1 \times 2 + 0 = 2)$
3	11 $(1 \times 2 + 1 = 3)$
4	100 $(1 \times 2 \times 2 + 0 \times 2 + 0 = 4 + 0 + 0 = 4)$
5	101 $(1 \times 2 \times 2 + 0 \times 2 + 1 = 4 + 0 + 1 = 5)$
6	110 $(1 \times 2 \times 2 + 1 \times 2 + 0 = 4 + 2 + 0 = 6)$
7	111 $(1 \times 2 \times 2 + 1 \times 2 + 1 = 4 + 2 + 1 = 7)$
8	1000 $(1 \times 2 \times 2 \times 2 + 0 + 0 + 0 = 8 + 0 + 0 + 0 = 8)$
13	1101 $(1 \times 8 + 1 \times 4 + 0 \times 2 + 1 = 8 + 4 + 1 = 13)$
20	10100 (You figure this one out.)
37	100101 $(1 \times 32 + 1 \times 4 + 1 = 32 + 4 + 1 = 37)$

So you see, by using only 1's and 0's we can write, in the binary system, any number that can be written in the decimal system.

Every number you can think of can be put down with ones and zeroes even though it may take many times as much space to write it. But electric brains don't care how long a figure is because they have one special trick that human brains haven't. Electric brains have the trick of being able to work at lightning speed. One of them can

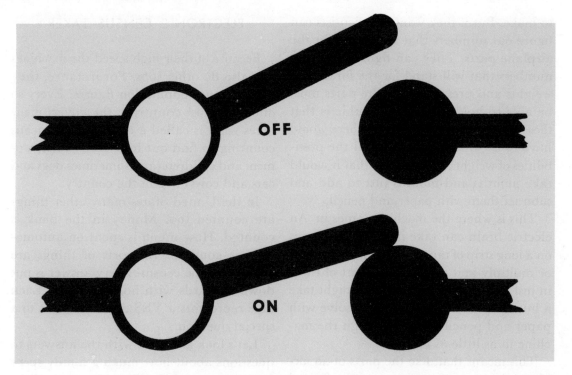

OFF

ON

handle thousands of numbers in a second, no matter how long those numbers may be.

This is the way it is done: The scientist makes the machine "think" of a number by working its controls. What really happens is that the machine's switches turn off and on in a special way.

SWITCH FIGURES

Suppose that when a switch is *off* it means zero. When it is *on* it means the figure one. Well, to make the machine think of the number 37, which we wrote out as 100101 in the binary system, this is the way the switches would go: ON-OFF-OFF-ON-OFF-ON.

Remember, each "On" means a figure 1 and each "Off" means 0. With the switches set ON-OFF-OFF-ON-OFF-ON it would be the same as 100101!

That is how the machine "thinks" of a certain number, by having its switches on and off according to the ones and the zeroes in the binary system.

Instead of actually punching buttons on the machine to make it think, however, the scientists use long tapes, like the tapes in a recording machine. These tapes carry "messages" composed of thousands of numbers in the binary system. The machine can take thousands, even hundreds of thousands, of these numbers and juggle them each second.

Let's look at a real problem and see how it's done.

When men build airplanes they have to test the wings and other parts to be sure they are strong enough. Each part has to be put under first one sort of pressure and then another. These tests take a long time to make. But if they want to, scientists can figure out numbers that will stand for the airplane parts. They can figure out other numbers that will stand for the forces and weights and pressures that the parts must be able to hold. The only trouble is that those numbers are so long, and there would have to be so many to cover all the possibilities of weight and pressure, that it would take months and months just to add and subtract them with paper and pencil.

This is where the machine comes in. An electric brain can take in all those figures on a long strip of tape and add and subtract or multiply and divide every part of them in just minutes. A problem that might take a hundred scientists a month to solve with paper and pencil will go through the machine in as little as an hour.

This means that, like the parts of an airplane, the parts of machines can be figured out by scientists without even bothering to go through the long drawn-out tests that once were needed.

ELECTRONIC CENSUS TAKER

Because of their high speed the machines can also do other jobs. For instance, they can compute population figures. Every so often, in most countries, the government takes what is called a census. That means counting to find out how many men, women, and children (and sometimes dogs and cats and cows) live in the country.

In the United States many other things are counted too. Money in the bank is counted. How much is spent on automobiles is counted. All sorts of things are counted in the census. Every answer is put down on cards with holes in them. Each hole represents a YES or NO answer to a special question.

Let's look at a card with the answers to questions about how much a family spent for an automobile. The first part of the card might ask "Did you spend more than $100 on your automobile?" Most cards would have a YES punched there. The next

A punch-card is being fed into an answering machine

question might be "Did you spend $200?"

Each question would go on up in cost. Suppose it got to a question that asked "Did you spend more than $2000?" and it still punched a hole for YES. Then the next question would be "Did you spend more than $2,100." Now, if you had only paid $2,050, you would have a NO answer punched on the card.

When that card's information was sent into an electric brain it would record that the person who answered had paid somewhere between $2,000 and $2,100 for his car.

Suppose someone wanted to know how many people in the whole country had paid between $2,000 and $2,100 for a car. All the cards of answers would go into the machine—although they would probably go in on tape rather than as separate cards. There might be cards from 20,000,000 persons who had bought cars. The machine would sort through them, or through the tape on which they had been recorded, at the rate of perhaps 50,000 answers per second. Within seven minutes it would have sifted through all 20,000,000 of them. And every answer recording between $2,000 and $2,100 would have been counted. In about seven minutes, then, an electric brain could "figure" just how many thousands of persons had spent that much.

ELECTRONIC TRAFFIC HELPER

Electric brains have been given problems to figure out having to do with things like

Preparing questions for the brain machine

traffic. Figures for the width of the streets, the timing of the red lights, the numbers of people crossing the street, and the number of cars passing the corner—all these can go into the machine to be figured according to whatever results of adding, subtracting, or dividing might be wanted.

In a few seconds there could be an answer that would tell whether the traffic jam would be less if the red light went off a few seconds quicker.

People sometimes speak of these machines as being able to "remember" things. They can—in a way. But they can "remember" only numbers written in the binary system. They "remember" these numbers on reels of tape, like the tape of recording machines that we mentioned before.

One reel of tape no longer than a phonograph record may be able to "remember" more than a million figures. Those figures can represent anything. By making certain numbers represent certain letters, the machines can even be made to "remember" words—a whole dictionary if wanted.

Perhaps the machine might be asked to try all the possible combinations of letters that would fit in a certain cross-word puzzle and to pick out a word that would fit. It could. Very quickly, just the way it handled the automobile cost problem—by going through all its numbers very fast and picking out the ones that would work. Since those numbers would actually mean letters in this case, the cross-word puzzle could be done in just seconds.

There seems to be no limit to the kinds of problems the huge electric brains can solve—so long as those problems can be done with numbers!

But no electric brain can handle any problem that can't be written in numbers. It can't solve the problem of where someone's sister hid his catcher's mitt. It can't solve the problem of why somebody is happy one day or unhappy the next. It can't say why one poem is thrilling and another dull.

What electric brains *can't* do, in other words, is to *think*. They can just figure—very fast.

Perhaps the best way to remember that is to think of one simple fact that any scientist will tell you is very true. Even when it comes to numbers, an electric brain can just give *answers*. It takes the wonderful mind of a human being to ask the *questions*.

Traveling in Space

From YOU AND SPACE TRAVEL
By John Lewellen

THUS far, no fuel has been developed that would send a big enough rocket to another planet or the moon, permit a landing there and a take-off to return to earth.

Gasoline or alcohol would do it, but the weight of the fuel that would have to be carried would be prohibitive. If a fuel were found with a higher exhaust velocity, and material developed that could stand such temperatures, the mass-ratio of the rocket would be greatly improved. That is, the weight of the fuel could be much less in relation to the weight of the rocket itself and the load of humans, food, and instruments it carried.

Atomic energy may provide the answer to the fuel problem. Work is now underway to adapt atomic energy to rocket motors.

Before man rides a rocketship to the moon, he probably will experiment with establishing a platform in space, much closer to the earth. This will probably be possible as soon as enough money is available to try it.

Suppose a rocket rose to 500 miles and then leveled off. If its speed were 18,000 miles an hour, the motor could be turned off and the rocket would circle the earth at that speed forever, just as the moon circles the earth.

The rocket would not lose speed because there would be no air resistance to stop it. Sir Isaac Newton, in another of his laws of motion, explained that any object in motion will continue at the same speed until some external force is applied to speed it up or slow it down. If it were not for friction— the force which slows it down—you could accelerate your car to 50 miles an hour, turn off the engine, and ride forever at the same speed. Above the earth's atmosphere there would be no friction to slow down the rocket.

However, at 500 miles from the earth, the earth's gravity would still pull on the rocket. It would fall. But it would never strike the earth. In falling, it would stay the same distance from the earth.

If you hold a gun level and fire it, and drop a bullet from your hand at the same time, the bullet from the gun and the one you drop will hit the ground at the same time. The force of gravity works on both bullets equally. However, the bullet shot from the gun has a forward velocity and may travel forward a mile or more, dropping all the while, before it hits the ground.

If a bullet could be shot forward at a speed of 18,000 miles per hour, and if it could maintain that speed, it would never drop to the ground. It would drop, to be sure, but the earth is curved, and the earth would drop out from under it at the same angle at which the bullet were falling. If the bullet could maintain that speed, it could drop forever and would never hit the earth. Literally, it would "fall around the earth."

A rocket above the earth's atmosphere *would* maintain that speed. Consequently, although it fell forever, its distance from the surface of the earth would never vary.

TRAVELING BY ROCKETSHIP

Once a rocketship were established in such an orbit, it could be visited by other rocketships which would take off from the earth at such times that they would intercept the "satellite" ship.

These visiting ships from the earth could bring materials which could be used in converting the original rocketship into a huge "floating" platform. Kitchens, bedrooms, and living rooms could be installed.

It has been estimated that it would take 68 tons of fuel to transport 1 ton of material to the space platform.

Even though the platform were circling the earth at 18,000 miles an hour, there would be no sense of speed aboard the platform. The earth moves, in its orbit around the sun, at more than twice that speed. But we on earth have no feeling of speeding through space, because everything around us is moving at the same speed we are. All things are relative.

Planets close to the sun travel faster than those farther away.

If a rocket took off from the earth in the same direction in which the earth travels around the sun, it would have the speed of the earth plus its own speed. This speed would be more than enough to offset the gravity of the sun, and the rocket would drift outward in space. In this manner it could intercept a planet such as Mars, which is farther from the sun than the earth is.

If the rocket went slower than the earth, it would drift inward toward the sun and could intercept the planet Venus.

The movements of the rocket and the plane can be calculated very exactly by methods long known to astronomers.

A trip to Mars would require 258 days. Then there would be a wait of 455 days until the earth, which travels faster than Mars, reached a position at which it could be intercepted on the return trip. The return trip would take another 258 days. Thus, the round trip would take 971 days, or about two years and eight months.

A trip to Venus would take 146 days, with a 470-day wait. The round trip would require two years and one month.

The temperature inside the spaceship could be controlled very simply, by having one side of the ship painted black and the other highly polished.

The black side toward the sun would absorb the sun's heat and the ship would become very hot. The polished side toward the sun would reflect the sun's rays away from the ship, and the temperature inside would become very cold. The ship could be turned until the desired temperature resulted.

It could be turned very easily merely by whirling a wheel on the inside of the rocket. As the wheel was turned one way, the rocket would turn the other way. Newton's Law of action and reaction, again.

LIFE WITHOUT GRAVITY

The strangest sensation in a spaceship would be the absence of gravitational pull. Unless you wore magnetic shoes or used some other device to keep your feet on the floor, you could walk on the ceiling just as easily.

Instead of putting a book on the shelf, you could leave it suspended in midair.

In fact, all movement would be accomplished with so little effort that the voluntary muscles would become flabby and deteriorate unless exercised regularly. But you could not exercise by lifting weights because they would weigh nothing. A one-ton block of iron could be lifted as easily as a feather. A device with a coil spring probably would have to be used to exercise the muscles.

Swallowing food and drink would be difficult because no force of gravity would help pull it down your throat. But it could be done; if there were any reason to, you could stand on your head and eat right here on earth.

If you insisted on feeling your feet push solidly against the floor, you could build a special room with the floor where a wall usually is. Then you could start the room to whirling rapidly—once started, it would keep whirling with no further effort—and the centrifugal force would push you out against the "floor."

To keep the weight of the spaceship as low as possible, you could economize on the amount of water needed for drinking purposes and the air needed for breathing.

Water vapor given off through breathing and evaporation of moisture from the skin could be recovered from the air inside the spaceship, condensed and purified, and used over and over again.

Living plants inside the spaceship could provide enough oxygen for the humans to breathe. Humans breathe in oxygen and exhale carbon dioxide. Plants breathe in carbon dioxide and exhale oxygen. It is estimated that 11 square feet of leaf surface would provide the oxygen needs of one person. Pumpkin plants would be good for this, although there may be other plants that would throw off even more oxygen per square foot of surface.

Those who would build spaceships are faced with many problems, the greatest of which is fuel. Yet so many of the problems have been solved already, it would seem that all of them are capable of solution.

In 1903 the Wright brothers sustained their first wavering flight for 11 seconds. It was only the dreamers who said, "In less than fifty years we will be flying around the world faster than the speed of sound."

Who knows? You may well see the day when spaceships are taking off for other planets.

380

The Challenge of Outer Space

By Karl Hess

Today we live in the space age. Fanciful predictions of space travel a few years ago are as real now as news of airplanes and automobiles.

Rockets from the earth have been fired past the moon and across the millions of space-miles between the earth and the other planets. Radio waves from earth are now beamed to the moon and beyond.

Television broadcasts can be sent back from devices spinning around the earth. We forecast the weather from mechanical eyes high in space that can see the entire surface of the earth. Men themselves have actually flown to the first frontier of space to hurtle around the earth at thousands of miles per hour.

These are just a few of the facts that make us realize how far along in the space age we already are.

FASTER AND FURIOUSER

It all happened so fast, and goes on happening so much faster, that no sooner do we get used to one adventure into space than along comes another to make the last one out of date.

Just think, there were only four years between the time that men were first able to send anything at all into space and the time when men themselves went up into space—first to circle the earth and then to plan trips toward the moon!

You might get a better idea of just how fast this has happened if you remember that it was thousands of years between the invention of the wheel and the invention of motors to make those wheels go faster than a horse can run. It was almost a hun-

dred years between the invention of the steam locomotive and the first airplane. And even then it was a whole lifetime between the first flight and the day that airplanes could circle the earth without stopping. But it was only four short years from the first fumbling efforts at reaching into space until the space age was well under way.

SATELLITES ARE LAUNCHED

On October 4, 1957, Russian scientists launched the first artificial satellite. Satellites, you remember, are bodies smaller than the bodies they whirl around. For example, our moon is a satellite of the earth.

The first artificial satellite was named *Sputnik,* the Russian word for satellite—or fellow traveler! It weighed 184 pounds, but the rocket that was used to push it up and propel it into a path around the earth, almost 600 miles high at its peak, weighed hundreds of times more.

Here is how it worked. The little metal moon, looking like a shiny basketball with rods sticking out of it to transmit radio signals, was perched up on the nose of a huge rocket. That rocket, in turn, was divided into separate sections so that when the power in one was used up it would fall away and let another rocket motor take over. Finally the last part, or stage, of the rocket released the artificial satellite itself and sent it whirling around the earth. Actually, that last part of the rocket also went spinning around the earth for a while, and it weighed nearly four tons.

HOW SATELLITES STAY IN ORBIT

Sputnik itself stayed in its path, or orbit,

around the earth for only a few months. Another satellite, called *Vanguard I,* launched by American scientists the following year will probably stay in its orbit for 1,000 years. Others may circle the earth forever because far beyond the atmosphere, where they travel, there is no air resistance to slow them down or wear them out.

One of these satellites is the amazing *Echo I* which American scientists launched in 1960. It is a balloon 100 feet in diameter, made of a thin shiny plastic film. Even though it is so fragile that it couldn't last a minute flying around in the earth's atmosphere, it can sail up in space without trouble and at a speed so great that it goes around the entire earth in just two hours.

Altogether, in just the first two years in which men could put such objects into space, Russian scientists launched six satellites and American scientists launched twenty-eight. Today the launching of a satellite is almost like sending an airplane off on a regular trip, and satellites are being used to help in everyday jobs such as television and radio transmission, weather forecasting, and the navigation of ships and planes down in the earth's atmosphere.

To get a better idea of a satellite's flight attach a toy rubber ball to the end of a long rubber band. Pretend that you are the earth, that the rubber band is the force of gravity, and that the ball is the satellite. If you whirl the ball slowly, the rubber band will tend to draw it back toward you. A slow satellite, or one that comes too close to the earth, is drawn back like that—by the force of the earth's gravity. If you whirl the ball faster it will go into a path that is farther away and you can keep it sort of "balanced" out there. A satellite can stay "balanced" like that against the pull of the earth's gravity.

WHY SOME SATELLITES HAVE TROUBLE

The path of a satellite is elliptical, or watermelon-shaped, rather than round. This is where they have trouble. If the path of a satellite is such that it noses too close to the earth on the flat or close side of the orbit, it will begin to meet just a tiny bit of resistance from the few particles of air that are sometimes found up that high. Also, of course, earth's gravity begins to tug at it more and more. Slowly it will start swinging closer to the earth each time it goes around. Finally it will re-enter the

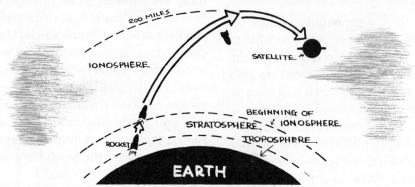

How a man-made satellite is launched into its orbit around the earth

earth's atmosphere. By then it is going so fast—as much as 18,000 miles per hour—that, unless it is made of very special metals, the friction of the air just burns it up.

The satellites that can circle the earth in space without this happening remain so far out in space that they have no real problem with air resistance. This means staying from 500 to 1,000 miles away from the earth at all times and traveling at speeds of approximately 18,000 miles per hour. The satellites that orbit closer and closer to the earth, and finally back into our atmosphere, have paths that come within only one or two hundred miles of the earth's surface even in the beginning.

ROCKETS CAN NOW PROPEL SPACE VEHICLES BEYOND ORBITING RANGE

But these circling space vehicles were just the first steps into space. Four times in the first years of space-flight, American and Russian scientists sent rocket-driven, metal-clad packages of radio instruments hurtling away from earth at the almost unimaginable speed of more than seven miles per second. Vehicles traveling at speeds as great as that don't go into orbit around the earth at all; they go whizzing on and on into outer space. It takes a speed of 25,054 miles per hour to do this. An American device named *Pioneer V* and a Russian one called *Lunik I* traveled more than 90,000,000 miles out into space and finally went into a path around the sun itself. *Pioneer V's* radio, could still be heard back on earth when it was—imagine!—22,000,000 miles away!

Today, going even farther, space "stations" are being planned to hover between the moon and the earth. From these stations rockets can be launched without being affected by the heavy pull of earth's gravity. Devices that use only the power of the sun's light to push them across space, as sailboats are pushed across water by the wind, are also practical. Atomic fuels will make all rockets easier to launch and allow them to travel longer.

ANIMALS BLAZED THE TRAIL FOR MEN

The most marvelous conquest of space was made by men. But before it was safe to send men up in space vehicles, the trips were checked by animals, and even bacteria. American scientists put samples of bread mold into some of the earliest vehicles that were sent around the earth to see what happened to the bacteria. Then mice and chimpanzees were sent up. The Russians used dogs for their checking flights.

The way the scientists got those space travelers back was very interesting. After the small metal containers in which the animals were put had orbited the earth a few times, electronically controlled rockets attached to them were set off. This jogged the containers out of their fixed orbit and propelled them back toward earth. Unlike most artificial satellites, these space vehicles were made of special metals that could resist the great heat of friction as they re-entered the atmosphere. Each was equipped with a parachute that opened automatically to let the container drift slowly to earth or into the ocean where it could be picked up. Several times American scientists were able to catch the containers—with nets stretched from airplanes—while they were still in the air!

All the animals on those trial flights were carefully examined by doctors, before and after. From these experimental check-ups scientists learned what the hazards of human space travel might be.

While the animals were making the trips, the men, who were called astronauts in America and cosmonauts in Russia, went through months of special training to prepare for their own adventures. Yet one experience they were wholly unprepared for was the magnificence they saw from their windows. They saw the stars shining, perhaps without any earthly dust or haze to dim them, and the celestial beauty of the sunlit earth spinning through emptiness.

FIRST MEN IN ORBIT

In 1961 the Russians announced that they had sent two cosmonauts into orbits in space, Yuri Gagarin and Gherman Titov, and that they had recovered them safely with their capsules intact, the latter after seventeen orbits. However, there was no advance notice to the world of these flights.

America's great day in space came on February 20, 1962, with all the world watching. With television cameras covering every moment, John H. Glenn, Jr., a colonel in the U. S. Marine Corps and one of the original team of seven American astronauts of Project Mercury, climbed into a one-man capsule named *Friendship 7* atop a giant rocket at Cape Canaveral, Florida. Anxious hours later, with all the details of checking and re-checking equipment finally finished, the rocket blazed to life and slowly lifted toward the skies. No one could say what might happen. Would the rocket work perfectly? Would it loft the capsule into a successful orbit around the earth?

It did wonderfully. Once, twice, three times, Colonel Glenn zoomed around the earth in space and then fired his retro-rocket for the capsule to be parachuted into the Atlantic Ocean. There naval vessels picked it up, its passenger mercifully safe.

In those five hours John Glenn lived through and shared with millions a day of miracles. Weightlessness to him was no problem. "I have had no ill effects at all from zero gravity."

On May 24, 1962, Lieutenant Commander M. Scott Carpenter became the second American astronaut to orbit the earth three times in his space capsule, the *Aurora VII,* and safely to survive the searing re-entry into the earth's atmosphere.

Can we hope that space exploration may become not a race but a mutual scientific effort? When the Russian cosmonauts Nicolayev and Popovich passed over the United States in their many-orbited flight of August, 1962, they wished "peace and happiness to the gifted American people." Perhaps there is hope in that.

MEN TO THE MOON—AND BEYOND

And then man reached for the moon. The United States government began working on a multi-billion dollar program, *Project Apollo,* to send manned expeditions to the moon—and then on to Venus and Mars. The National Space and Aeronautics Administration hopes to land three men on the moon before 1970, and the cost to the United States taxpayers is estimated at more than *twenty billion dollars.* (Yet think of what twenty billion dollars could do to improve conditions on our own earth!)

There are still staggering problems to be solved before man can explore other solar systems. The distances between them are so vast that it would take hundreds of years to get from Earth into the next solar system—even in the highly unlikely event that man could ever travel *faster* than the speed of light (186,000 miles per second). There are challenges aplenty in the dark star-filled reaches of the endless road into space.